In Praise of Fair Colorado

The Practice of Poetry, History, and Judging

Clay

May the many voices you convey continue to help citizens of this great land to find theirs.

Greg Hobbs
4/2005

"Justice Greg Hobbs' extensive and impressive anthology *In Praise of Fair Colorado: The Practice of Poetry, History, and Judging* is a significant contribution of thoughtful poems, detailed diaries, eloquent speeches, short essays, personal letters, substantive articles, and judicial opinions by a man who sees the State of Colorado with eyes that admire its wilderness and beauty and are amazed at its resources and power. They are the same eyes that are guiding the development of its laws and perceiving the opinions that govern its society. Throughout, all of his writings are *in praise of fair Colorado*, reflecting his love for and commitment to all of Colorado that he has observed.

"His expertise as a water lawyer is amply displayed. Few authors could claim the background and experience of Justice Hobbs on these issues, and none could match his passion for the subject and thorough research in his writings.

"Finally, nowhere is his intimate writing style more appreciated than in his judicial opinions. His analysis of the constitutional and practical issues is thoroughly researched and well reasoned, and his order reflects his perception of the sensitivity of the issues and desire for a practical, rather than controversial, legal solution."

—John Moye, Moye Giles LLP, past president
of the Colorado Bar Association

"This is an irresistible river trip with a guide whose pack is crammed with poetry, maps, passion, The Code of the Mountains, water bottles, love of the law, lore of the west, and fishing gear. Rounding each bend of the river brings forth unexpected vistas of the pursuit of justice, and the community of men and women.

"There are dangers. Once you start, you will be unable to close the book. But what a joy to be able to enjoy such a journey with guide Justice Greg Hobbs!"

—Lucy Marsh, Professor of Law,
University of Denver College of Law

"Justice Greg Hobbs praises our glorious landscape and democratic institutions while reminding us that the true measure of our greatness lies in the justice that we reserve for humble places, unpopular ideas, and unconventional people. This is a book that all Coloradans should read and contemplate while we make our way through these perilous times.

"Greg Hobbs possesses a razor-sharp mind, a strong character, and a deft touch with the English language. In his essays, speeches, reviews, treatises, opinions, and poems, he illuminates the fine points of law while reminding us of our democratic heritage and our obligations to justice."

—Mark Fiege, Associate Professor of History,
Colorado State University

In Praise of Fair Colorado

The Practice of Poetry, History, and Judging

Justice Greg Hobbs
Colorado Supreme Court

BRADFORD PUBLISHING COMPANY
Denver, Colorado

DISCLAIMER

This book is intended to provide general information with regard to the subject matter covered. It is not meant to provide legal opinions or to offer advice, nor to serve as a substitute for advice by licensed, legal or other professionals. This book is sold with the understanding that Bradford Publishing Company and the author(s), by virtue of its publication, are not engaged in rendering legal or other professional services to the reader.

Bradford Publishing Company and the author(s) do not warrant that the information contained in this book is complete or accurate, and do not assume and hereby disclaim any liability to any person for any loss or damage caused by errors, inaccuracies or omissions, or usage of this book.

Laws, and interpretations of those laws, change frequently, and the subject matter of this book can have important legal consequences that may vary from one individual to the next. It is therefore the responsibility of the reader to know whether, and to what extent, this information is applicable to his or her situation, and if necessary, to consult legal, tax, or other counsel.

Library of Congress Cataloging-in-Publication Data

Hobbs, Greg.
  In praise of fair Colorado : the practice of poetry, history, and judging / Greg Hobbs.
    p. cm.
  Includes index.
  ISBN 1-932779-02-7
  1. Law--United States--Miscellanea. 2. Law--Colorado--Miscellanea. 3. Conservation of natural resources--Law and legislation--United States--Poetry. 4. Civil rights--United States--Poetry. 5. Colorado--Poetry. 6. Law in literature. I. Title.

KF389.H62 2004
978.8--dc22

2004021430

Copyright © 2004 Gregory J. Hobbs, Jr.
All rights reserved.
No part of this book may be reproduced in any form or by any means, without permission in writing from the publisher.

In Praise of Fair Colorado: The Practice of Poetry, History, and Judging
ISBN: 1-932779-02-7

Published 2004 by Bradford Publishing Company
1743 Wazee Street, Denver, Colorado 80202
www.bradfordpublishing.com

To Bobbie, Dan, and Emily,
Joni, Kyle, Shannon, and Ella,
Alison and Mark

The author has assigned all of his royalties from the sale of this book to:

Legal Aid Foundation of Colorado
1900 Grant Street, Suite 1112
Denver, CO 80203

(303) 863-9544

About the Author

Greg Hobbs is a Justice of the Colorado Supreme Court. He serves as a co-convenor of the Western Water Judges Educational Project, Dividing the Waters, and is vice president of the Colorado Foundation for Water Education.

Justice Hobbs practiced water, environmental, land use, and transportation law prior to becoming a Justice on May 1, 1996. He is a graduate of Boalt Hall, University of California, Berkeley, J.D., 1971, Order of the Coif, Supreme Court Editor for the *California Law Review*; and the University of Notre Dame, A.B., History, 1966, *magna cum laude*. He taught sixth grade in New York City and served in the Peace Corps before law school. He was law clerk to Judge William E. Doyle of the United States Court of Appeals for the Tenth Circuit, an enforcement attorney for the Environmental Protection Agency, a First Assistant Attorney General for the State of Colorado, and a partner with the law firms of Davis, Graham & Stubbs and Hobbs, Trout & Raley.

He served as vice chairman of the Colorado Air Quality Commission from 1982 to 1987 and, at various times, as a member of the Metropolitan Air Quality Council, Regional Air Quality Council, Metropolitan Transportation Development Commission, and the Colorado Governor's Metropolitan Water Roundtable, Transportation Roundtable, Environment 2000 Citizen's Advisory Committee, and Wilderness Air Quality Values Task Force. He is a frequent writer and speaker on water and environmental matters, and a member of the Colorado Authors' League.

Justice Hobbs is a member of the Denver Bar Association, Colorado Bar Association, American Bar Association, a fellow of the Colorado Bar Foundation and American Bar Foundation, and a member of the American Bar Association's Section of Environment, Energy, and Resources. He is the Colorado Supreme Court's Liaison Justice to the Colorado Bar Association Board of Governors, the Judicial Advisory Council, and the Access to Justice Commission.

Table of Contents

Foreword		xiii
Preface		xix
Acknowledgements		xxv
I.	I've Seen the Mountains Falling	1
	I've Seen the Mountains Falling	3
	Sense of Place	4
	Finding Colorado	7
	Motion for Appearance and Late Filing	9
	In Relief	10
	Mountains Call	12
	Colorado Comes Back Round Again	13
	A Poet with the Heart of a Fighter	15
II.	The Great Divide Community	19
	Welcome!	21
	Swearing-In	23
	The Practice of Poetry, History, and Judging	25
	Colorado's Independent Judiciary	40
	Scouting for All	48
	Marriage of Maggie Fromholtz and Casey Vanderbeek	52
	Can't You Feel the Ground Waking?	55
	Leadership Denver Graduation	60
	Settling In	62
	To See the Mountains: Restoring Colorado's Clear and Healthy Air	67
III.	Lawyers and Judges, Trail Guides and Mapmakers	119
	Turning Forward	121
	On Starting Law School	122
	The River Trip of Your Life	124
	Ethics and the Law for Water and Environmental Lawyers	130
	Taking our Constitutional	136
	Light Bearers	141
	A Former Water Lawyer's View of Torts	143
	Tribute to Clyde O. Martz	148
	Persuading the Decision-Maker	154
	Book Review: *Thinking Like a Writer*	157
	Swearing In New Attorneys	160

IV. Fishing and the Supreme Court 165
    Out the Window.. 167
    Fishing and the Supreme Court—Making the Transition
        from Private Practice....................................... 168
    Protocols of the Colorado Supreme Court 173
    May Day Anniversary: On Being an Imminent Jurist............... 179
    Two of a Piece 182
    State Water Politics Versus an Independent Judiciary:
        The Colorado and Idaho Experiences.......................... 187

V. Water and the West.. 213
    One Body, One Spirit, Many Futures 215
    Historical Perspective on Western Land and Water Law........... 216
    Machu Picchu Book Reviews...................................... 227
    The Role of Climate in Shaping Western Water Institutions 232
    Mesa Verde Journal... 270
    Book Review: *Silver Fox of the Rockies: Delphus E. Carpenter
        and Western Water Compacts*................................. 280
    Inside the Drama of the Colorado River Compact Commission:
        Negotiating the Apportionment 285
    Prior Appropriation and Instream Flow: The Struggle to
        Integrate Instream Flow Rights into Western Water Law 318
    How Like a River, The Evolution of Western Water Law........... 322
    Tribute to Marc Reisner 327
    Delight for Waterbugs, A Colorado Education 330
    A Sonnet to a Problem River..................................... 335
    Lessons from History: How Drought Shapes Colorado
        Water Law and Policy.. 337
    A Primer on Colorado Water Law.................................. 341
    Celebration of Colorado's Instream Flow Law 347
    Ev/Ann Long View 349
    Working with Water 353
    Where We Are, Where We've Been 358
    Additional Water Writings....................................... 363

VI. Constitutional Perspectives 365
    I Am the First Amendment.. 367
    People v. Schafer... 369
    Board of Education v. Wilder 379
    People v. Kobe Bryant 387
    Book Review: *The Colorado State Constitution:
        A Reference Guide*.. 407
    The Trial of the President 410

Index of Poems
By Justice Hobbs
(in order of appearance)
© 2004 Gregory J. Hobbs, Jr.

William Stafford's Yarn	xv
I've Seen the Mountains Falling	3
Welcome!	21
On Being Sworn	24
Judges Must Be Students	26
Coloradans	26
Code of the Passing Through People	29
They Call Me Squaw Man	33
Which Colorado Shall We Be?	35
Out on the Road Today	37
Fisherman's Knot	39
Of All the Stars	41
Durable Goods	41
Lewis and Ives	43
Compass	44
Our Own Peaches	45
One's Calling	46
Canoe	46
I Like the Feel of a Book	56
Ellipse	64
Turning Forward	121
Graduation	124
Lucy's Civil Procedure	127
Do Not Shy	139
Easy on the Water	155
Tables	161
Polis	162
Out the Window	167
I Stand to the Waterfall	168
The Phone Almost Never Rings	169
Pool	171

Talk about a Fix	180
Muster	183
Easy Strides	184
Just Desserts	185
One Body, One Spirit, Many Futures	215
Carrying My REI Water Bottle	216
Sixteen Fountains	231
Pueblo People of Mesa Verde	239
Good Colorado Headwaters Education	269
A Divide	334
Colorado Mother of Rivers	348
The Ev/Ann Long View	350
Come On Back All You Graces	351
I Am the First Amendment	367

Foreword

Greg Hobbs: Poet-Judge
By Carol Sullivan

When I think of my good friend Greg Hobbs, I am reminded of Sir Thomas More as he is portrayed in *A Man for All Seasons*. Chancellor of England More clashed with Henry VIII when More insisted on the sanctity of oaths. Like Chancellor More in the Renaissance, Supreme Court Justice Hobbs of Colorado dons a black robe, bears a lofty title, and is unassuming—though it is unlikely that Hobbs is headed toward More's fate of martyrdom and sainthood. In a poetry class last year, a fellow student asked Hobbs what he did for a living, and he answered, "I'm a judge." His wife Bobbie, who was also taking the class, as was I, didn't even roll her eyes at this understatement. And his longtime teacher, the poet Kathryn Winograd, declined to parade his credentials. Instead, Hobbs was riveted, as was the rest of the class, on poetry. "Wait…that tastes good…already it is on the wing," declares Rainer Maria Rilke, one of the poets we studied. As I read and ponder Hobbs' poetry, judicial opinions, and essays, I caution myself: *Wait!*—Hobbs' work is "already on the wing."

Hobbs—judge, poet, historian, husband, father, and lover of Colorado's magnificent landscape—marshals a breadth and depth of interest and expertise that remind me of More. Yet I also see in Hobbs a likeness to the Common Man in Robert Bolt's play *A Man for All Seasons*. The Common Man enacts roles that seem simple or benighted, but events show that in these many guises the common person undergirds society's well-being. Like More, Hobbs treats each person with courtesy and respect. In our democracy, Hobbs speaks as one citizen to another. He never patronizes but instead prides himself on being a common man—a human being and a citizen. Clearly, Hobbs binds himself to community and landscape. Dip into his work, and you will discover for yourself those bonds.

Consider Hobbs' "Letter to his daughter," welcoming her into the legal community as she starts law school where she can continue to practice her "zest for debating the alternatives," and where she will experience "the humility of the searcher." As a father and a lawyer, he attests to the character of both his daughter and the law: "Being a fine person in community with problem-solving ability is what good lawyering is all about. You can do this because you know what the fight for your own voice really means and costs. So you can help others find theirs, so they may be treated fairly." (pp. 122-23). Has Hobbs articulated for his daughter a golden rule of the legal profession?

When the Colorado Supreme Court swore in new Colorado lawyers in 2003, Hobbs spoke again of good lawyering, this time as a calling "to serve with scholarship and common sense, the workings of justice—incident by incident, matter by matter, case by case, in community." (pp. 160-63). On another occasion, Hobbs emphasized that judges, like all lawyers, serve the citizenry. In

Hobbs' memo to law clerks and brief writers of the Colorado Supreme Court, he advises: "Opinion writing is our primary obligation and privilege. The other two branches of government need not explain their decisions. We must. We do so publicly.... Clarity begins immediately and never ceases—active tense, active sense. Good writing is good thinking, good execution.... Good judgments do not dwell in ether. They are windows on Colorado's experience." (pp. 182-86). Good citizenship, steeped in service and in reflection on experience, offers a pathway to community, Hobbs stresses.

In his paean to Delph Carpenter, we see many of Hobbs' treasured values: Colorado, the West, the outdoors, the Colorado River, affirmation of commonality among adversaries. Hobbs hails Carpenter as "a small-town water lawyer who became a national statesman of rivers," architect of compacts to settle interstate water allocation disputes. "Carpenter's life mirrored the Great Divide he revered. He loved the shining mountains and the Great Plains that take one inevitably to them. He drew from them strength as a husband, father, lawyer, legislator, and craftsman of treaties. When litigating for Colorado against Wyoming in the United States Supreme Court, for example, he climbed to the source of the Laramie River to understand the lay of the land and how the waters flow." (pp. 280-84).

The reader witnesses the drama of interstate compacts forged by Carpenter and other negotiators in Hobbs' staging of the commission meetings that yielded the Colorado River Compact of 1922. His script describes Carpenter, who represented the state of Colorado, as "self-possessed, bordering on the arrogant, but...constantly aware that this great enterprise must be successful and he bears a heavy burden." At one point Carpenter asks of the Arizona State Water Commissioner W.S. Norviel, "Isn't your attitude that no matter how terrible a drought...isn't it always your disposition to get assurance for your dry deserts below [in Arizona, California, and Nevada], and ask us [in Colorado, Utah, Wyoming, and New Mexico] to bear the brunt of that visitation of drought?" Norviel, "caught in the middle between the skillful Colorado Carpenter and (his potential nemesis) Californian [W.F.] McClure," backs off, saying Arizona wants only "our legal rights." (pp. 285-314). Carpenter is able to find common ground among the negotiators, and the Colorado River Commission adopts a compact that is ratified by Congress in 1928. Hobbs observes that Carpenter, once "a win-at-all-costs litigator...became a peacemaker because [of] the reality of water scarcity and necessity." (p. 281).

Community, the crux of many of Hobbs' convictions, never is a feel-good, anything-goes, hazy notion. In some circumstances, community means freedom from government intrusion in the home—however so humble. Hobbs declares in *People v. Schafer* (1997), "A tent is a home for Fourth Amendment purposes." In this case a young man who lawfully set up his tent in Cortez, Colorado, found the inside "ransacked" when he returned—police having conducted "a warrantless search of a tent whose flaps were closed and its entrance zippered shut." Hobbs finds that both the Fourth Amendment "right of the people to be secure in their persons, houses, papers, and effects, against unreasonable searches and seizures," as well as the Colorado Constitution's protection from such warrantless searches, are guaranteed to this man, even though he was perceived by local citizens as a "transient." In building his argument, Hobbs draws on legal precepts as well as the journals of Lewis and Clark, Major Stephen Long's report to Congress on his expedition in Colorado, a watercolor by Samuel Seymour depicting the expedition's tents, the field book of the Boy Scouts of America, and history of the Ludlow massacre of 1914 when women and children died underneath their tents in Colorado labor strife. Hobbs concludes: "Though it cannot be secured by a deadbolt and easily may be entered by those who respect not others, the thin walls of a tent nonetheless are notice of its occupant's claim to privacy unless consent to enter be asked and given." (pp. 369-78).

Hobbs seeks the truth, and he understands that "I'm not God," as More said in Bolt's play. Plainly, Hobbs' intellectual home is the law. More's words could be Hobbs' credo: "The currents and eddies of right and wrong, which [some] find such plain sailing, I can't navigate. I'm no voyager. But in the thickets of the law, oh, there I'm a forester." While Hobbs never loses that ethical compass that led him to study one year in a seminary, he never lets go of his allegiance to the law.

To reach the deep well of Hobbs' thinking, we move deeper into stories—stories drawn from history, precedent, and imagination. History—our common story—courses through Hobbs' judicial opinions, his poetry, his essays. Each generation renews history, he reminds us: "The great idea of progress in history is to share with friends and strangers, at the scarce and genuine watering hole, the drinking gourd of justice—a sip at a time." Imbibing justice, we may find ourselves riven by conflict. "We become holders in due course of the commitment our ancestors made to us when we negotiate in good faith—when we wake up in the morning to the land that Black Elk, a Native American, recalls when he intones...'A thunder being nation I am.'" (p. 160).

And how do we negotiate in good faith? In his dissent from *The Board of Education of Jefferson County v. Wilder* (1998), Hobbs offers legal and aesthetic precepts for self-governance, which thrives on vigorous debate. In the *Wilder* case, the majority upheld the school board's firing of an English teacher for showing his students the film *1900*, which depicted Italy from 1900 to 1945. Wilder taught at Columbine High School before the shooting deaths in 1999. Hobbs' dissent contends that the film helped students to think deeply about socialism, fascism, and personal corruption. He warns, "When we strip teachers of their professional judgment, we forfeit the educational vitality we prize. When we quell controversy for the sake of congeniality, we deprive democracy of its mentors." The film "inspires and instructs," says his dissenting opinion. Like all skillful art, it "inspires thought by rooting in the heart the image of justice versus injustice." (pp. 379-386).

The theme of "Fair Colorado," its people and its landscape, flows through this book. Hobbs offers us a love as vast as Whitman's for the land and its people. He hears the songs of prairie, mesa, canyon, and mountain. He roams with his brother Will along the great bend of the Continental Divide. For brother Will Hobbs, these mountains yield the setting for his riveting young adult novels *Bearstone* and *Beardance*. For Greg Hobbs, these mountains inspire his history of citizen efforts to control air pollution—"To See the Mountains: Restoring Colorado's Clear and Healthy Air" (pp. 67-118). Poems open each of the six chapters in this book. Each poem sings out in praise of Coloradans past, present, and future, fortunate citizenry who live in a fair land that stirs its people to be fair. In the lyrical essay "Sense of Place" (pp. 4-6), we enter into the awe and mystery that Hobbs and his brother felt when entering the ancient Puebloan kiva perched between the twin peaks of Chimney and Companion Rocks. Coloradans, Hobbs maintains, are marked by humanity's passage through the great Continental Divide.

Walt Whitman and Shakespeare before him remind us of the vital nexus between truth and beauty, logic and lyricism. Shakespeare tells us in *A Midsummer–Night's Dream*, "Imagination bodies forth/The forms of things unknown, the poet's pen/Turns them to shapes." Whitman speaks of the "equable" poet who judges: "He sees eternity in men and women—he does not see men and women as dreams or dots." In *Poetic Justice*, Martha Nussbaum interprets Whitman as creating a poet-judge who illumines rich, concrete moments to become, in Whitman's words, "the equalizer of his age and land." Pursuing this ideal, Hobbs writes to forge bonds that equalize our age, our land.

Sometimes he ties together both playfulness and social commentary, as when he quips in the opening stanza of "Lucy's Civil Procedure":

> Plaintiff, defendant,
>
> cross-claim, counter-claim,
>
> third party claim,
>
> surely someone is to blame! (p. 127).

On another occasion he links foibles of both writing and writer. Hobbs observes, "Lawyers and judges are literate people. They master words and their nuances. They explain the law and justice clearly and concisely to decision makers and the community. Until they start writing!" (p. 182).

At his best, Hobbs binds us to timeless wisdom and to humanity—yesterday, today, and tomorrow. In his letter to his daughter, he cites Emily Dickinson's lyrics on time, eternity, and home:

> Forever—is composed of Nows—
>
> 'Tis not a different time—

> Except for Infiniteness—
> And Latitude of Home—

Hobbs tells his daughter, who shares the poet's first name: "You're an Emily," and he notes that Dickinson's father was a lawyer. "I'm glad," he says, "to be your Dad." (p. 123).

Wander through the pathways of Greg Hobbs' mind as his thinking meanders, eddies, and races like a river in this volume, and you may "part the dark" as you find that forever is not so different from today (p. 163). May you also find your own infinity, your own latitude of home. In these pages, citizen-reader, may you plumb your own capacious spirit.

Chair of the Colorado Air Quality Control Commission when Greg Hobbs was a commissioner, Carol Edmonds Sullivan appointed Hobbs to rewrite the commission's protocols. She recalls that his work brought to the table intelligence, diplomacy, and procedural ease as the commission wrestled with air quality, oil shale development, and emissions from coal-fired power plants and motor vehicles. When he completed his term of office, she wrote to tell him that he reminded her of Chaucer's humble, noble knight, first among pilgrims, possessed of gentilesse, *a certain gentility, capability, and grandeur of spirit. Sullivan is a yoga teacher and author of the biography of a Colorado Congressman,* Wayne Aspinall: Mr. Chairman. *Her doctorate in English is from the University of Denver. She has been a state legislator and adjunct associate professor at the Colorado School of Mines.*

Other works cited:
Bolt, Robert. *A Man for all Seasons*. Vintage, 1960.
Hobbs, Will. *Beardance*. HarperCollins, 1993. Also see http://www.willhobbsauthor.com.
Hobbs, Will. *Bearstone*. HarperCollins, 1989.
Nussbaum, Martha C. *Poetic Justice/The Literary Imagination and Public Life*. Beacon, 1995.
Whitman, Walt. "As I Sat Alone by Blue Ontario's Shores." *Leaves of Grass*. [1867].

Preface

Lucky to Be a Coloradan

I am up at night thinking about why I want to make these writings public. Since I took this job in May of 1996 my sleep pattern has been irregular.

Night time is the perfect time for Supreme Court justices not to be seen or heard. Don't they prefer to be hidden away from public view? Doesn't "judicial activism" thrive on these black-robed, largely anonymous, publicly silent individuals hatching up new schemes to overthrow the Republic?

Just this summer, I was up many a night trying to figure out how to "take away the First Amendment right of the press to report" the sexual conduct of a young woman who accused a famous basketball star of rape. Several years ago, in dissent, I wrote a "movie review" about a fired high school senior speech and debate instructor who showed a smutty movie to his class instead of teaching them public virtue. And, before that, tracing the history of the tent in the American West, I let a guilty motorcycle-riding convenience store robber "off" because the police went into his tent—which could have been moved at any minute—to find the evidence.

At least that's how various editorialists, reporters, and newspaper readers saw my opinions in those cases. These controversial opinions are included in the sixth chapter of this book. I hope you will read them, and ask yourself: Did Hobbs and the justices who concurred with him get it right? Or not?

You would think from press reports that my attention is fixated on sex and crime. You would be right. Of course, the job requires me and the other six justices of the Colorado Supreme Court to focus on how people steal and do mayhem on each other. But the criminal law also involves the protection of citizen privacy against unwarranted police searches, and the law grants the accused the right to have a jury determine an individual's guilt or innocence.

Judges have the privilege of seeing that the government abides by the constitutions and laws of the State of Colorado and the United States. In addition to criminal cases, we decide water, land use, business, employment, insurance, worker's injury, automobile accident, tax, wrongful death, ballot title, congressional redistricting, school, freedom of speech, and family cases. In fact, we get to see every type of legal problem the citizens of Colorado happen to get themselves into. This is a fascinating job involving real and sometimes really strange stories of people in their everyday lives.

Judicial opinions must speak for themselves; judges cannot respond to the press about their deliberations. Believe me, it is hard to sit quietly when you don't think the comment or report is accurate or fair. But we must not respond. Even thinking about responding would insert into our deliberations, in the first instance, a political consideration consisting of speculation about the reaction of the press or the legislature or this or that group to what we are about to decide. Then we would be attuning our words not to the law but partisan considerations.

Fortunately, under Colorado's constitution, judges are removed from politics. We cannot attend political meetings, give campaign contributions, solicit funds for any organization, or take a public stand on candidates for office. No yard signs! We have taken an oath to decide each case on its facts and the applicable law, as fairly and as accurately as we can, and move on.

The job is full of beauty. Judges must listen carefully to the written and oral arguments of attorneys representing people with terrible problems that rob their peace of mind and upset their families. Though such troubles are not beautiful, the lawyer's art of illuminating a resolution the law offers can be.

The job is beautiful because I get to look at what the elected representatives of the people have to say about the law in the statutes they pass and what other courts, going way back in history, have had to say about similar cases. Then I help decide, together with my six colleagues, what to do about the problem, and move on to the next interesting window on Colorado's ongoing experience.

It is beautiful because I get to go out of the courthouse and visit with citizens in every part of this magnificent state. So long as I don't speak about the merits of a pending case, or get involved in partisan politics and accomplish all my judicial work, the Colorado Judicial Canons of Ethics allow, even encourage, me to speak and write about the law and justice.

Improving access to justice for all citizens and preserving judicial independence to make decisions free of political interference are the top two priorities of the Colorado judiciary, in addition to deciding every case that comes before us. To do this adequately, let alone well, judges must be visible to our fellow citizens, as active participants in non-partisan community groups and forums, exercising our teaching and writing voices. Colorado's magnificence includes not only its natural landscape, but also the vitality of its service, cultural, artistic, educational, and civic organizations.

That's where the middle-of-the-night tapping on the keys of this laptop figures in. To do my part I need the weekend and quiet time to reflect and prepare.

Since I'll be 60 in December, maybe I don't need as much sleep as I did when I was appointed to this court nearly nine years ago. No matter the late nights, my eagerness to start another day afresh reminds me of the poet William Stafford, who cut short the other end of the night. He awakened before the stars had broken. Here's my personal view about how this wonderful western poet and poetry teacher set the discipline for his thinking and writing:

WILLIAM STAFFORD'S YARN

William Stafford at his desk in early morning took his pen in hand and let the pen tell him where it wanted to go. Most often the pen stayed within the room and played, as a cat will, with a ball of yarn. The yarn unraveled itself, going where it wanted to go. Many mornings the yarn took itself out the door, down the street, down to the river, beyond the lights, over the hill, and the one after that, to a place where the yarn would un-ball itself on the shore of the river of stars.

Each morning the yarn would pick one of the morning stars to visit. Sky, Open Doors, The Sleep of Blue, Clear Days, Promises, Father, Mother, Others, The Blue Voice, Roof All Day, Arches, Turn Away, Reach Far Within Me, So Sure, Whatever Is Hiding, Nothing. Then the yarn would roll itself through the window back up to have coffee with William Stafford, his cat, and his pen about the time dawn began to look through for them.

Stafford is one of many poets I've befriended and from whom I have learned many a turn of word and window on the world, although we never met across the table. I've been writing poetry longer than I have been a lawyer and a judge. From my chambers, I can see the State's gold-leafed capitol dome, Civic Center Park, a wedge of Denver office buildings, and the blue-blue/snowy Indian Peaks of the Great Divide. I like to write poems about what I see.

I like to look people straight in the irises and talk with them. I talk with them about the law and the administration of justice, and I often use poems to illustrate the theme on which the meeting or event they have invited me to, turns. A well-tuned poem can cut to the heart and tell the story in a concise, incisive way. A gifted high school rhetoric teacher liked to tell me and my classmates, "Use the purple patch." By that he meant weave into the talk the passage that captures instant recognition of a similar story in the listener's own life, or paints the picture with splashes of colorful detail.

Poems have the power to paint our purple mountains majesty—the ones we Coloradans see right out the front window, every day. But you'll not see poems in my judicial opinions; they are reserved for other settings. Fishing rod handy, I often scratch incipient poems on loose-leaf paper, napkins, or envelope backs when I'm out about the land and waters. Sometimes they pop back up in a talk, essay, or article.

I have a joyous job. The writings and the talks collected in this book flow from my experience in this place of headwaters, the mother of rivers, Colorado—and from many a Western place where I've lived, camped, and hiked with members of my family and with our dear dogs. You will see, I hope, echoes of many of your personal experiences and your historical background reflected here. Imagining the audience I am speaking with or addressing birthed the poems, talks, essays, articles, and scripts in this book.

I help serve as a Western water bearer, and I do love the desert so. It keeps me thirsty and humble, so I can appreciate all the more the flowers of a scarce and sudden rain.

We have inherited the opportunity to live in this magnificent Western place, we Coloradans. Native Americans and Hispanos preceded most of us here, but they also moved into this land relatively recently. Carved in all the rocks we see up-titled or rinsed-off clean are fossil memories, the history of streams and oceans vanished and come back round again—the yearning of a creative geography to reinvent itself.

It's a privilege to be a Coloradan living in a fair land working for a fair Colorado in all its personal and community relationships. So much beauty is revealed on the surface and finds its source from the depths. So much deprivation, too. The Utes loved their Shining Mountains—all of Colorado's Western Slope—

only to see it chipped and pieced from them, so now the remaining bands are perched along the Pine and Mesa Verde environs. A peaceful band of Cheyenne—some intermarried with early white traders—were exterminated at Sand Creek on the eastern plains by Chivington and the Colorado Militia.

We must live with this heritage, as well as the acid drainage left from mining mountains. And we must not despair—but let us garner and harvest hope. We start with what we have and where we are, and we pass through and move forward. Every mountain pass, every prairie blade of grass, parts to let us through or to let us linger apace.

I am lucky to be a Coloradan. Research, survey, distillation, synthesis, articulation, passing through the events and revelations of each day and moment, these are critical to the practice of poetry, history, and judging.

This work has sprung from invitations citizens have extended to me to speak, teach, write, and provide the keynote for events, ceremonies, and commemorations. I celebrate Coloradans for what they do in community. I make this middle-of-the night/all-day work visible because stories, mine and theirs, have a place in this great land.

The poems here are mine, except those shown by attribution to other authors. Poetry is a very personal form of public speech. W.B. Yeats, Walt Whitman, Emily Dickinson, Thomas Hornsby Ferril, William Stafford, Wendell Berry, Terry Tempest Williams, and John Neihardt appear in this work because their insights, rhythm, and civic pitch flow naturally from the tongue and heart's own ear. Every time we give voice to their intonations, we continue on the ever-present journey into the West.

Wallace Stegner—full of wisdom and plentitude in the midst of scarcity—warned us of destructive propensities and the magnificence of our inherited western geography, sometimes shouting hosanna, at other times scolding, always redemptive. He is alive in these pages, too. Stegner and many a historian whom I've researched and cited draw my fidelity and allegiance. Law review articles and judicial opinion footnotes are the stirrups upon which the work of these persons continues to ride in my work.

In many ways, this book reflects the well I draw from for both my opinions and my poems. Journals of travelers, maps, photographs, sketches, paintings, historical and contemporary commentary about the western experience, in each of these and the more traditional legal literature are sources of profound inspiration and firsthand scholarship. I consult them frequently in researching and preparing judicial opinions and in commenting on the draft opinions of my colleagues during deliberation, another duty of this office.

Because some of the talks, essays, and articles included here contained overlapping materials, they have been trimmed in places. The essays in the first chapter are from books of poems I authored and privately published in 1977, 1990, 1992, and 1995. They were written before Governor Roy Romer appointed me to the Supreme Court on May 1, 1996. They show, I think, how I came to be a Coloradan. The rest I've written since.

Many thanks I owe to the making of this book: to Molly McGill and Greg Smith of Bradford, my editors; to Reda Martin of Bradford whom I had worked with as Liaison Justice to the Civil Rules Committee—she believed in collecting these writings and publishing them; to my reviewers John Moye, Lucy Marsh, and Mark Fiege; to Carol Sullivan, Foreword writer; to Kathryn Winograd, Colorado poet/my teacher; to my law clerks who have helped me birth the many judicial opinions I have written; to my esteemed colleagues of the Colorado Supreme Court, whose thinking and writing continues to inspire and educate me; and to my wife, Bobbie; to our children, Dan and Emily; to our son- and daughter-in-law, Alison and Mark; and to our four grandchildren, Joni, Kyle, Shannon, and Ella.

The most beautiful occurrence ever happening in my life is the day I met Bobbie on the face of Baldy Mountain at Philmont Scout Ranch outside of Cimarron, New Mexico, when we were camp counselors in the 1960s, and every day since.

If the work between these covers speaks and sings truly of the Great Divide community, it finds its voice in the citizens of Colorado who called me to this office.

Justice Greg Hobbs
September 2004

Acknowledgments

Poems by Justice Hobbs in this book have appeared in *High Country*, the magazine of the Philmont Staff Association; *University of Denver Water Law Review*; *The Legal Studies Forum*; *Denver University Law Review*; *Colorado River Project Symposium Proceedings* published by the Water Education Foundation; *The Colorado Lawyer*; and *Colorado Mother of Rivers, Water Poems by Justice Greg Hobbs*, published by the Colorado Foundation for Water Education.

Poems by authors other than by Justice Hobbs in this book are identified by the poet's name. These poets include Walt Whitman, Emily Dickinson, William Stafford, Thomas Hornsby Ferril (poems reprinted by permission of The Thomas Hornsby Ferril Literary Trust), Wendell Berry, Terry Tempest Williams, and John Neihardt.

With permission of the original publishers, the following are collected and reprinted in this book:

Where We Are, Where We've Been, in CONJUNCTIVE MANAGEMENT OF GROUND AND SURFACE WATER, Colorado Water Newsletter of Colorado State University (April 2004), available at http://www.cwrri.colostate.edu/pubs/newsletter/newsletter.htm.

To See The Mountains: Restoring Colorado's Clear and Healthy Air, 75 U. COLO. L. REV. 433 (2004).

The Role of Climate In Shaping Western Water Institutions, 7 U. DENV. WATER L. REV. 1 (2003) (followed by Mesa Verde Journal).

The Practice of Poetry, History, and Judging, 80 DENV. U. L. REV. 756 (2003).

Book Review of Tim Terrell, Thinking Like A Writer: A Lawyer's Guide to Writing and Editing, 32 COLO. LAW. 60 (Dec. 2003).

How Drought Shapes Colorado Water Law And Policy, 1 HEADWATERS 4, Colorado Foundation For Water Education (Oct. 2003).

Inside the Drama of the Colorado River Compact Negotiations: Negotiating the Apportionment, Water Education Foundation, Colorado River Project Symposium Proceedings (Sept. 17-19, 2003).

A Primer on Colorado Water Law, No. 977 TRAIL & TIMBERLINE 16, Colorado Mountain Club (May-June 2003).

Two of a Piece, 32 COLO. LAW. 39 (April 2003).

Delight For Waterbugs, A Colorado Education, WATERNEWS, Northern Colorado Water Conservancy District (April 2003), at 16.

Book Review of Daniel Tyler, Silver Fox of the Rockies: Delphus E. Carpenter and Western Water Compacts, 6 U. DENV. WATER L. REV. 566 (2003).

How Like A River: The Evolution Of Western Water Law, excerpted in A. Dan Tarlock, James N. Corbridge, Jr., David H. Getches, WATER RESOURCE MANAGEMENT, A CASEBOOK IN LAW AND PUBLIC POLICY, Fifth Edition 158 (2002).

Book Review of Dale A. Oesterle and Richard B. Collins, The Colorado State Constitution: A Reference Guide, 31 COLO. LAW. 39 (Dec. 2002).

A Sonnet To A Problem River, Book Review of G. Emlen Hall, High and Dry: The Texas-New Mexico Struggle For The Pecos River, Vol. 34, No. 13 HIGH COUNTRY NEWS 16 (July 3, 2002).

Book Review of Kenneth R. Wright and Alfredo Valencia Zegarra, Machu Picchu, A Civil Engineering Marvel, and Ruth M. Wright and Alfredo Valencia Zegarra, the Machu Picchu Guidebook, A Self-Guided Tour, 6 U. DENV. WATER L. REV. 137 (2002).

State Water Politics Versus an Independent Judiciary: The Colorado And Idaho Experiences, 5 U. DENV. WATER L. REV. 122 (2001).

May Day Anniversary: On Being an Imminent Jurist, 30 COLO. LAW. 61 (Sept. 2001).

Persuading the Decision-Maker, 29 COLO. LAW. 63 (Sept. 2000).

Protocols of the Colorado Supreme Court, 27 COLO. LAW. 21 (Mar. 1998).

Historical Perspective on Western Land and Water Law, Water Education Foundation, 75th Anniversary Colorado River Compact Symposium Proceedings (May 28-31, 1997), at 112.

Fishing and the Supreme Court—Making the Transition From Private Practice, 25 COLO. LAW. 31 (Dec. 1996).

I've Seen the Mountains Falling, Poems of Colorado, Philmont, Southwest, Philmont Staff Association (1995).

"Justice Gregory Hobbs: A Poet with the Heart of a Fighter," in *Ag Journal* (Dec. 2001).

Poem reprinted from *Black Elk Speaks: Being the Life Story of a Holy Man of the Oglala Sioux* by John G. Neihardt by permission of the University of Nebraska Press. Copyright © 1932, 1959, 1972 by John G. Neihardt. © 1961 by the John G. Neihardt Trust. © 2000 by the University of Nebraska Press.

Excerpt from *Where the Bluebird Sings to the Lemonade Springs* by Wallace Stegner, copyright © 1992 by Wallace Stegner. Used by permission of Random House, Inc.

William Stafford poems "Ask Me," "West of Here," "Looking for Gold," "Walking the Borders," "Home State," and "The Dream of Now," copyright 1977, 1981, 1987, 1991, 1998 by the Estate of William Stafford. Reprinted from *The Way It Is: New & Selected Poems* with the permission of Graywolf Press, Saint Paul, Minnesota.

Excerpt from *Hour of Trial: The Conservation Conflict in Colorado and the West 1891-1907*, by G. Michael McCarthy. Copyright 1977 by the University of Oklahoma Press.

Wendell Berry, "Sowing," in *Farming: A Hand Book* (Shoemaker & Hoard, 1970). Reprinted with permission of the publisher.

I've Seen the Mountains Falling

I'VE SEEN THE MOUNTAINS FALLING

I've seen the mountains falling,
heard the mighty canyons ring
with Colorado thunder
and clear blue mountain streams,
I've seen the nights grow brighter
and the days just shine in gold,
been looking for El Dorado
in the mountain of my dreams.

I hear the eagles calling,
see torches in the sky,
went off to Colorado,
had a gleaming in my eye,
there I found my measure
was a bird upon the wing
and the mountains' greatest treasure
is the way the aspen sing.

I guess you might get crazy
thinking you're going to die,
you drive your body pounding,
waste beauty on your way,
you turn your only fortune
into gambling your life away,
when El Dorado's being
on a Colorado Day.

I wish I'd seen the world,
been a woman and a man,
felt the grip of dry starvation
and sailed the Rio Grande,
I'd be a farmer, mountaineer,
write a book about the mind,
but lay me down a fossil
in Colorado land.

Sense of Place
January 1977

West of Wolf Creek Pass, between Pagosa Springs and Bayfield in southwestern Colorado, an east-west ridge cuts across the prevailing pattern of north-south canyons. This geographical anomaly of itself would not interest the traveler hastening to Durango, Silverton, and Ouray where the awesome San Juan Range, christened Weminuche by the mountain Utes, can be seen in towering moods along the great bend of the Continental Divide.

Yet even the most hurried pilgrim must slow his pace in wonder at two colossal features of the ridge: a perfectly formed chimney and the other, a rather unshapely outcrop that stands alongside in solemn vigil.

Chimney and Companion Rocks are well-named, but they are not homelike as their names would seem to indicate. Thunderheads often nest atop the two and lightning plunges back with hawkish talons. Stones are split into pebbles and join the fossil fronds and fish that gather in the gullies. Most of Colorado is a primeval sea thrown up for the wearing down. Here old inhabitants are possessed to show themselves; the place is alive with fossils.

My brother Will and his wife, Jean, live in Cabezon Canyon, from which they have a constant view of the Chimney and its mate. Their 20 acres between the rimrock are peopled with goats they raise for food, milk, and companionship. There are no human neighbors. When Sally, Snowstorm, and the kids grow too familiar and their conversation tiresome, the coyotes visit—below the goat barn on keen fall nights they startle with the pitch and rhythm of their intelligences, as if their beast-like tongues had been loosed by some great teacher.

Will and Jean have set a sign at the mouth of the canyon: "No Hunting!" They are listeners. The place abounds with neighborly sounds: owl on her nightly cruisings, packrat scurrying with bits of fur and bone, wasting nothing for his home, mule deer nibbling willow shoots by the creek, bobcat feet. The rimrock also carries on a daily conversation as befits an aged prophet, by facial expressions. On its countenance appear fantastic forms of birds, beasts, and men faintly etched but discernable nonetheless, like clouds sometimes do, a metamorphosis of shapes depending on the light of seasons and the perceiver. From the rimrock's perspective, the native peoples viewed clouds as their departed relatives watching over them.

During the New Year's holiday just past, Bobbie, Dan, Emily, and I returned to the canyon and found that the visage of this homeland was being altered in other ways. Since our last visit in late summer, a local farming family—they live along the Stollsteimer on the way to Navajo Lake—had leased their pasture land for stripping coal; their goats' own hill was being laid as low as a body without its marrow bone. Another pasture and a pond have been promised in return. But the country is rain-poor, and for two seasons now snow has been scarce.

This the General Assembly cannot abide; it voted last week to seed the sky over the San Juans and other western peaks. A good part of the hoped-for west slope snowpack is being wrapped for transmountain diversion and for energy development. Water rights have become as negotiable as shares of stock, though once parted from the land the family water's gone and there's little reclamation without it once the stripper's job is done.

Agents of the San Juan Lumber Company operating out of Arizona in the summer of 1976 successfully stopped a wilderness designation of the Piedra River watershed, which runs from the high range past Chimney Rock on the west. Their argument to the local folk: trees alone are left for work and a man won't know his wife and children when they're hungry, wilderness stands between you and your next meal. Opposition to preserving the forest was compelling to locally elected officials.

When the land and water's gone, families grow lawns, live in town, and vote.

Will and I climbed the east-west ridge on New Year's Day, up through the silver sage, gnarled green piñon brakes, the fossil fronds and fish, brown with age—the sky so blue it seemed the primeval sea had turned upside down for swimming. We struggled up a narrow channel of rimrock, shaped like palisades of the parted Red Sea, to the top. Will called it Holy Ground.

It was my first time there. At the penultimate point of the ridge they stand alone, Chimney and Companion Rocks, twin pinnacles of wind-eroded stone, and sloping down from them, the muted kiva mounds deep within the wounded spirit wombs, self effacement, communality and awe, out of which a singular lineage once emerged, grandfathers, sons and daughters, deer, the sun, pebbles, all as one.

We came down in nightfall in lightly spreading snow. The parched hills were glad of it. They spoke of knowledge, power, and those who would hear of both.

If ever Mother Earth should lead her people forth again, there to welcome them will be the mountains and their kin. It seems strange they could use our help to maintain their sense of place.

Finding Colorado
February 1977

Each of us has a special place in nature. Deprived of it, we stray until an event, a person, or a location of great beauty reorients our spirit. When I was a boy in California, I had a favorite place by a creek to go for thinking under a huge oak tree with crawdads scuttling in the water and blue-bellies flashing on and off the rocks. On returning from college one summer, I found the creek had been buried in a culvert and the oak tree cut down for a parking lot. Crayfish and lizards were extinct. This bothered me considerably at the time. Fortunately, the incredible Rocky Mountains intervened.

I met my wife, Bobbie, on Baldy Mountain in 1966, my fifth summer as a ranger and camp director at Philmont Scout Ranch high in the Sangre de Cristo Range outside of Cimarron, New Mexico. We married in Denver, her home, the next summer. Throughout Peace Corps service in South America and the turbulent halcyon days at Berkeley, we kept thinking of the mountains where our love began. We returned here in 1971.

My work is shaped from love of Colorado, the Southwest, and family. Coming to feel fully of each has been intense, disruptive, and wholly wonderful. Personal and professional lives have been synthesized in the process. While arguing the State's case against industrial polluters in my daily work as a lawyer in a smog-sprawled city beneath magnificent mountains whose history is long and has only begun, I have become aware of the fearful struggle that rages worldwide between the corporate-state economy and nature's economy. As husband and father growing with wife and children in this environment, I have learned that the human economy is precariously linked to economies of the time and place we find ourselves.

Our passionate spirits, so capable of destroying and being destroyed, are also susceptible of being reborn to the natural world and to each other as, through with yet another search, the endangered peregrine falcon flies home to his like-wandering mate and their struggling young in some high and sheltered place. If allowed to live, peregrines can nest in the wild or on tall urban office buildings. So can we.

This land we love is a spirit that calls to kindred spirits in varied harsh and subtle tones, as it did the native peoples and their spiritual forebears, as it does their progeny. Whatever the rhythm and lyric of the singer, psalms are poems of mankind's earthly spirit reawakened to the search for harmony.

Here, there is a source of power that has no need of nameplates; hence no fear of being labeled romantic, impractical, idealistic, simplistic. As the wild and beautiful seasons are manifestations of the earth in its orderly turn through the universe, so are we. Discovering this has always been the essence of revelation.

Last summer my son Dan and I hiked into the Holy Cross Wilderness. We camped by a creek under a huge spruce tree, watched rainbow trout flash in the water and marmots scuttle across the rocks. When my daughter Emily's old enough to backpack, just a year or two now, she'll go. I believe the kids will want to lead their children there, too.

Motion for Appearance and Late Filing
March 1990

Lawyers author appellate briefs on behalf of clients to seek reversal of an adverse decision by the court below, or to protect a favorable decision from being overturned. Effective briefs argue the applicable facts and law succinctly, understandably, and with conviction. It is customary to file with the Brief a set of Appendices, consisting of excerpts from statutes, rules, legislative history, pleadings from the court below, and exhibits that counsel deems particularly important to full consideration of the merits by the appellate court.

As an Assistant Attorney General in the mid- to late-seventies, the undersigned argued cases on behalf of the State of Colorado. Subsequently, in private law practice, he has learned that one's view of the "public interest" is colored by his or her occupation and preoccupations. A land developer sells "affordable housing and a decent place to live." A farmer takes stock in "food and fiber for the nation." A coal miner tries to keep "the wolf from the door." An ecologist argues that "in wilderness is the preservation of the world." Attorneys are retained to argue for all perspectives.

As Coloradans and inhabitants of the Southwest, we are united by love for the land, the air, and the waters. Inexplicably, we also claim the right to abuse them and each other—at least, the evidence of our short human history here proves that proposition. Taking our proper place in the magnificence that surrounds us is a lifetime process of choice and inspired recognition.

Together we represent an overwhelming force that the earth cannot reckon with, unless we choose to honor the invariable truth of Colorado: that the seasons, and all creatures who live through them, change invariably in patterns of unpredictable days. Separately, each of us exhibits a facet of the truth; together, we are the workings of justice in community.

Lawyers licensed to practice law in this state may appear before its courts and, with leave, may file late or additional pleadings. The appeal herein is made by a citizen/attorney to fellow citizens: that we may share the blessed power this remarkable region holds for each of us.

Therefore, in the interest of justice and equitable consideration, leave is sought at this time to appear and make a late consolidated filing. No objection will be made to a lengthy extension of time for filing of an Answer Brief.

WHEREFORE, Appellant prays.

> Respectfully submitted,
> Gregory J. Hobbs, Jr.
> Colorado Attorney Registration No. 0009

In Relief
May 5, 1992

When traveling together, whether for distraction or experience, years take on the accent of road maps, trail maps, topographical maps. Relief maps are a tactile universe; one can feel oriented until arrival becomes confused with deterioration announced by weathered signs like "road work ahead," "detour," or that definitive statement about going nowhere, spotted in the Navajo homeland: "road closed."

Why closed? For lack of interest, by way of charitable warning, because tourists run out of gas, banditos abound, bedrock has disappeared into the abyss, or governmental budgets don't cover all the potholes there are to go around? The traffic circles of medieval Spain, while most other consequences of noble inbreeding have declined, continue to confront visitors with this historical truth, that modern European cities like Seville were built to accommodate donkey paths.

Through that unaccustomed means of circumlocution—walking in the age of motor cars—is revealed the discovered country through whose bourne the traveler can return. In the jungle of the Yucatan, aqueducts for conveying rainwater to 12 encircling reservoirs served, in drier days, as highways for foot traffic passing in and out of the sacred ceremonial heart of Tikal. From the top of an enduring stone wall, perfectly fitted without mortar between the Sun Gate and Huayna Pichhu, a condor can be seen wheeling skyward from Machu Picchu, stronghold of stargazers. Sally crabs scutter across volcanic rock while fur seals flip and sea lions roar, on Santiago Island, in the Galapagos where Darwin redefined God and Nature through observing that adaptation, not doctrine, is the essence of revelation.

In the spray of Angel Falls, a mighty stream plunging from a Tepui pours through the Rio Carrao to the Orinoco to the Amazon up past Florida, taking the New World to the Old in a great sweep. Nile temples of Karnak, carved Nabatean hallows of Petra, protruding Mayan pyramids on limestone caprock, bear witness to a migration of fervor, intellect, and hard labor as sure and capricious as the ever-encroaching rainforest, desert, or civilization.

Trade routes running north out of Peru through Mexico carried to the canyon outposts of the Southwest a multi-partisan tradition of far-flung togetherness, long before the Extremadurian conquest unloosed from the Americas back to the Old World their life-sustaining gifts: corn, potatoes, squash, and chile peppers.

Exploitation yields to tourism, then to enlightenment. The principle of conservation of matter and energy, of travel and gearing up for travel, is that nothing is truly lost, all is transformed, accounts are due when the journey is done.

Mountains Call
January 1995

Before he wrote *Changes in Latitudes, Bearstone, Downriver, The Big Wander,* and *Beardance,* my brother Will and his wife Jean lived in the Cabezon Canyon within sight of Chimney Rock in southwestern Colorado. They taught school and managed goats. With Suzy, their beloved Australian Shepherd, they climbed the nearby rocks and ridges. Having explored nearby environs, in July of 1975 they led us forth on the first of many family treks into the Weminuche Wilderness along the great bend of the Continental Divide.

Will and I first saw Chimney Rock in 1964, on a long weekend break from ranger duties at Philmont Scout Ranch outside of Cimarron, New Mexico....

The Sangre de Cristo mountains of Philmont and Colorado San Juans have become enduring bastions of strength and inspiration for our family. Australian Shepherds Suzy and Pepsi (daughter of Suzy's first and only litter) always ran ahead of us into the mountains, turning constantly to check that we were following, returning to herd us forward if our resolve to reach the next bend or summit might be flagging. Suzy's life was tragically destroyed on Will and Jean's property by poison bait (perhaps intended for coyotes). Pepsi, too, has crossed the Divide, having grown old among the very highest crags. Our kids are grown.

The mountains, mesas, canyons, and rivers still call us to live within that magnificent landscape that fires the imagination of each new generation of westerners. After parenting, there's husbandry. Legal energy is worth spending for this: honest clients with just or hard causes; a sufficient supply of good water for drinking, growing living things, fishing, and floating on; clean air; and wild places where there's nothing between a person and the crest of the Divide but feet, family, a fine canine, and up ahead, a mighty pass to push on through.

Colorado Comes Back Round Again
April 1995

As 1990 turned, following ample precipitation in the eighties, drought again settled in on Colorado's western slope, particularly throughout the San Juan Basin from Wolf Creek Pass to Pagosa Springs and Durango to Cortez. Irrigation water ran low through ditches plumbing McElmo Creek behind Sleeping Ute Mountain.

Just across the border in Indian Country, enormous twin-tank tractor/trailer rigs hauled across the Navajo Reservation, bearing water for scattered families who perch on that brown, red, and rifted landscape, as their ancestors did before them. The fractured towers of Hovenweep—on massive sloping boulders and rimrock headwalls—stood watch over the Colorado Plateau, from the thinly snow-capped Uncompahgre Mountains on the east to the multifingered western gulches of Cedar Mesa. Aridity returned.

Westerners, we observe seasons and the cycle of man. In the late seventies, skyscrapers boomed upward along Colorado's Front Range as contractors and drill crews fanned out over western Colorado. Carbon monoxide violations in the Denver metropolitan area peaked at 154 per year. The "brown cloud" sloshed its way darker and denser down the Platte Valley from the foothills to Fort Morgan. The Mile High City burgeoned with relocated corporate headquarters, sprawling subdivisions, and penny stock brokers banking on western slope resource extraction. Colorado Springs was heralded as the "Star Wars Capitol." Universities—Mines, C.U., and C.S.U.—turned out engineers of all types (mining, agricultural, oil, hydraulic) in order to serve hot job prospects.

A million-barrel-a-day shale oil industry seemed imminent. Colorado Ute geared up for the construction of additional power plants and transmission lines. Grand Junction built a gleaming new airport and the Hilton Hotel came to Horizon Drive. Then came "Black Sunday," May 2, 1982. Like a huge tanker veering off for other climes, Exxon made "The Announcement," leaving the shoals of the Grand Valley in its wake, stranding Battlement Mesa for a retirement community.

One by one, the building cranes vanished from Denver, along with scores of families on both sides of the Divide who tracked on to seek a living elsewhere. Businesses folded. Those who love the mountains and the plains, the mesas and the river valleys—the gritty and the lucky ones—dug in.

Colorado goes and comes back round again.

Faltering growth and intervening perspectives have spurred another kind of progress. As the nineties turn to middle age, a brief report is that carbon monoxide violations have fallen to one in the Denver metropolitan area. The St. Vrain nuclear power plant is shut down—permanently, it appears. Due to compromise between environmentalists and water supply interests, a 75-mile stretch of the Cache la Poudre River has been designated as a National Wild and Scenic River. Public Service Company is stressing conversion of wood-burning fireplaces and motor vehicle fleets to natural gas. Two Forks Dam foundered on a question of beauty, and the Denver Water Department is promoting conservation as a requirement of life in the metropolitan area. Governor Romer received the Environment 2000 report from the Citizens' Advisory Committee. It began with this nineteenth-century question of a western Native American:

> When the buffalo are all slaughtered, the wild horses tamed, the secret corners of the forest heavy with the scent of many men, and the views of the ripe hills blotted by talking wires, where is the thicket?
>
> Chief Joseph of the Nez Perce

In August of 1993, the long-delayed Colorado Wilderness Act, which now includes portions of the pristine Piedra River canyon as wilderness, was signed into law by the President.

Nationally, the election of 1994 was termed a watershed. But the Governor's "smart growth" message captured Colorado. Up higher, from the Window—where mountains fall away into the Atlantic and Pacific watersheds—climbers discover why a livable land for all creatures is a sacred trust that each of us may carry for a time certain.

Justice Gregory Hobbs: A Poet with the Heart of a Fighter

By Liz Dunn
Ag Journal, reprinted with permission
December 7, 2001

Justice Gregory Hobbs is a poet, a teacher, an historian, a conservationist, and a writer. He is a father, a husband, a Colorado Supreme Court Justice, a lover of the Southwest, and a student of western water law.

"I was born in Gainsville, Florida in 1944. My dad was in the Air Corps during the war, and then he went with the Air Force," Hobbs said. "I knocked all around the country basically, especially the West."

Hobbs eventually ended up studying history at Notre Dame, and graduated *magna cum laude* in 1966. He went on to graduate school at Columbia University. "I found out pretty immediately that New York was such a grand place, and graduate school was not, that I ended up spending a semester getting to know New York." Hobbs said.

After dropping out of graduate school, Hobbs taught sixth grade for a semester at St. Paul's Catholic School in Manhattan. "That's the hardest job I've ever had in my life! But it was wonderful, too." He then spent a year in the Peace Corps in Latin America, after which Hobbs came back to the United States to begin his law career.

"I started law school in the fall of 1968 at Berkeley, needing a useful occupation," Hobbs said. After law school, Hobbs clerked for Judge William Doyle on the 10th Circuit. "When I saw what a fine person he was and the role judges play in our society, I decided I wanted to be a judge."

Hobbs tried private practice in San Francisco for 11 months, but missed the mountains of Colorado. Hobbs moved back to Denver in October of 1973, where he found a job with the EPA doing air pollution enforcement. He then moved on to start the Natural Resources section of the Attorney General's office, where he began to learn water law.

Eventually, Hobbs returned to private practice, joining Davis, Graham & Stubbs in 1979. "I was hired to help get the permits for the Windy Gap water project, and that was when I first started to work for the Northern Colorado Water Conservancy District," Hobbs said. "Nobody could want a better water client than the Northern District. That board is totally dedicated not only to the seven counties it serves, but to the role of water agencies in society."

As general counsel for the Northern District, Hobbs worked with the legislature, the courts, farmers, developers, and community leaders in Northern Colorado.

On April 18, 1996, Hobbs was appointed to the Colorado Supreme Court by former Governor Roy Romer. Colorado voters retained him for a ten-year term, which expires in 2009. During his time on the court, Hobbs has seen every type of law in Colorado, but water law continues to be his chief interest.

The future of water law in Colorado is of primary concern to Hobbs. "Part of the water business is the changing values and attitudes. I think we have a very flexible water doctrine in Colorado," Hobbs said. "The water law builds on the values and customs of the people."

"We've always had these two chambers of our western heart, beneficial use and preservation. Even from the earliest times of settling the West, you can see that with the setting aside of Yellowstone, the Grand Canyon, and Yosemite," Hobbs said. "In the meantime, we were out there encouraging people to settle the land, take the water from the streams to grow crops, grow cities, grow kids, and make the businesses.

"The twenty-first century is going to be more of the same. Our agendas of beneficial use and preservation bumping up against the basic need of people and the environment for water will continue," Hobbs said. "I'm confident that the people of the West can deal with this. A basic manifestation of westerners is their optimism and innovation, as well as their commitment to property rights and their understanding of informed public policy choices."

Hobbs is also concerned about the continuing urbanization of Colorado. "Educating the urbanites regarding the history and culture of the water policy and the law is absolutely critical, or we will not have support for having stable systems of allocation and administration," Hobbs said.

In addition to a love of the law, Hobbs has a love for westerners and living in the West. "I've been writing poetry for over 30 years. Naturally my subject is the West, the mountains and plains, the rivers of Colorado, New Mexico, Utah, and California," he said. "You can't help but be moved by this great land heritage that we have in the West. There is nothing like it."

In addition to his passion for poetry and the West, Hobbs also enjoys collecting historic water maps of the Southwest and participating in an educational group for water judges called "Dividing the Waters."

Although Hobbs can count among his achievements helping in the compromises that produced the northern water district's Windy Gap Diversion Project, the 1986 Wild and Scenic River Act on the Poudre River, the northern district's Southern Water Supply Pipeline, and the 1993 Colorado Wilderness Act, his greatest achievement and privilege is his family. Hobbs and his wife, Bobbie, have one son and one daughter, three grandchildren, and another grandchild on the way.

The Great Divide Community

WELCOME!

Welcome to Colorado,
welcome home!
Hope you feel good
about moving on—
moving here,

Where'd you come from—
Kansas, Ohio, California,
Bosnia, Pakistan,
Israel? Welcome home,
welcome here! A basic

Truth, beside the land,
beside the sky—all of us,
we entered here, Ute,
Cheyenne—moving up
the rivers, moving 'cross

The plains, from Santa
Fe, Spain, China, Japan,
Ireland—on horse, on foot,
board the iron horse, board
the aero-plane—our oldest

Ruins, why, just yesterday
people into Hovenweep
settling the southwest sun,
moving disappearing water
from disappearing creeks,

Building towers, too, they
looking for enemies? Looking
for friends moving up the trade
routes from Central, from South
America—they pray, make

Mistakes, cruel and kind, families
discover much, prosper, bust out,
love the whirling storms—then,
just as suddenly, sky-on-fire scarlet,
swoop of hawk, sweep of the long 360,

Lope of coyote, Ponderosa pollen,
miller moths moving on through—
fluttering round the lights, borrowing
the land, the sky, hatch on the
waters—borrowing Colorado, each

Other. Welcome!

Justice Hobbs' Swearing-in Ceremony
Speech in the Courtroom, Colorado Supreme Court
May 1, 1996

Dear People of Colorado:

I thank the Governor and the members of the Judicial Nominating Commission for their trust, their confidence, this great challenge. I thank the Chief Justice and the People of the State of Colorado for the oath I have taken. I thank my longtime friend David Robbins for showing me how rugby players can smash into each other on the field and in the courts, and shake hands. With joy, enthusiasm, with awe and dedication to the work of the courts, I accept this call to serve Colorado—once again—to the best of my ability.

My family, my friends: Thank you for honoring Bobbie and me, and the members of this Court, by being here with us. You are teachers, farmers, actors, poets, legislators, businessmen and women, Scouting leaders, community workers, government officials, lawyers; you are backpackers, fisher persons; you are doers, thinkers, neighbors, parents, children. You are Colorado.

Could there be a better land to air our differences, to breathe the common air, to hear the waters sing? Each of you has placed an item in my pack—map or compass, the fire starter, poncho for the rains, a sturdy pair of boots, some funny saying, sneakers for relaxing around the campfire, your strength for new mornings after a restless night on the ground. With gratitude, I cinch again the shoulder straps. May I hike along with you! A mighty pass awaits some awesome views.

For you my dear wife and children, my dear mother and friends, for you my new colleagues, I mark this start, this day, with a poem and a prayer:

ON BEING SWORN

I can help you with your pack,
you can help me, too

We've each a mighty load to carry on,
there's lots of fishing left to do.

Don't forget the meadow frisbee
and the cards for Hearts and War,

We'll switch the lead from time
to time, when I might lag

And you're all speed. Guess I ought
to say it now, before we start to

Strain and sweat, the view ahead
is what we'll earn and not

A finer day for hiking through.

The Practice of Poetry, History, and Judging[*]
Denver University Law Review, Judges Symposium Issue
2003

I am delighted to accept the *Denver University Law Review*'s invitation to share a perspective on a law topic of personal importance. Judges are not often asked for their personal viewpoint. There is good reason for this: judges cannot allow their personal views to stand in the way of their sworn judicial role.

The mystery is this: We get to become judges because the perspective we have gained as individuals in the community led to our nomination and appointment to the bench. Having called us to service, the Judicial Nominating Commissions and governors who select us—and the citizens who retain us in office—certainly expect that we will bring our personal resources to bear in performing the public's work. These personal resources include our personality, education, experience, skills, expertise, and what we like to do.

. . .

Blessings are of water and the spirit. History was my college major at Notre Dame. I've been writing poetry longer than I've been a lawyer; I am glad to include in this essay poems I have written of living and working in Colorado. My first law job after graduation from Boalt Hall, Berkeley, was law clerk to U.S. Circuit Judge William E. Doyle. He served on the Colorado Supreme Court before joining the federal judiciary. I pass his picture every day in the hall outside the door of my chambers.

When I left Colorado, after the clerkship, to practice in San Francisco, Judge Doyle's parting reproach/challenge to me was, "Why don't you make your stand here?" I'm still standing on the strength of that question.

Judge Doyle began to teach me the practice of judging. Judging is the practice of translating the experience of the community into a just decision grounded firmly on scholarship and common sense, responsive to the facts and the law of the case.[1]

---

[*] 80 DENV. U. L. REV. 756 (2003). Reprinted with permission.
[1] History can resonate in a state supreme court's consideration of a contemporary legal problem. I cite instances in the footnotes that follow.

JUDGES MUST BE STUDENTS

Law is the written experience
of the People

Wise for being slow to change,
courage for the changing

In the strength of individual experience,
one Nation

Joined to the community
of individuals,

Judges must be students
of the experience of the community.

Becoming a Coloradan

We are blessed to live in the land of the Great Divide. Surely, it's a place of poetry,[2] nature, men and women, words, passion, spirituality, delight, tragedy, insight, wit, brevity, discipline, melody, a profound sense of passing, and so a profound sense of gratitude for the opportunity to be here, at this time, in this place, with this person, this bird, this tree, this flower, this river, that hill, the one behind it, so on up to altitudes and attitudes, where oceans gurgle from snow seeps, in multiple directions, drawn by gravity to destinies far and near.

COLORADANS

To each of us
the land, the air, the water,
mountain, canyon, mesa, plain,
lightning bolts, clear days with no rain,

---

[2] On the day he appointed me to the Colorado Supreme Court, Governor Roy Romer requested that I not put poetry into my judicial opinions. But he also wrote me a note eight days after I was sworn in, saying, "I hope you still take time to enjoy your poetry, hikes and other important parts of life." I am honoring these requests and hopes.

At the source of all thirst,
at the source of all thirst-quenching hope,
at the root and core of time and no-time,
the Great Divide community

Stands astride the backbone of the continent,
gathering, draining, reflecting, sending forth
a flow so powerful it seeps rhythmically
from within,

Alive to each of us,
to drink, to swim, to grow corn ears,
to listen to our children float the streams
of their own magnificence,

Out of their seeping dreams,
out of their useful silliness,
out of their source-mouths
high and pure,

The Great Divide,
you and I, all that lives
and floats and flies and passes through
all we know of why.

Thomas Hornsby Ferril worked for the Great Western Sugar Company. He was also a poet. He knew how water and well-prepared soil can siphon sugar to a poem and sugar beets. He loved Colorado history—plains history, stream history, mountain history—the history of rocks and rivers and how they came before and will outlast us. He wrote *Two Rivers*[3] about the confluence of the South Platte and Cherry Creek, from which Denver sprang as a result of an 1858 gold find. His poem sings of the wagon people and the invitation of the waters: "If you will stay we will not go away."[4]

---

[3] Thomas Hornsby Ferril, *Two Rivers, in* THOMAS HORNSBY FERRIL AND THE AMERICAN WEST 122, Robert C. Baron, Stephen J. Leonard, and Thomas J. Noel, eds. (Fulcrum Publishing, Golden, Colorado and the Center of the American West, University of Colorado at Boulder 1996).

[4] *Id.*

Living through the Dust Bowl, Ferril knew enough of water scarcity to also write a poem he titled *Drouth—1824*: "Hear how the wagons crack/ In the copper drouth of the prairie."[5]

Another great western writer, Wallace Stegner, said: "Adaptation is the covenant that all successful organisms sign with the dry country.... [W]ater is safety, home, life, place. All around those precious watered places, forbidding and unlivable, is only open space, what one must travel through between places of safety."[6]

Stegner's calling was to write about the joy and scarcity of the watering holes. He showed us how to relate our kinship to each other and to every other living thing that depends on water for a living. He softened no blows about our wasteful habits and busted hopes. "The town dump" is "our poetry and our history"[7] he said in *Wolf Willow*,[8] his reminiscence about growing up as the child of homesteaders on the plains of southern Saskatchewan, very near Montana's border.

What a concept, by our garbage are we known! What Stegner found in the dump as a kid was every sort of trace of what westerners prize and discard in trying to perch a toehold. What he meant to say—as always—he said tartly and wisely: "The lesson they preached [from all these throwaways] was how much is lost, how much thrown aside, how much carelessly or of necessity given up, in the making of a new country."[9]

Stegner match-paired his critical eye with his hopeful eye. Optimism and community he thought to be the West's future legacy:

> Angry as one sometimes gets at what heedless men do to a noble human habitat, one cannot be pessimistic about the West. This is where optimism was born. And when the West learns more surely that co-operation, not rugged individualism, is the quality that most characterizes and most preserves it, I will seize the harp and join the boosters, for this will be one of the world's great lands.[10]

---

[5] Thomas Hornsby Ferril, *Drouth—1824*, in THOMAS HORNSBY FERRIL AND THE AMERICAN WEST, *supra* note 3, at 16.
[6] Wallace Stegner, *Living Dry*, in MARKING THE SPARROW'S FALL: WALLACE STEGNER'S AMERICAN WEST 226-27 (Page Stegner ed., 1998).
[7] Wallace Stegner, WOLF WILLOW: A HISTORY, A STORY, AND A MEMORY OF THE LAST PLAINS FRONTIER 36 (Penguin Books, 1990) (1962).
[8] *Id.*
[9] *Id.* at 35.
[10] Wallace Stegner, *The Rocky Mountain West*, in MARKING THE SPARROW'S FALL: WALLACE STEGNER'S AMERICAN WEST 259 (Page Stegner ed., 1998).

Waste, necessity, opportunity, community—these are characteristic Western experiences. Despite our go-it-alone pretensions, enduring amidst this magnificent and capricious landscape has always meant pulling together. Those who get greedy and cannot cooperate will be exposed by the land and their neighbors for what they are, destructive of community and of themselves.

We are still a wagon people. We are immigrants, homesteaders. We are yet settling into this great land. We are marked by what we take—and what we give back—to the land and to each other. We are contemporaries passing through what has been, what is, and what shall be. We are tenured to this place of boom and bust hopefulness. We must see and hold on to what we value most.

CODE OF THE PASSING THROUGH PEOPLE

Pack our wagons, so the axles ride a little
higher than the wagon-tearing stones, not so high
a capsize-wind will blow over the edge all we
carefully stowed, or in mire-hole sink beyond

Resurrection. Pack only what we're needing and
hope chest bear for when we homestead arrive, and there's
cause for remembering what of our ancestors
at table before us spread, to remember theirs.

And do not expect what we do not earn, and thank
always for what is given us. And do not waste
what tomorrow we may need, or blind to another's
need, in grace and privilege, we may choose to freely

Give. Sharpen our axes, oil our guns, for they are
tools, like the hammer, nail, stool, hand, and milking pail,
lamp, wick, candle, planed-off plank and any good book,
needle, thread, spindle, spool, crank, flume and headgate wheel,

Self-defense a right, but never to pick a fight
or intimidate or disregard innocents
or refuse to forgive or ask for forgiveness.
Insist that conscience begins in living it, string

String, every string, so every string plays of future
well-being. How the red wing blackbird morning sings
and barn owl hunts the fluttering evening, cherish
every creature for that creature's form of speaking

And every intonation and form of being.
And when we borrow another person's strength or
natural feature, honor and repay, in how we
transforming live and love and better pass on through.

We are part of developing a new country, a country of law, justice, love, individual rights, and community rights. This is a work of duty and the public interest forged of humility, hard work, and the friction of conflicting voices and ideas which ignite the spark—induced by the oxygen of inspiration—that lights the way.

To help this light shine more clearly, we must understand the dark of our history as well as the bright.

Carved Out of the Public Domain

Congress carved the western territories and states out of the public domain, acquired by purchase, exploration, conquest, and negotiation, forged into highly consequential legal instruments: the 1803 Louisiana Purchase, the 1846 Oregon Compromise, and the 1848 Treaty of Guadalupe Hidalgo.[11] This vast expanse—from the Mississippi River to its headwaters on the Continental Divide, from the Snake and the Columbia Rivers to the Pacific Ocean, from the San Luis Valley of the Rio Grande and the Colorado River from its source on the western side of the Great Divide to the California delta, across the Great Basin to the Sierra, from its foothills to the long western shore—this vast and incomparable expanse gave birth to the Public Land States, 30 in all, creatures of the federal determination to follow the lead of those who were already going there.[12]

---

[11] Loren L. Mall, PUBLIC LAND AND MINING LAW: TEXT AND CASES 4-7 (3d ed. 1981); *see also People v. Schafer*, 946 P.2d 938, 942-45 (Colo. 1997) (discussing, in the context of the Fourth Amendment's reasonable expectation of privacy the tent as habitation in the West from Lewis and Clark to the contemporary tourist); *Lobato v. Taylor*, 71 P.3d 938, 945-57 (Colo. 2002) (discussing, in the context of deeds to land of the Sangre de Cristo Grant in the San Luis Valley, Mexican land grant, settlers' rights, and Colorado territorial law).

[12] Mall, *supra* note 11, at 7-8.

The job of the mapmakers was to reduce the scale of the West to features and contours, to show the lay of the land, where the rivers fall from peak to forest through the livestock grazing zones, then to the agricultural bottom land capable of cultivation by irrigation from the streams, exposing geological formations where might lie the valuable minerals.

Those explorers who mapped the west, Powell, Hayden, Wheeler, and King,[13] brought with them sketchers, photographers, and landscape artists—among them, Holmes, Jackson, Bierstadt, Moran, and Egloffstein—to portray the book of the western wilderness—magnificent, savage, alarming, and alluring.[14]

The job of the artists was to fire the mind with the sublime. Here the Creator had done the most glorious work: the falls of the Yellowstone, the chasm of the Grand Canyon, the sliced-off magnificence of Yosemite's Half Dome, and the sheer precipice of El Capitan. Out here, in the language and concepts of Manifest Destiny, Providence wrote Independence, Freedom, Challenge, Promise, and Fulfillment on the face of every feature of nature's blessing. Here, Salvation and all the tools needed for Sustenance and Deliverance had come together.

All in the interest of settlement. From their outset, the territories and states preoccupied themselves with reducing the land, the waters, the timber, and the minerals to possession. For example, the very first session of Colorado's territorial legislature in 1861 adopted a statute that defined "real estate" as "any right to occupy, possess, and enjoy any portion of the public domain."[15] It also passed a water law that allowed any person to cross the lands of another to access, and remove from the streams, water necessary to work mining claims, irrigate farm land, and supply the factories, however far removed those uses might be from the stream.[16]

---

[13] William Goetzmann, NEW LANDS, NEW MEN: AMERICA AND THE SECOND GREAT AGE OF DISCOVERY 412-14 (Penguin Books, 1987) (1986).

[14] *See generally* William H. Goetzmann & William N. Goetzmann, THE WEST OF THE IMAGINATION (1986).

[15] *Gillett v. Gaffney*, 3 Colo. 351, 358 (1877); *Bd. of County Comm'rs v. Vail Assoc.*, 19 P.3d 1263, 1275-78 (Colo. 2001) (discussing taxation of private ski area on U.S. Forest Service Land in context of Colorado and United States public land law).

[16] *Bd. of County Comm'rs v. Park County Sportsmen's Ranch*, 45 P.3d 693, 705-08 (Colo. 2002) (discussing English common law and Colorado water law in the context of federal and state public land law); *Yunker v. Nichols*, 1 Colo. 551 (1872); COLORADO FOUNDATION FOR WATER EDUCATION: CITIZEN'S GUIDE TO COLORADO WATER LAW 4-5 (2003) (discussing Native American and Hispanic water uses and water structures).

From the mines, from the farms, grew the towns and cities. Agriculture, mining, manufacturing, every form of commerce, recreation, tourism, transportation, education, and that most adaptable and necessary resource—people moving here to build and shape community—these are the sticks in the bundle of Colorado's heritage, past, present, and future. This legacy always takes shape from the land, the water, the sky, the vistas, and the limits we impose on our use of them.

Don't Go There! (But We Must and We Shall)

John C. Fremont was called the great pathfinder. But his risk-taking in the face of due warning about the elements led others to disaster. He persuaded Bill Williams to guide him up into the teeth of the Big Winter of 1848.[17] The warnings came from other mountain men at Bent's Fort and Pueblo.[18] Senator Thomas Hart Benton, Fremont's father-in-law, conjured up Fremont's fourth expedition to resurrect his son-in-law's reputation after Fremont had been court-martialed.[19] Various groups were vying for the glory and reward of having the transcontinental railroad route.[20] Senator Benton convinced St. Louis investors to finance Fremont. Bill Williams just barely escaped the disaster; the persistent rumor is that he and other survivors resorted to cannibalism after Fremont got out to Taos and went on to California.[21]

Fremont declared the expedition a success, despite the ten who died.[22] He became a California senator and, in 1856, the first Republican candidate for President after getting rich on a Sierra foothills land grant. His wife Jessie, a fine writer, is credited for ghostwriting his adventurous accounts of exploration.

Abraham Lincoln ran in 1860 on a platform supporting passage of the Homestead Act and the Railroad Act.[23] The Colorado Territory came into being in 1861. The Colorado militia under Chivington exterminated a peaceful encampment

---

[17] Andrew Rolle, JOHN CHARLES FREMONT: CHARACTER AS DESTINY 115 (1991).
[18] *Id.* at 114.
[19] *Id.* at 123.
[20] *Id.*
[21] *Id.* at 118.
[22] *Id.* at 120.
[23] Stephen E. Ambrose, NOTHING LIKE IT IN THE WORLD: THE MEN WHO BUILT THE TRANSCONTINENTAL RAILROAD 1863-1869, 67, 79-80, 172 (2000); *see also McCormick v. Union Pac. Res. Co.*, 14 P.3d 346, 352-53 (Colo. 2000) (discussing the federal railroad acts and land patents from the public domain).

of Native Americans at Sand Creek in 1864, a year of escalating scalpings and killings by Indians and whites.[24] The coming of the railroad cleaved through the two cultures of the Squaw Men, a singular generation of a few white men who lived in community with Native Americans.[25]

THEY CALL ME SQUAW MAN

They call me squaw man. On account
of the Cheyenne woman I live with.
There weren't no other women here
when I came out. Her people took me
in. We'd skinned along the cottonwood
bottoms, at Big Timbers on the Arkansas,
set our poles and wrapped our hide tight
to the raw smoke opening at the top,
strangle berries was already freezin'.

That's when the Pathfinder come through,
says he discovered South Pass, crossed
the Sierra in a big snow, liberated Californi'.
Says he knows where the Railroad's got to go,
from St. Louis out the Arkansas, up and over
the 38th Parallel.

I says to him, Don't go up there. We been
chunkin' ice out of river edges since
September just to get a drink. Up in the hills
deer and bear been growin' more than usual
hair, and it ain't strange ten feet or more
of snow up there with early signs like this.

"Old Fool," he says. "I've done it all before.
Follow me, Men, don't listen. Just up
and over the other side to California!"

---

[24] Carl Ubbelohde et al., A COLORADO HISTORY 106-09 (8th ed. 2001).
[25] *See id.* at 109.

He tries the San Juans in December,
gets hisself and the men stuck in a notch
between the Rio Grande and whatever.
Bogs down at Christmas. The mules was
freezin' in their tracks and there wasn't
any eatin' left a civilized man can mention
once they was down and the flesh stripped.
The Pathfinder skedaddles out of there
to Taos and Californi.

There's ten men didn't. Left their marks
on the bark where a Griz can't reach
and claw when the snow melts.

We almost didn't make it neither. There was
nothin' for us to cut but rabbit, coyote.
Grandfathers stirred their story sticks into the
coals, said of the ice that never melts up in the
Yellowstone country. We drew buffalo on the
inside of tipi walls with cold smoke the fires
made when the old men fell quiet, and let
the children gnaw the bottom thongs. River
finally loosed and we scraped into the Sand Hills.

My woman died of the pox. Chivington gutted
her family a year later. The railroad's chasing
the old Smoky Hill trail into Denver. They've
carved through Cheyenne for the trans-continental.
I spend my days hacking around Fort Lyon,
the white people tell their children

Don't go near that squaw man!

Our state has had great moments of progress and great moments of shame. Entrepreneurial enterprise has been present from the start. After the Civil War, General William Tecumseh Sherman was assigned military jurisdiction over the West. He decided he needed to see what was there. He traveled up the Platte Trail and then came down the Front Range from Fort Laramie.[26] He most looked forward to seeing and being in the Rocky Mountains. He was a private person; he hated receptions and having to make speeches.[27] Wouldn't you know! The civic leaders of Denver came out to see him and to invite him to a reception and to give a speech.[28] Their motivation: to get the Army to build forts in Colorado so Denver merchants could sell them supplies.[29]

Our state has had its moments of great shame: the Sand Creek Massacre, riots against the Chinese in downtown Denver in the 1880s, the Ludlow Massacre of 1914, Ku Klux Klan marches in the 1920s, and *de jure* discrimination against African-Americans in the Denver public schools as recently as the 1960s.[30]

The hospitality that Governor Carr showed to the Japanese people interned here during World War II;[31] the federal court orders against segregation in the schools; our efforts at opening up trade routes to Africa, Central and South America, and Asia; our election of Hispano, African-American, and Japanese-American leaders—these demonstrate a Colorado compassion and commitment to a community that, despite difficulty and temptation, points to achieving what is fair and just.

We have a choice, the choice that every generation of Coloradans gets to make.

WHICH COLORADO SHALL WE BE?

> I wander through a state that's grown
> from out of prairie grass, a state of roots
> in confluence of creek and river path.
> I loathe this state, I love this state, for what
> it's been and is, mean and dusty, lovely, green,
> which Colorado shall we be?

---

[26] Robert G. Athearn, WILLIAM TECUMSEH SHERMAN AND THE SETTLEMENT OF THE WEST 74 (1995).
[27] *Id.* at 75.
[28] *Id.* at 76-78.
[29] *Id.*
[30] *See* Carl Abbott et al., COLORADO: A HISTORY OF THE CENTENNIAL STATE 153, 283-87, 322 (3d ed. 1994); Louisa Ward Arps, DENVER IN SLICES 23 (1959).
[31] Abbott, *supra* note 30, at 365-66.

> I'm the state of Chivington, of hounding out Chinese,
> of walking through the streets in sheets and
> fixing school boundaries to keep them Afros out.
> I'm the state of parks and trees, of getting exercise,
> of welcome you, I'd like to help, what interests you?
> which Colorado shall we be?

Thirst at the Watering Hole

Justice is not a vaporous ideal. It's the thirst for searching out the watering hole. To smell the oasis and then, unerringly, to humble on the path that leads some other there—and they to others. Consider humor, honesty, humility—the three "uh huhs"! When we look to those we truly admire, isn't it their grace, their judgment, their kindness, their practicality, their intellect, their skill and craft, their unique madness and magic, their counsel and wisdom, their art, their passion, and their generosity that fills us with gratitude and profits us to the core?

Judging well in community benefits from having worthy mentors and colleagues, and focusing on the heart of the job. State and federal appellate judges must exercise scholarship and common sense. All judges have this responsibility, of course. But appellate judges, in particular, have a duty to articulate justice and the law, in writing, for public guidance.

The third branch of government, the judiciary, governs primarily through the written judicial opinion. Authoring a written opinion for an appellate court can be very humbling because of the work it takes and the impact court decisions can have on citizens and the community.

The work is hard and important.

First, the appellate judge needs to thoroughly research, read, and write the proposed opinion to be as correct as one can based on the law and the facts of the case. A judge is making a judgment on what others have done or left undone in their lives. The judge always owes the parties to the appeal the courtesy of fair and diligent consideration.

Second, the appellate judge needs the vote of a majority of the judges or justices who must decide the case. Otherwise, the judge's opinion will never see the light of day. One of a judge's colleagues may end up authoring the court's decision, simply by proposing a concurrence or dissent that gains enough votes to become the court's judgment.

For example, the Colorado Court of Appeals sits in three-judge panels to decide a case; a judge needs the vote of at least one other judge besides his or her own. Our Colorado Supreme Court—which chooses which of the decisions of the Colorado Court of Appeals we will undertake to review—has seven justices; a justice needs the vote of at least three other justices.

The appellate judge must never give in to anger or pettiness. The law's not about the judge anyway. It has to do with people in community. Next time around, when the judge gets the next assignment to write the proposed majority opinion, he or she will have the privilege of convincing colleagues yet again.

Third, and most important, the appellate judge must learn never to give up listening and learning about people and the law, and how the work of justice is the crucial work of any civilized society, in all ages. Growing into the job—every day a judge gets to do the job—is the mark of settling into the role and responsibility of being an appellate judge.

. . .

Judges look through the windows of their cases onto the landscape of what actually happens in the lives of citizens. They are reporters, educators, guides, scholars, idealists, pragmatists, and decision-makers. They are bound by principle to articulate principles the best they can discern and apply them, window-by-window, case-by-case, upholding the rights and the responsibilities of individuals and the community. They must be sign readers of the facts and mapmakers of justice and the law.

OUT ON THE ROAD TODAY

A.

Can't make it on the cleaning stints,
gotta' get good tips tonight,
just can't get kicked out
of another apartment,

Damn bus is late again,
Momma's got the baby,
hope she's not too sick,
what if I get sick, no benefits?

Two guys snigger, leer at her,
She huddles in her slicker.

B.

I'm just hanging with the brothers
at the Points outside the bar,
I see them coming, I start walking,
they pull a patrol car onto the sidewalk,

Hey you, they say! I just keep on stepping,
hey you they say, stop right there!
Get on over here! My fist is clenched,
that's proof enough for them.

He doesn't hang at the bar with
The guys who buy at Cherry Creek.

C.

I get to the King Soopers, wait in line
at the pharmacy counter, sorry we can't
do that, they say, hasn't been approved,
call your insurance company,

Car smokes, emission test is due,
another $500.00 to the mechanic
maybe gets it through, what if I forget
and drive with the registration out?

A grandfather on oxygen tries to steer into traffic,
Park it or walk it! screams the driver behind.

D.

Will the young mother raped
outlast her cross-examination?

Is the constitution in place for a
black stop in a "bad" neighborhood?

Will the jury see those teen-aged epithets
caused one of the elders to crash into a pole?

What if they, what if we, what if I
Just don't care?

E.

Call the next case![32]

Upstream

Ferril spoke of how his father took him fishing, how he took his father's ashes back to the river, and how the rocks and the waters will outlast.[33] I thank my father for the fishing; my mother for the blessing; my wife for the loving inspiration.

FISHERMAN'S KNOT

Lord, my hands tremble,
I must take off my glasses,
hold the line to my eye
and twist three or four
times. This space between
the loop, Lord, help me
hold it here, grant me
just a little more light
to thread the gap between
my thumb and forefinger,
let me cinch my filament
to your swivel. Lord, I am
complete, I hear the stream
behind me continuing.

---

[32] *Outlaw v. People*, 17 P.3d 150, 153-54 (Colo. 2001) (discussing the unwarranted stop of an African-American person in Denver's Five Points neighborhood).

[33] Thomas Hornsby Ferril, *Fishing Upstream With My Father* and *Time of Mountains*, in THOMAS HORNSBY FERRIL AND THE AMERICAN WEST, *supra* note 3, at 21, 114.

Colorado's Independent Judiciary
Speech to the Rotary Club
Commerce City, Colorado
December 31, 1997

Thank you for your invitation. Gary Gibson said I should speak from the heart. You invite me here the last day of the year; each day—from dawn to starlight—is a day for reflection, promise, and action, but the last day always takes on a particular luster of summing up and looking ahead. I asked Gary if I could read some poetry, for the heart cannot be engaged without a voice to give it song. I hope to reflect with you how each of us contributes to Colorado's changing sense of justice.

First, thank you for the opportunity you have provided me to serve as a Justice of the Colorado Supreme Court. Under our state constitution, citizen commissions interview applicants and select three nominees for each judicial vacancy. The Governor appoints one of the three and that person serves until the next general election. A citizen judicial performance commission reviews the judge and submits a public report prior to the election. Then the people of Colorado vote to retain or not retain the judge in office.

Other states provide for contested election of judges. In those states, the judges solicit campaign contributions, including from lawyers who appear before them in court. In Colorado, judges are removed from the political process. We cannot contribute to or participate in political campaigns and we cannot accept contributions, because the people of Colorado have determined that judges should have independence to examine each case before them fairly and impartially.

I am privileged to serve with a collegial court of seven persons who reflect Colorado's membership and values. Our Chief Justice, Tony Vollack, is a former Colorado State Senator and District Judge. Our next senior justice, Mary Mullarkey, served as Solicitor General of the State of Colorado and an employment law specialist in public and private practice. Gregg Scott, the first African-American to participate on the Colorado Supreme Court, was a University of Denver business law professor and securities law expert. Rebecca Love Kourlis, daughter of Governor John Love, practiced natural resources law and was a District Judge and Water Judge on Colorado's western slope. Alex Martinez, former public defender and County Judge and District Judge from Pueblo, is Colorado's first native-born Hispanic appointed to the court. Mike Bender, a member of Colorado's Jewish community, distinguished himself as one of Colorado's foremost criminal defense trial attorneys.

Each of these persons brings his or her personality, scholarship, expertise, and common sense to the discussion of each case we review. I say to you that excellence and a broad mix of community and cultural background constantly aid our work to figure the vista and the way of each case.

The aim of this work is the fair application of the law to the facts. It's hard, humbling, and invigorating work. Each case is a direct window on Colorado as we see people in conflict, either of their own making or visited randomly upon them by others. To find out what happened and why and to apply the principles of constitutional, statutory, and common law the best we can requires concentration, practical judgment, and a strong sense of the rights and values of the community and of individuals. The only way to pursue life, liberty, and happiness is to work at each of them in every way we may, every day.

You know this. That's why you're here to share the common table and better understand how to serve. I congratulate you. You would not be here without a strong sense of self, of family, of place, of community.

My wife, a pre-school Montessori teacher, tells me that the skin and brain are the first two organs of the human embryo that start to grow, and they develop in close relationship out of the same layer of embryonic tissue. Throughout life, the outer environment stimulates the inner. Instructed, the galaxy of the mind reaches out to the universe as you experience that inner glow of confidence that helps to light the way when most needed.

OF ALL THE STARS

Of all the stars
the brightest star is
where you are when dimmer
stars are least likely to appear.

That locating sense of confidence begins in family through joy, fair play, discipline, mercy, and abiding love, by which the boundaries of rights and duty to others (elements of justice) are illuminated or slip into obscurity, depending on adult paradigms. Durable goods are those that settle in the mind from the cultural and natural environment when all the expendable toys have served their time.

DURABLE GOODS

With regard to children
we want to think in terms
of durable goods, climbing

heights Abraham argued
for a chance to match

A young soul with experience.
Parenting, he asserted,
requires opportunity and raw
available material, water,
a tent, some time and trees

Occasionally. The old man was
less willing to submit to less,
in this he struggled that the pride
of his disappearing years might
suddenly disappear

His heritage knew enough
of justice to escape mercy.
His sense of expectation had
not been honed to being spared, yet
he said: "Make it so."

Would any parent in a similar
circumstance acquit as well his
kin without prior assurance?
This is not about cars
or refrigerators.

We are blessed to be American Westerners. The nineteenth-century explorers who led the way beheld those natural wonders the Native Americans knew and revered so well: the tall grass prairie, herds of buffalo, the shining mountains, plunging streams, fish and eagle, the sandstone cliffs. Always the preconceptions and the misconceptions give way to the joy of the generations, one by one, finding their own western way.

Jefferson thought there was a waterway to the western ocean and in 1804 sent Lewis and Clark to pilot it. They ditched the boats at the great falls of Missouri and up and up they struggled only to encounter the stronghold of the Bitter Roots. They surely would have perished without the help of the Shoshone and the Nez Perce.

In 1858, Lieutenant Ives thought to navigate the Colorado River by steamboat from the Gulf of California. After he crashed the boat upon the rocks of the Black Canyon where Lake Mead now stands, he crossed overland to the rim of the Grand Canyon and declared the whole region so inhospitable that surely no one else would ever bother to visit. Within a decade John Wesley Powell—the one-armed Major tied to a wooden dory—boomed into the gut of that primordial canyon which is a highly visited world treasure.

LEWIS AND IVES

A River always bends its course against
the confident.

Said the President, "Your mission is single,
the direct water communication from sea to sea
formed by the Missouri."

Lewis holding forth on foot
crossed the Bitter Roots.

And Lieutenant Ives
who from tide to source would power
up the Colorado

Foundered on a rock,
his steamer split apart.

"Ours has been the first, and will
doubtless be the last to visit
this profitless locality," said Ives.

Just up the pike, Las Vegas lights.

Our beloved West is rapidly urbanizing; 85 percent of us live in cities and metropolitan areas. By the mid-twenty-first century, another 26 million people will be added. Hard work and optimism, the beneficial use of natural resources and the preservation of great natural wonders and open space, opportunity of work, play, and economic livelihood have always marked the best part of our maturing frontier personality. We have continued need of compasses. To use a compass requires imagination, a sense of self, family, place, community.

COMPASS

Set the compass
in your hand
and imagine

You radiate
to every direction
all degrees.

You may choose
the course
and variation,

Return insightful,
or remain
where you are

Centered.
If you stay,
draw confidence

From your geography,
friends will you
locate.

What a magnificent place we share. The Continental Divide is our spine. Glorious mountain parks, North Park, Middle Park, South Park, the San Luis Valley, hold our interior high and wide. Mountain and prairie streams have given birth to towns and cities. Economic, cultural, recreational centers have arisen from the early farming and mining communities. Twenty-four wilderness areas preserve magnificent ranges, bid you welcome by foot or horse. Or you can choose to stay away, knowing they will always be there. People of the world are attracted here. We have the opportunity to include them in a fair and just society we help to make by daily choice.

We might think of justice as a bushel of Orchard Mesa peaches, ripe and delicious. Each has been nurtured to maturity. The rights of individuals and the rights of the community are like that. Water them well and let them capture the sunshine deliciously.

A very gifted family therapist, Susan Heitler of Denver, teaches that "and" is the way of understanding and of living together, of being inclusive. "But" is always the method for taking exception, fostering disagreement, promoting exclusivity. Rights *and* duties, like skin *and* brain to the growing embryo, are interdependent.

OUR OWN PEACHES

Every legal case begets of rights
and responsibilities.
If I promise and perform
a duty which we both agree upon,
I have the right that you will too.

When one of us fails without excuse,
or leave of the other, a breach occurs
and, rather than speaking of it openly, we demur
to speak at all and so dismiss the other's right.
In this deny our own responsibility.

The art of sealing breaches starts
with peeling back excuses,
so juice of mutual promises
will renew our taste
for tasting rights
of others,
as our own Peaches.

The America we know today is not the America of the founding fathers. It's richer, more inclusive, and holds even greater promise for the future. When the Constitution was adopted, black people were slaves; women could not vote; Native Americans were exotic and threatening; wilderness was to be conquered.

But they sure did hand us a mighty compass, didn't they? Three branches of government to energize and spell each other off; a bill of rights to protect the individual against the tyranny of the majority; unbounded hope in destiny. They call; we answer.

Each generation of Americans has contributed to advancing the embrace of maturing justice based on individual and community respect. Our parents and grandparents fought in world wars to preserve that opportunity; our generation has contributed the Peace Corps and a worldwide economy through which dedication to the betterment of the world's people should be a motivating aim.

There are many callings among us. We are called to teach and learn, to help others, to conserve time to ourselves for reflection and recharge, mostly to love the time and revere the place of our being here. How we may serve is revealed in the wind that touches our skin, the brain that answers back when we hear God and the universe calling.

ONE'S CALLING

Whence comes my calling?	Whence? returns the wind.
Can I know how?	How? squawks a raven.
When shall I begin?	When? the tide comes in.
Will I do well?	Well? reflects the water.
What then?	Then? be answering.

Each day we work in community—whether the last day of the year, in spring or fall, or the quickening moments of a long summer evening, beyond the niches of our doubts—peace and beauty surround us. Into our hands we receive the paddle of grace. Across the mirrored waters, we take heart. Islands and continents, take us home again!

CANOE

Help me summon up the strength
to do the good I can each day,
at least a little space with you
between despair and opportunity.

To dip my shiny stirring blade
in waters deep and welling full
and let my muscle ache desist
to sit a-center my canoe.

Quiet would you spread to me
hums and hums of sinewing,
nimble tissues at their work
of joining joy to drudgery.

Thank you for this resting me,
for the whys persisting me,
I take this heel to my hand,
paddle, Lord, this promised land.

Thanks for asking me to share this time and place with you.

Scouting for All
Denver Area Council Boy Scouts of America
Frontier District Annual Recognition Dinner
Denver, Colorado
March 12, 1998

Thank you for your invitation. I am glad to join you in celebrating your joy in serving our community through Scouting. Tonight we recognize those whose example we wish to honor. Great work begins in the honesty of the heart, seeking not recognition, being grateful when it is bestowed by those whom we respect.

To the honorees we single out tonight for their contributions to Cub Scouting, Boy Scouting, exploring, and learning for life—thanks especially for the many times you were passed over when others were being honored and you were truly glad for them. Your turn is now. We are grateful for the opportunity to do this good turn for you, men and women of Denver, Colorado. We the volunteers and professionals of the community of Scouting say to you, "Well done! Thank you!"

Look at each other, will you? Neighbors, friends, those from across town, those of all different callings, complexion of heritage, upbringing—wrought together by the very high importance you place on the education of young people. That they may know the joy of self confidence, the challenge of surviving in the city, on the plains, in the mountains. Of feeling what it's like to work with each other and have the intoxicating smell of ponderosa pine suffuse their brain and breath, far from car exhaust and the noisy street. Of setting up their tents in the wind and storm and waking up to a stronger, fresher morning.

To join together as a den or a patrol, or a crew. To sweat hard in the gaining of a mountain pass on foot, pack on back. To hear the song of the brook slipping off the rock, the squawk of kindred raven wheeling in the sky. To rejoice in the vista of high places shared with those who labored there with you! To return to the reality of daily living, refreshed, inspired, ready for the digging in, strong for the inevitable surprises, those momentary bouts of self doubt that must be struggled through. To be prepared, and always preparing to sling the pack back on and start once again on the long climb.

This is Scouting! And through the dedication of those adult leaders, like you, who provide the opportunity, we learn when we are young how to gather in the quiet, hear our calling whisper to us, set our blade to deeper waters.

Such a wonderfully curious organization Scouting is. We dress in uniforms that are reminiscent of nineteenth century worldwide colonialism achieved by armed occupation of native peoples. Yet our only weapon is a 12-point "law" featuring civility, friendship, respect for each other and reverence for the natural world and the divine spark that animates this beautiful, constantly surprising universe. Think about this—the basic weapon of Scouting is universal justice. And we Scouts and Scouters are very much a work in justice-making progress.

We started the twentieth century in brotherhood. We look forward to the twenty-first century in sisterhood and brotherhood. Look at each other, you men and women of Denver, Colorado, you Scouters. Scouting is and should be the mirror of community. The more we work to be inclusive of the various communities comprising our community, the more we can fulfill our great calling of service to God, country, each other, ourselves.

. . .

Tonight, you sit at tables with your Scouting friends. When we work and play together, our preconceptions are generally transformed by the common effort. Discrimination bears a terrible price. My mother told me what it was like being an Irish Catholic growing up in an Eastern city, granddaughter of an immigrant household servant. She was nothing but a lowly "Mick" to some. Thank God for "Micks" and all the rest of "them" we Americans are!

When the controversy about homosexual Scouters began to boil in the early nineties, I thought about my fellow Philmont Staff member, Larry Murphy, a homosexual male and professional historian, now deceased, who published histories of Philmont and the Maxwell Land Grant of Northern New Mexico and Southern Colorado. He was a fine man, a good friend, and a great Scouter. A Scout is friendly! Friendship is the key to overcoming bias.

To my knowledge, Larry never broke the trust each of us owes to young people—now expressed in Scouting's youth protection program. Weren't we all shocked and ashamed here in Denver to learn in the early nineties—at the same time that homosexual membership in Scouting was questioned—that the person after whom our Council Scouting Headquarters center is named sexually abused his daughter for years as she struggled to grow up?

Criminal conduct cannot be tolerated, whether committed by heterosexuals or homosexuals. We know how to draw the line against unacceptable conduct that is incompatible with Scouting. We know how to set and enforce standards of trust and responsibility to protect our youth and respect each other.

We must also have humility enough to learn and grow. I am confident, within this magnificent geography of nature—natural, human, and divine—that we will find our heart again and welcome Larry back.

Learning For Life is what we call our program for young men and women 14 years and older. Urban Scouting and Career Scouting are tucked within this expanding tent. You will recall that Frontier Scouting began right here in urban Denver with our district. Through the leadership of Van Lucero, the Denver Area Council started in the 1980s an after-school and weekend program for urban young men of Scouting age who weren't in traditional Scout troops. These young men often came from single-parent families led by women, and their sisters would often accompany them, wishing to participate. Instead of being turned away, they were welcomed!

Centered in the recreational centers of the City and County of Denver, with partially paid paraprofessional leadership supplied by the Denver Area Council to make up for the absence of traditional Scoutmaster leadership—which essentially proved to be unavailable—this pioneering urban Scouting program expanded to include computer training, bike trips to Cherry Creek Reservoir, fishing in the mountains, and other opportunities previously unknown to these kids.

As happens so often in an organization that ultimately depends on local volunteers, community values surfaced from local arenas. Because of similar experiences in Houston and Chicago and other cities, National Council began to embrace emergent forms of Scouting, borrowing elements of the traditional program without being committed only to perpetuating the hierarchical forms of advancement and membership characterizing the traditional Boy Scout Troop.

Within the past two weeks, National Council has announced that sponsoring local Learning For Life units, excluding criminal conduct, may set their own membership criteria. Wonderful! Scouting has a long tradition of the local unit choosing or discharging its own leadership through the unit committee. There is no substitute for understanding and control at the local level, where adults and young people can take responsibility for their leadership choices.

Thus, National Council has indicated, I think, that Learning For Life units may admit young men and women regardless of their sexual orientation or their religious beliefs. Certainly, then, the National High Adventure bases—New Mexico's Philmont, the Minnesota Canoe Base, the Florida Sea Base—must be open to attendance to anyone who is eligible for participation in Learning for Life programs, as well as Explorers and older Boy Scouts. Staff members should be drawn from our finest young adults throughout this country and, increasingly, the world regardless of race, gender, family background, financial means, or sexual orientation. This should not surprise us—this is America, the world's most diverse democracy, honored for its optimism and ability to include and defend the rights of others.

We are Rocky Mountain western Americans. The challenge of some of the finest topography in the world, the glorious spine of the continent, resides in our front yard. Population projections are that 26 million more people will inhabit the western states within the next quarter of a century. Hispanic, African-American, Asian, Native, Anglo—the world's peoples are reflected in our people, Americans all. "Be Prepared!" is our watchword. Starting here and now, building on what we know how to do best—teamwork through Scouting—we load our packs, we tune up a hiking song, confident in those who would join our movement, we move on! Our calling to service calls to us.

Congratulations to those we honor tonight by their example. Thank you for the honor of sharing this time and place with you.

Note: Justice Hobbs, an Eagle Scout, was a scoutmaster of a Denver Boy Scout troop for eight years; chairman of Denver's Frontier District for four years; and a member of the Ranch Committee, Philmont Scout Ranch, National Council of the Boy Scouts of America, but was not reappointed to the Philmont Board following this talk.

Marriage of Maggie Fromholtz and Casey Vanderbeek
In Chambers, Colorado Supreme Court
June 19, 1998

Casey and Maggie,

This is your day of joy, the day you say your vows of faith, hope, and love to each other. Marriage happens day by day as you rise, as you lay you down to sleep, as you talk and eat and hike and see the arc of the summer and the winter sun take its journey across the sky and the moon come up on all your thoughts and songs and hurts, in all the days that you shall have together.

Love each other well. This is the joy of life.

From your love you shall gain the peace that passes understanding. All that was before, your families, generation on generation, all that is and ever shall be, is joined in you as you set upon your way together.

Take it day by day, hour by hour, minute by minute. You shall disagree; you shall need your time apart; from time to time each of you shall carry a heavy pack. And when you shall flag the other shall say, "I am here for you." And you shall gain the pass together; and you shall see the farther peaks. You shall take your rest between the crags and the wildflowers.

In all of this, you shall gain the peace that passes understanding. Marriage is a sacrament and a means of survival. A state of grace and of necessity. You marry each other by exchanging your vows. Marriage is not conferred upon you by any other power; you are your own authorities, other authorities are your witnesses.

Please hear this eighth-century poem of wisdom from the Tao Te Ching:

> The supreme good is like water,
> which nourishes all things without trying to.
> It is content with the low places that people disdain.
>
> In dwelling, live close to the ground.
> In thinking, keep to the simple.

> In conflict, be fair and generous.
> In governing, don't try to control.
> In work, do what you enjoy.
> In family life, be completely present.
>
> Be content to be simply yourself.
> Don't compare or compete.
> Everybody will respect you.
>
> Lao Tze, *Tao Te Ching*, chapter 8, poem 1.

Casey, do you come here today of your own free will to marry Maggie and hold her and love her and treasure her forever?

Casey's response: "I do."

Maggie, do you come here today of your own free will to marry Casey and hold him and love him and treasure him forever?

Maggie's response: "I do."

Casey, you have a ring for Maggie. The ring is a symbol of union—of your faith and hope and love. Now, Casey, take your lover's hand, place the ring on her finger, look into the eyes of the soul you love and repeat after me.

I, Casey, take you, Maggie, to be my lawfully wedded wife, to love and to cherish this day forth, to have and to hold, for richer, for poorer, in sickness and in health, in good times and in bad, for as long as I shall live, until death do us part.

Maggie, you have the ring that Casey has given you as a symbol of his love for you. May you hear the mountain waters sing and love him. You are the soil, the breath of life and of truth to each other. You are the spark, the touch of life and of faith to each other. Maggie, you have a ring for Casey. Now, look into the eyes of the soul you love and repeat after me.

I, Maggie, take you, Casey, to be my lawfully wedded husband, to love and to cherish this day forth, to have and to hold, for richer, for poorer, in sickness and in health, in good times and in bad, for as long as I shall live, until death do us part.

May the God of all creation hold you and love you the rest of your days, for as long as mountains sing the mountain waters, and when they join the sea again, and beyond.

Now in the eyes of these witnesses, and in the sight of God, by the power vested in me by the State of Colorado, I pronounce you husband and wife. You may kiss each other and be glad!

Can't You Feel the Ground Waking?
Speech to the Colorado Association of Law Librarians (CoALL)
Annual Institute for Law Librarians and Friends
Denver, Colorado
February 24, 2001

Thank you for your invitation! Can't you feel the ground waking? In this morning's mist you can hear how happy the birds are.

I love the name CoALL—Colorado, community, cooperation, all of us together. What a great acronym! Who thought it up? No matter, keep it. And continue living up to it! Our profession—I include all of us in this, lawyers, judges, you who help to find and disseminate the information—we are all necessary to the important work of locating that geography of scholarship and practicality that animates each decision we are called upon to make.

The law is a reflection of the customs, morals, and ethics of a people. You help us locate the historic and legislative materials we need to know in understanding the context of the constitutions and the statutes. How did those who thought it up—and wrote it down—come to this particular formulation? In each case, we must look through the window of the facts before us to the landscape of the precedent, in order to have a clearer view in formulating resolution to a current dispute. So congratulations on your choice of a valuable profession!

And thanks for sending me to Philadelphia this past July for the national meeting of law librarians. People from other countries were there, too. During breaks, I was able to visit the home of the American Philosophical Society, where Thomas Jefferson conceived the idea of a great scientific mission of exploration into the unknown West. And to see the meeting house of the Pennsylvania legislature, where the Constitution was written—what a privilege!

At the national meeting I learned that many law libraries throughout the country are experiencing a decline in face-to-face patronage, as more and more lawyers and courts turn to electronic research. However, as we are finding with the Colorado Supreme Court law library, *pro se* patronage is more frequent. About 50 percent of our district court matters involve people who have no lawyer. We all, CoALL, you all, need to be in the business of customer service to discover and meet the changing needs for information and the available ways to get and deliver it. The goal before us—always—is access to justice.

Of course, you should not be expected to give legal advice, but the difference between providing information and giving legal advice is not all that clear cut. We should err on the side of giving information to those who need it. That's where you come in!

Our court has adopted an "unbundling rule," which allows attorneys to help those who are going to represent themselves draw up their pleadings. The problem and the fear of "ghostwriting"—the unidentified voice in the background—are resolved by requiring the *pro se* litigant to disclose the name of the attorney who assisted in writing the document. By assisting in this way, the attorney is not making an entry of appearance—and the attorney may not appear to argue in court—unless the client retains him or her for that purpose.

Due to the high cost of obtaining full legal counsel and the constitutional right of persons to proceed without a lawyer in court, if they choose, the experience of the Colorado judiciary is that some legal assistance, even if only in the background, is better than none. Our rule applies only in state courts; and even with it in place, many persons will not have any lawyer assistance at all. They will be looking to you to help them find what may help them. What a challenge! What a call to service!

Of course what information you can provide—in cooperation with each other—is essential to the ability of judges to do their jobs. Attorneys are advocates for a particular result on behalf of their clients. They must be as well prepared as they can be to help point the way. But often, it seems, they get caught up in arguing with each other, and so lose sight of their essential role to assist decision-makers in locating, amidst the landscape of the case, a sound judgment.

Appellate judges have the assistance of law clerks. Part of our job of mentoring is to teach the joy of research. I don't mean just the electronic research. The recent law school graduates come to us knowing how to do this, and they do it very well. I'm talking about using the books! Last night, thinking about what I wanted to say to you, I wrote this poem:

I LIKE THE FEEL OF A BOOK

> I like the feel of a book,
> the way it cradles in your palm
> and peels open to thumb
> and forefinger, I like turning
> leaves, on every leaf engrained
> by some creator, a story of
> discovery, I would dwell in a
> forest of leaves, way up
> in the canopy, to see the river
> traders pass below with coconut

>   and crocodilians, or along the
>   route of caravans, perch in
>   a lone acacia tree to spy
>   a sway of camels conveying
>   silk to Byzantium, and why spiders
>   have so many eyes. I should like
>   to hear the troubadours sing of
>   lost and gallant warriors falling
>   in the train of Charlemagne or
>   sailing off beyond the Hesperides,
>   and how to tie a caddis fly
>   and set it gently down upon
>   the spine of rising waters.

This book I am holding up to you is *A River Running West: The Life of John Wesley Powell* by Donald Worster (Oxford University Press, 2001). It's the new biography of the man who first ran the Colorado River and then became Director of the National Geological Survey and Director of the Bureau of Ethnology. The Powell biography that preceded this is Wallace Stegner's great work, *Beyond the Hundredth Meridian*.

During the summer of 1867, Powell came to Colorado to collect specimens for the Illinois College where he was teaching. During a visit into Middle Park to Hot Sulphur Springs, he got into a conversation with a mountain man about the Colorado River—and thence conceived the idea of running the long-unexplored reach of it, which of course he did, not once, but twice.

I love this wonderful passage:

> If the test of a good manager is whether she or he can recruit first-rate talent and then allow that talent the freedom to do its best, then Powell met the test. He ought to have, for he had learned management the hard way by patching exploring parties out of anarchic fur trappers and frontier runaways, college students, pious, valetudinarian ministers, disgruntled military men, assorted family members, complainers, dabblers, dreamers—the standard American lot.
>
> Worster at 329-30.

Don't we recognize that this collection of easterners transformed into westerners, just by the process of passing through here and then settling in—is yet—us?

Many of you have seen me in recent months and are wondering when you are going to get your books back. Our court has had a series of cases involving public land and water law. We have pulled on your resources to locate the geography of the legal issues presented. We've obtained government documents dealing with the Colorado River Compact and the Colorado River Storage Project Act at the Denver Public Library and the Colorado State Publications Library. We've checked out mineral and public land treatises from the University of Colorado and University of Denver law school libraries.

These materials, typically not cited in the briefs, helped us to formulate and reformulate our draft opinions—in combination with the briefs of the parties and the electronic research—as we worked our way through draft after draft to final decisions. A water case (Arapahoe County Gunnison River), an oil and gas case (McCormick), and a tax case (Vail) were cases involving issues tracing back to Colorado's creation out of the public domain.

. . .

Today, 36 percent of Colorado is still public land, and the state depends upon it for open space and recreation, which has proved to be a treasure more enduring than the valuable resources mined from the mountains.

The Colorado courts will continue to get cases like this where the customs and laws grew directly out of our public land heritage and western experience. I like to help my law clerks see how the treatises and historical materials can illuminate the context of the legal issues presented. We are general practitioners practicing in somebody else's field of expertise, and we need to know what those who have studied the area have to say about it. And we need to trace what the state and federal legislatures have done about it. And we need to honor the constitutions the people wrote in assigning duties and responsibilities in community and preserving rights to individuals.

I love to take out and turn the leaves of the books in my chambers, the reports of court decisions going straight back to 1861 when that first territorial legislature began to grapple with the realities of settling into this vast and irregularly watered vista that makes up our state of the Great Divide.

So this is where we all come in, to serve the community with scholarship and common sense. Our libraries are facing declining face-to-face patronage, but the need for access to information by citizens who are struggling to know and vindicate their rights on their own is increasing. After the Philadelphia meeting, we formed a Supreme Court Law Library alternatives study committee. It includes several of your members working in public and private law libraries.

The committee is urging the Court to consider opening the Supreme Court Library on Saturdays from 10:00 to 4:00, because the Denver Public Library across the street gets citizen visits on Saturday, which would be referred to the Supreme Court Library were it open. The committee also recommends extending the library hours from 5:00 to 7:00 p.m., so lawyers and citizens after work hours can avail themselves of the library's collection. We are glad that our judicial contract for electronic research includes use by the public in our library. This is an important part of our negotiation with the providers.

The committee suggests holding clinics in the library on nights or weekends for citizens, on topics such as family law and contract rights and remedies, in cooperation with lawyers who are willing to provide pro bono instruction. Colorado ethics rules set forth an aspirational goal of 50 hours of pro bono service per year by each attorney licensed to practice law in the state. Can we match this energy with the need of citizens for legal information? Of course we'll try, but how much we can do likely depends on funding and readjustment of existing resources and continuing to build on your cooperation. But I know that our excellent staff—and we have heard constant praise of their attitude and expertise during our committee-initiated surveys—will rally to doing what we should be doing.

Thanks for your invitation. We promise to get the books back!

Note: The expanded library hours have not occurred due to lack of state funding. Also, because of budget cuts, the Denver Public Library has had to restrict its hours.

Leadership Denver Graduation
Denver Metropolitan Chamber of Commerce Foundation
June 7, 2001

Thank you for your invitation to talk about leadership on your graduation from Leadership Denver. During the past year you have been in community in ways you haven't been before. You have made friends who, in your lifetime, will continue to intersect the intersections of your personal and professional journeys. Congratulations!

You are not alone. Look to each other, take comfort and inspiration. It's not what each of you has done, it's not what each of you shall do. It's how you reflect and speak and act that brings joy and peace and inspiration, first to yourselves, and then to others. There's your commencement, your starting point.

Don't you find that the most interesting conversationalists are those who like to know where you're from and where you're coming from? Instead of asking, "What do you do?" or having them ask this of you—engaging in verbal sorties to determine your relative worth—you might now think of saying, based on your exposure to the wider community of public and private interests, "What interests you most?" If the person says "My job!"—by all means find out about that job.

What do you say when someone asks you this question? To this question, you will likely answer from the heart. You may answer, "I like to read, I like to sing, I like to garden, I like to watch my kid playing lacrosse, I like working with _____," and then you name the organization you currently volunteer with.

The question "What do you do?" is medieval, unless it springs from democratic opportunity. A status-conscious society judges people, not by the values they pursue, but by power, prestige, possessions—the three plosives that value big noise and deafen responsibility. We replaced kings so that citizens could govern themselves on an equal basis; but the working out of this promise took a civil war and continues to require our constant efforts.

. . .

Business without commitment to the wider public interest is just...business. Commerce and community—isn't that what your most recent schooling has been about? Aren't you amazed at the variety of jobs people do? Many of these are jobs we would never consider doing, yet depend upon. When I start to get angry about not getting service quick enough, or being sent around the bureaucratic bumble bush, I like to ask, "Would I want that job, would I want to do anything for anyone who's acting like me?" Then my jets begin to cool, then I say thank you, then I'm glad to pay others for what I can't or won't or don't have time to do but need to have done to get through the day.

The person that ladles out venom and disrespect earns the returning poison. Commerce is the interaction of each of us doing our jobs, enjoying our art, in a highly interdependent community. Those who go before, those who join you in going forth this day, those who have not yet experienced you—they wish you well, they travel beside you, they await you.

Don't forget that the strength you bring can proceed only from your inner strength. Your inner strength depends upon your mind, body, and spirit collaborating in tandem through your hand, tongue, smile, your eyes and ears. Seeing, hearing, feeling, doing what's right and fair and needs to be done and said in the interest of service, community, justice, peace.

. . .

We are blessed to live in the land of the Great Divide. Surely, it's a place of poetry, nature, men and women, words, passion, spirituality, delight, tragedy, insight, wit, brevity, discipline, melody, a profound sense of passing, and so a profound sense of gratitude for the opportunity to be here, at this time, in this place, with this person, this bird, this tree, this flower, this river, that hill, the one behind it, so on up to altitudes and attitudes, where oceans gurgle from snow seeps, in multiple directions, drawn by gravity to destinies far and near.

. . .

The entrepreneurial spirit and the great natural beauty that surround us continue to attract people from all over the world. We have a great duty of trust to take care of this land and this city, for ourselves and for the generations.

. . .

Settling In
The Colorado Municipal League
2001 Annual Seminar on Municipal Law
Steamboat Springs, Colorado
October 6, 2001

Thanks for your invitation. What a beautiful fall day here in Steamboat Springs. The air is crystal. Peaks shine in the morning sun. Like the river, which flows serpentine, I shall come round to the topic you requested me to address this morning, "Effective Appellate Advocacy: What Works and What Doesn't."

But today is Saturday, poetry day around our house—Bobbie and I have attended workshops of gifted poet and teacher Kathryn Winograd. Now, Saturday is our day of errands and observing community in the neighborhood or going to the mountains into the Ponderosa Zone—and writing and reading poetry.

In view of the events of this past month, September the eleventh, I would like to read you a poem of the great Manhattan poet, Walt Whitman, who was celebrating this land and the immigrants from all over the world to this land, 140 years ago, in *Leaves of Grass*—a professor of the classics expressing the wisdom of the ages for his students:

THE BASE OF ALL METAPHYSICS

And now gentlemen,
A word I give to remain in your memories and minds,
As base, and finale too, for all metaphysics.
(So, to the students, the old professor,
At the close of his crowded course.)
Having studied the new and antique, the Greek and Germanic Systems,
Kant having studied and stated—Fichte and Schelling and Hegel,
Stated the lore of Plato—and Socrates greater than Plato,
And greater than Socrates sought and stated—Christ divine having studied long,
I see reminiscent to-day those Greek and Germanic systems,
See the philosophies all, Christian churches and tenets see,
Yet underneath Socrates clearly see—and underneath Christ the divine I see,
The dear love of man for his comrade—the attraction of friend to friend,

Of the well-married husband and wife—of children and parents,
Of city for city, and land for land.

> Walt Whitman, *Leaves of Grass*,
> 1891-1892 Edition (Random House, Inc.).

"Of city for city and land for land." So too and not so long ago—while Whitman was writing from his eastern habitation looking often with longing and anticipation to the West—the fifty-niners came to Colorado and began to discover and settle the land of the Great Divide, Hispanic families having already moved up from northern New Mexico to the San Luis Valley in the early 1850s. Hear what our poet laureate Thomas Hornsby Ferril wrote on viewing the confluence where the mountain river and the plains river join each other, from where Denver grows:

TWO RIVERS

Two rivers that were here before there was
A city here still come together: one
Is a mountain river flowing into the prairie;
One is a prairie river flowing toward
The mountains but feeling them and turning back
The way some of the people who came here did.

Most of the time these people hardly seemed
To realize they wanted to be remembered,
Because the mountains told them not to die.

I wasn't here, yet I remember them,
That first night long ago, those wagon people
Who pushed aside enough of the cottonwoods
To build our city where the blueness rested.

They were with me, they told me afterwards,
When I stood on a splintered wooden viaduct
Before it changed to steel and I to man.

They told me while I stare down at the water:
If you will stay we will not go away.

> Robert C. Baron, Stephen J. Leonard, Thomas J. Noel (eds.),
> *Thomas Hornsby Ferril and the American West*
> (Fulcrum Publishing, Golden, Colorado and the Center of the
> American West, University of Colorado at Boulder 1996) at 122.

"If you will stay, we will not go away." So we are here, and so the rivers are. Last Saturday night I was privileged to perform a wedding for a young couple starting off on their journey and passage together.

After the ceremony and while the reception was going on, I stepped outside the Denver Art Museum, looked at Civic Center Park in front of me, to my right, the east, the State Capitol, to my left, the west, the City and County Building, across the park, the *Denver Post* building and the other buildings of downtown daily life and commerce. Surveying the ellipse that holds this core of the community together, I wrote this poem thinking of my opportunity to talk with you today:

ELLIPSE

South side of the ellipse
in the heart of the city—
interposed between local
and state courts—art museum
and the public library,

On the east axis, the golden
dome of the capitol—dipped
in dawn, glowing sentinel to
a westering sky—looks to the
heart of the Continent,

Round the north curvature,
the press and downtown businesses—
commerce and the stuff of daily
commentary—offset history,
culture, with contemporaries,

The people come and go
across their park at the center—
gather and retreat along diagonals—
The People's Fair, Festival of
Mountains, Festival of Plains,

Every step they take, here history,
here art, here business, here
government, here the common

space—here the future, here the past—
always present, always different.

We serve a public purpose, we serve community.

I know that you are from big cities and small towns across the mountains, mesas, canyons, rivers, and plains of Colorado—and I am not one who believes that small towns on the eastern plains should be returned to the Buffalo Commons. Serving as *ex officio* chairperson to local judicial citizen nominating commissions, I have seen the power of integrity and community purpose these citizens bring to the process of nominating persons to whom—as judges—they would be willing to entrust their most important personal and business interests to a fair, impartial, just decision.

And the Western Slope, home to the mining economy that has come and gone and come back round again, and always present—the recreational, tourist, and health business that brings many a person to visit, here to stay: women in their long dresses with walking staffs climbing the mountain paths in the nineteenth century; tuberculosis patients seeking rest and revitalization at Glenwood Springs and Colorado Springs.

And so I use Denver as a metaphor for this settlement and growth and our continuing role in developing livable communities in a livable land, as we respect each other and the creatures and the landscape through which we make our passage.

I hold here the Hafen reader about Colorado so many students of our state used to learn from. This is a description of Denver at the time settlement on the Two Rivers began to take place:

In early 1859, the best houses were rude log cabins with dirt floors and canvas or dirt roofs. Of their furnishings A. D. Richardson, a pioneer newspaperman, writes: "Chairs were glories yet to come: stool tables and pole bedsteads were the staple furniture, while rough boxes did duty as bureaus and cupboards. Hearths and fireplaces were of adobe, as in Utah, California and Mexico. Chimneys were of sticks of wood piled up like children's cob-houses and plastered with mud. A few roofs were covered with shingles split by hand, but most were logs spread with prairie grass and covered with earth."

LeRoy R. Hafen and Ann W. Hafen, *Colorado,
A Story of the State and its People* (1947) at 178.

Contrast this description of Denver with what a *Harper's Weekly* writer said only two decades after formation of the Colorado territory:

> If the city were less substantial in appearance than it is, if it possessed certain glaring peculiarities, it would be much easier to describe it. But it so belies its age, and seems so much older than it really is, that one falls to taking for granted that which should be surprising. Wide, shaded, and attractive-looking streets, handsome residences surrounded by spacious grounds, noble public buildings, and the many luxuries of city life, tempt one to forget that Denver has gained all these excellencies in less than twenty-five years. Every tree that one sees has been planted and tended; every attractive feature is the result of good judgment and careful industry. Nature gave Denver the mountains which the city looks out upon; but beyond those hills and the bright sky and the limitless plains, she gave nothing to the place which one has only to see to admire. The site originally was a barren waste, dry and hilly. Never was it green, except perchance in early spring, and not a tree grew, save a few low bushes clinging to the banks of the river. Surrounded on the east, south, and north by the extended prairie lands, fast being converted into productive farms, and having on the west the mountains with their treasures of gold, silver, coal, iron, and lead, Denver is the natural concentrator of all the productions of Colorado. From it are sent forth the capital, the machinery, and the thousand and one other necessities of a constantly increasing number of people engaged in developing a new country.
>
> THE WEST: A COLLECTION FROM HARPER'S MAGAZINE 52-53 (1990).

And so we are still engaged in developing a new country, you and I, a country of law, justice, love, individual rights and community rights. This is a work of duty and the public interest forged of humility, hard work, and the friction of conflicting voices and ideas that ignites the spark—induced by the oxygen of inspiration—which turns to flame to warm and light the way.

Effective advocacy of any type is the art of persuasion—vision and constant revision—presented to decision-makers in words of scholarship and common sense turned to problem-solving, appealing to the policy and sense of public purpose that animates their deliberation and collaboration.

. . .

Thank you very much for inviting Bobbie and me to spend a part of this lovely morning with you.

To See the Mountains: Restoring Colorado's Clear and Healthy Air*
University of Colorado Law Review
Spring 2004

> Off to the west
> Where my elm tree used to be
> Before the beetles killed it
> I see the Rocky Mountains
> Trying to shoulder up
> Above the violet-ochre smog...
> The smog is drifting my way,
> I can taste it...[1]

The mountains are before us always.

In this state of the Great Divide, we look west, we look east to them. Shining out of the plains, they continually draw us to their constant promise. Native Americans, including the Pueblo People, the Navajos, and the Utes, considered them sacred.[2] Hispanos moving into the San Luis Valley from Northern New Mexico depended on them for home-building, firewood, and live stock grazing.[3] The 1859ers rushed into them for mineral treasure.[4]

Since the founding of the Colorado Territory in 1861, farmers, cities, and businesses have depended on the mountain waters for beneficial use. Skiers, backpackers, hunters, kayakers, and fisher persons from all over the world check their heart-travels by the gauge of mountain vistas, and—exalted at the sight of

---

* 75 U. COLO. L. REV. 433 (2004). Reprinted with permission of the University of Colorado Law Review.

[1] THOMAS HORNSBY FERRIL, *Stories of Three Summers, Colorado 1776*1876*1976*, in THOMAS HORNSBY FERRIL AND THE AMERICAN WEST 96, Robert C. Baron, Stephen J. Leonard, and Thomas J. Noel eds., (Fulcrum Publishing, Golden, Colorado and the Center of the American West, University of Colorado at Boulder 1996).

[2] VIRGINIA MCCONNELL SIMMONS, THE SAN LUIS VALLEY, LAND OF THE SIX-ARMED CROSS 17 (2d ed. 1999); LEROY R. HAFEN & ANN W. HAFEN, COLORADO, A STORY OF THE STATE AND ITS PEOPLE 69 (1943).

[3] *See Lobato v. Taylor*, 71 P.3d 938, 945-57 (Colo. 2002) (in the context of deeds to land of the Sangre de Cristo Grant in the San Luis Valley, discussing Mexican land grant, settlers' rights, and Colorado Territorial law).

[4] ROBERT G. ATHEARN, THE COLORADANS 16 (1976).

them—breathe deeply. Waking to the backbone of the Continent, Front Range residents can hardly wait for the weekend to be among "their" mountains.

To see the mountains clearly is a Colorado heritage. To breathe healthy air is a necessity of life. To keep the air clear and healthy has been and continues to be a public policy priority for each and every Colorado generation. Bad air not only brings on and aggravates injuries to persons who suffer diseases such as asthma, it is also suspected to trigger processes that cause heart attacks, strokes, and Alzheimer's disease.[5] Bad air also impairs the economic viability of tourism to a state that has been reputed throughout the world from the early days of the Colorado Territory as a recreational mecca.

Colorado's bad air problem built towards a crisis in the 1950s and '60s. The poem Ferril wrote in the 1970s testifies dramatically to the filth Denver residents saw and breathed. For example, in the benchmark year of 1972—shortly after the passage of the major 1970 Colorado and federal clean air acts but before pollution controls set in—Denver air violated the national health standards for carbon monoxide more than 154 days that year.[6] In 1977, the downtown monitoring station at 21st and Broadway reported 42 days of violation for ozone.[7] Concentrations of total suspended particulates were at 136 micrograms per cubic meter while the federal ambient air standard was 75 micrograms per cubic meter.[8] In addition, levels of nitrogen dioxide violated the national standard at the downtown station.[9]

Denver was not the only city in Colorado experiencing problems. Greeley and Fort Collins often violated the national health standards for carbon monoxide, ozone, and total suspended particulates.[10] Pueblo and Grand Junction also violated the standard for total suspended particulates.[11]

The polluted air was not the sight tourists hoped to see. Visitors to rural valley towns surrounded by incredible mountains—like South Fork, Pagosa Springs, and Durango—were disappointed to find that wigwam waste-burner wood smoke caused a huge foul-smelling pall that obscured the vistas. Visitors to Rocky Mountain National Park and the Front Range mountains south to Pikes' Peak passed through a ghastly Brown Cloud, still hoping to see the miraculous sights

---

[5] Kris Newcomer, *Researchers Study Polluted Air as Trigger for Disease*, ROCKY MTN. NEWS, Oct. 28, 1990, at 8.
[6] COLORADO AIR POLLUTION CONTROL COMM'N, 2 REPORT TO THE PUBLIC 46 (1978).
[7] *Id.* at 136.
[8] *Id.* at 35.
[9] *Id.* at 53.
[10] *Id.* at 8, 10.
[11] *Id.* at 11, 13.

Zebulon Pike,[12] Stephen F. Long,[13] John C. Fremont,[14] John Wesley Powell,[15] Thomas Moran,[16] W.H. Jackson,[17] and a host of unnamed visitors and settlers described, painted, photographed, and revered.

The restoration of Colorado's clean air is a great story of natural resource restoration. It took nearly half a century to accomplish. Wishing for cleaner air became a public aspiration. Disgusted with air that looked and smelled like rotten soup, citizens grew tired of hoping that a great wind would blow the pollution away, or that the temperature would change and the latest pollutant-trapping inversion would lift. For five decades, unrelenting press attention focused on Colorado's pollution black-eye and virtually every step in cleaning it up. Fortunately, air is a common

---

[12] From the prairie along the Arkansas River, Pike in mid-November of 1806 first sighted as "a small blue cloud" the mountain in Spanish territory that would later bear his name. CARL UBBELOHDE, MAXINE BENSON, & DUANE A. SMITH, A COLORADO HISTORY 21 (8th ed. 2001).

[13] Traveling up the South Platte, Long's party spotted from a great distance the great escarpment of the Colorado Rockies:
> From this encampment, we had a plain but still distant view of the mountains.... They stretched from north to south, like an immense wall occupying that portion of the horizon, lying to the northwest, west, and southwest. We could now see the surface of the plain, extending almost unvaried to the base of the first ridge, which rises by an abrupt ascent above the commencement of the snow.

FROM PITTSBURGH TO THE ROCKY MOUNTAINS, MAJOR STEPHEN LONG'S EXPEDITION 1819-1820, at 198 (Maxine Benson ed., 1988).

[14] With Fremont in 1853-1854 on his fifth expedition, daguerreotype photographer Solomon Nunes Carvalho described the view from Bent's Fort near La Junta on the Arkansas: "When the weather is very clear, you can see the snow peaks of the Rocky Mountains from Bent's house, which is seventy [sic] miles distant." ROBERT SHLAER, SIGHTS ONCE SEEN, DAGUERREOTYPING FREMONT'S LAST EXPEDITION THROUGH THE ROCKIES 81 (2000). The distance from Bent's house to the peaks is actually 120 miles.

[15] In his 1867 and 1968 field seasons in Colorado, Powell and his party, including wife Emma, climbed Pike's Peak and Longs Peak to gain the vistas. Amateur newspaper correspondent, Joseph Hartzell with Powell on the Pike's Peak climb in 1867, wrote rhapsodically of a hundred mile vista:
> With a picturesque landscape of hundreds of miles in extent spread out beneath us, the clear, blue arch of heaven above, no wonder that it seemed to our rapt vision something like enchantment. Surely the Creator intended the grandeur and beauty of the world as a foretaste of the hereafter.

DONALD WORSTER, A RIVER RUNNING WEST, THE LIFE OF JOHN WESLEY POWELL 122 (2001).

[16] In August of 1874, having heard of the fabled Mountain of the Holy Cross as a member of Ferdinand Hayden's survey party, Thomas Moran ascended into the mountains from Morrison to find and sketch that stunning view of the mountain's cruciform which—translated into his great painting—fired the imagination of the westering nation. Camped on the South Platte River in South Park he described Pike's Peak looming 50 miles or so to the south. THURMAN WILKINS, THOMAS MORAN: ARTIST OF THE MOUNTAINS 138 (2d ed. 1998).

[17] See, e.g., Jackson's 1892 photograph of the Central Front Range from Longs Peak to the Indian Peaks taken from northwest Denver and the late 1990s companion photograph following Denver's air quality restoration, in WILLIAM HENRY JACKSON & JOHN FIELDER, COLORADO 1870-2000, 20-21 (2000).

resource shared by all. At common law, no right of property ownership to pollute the public's air vests by law. Uncontrolled nuisance more accurately described air pollution's legal status in mid-twentieth-century Colorado.

Early local efforts to control smoke could not get the job done. It took the very strong CAA and its amendments in 1970, 1977, and 1990 to provide a mandatory health-protection framework that complemented and drove implementation of Colorado's 1970 air statute and its subsequent amendments. The automobile and manufacturing industries had no choice but to comply with national standards designed to force the development and installation of air pollution technology as rapidly as possible.

But something else was going on in Colorado just as important. The state's business community came to see that its interest in economic development must be paired with cleaning up the state's air and developing a transportation network that included rapid transit in the Denver metropolitan area. After all, tourism and homebuilding depend on citizen enjoyment of the air resource for its own sake—to see Colorado's glorious landscape.

Press reports focused on how Colorado suffered national ridicule for its horrible air pollution. The most notable incident occurred in 1988 after the Denver Broncos suffered their third Super Bowl loss. The CBS Evening News proclaimed that Denver was "a town that's never been No. 1 in anything but carbon monoxide levels."[18] Soon thereafter, the Greater Denver Chamber of Commerce lent its considerable prestige to coordinate the Brown Cloud Study and support clean air action measures.

"Let's do something about this filthy air!" took hold as a top public priority. Starting in the 1950s, citizens came to recognize that they were part of the problem, as a result of burning trash in their backyards, driving smoky cars, and burning wood in their fireplaces, for example. The struggle for voluntary, then mandatory measures for air pollution clean-up has been long, costly, productive, and satisfying.[19]

On August 9, 2002, the United States Environmental Protection Agency announced that the Denver Metropolitan Area had achieved compliance with federal health limits for all six major pollutants regulated under the CAA:[20] particulates, ozone,

---

[18] REGIONAL AIR QUALITY COUNCIL, DENVER METRO AIR QUALITY: 25 YEARS OF PROGRESS 3 (Air Exchange Supplement) (Aug. 2001), *available at* http://www.raqc.org/newsletters/AirExchange/Retrospect.pdf [hereinafter DENVER METRO AIR QUALITY]; Mark Obmasick and Michael Booth, *We Can See Clearly Now*, DENV. POST, Dec. 8, 1996, at A1; *see* Todd Hartman, *Denver Breathes Easy with EPA's Blessings*, ROCKY MTN. NEWS, Aug. 10, 2002, at 19A.

[19] Todd Hartman, *At Long Last, Metro Area Breathes Easy*, ROCKY MTN. NEWS, July 29, 2002, at 1A.

[20] Todd Hartman, *Denver Breathes Easy with EPA's Blessings*, ROCKY MTN. NEWS, Aug. 10, 2002, at 19A.

carbon monoxide, nitrogen oxide, sulfur dioxide, and lead.[21] Further, the Denver Broncos won two Super Bowls in the meantime! Colorado is no longer seen as a national loser in football or air pollution.

Incredibly, compliance with the national air health standards and the resulting significant visibility improvement occurred despite Colorado's growth from two million to four and a quarter million people between 1970 and 2000. The state and CAA provided the legal platform, but the persistent will of Colorado and United States citizens made achievement of clean air goals possible.

Nevertheless, the Front Range area still violates the state's visibility standard 55 times a year[22] and—after a period of compliance—must now implement additional measures to control ozone pollution to meet the newly enacted eight-hour national ozone standard.[23] Clearly, the constant attention of Coloradans on keeping a restored air resource in place is crucial.

Because it took Colorado half a century to crack the terrible air problem, I cannot hope in this article to provide a comprehensive account of all the persons, efforts, and events that have contributed to the state's clean air restoration. But, I can say from historical and legal research, informed by personal experience in Colorado air quality matters since the early 1970s, how bad the problem was, how irresistible the public commitment to air pollution control became, and how glorious the healthy air and the vistas are that we can share.

In this article, I set forth the clean air public policy progression largely in chronological order. I also focus on significant stages of air pollution control. The article considers citizen realization about how bad the air was and it examines the visible progress made through the adoption of strong federal and state air pollution control statutes. In addition, the article discusses significant litigation that established enforcement precedent, and the role that stationary source control, mobile source control, and transportation, land use, and air quality planning played in the restoration of clean air in Colorado. The article also reviews the Brown Cloud study, subsequent emission reduction measures, and Colorado's achievement in meeting national health standards.

---

[21] *See* DENVER METRO AIR QUALITY *supra* note 18, at 3. *See also* 42 U.S.C. § 7409(a)(1)(A) & (b)(1); 40 C.F.R. §§50.4 to 50.12 (2003).

[22] COLORADO AIR QUALITY CONTROL COMM'N, REPORT TO THE PUBLIC 2 (2002). *See also* Regional Air Quality Council, *Update on the Blueprint for Clean Air*, AIR EXCH. (Winter/Spring 2000), *available at* www.raqc.org/reports/blueprintforcleanair/bpupdate.htm.

[23] *Our Ozone Problem Is Real*, DENV. POST, Dec. 6, 2003, at 15C; Joey Bunch, *Denver Area Returns to Dirty-Air List*, DENV. POST, Dec. 5, 2003, at 1A. *See* Christopher M. Kamper, *Colorado Addresses New EPA Ozone Standard*, 33 COLO. LAW. 67 (Feb. 2004); Allison D. Wood, *Implementing EPA's 8-Hour Ozone Standard, Round Two*, 18 NAT. RES. & ENV'T 16 (Winter 2004).

Part I addresses how bad the air quality problem was in the 1950s up until the 1970s. Part II discusses how the 1970s brought about visible progress in controlling stationary pollution sources. Part III tells how the crucial air quality control decade of the 1980s dealt with transportation, land use, and air quality planning in the quest to bust the brown cloud. Part IV reveals how Colorado achieved the national health standards for air by the end of the 1990s. Part V cautions about new challenges in light of twenty-first century growth and the need for continued dedication to Colorado's air quality control priority.

I. How Bad It Was: The 1950s to 1970s

It seemed to Colorado "natives"[24] that the world was flocking here after World War II. Together, all we nestlings helped to foul the place; then came the inevitable process of cleaning up our mess.

A. *Citizens Learn to Detest "The Sewer of the Air"*

Coloradans hate not seeing the mountains. In 1959, an airline pilot based at Stapleton lamented the "deterioration of Denver's once crystal-clear air...it rivals any large city in smoke concentration—even Los Angeles."[25] A first and largely ineffective poke at controlling air pollution had actually started a decade earlier, but the ignorance of citizens about their own contribution to the problem and a pro-business attitude among state legislators prevented any real progress. Clearly, the air had to get worse before it got better. Citizen concern later turned into citizen contempt for public inaction and finally spurred legislators to act.

Denver adopted its first anti-smoke ordinance in 1948, but the building department rarely enforced it.[26] Fifty thousand backyard ash pits burned trash at home, contributing to "a perpetual haze hugging the Platte River valley...."[27] Inspectors were sent to knock on the doors of those whose pits were smoking badly and to implore them to burn their trash a little better, if they could figure out how to do that.[28]

By 1954, there were 100,000 homes with polluting incinerators. They combined with factories, oil refineries, and motor vehicles to produce episodes of "eye-smarting pollution."[29] Denver established the post of Air Pollution Inspector, a

---

[24] Indicating those who arrived just a little less recently than the others.
[25] *Denver's Air So Bad It Rivals L.A., Airline Pilot Warns of Increased Smog*, Denv. Post, Jan. 18, 1959, at 3AA.
[26] John Buchanan, *Denver Firms Spending $500,000.00 to Fight Smoke*, Denv. Post, Apr. 13, 1952, at 17A.
[27] Jack Gaskie, *Ash Pits to Blame for Some of Pall Over Platte, Smoke Nuisance in Denver Cut 80 Percent in Past Two Years*, Rocky Mtn. News, Mar. 24, 1951, at 41.
[28] *Id.*
[29] Bill Jones, *Denver's Air May Turn in 10-Years to LA-Like Smog*, Rocky Mtn. News, Dec. 4, 1954, at 5.

public official whose job was to take pictures of industrial smoke stacks and send cease and desist notices to the operators. Such orders were largely ineffective because it took a court case to establish the existence of a nuisance and collect fines.[30]

In 1957, the U.S. Public Health Service issued a 78-page report stating that pollution levels in Denver were a year-round problem. It recommended an inventory of air pollution sources, a meteorological study "so that further growth can be planned to avoid poisoning the general atmosphere," and adoption of an air quality control program.[31] A survey of air pollution sources included motor vehicles, refuse burning in landfills and backyard incinerators, manufacturing plants, heating of homes and buildings, and power plants.[32] Newspapers printed photograph after photograph displaying Denver's "smokescape" and "sewer of the air."[33]

B. The Press Gets Interested and Legislators Partially Respond

Then called "smaze,"[34] Denver's filthy air rapidly became a political liability due to focused media attention. For example, the *Denver Post* in 1962 displayed a full page photograph of Mt. Evans rising out of a murky brown soup masking Denver below. The caption read: "Suspended filth hides Denver's rooftops. Mt. Evans gleams white from 2,000 feet up, but from the ground it is obscured."[35]

Seeing clearly was not the only issue. Citizens were suffering the health effects of bad air. Dr. William F. Spence of the University of Colorado Medical Center reported that, "the incidence of certain pulmonary diseases, such as chronic bronchitis, has increased to a marked degree in the past few years.... [and] a more serious condition, pulmonary emphysema...."[36]

As the unabated pollution problem continued to hamper citizen health and clear mountain views, state lawmakers began to take notice. The stupendous golden-domed Colorado state capitol building sits on a mile-high hill looking straight west to the Continental Divide. Legislators were also unable to see Mt. Evans, and they clearly heard a rising citizen howl.

In 1963, a Denver state legislator, William Griffith, introduced a bill in the General Assembly to create special enforcement districts for air pollution control.

---

[30] Bill Jones, *Denver Plans to Crack Down on Air Pollution*, ROCKY MTN. NEWS, Feb. 5, 1955, at 5.
[31] *Pollution of Denver Air Scored*, DENV. POST, July 2, 1957, at 11.
[32] *Id.*
[33] Gene Lindberg, *'Sewer of the Air,' Air Pollution over Denver Held Metropolitan Problem*, DENV. POST, Jan. 10, 1960, at 13A.
[34] J. Bob Lucas, *U.S. Public Health Group to Make Survey of Denver Smaze Problem*, ROCKY MTN. NEWS, Nov. 27, 1956, at 31.
[35] Bob Jain, *Denver's (and your) Air Pollution Problem*, DENV. POST, Jan. 21, 1962, (Empire Magazine), at 4.
[36] *Id.*

District court orders would trigger an election to establish a district in the local area, and, if formed, the district would have taxing authority and the power to employ an air pollution control officer and staff.[37] Deferring to local units of government has been the typical initial approach of Colorado legislators for dealing with difficult environmental and land use problems. However, because the bad air knew no jurisdictional boundary, the General Assembly began moving toward state-wide legislation. In 1963, it enacted the state "air sanitation act"[38] rather than the Denver legislator's local district proposal. Though inadequate, this legislation empowered the State Board of Health to establish air quality standards, including standards for motor vehicles,

> to reflect the relationship between the intensity and composition of air pollution and the health, illness, including irritation to the senses, and death of human beings, compatible with the preservation of public health, as well as damage to vegetation and interference with visibility.[39]

The act established a nine-member air pollution advisory board composed of government officials, industry representatives, and citizens. The advisory board was to consult with the Board of Health during the process of proposing suitable standards, which were to be considered at a public hearing, then adopted and submitted to the General Assembly for consideration. In connection with other air act revisions in 1964, the General Assembly adopted the standards that emerged from this process.[40]

C. Inadequacy of Initial State Program

The 1963 and 1964 legislation provided no comprehensive means of ensuring compliance. Enforcement of air pollution control standards depended on local ordinances and agencies.[41] As its population grew, Colorado's air got worse. Denver was not the only highly-polluted region in the State. Pueblo had more air pollution than all of the 11 Colorado counties tested during the final quarter of 1965.[42] Boulder, Colorado Springs, Fort Collins, Grand Junction, Greeley, and Longmont also failed air quality standards.[43]

In 1966, the General Assembly adopted revisions to the air statute, creating the Air Pollution Control Division, which could enforce Board of Health standards by

---

[37] *Air Pollution Control Bill Widely Backed*, DENV. POST, Jan. 17, 1963, at 3.
[38] Act of Apr. 15, 1963, ch. 150, 1963 Colo. Sess. Laws 549, (codified at COLO. REV. STAT. § 66-24-1 to -5 (1963)).
[39] § 3(1)(a), 1963 Colo. Sess. Laws at 550 (codified at COLO. REV. STAT. § 66-24-3(1)(b) (1963)).
[40] Act of Mar. 18, 1964, ch. 58, § 4, 1964 Colo. Sess. Laws 483, 484-85 (current version at COLO. REV. STAT. § 25-7-102 (2003)).
[41] *See generally* Act of Apr. 15, 1963, ch. 150, §3, 1963 Colo. Sess. Laws 549, 550; Act of Mar. 18, 1964, ch. 58, § 6, 1964 Colo. Sess. Laws 484, 485.
[42] *Pueblo Gets Worst Mark in State Air Pollution Tests*, PUEBLO CHIEFTAIN, Jan. 28, 1966, at 1A.
[43] *Id.*

issuing cease and desist orders.[44] The Board of Health designated four air pollution basins centering on the cities of Denver, El Paso, and Pueblo, as well as Grand Junction.[45] The 1966 legislation also established a statewide Air Pollution Variance Board for the purpose of adjudicating appeals from Division compliance orders and for reviewing variance applications requesting temporary exemptions for polluters who needed time to comply with clean air standards.[46] The 1966 act exempted backyard trash burning from regulation.[47]

D. In Your Face Newspaper Photography and Disease Reports

Newspaper photography continued to expose a horrible air pollution problem. A 1966 article compared the once-clear view Denver residents enjoyed of the mountains with the "valley of the big smokes."[48] The captions read:

> The vista Denver was famous for is now too often found only "on a windy Sunday morning when the foundries, chemical plants and steam boilers are shut down, before people fire up their incinerators and when traffic is light," according to a meteorologist.
>
> This "valley of the big smokes" is the South Platte River bordering S. Santa Fe Dr. Chimneys contributing to growing smoke cloud belong to power generating plants and auto wrecking yards near the Hampden Ave. interchange.[49]

The accompanying text reported one Colorado citizen as saying, "it was 'quite unusual' to see any pall over [Denver]" in the early 1950s, but now in the mid-60s "it is unusual to see any city at all. Denver has disappeared in the gloom of its wastes."[50]

Citizens were outraged about the air pollution, but many could not see their own part in causing it. A beleaguered five-county association of Denver area cities and counties, known as the Regional Air Pollution Control Agency, labored to develop an ordinance to control, by 1968, "that odious neighborhood nuisance, the

---

[44] Air Pollution Control Act, ch. 45, §§ 7 & 14, 1966 Colo. Sess. Laws 210, 217 & 224 (current version at COLO. REV. STAT. §§ 25-7-104, -121 (2003)).

[45] Air Pollution Control Act, ch. 45, § 8(1)(c), 1966 Colo. Sess. Laws 210, 219 (codified at COLO. REV. STAT. § 66-29-8(1)(c) (Perm. Cum. Supp. 1967)); Air Pollution Fight Charted, DENV. POST, Apr. 14, 1966, at 19.

[46] Air Pollution Control Act, ch. 45, § 7 & 11, 1966 Colo. Sess. Laws 210, 217 & 222 (codified at COLO. REV. STAT. §§ 66-29-7, -11 (Perm. Cum. Supp. 1967)); Rendall Ayers, Hearing Held on Air Pollution, DENV. POST, May 5, 1966, at 59.

[47] Air Pollution Control Act, Ch. 45, § 5(4)(b)(ii), 1966 Colo. Sess. Laws 210, 213-14 (current version at COLO. REV. STAT. § 25-7-108 (2003)).

[48] Mark Bearwald, How Denver Is Strangling Itself, DENV. POST, Jan. 30, 1966 (Empire Magazine), at 5.

[49] Id.

[50] Id.

backyard incinerator."[51] But, "[c]ity fathers in Denver, Aurora and Boulder who considered banning these smudgepots" were

> besieged by aroused citizens who feel the freedom to smolder sodden trash is among the inalienable rights of man. Indeed, much of the mail generated by recent discussion of air pollution has come from irate householders who heap scorn and calumny on the automobile, the Public Service Co. and all industry while extolling the basic goodness and utility of the clean-burning incinerator.[52]

After looking out of his window in May of 1967 and seeing how bad Fort Collins' air had become in just six years, Dr. Elmar Reiter, a Colorado State University professor of atmospheric science, predicted that if nothing were done, citizens would suffer serious health problems, even death, and

> '[c]ertainly by the end of this century we're going to have to put up direction signs pointing to the mountains—because people won't be able to see them any more.
>
> . . .
>
> To really attack pollution we must combine the forces of meteorology, chemistry, political science, sociology, perhaps theology—because we have to design a new society which provides for life with health and a future.[53]

Dr. Reiter should have included all the natural and political sciences and theology, too! This cosmic forecast about what it would take for a successful community effort to clean up Colorado's air turned out to be quite accurate. Citizen advocacy to spur legislators to action was clearly needed, and predictably it arose as the problem got worse. The source evidence was overwhelming—Denver air really was as bad as Los Angeles air. A visitor from Cleveland arriving for a medical convention exclaimed, "Oh, no! Not here, too!"[54] In reporting this in a piece entitled, *The Sky IS Falling Down*, the news writer summed up a dismal scene:

> Snuff out the smokestacks and there are the burning dumps. Snuff the dumps and you have the back yard burning. Squelch all these sources and the nastiest smog producer of them all still pours deadly gasses into the air, the cars, buses, trucks, and those sleek jets coursing in and out of Stapleton.[55]

---

[51] *Id.*
[52] *Id.*
[53] William Logan, *Purify Air or Die, Says CSU Scientist*, ROCKY MTN. NEWS, May 28, 1967, at 20.
[54] Dirk Van Loon, *The Sky IS Falling Down—First of a Series, On a 'Bad Day' Denver Is Like L.A.*, ROCKY MTN. NEWS, Jan. 21, 1968, at 16.
[55] *Id.*

Much needed to be done.

E. Snuffing the Backyard Smokers and Dreaming of Mass Transit

For starters, citizens had to change their burning habits. And cities had to make this possible by hauling the garbage away for land disposal. By January of 1968, the counties of Adams, Arapahoe, Boulder, Jefferson, and El Paso had a ban on backyard incineration in effect.[56] Denver delayed implementation of its ordinance pending acquisition of equipment for additional trash pickup.[57] Local officials were nervous about enforcing their ordinances.[58] Foreseeing the difficulty in enforcing local ordinances, the General Assembly in 1967 adopted a ban on backyard refuse burning, except in sophisticated and expensive incinerators that no citizen was likely to buy. The ban was to take effect by January 1, 1970.[59] With the finger pointed at them and trash pickup available, citizens finally relinquished a very dirty habit.

As a result of the 1967 federal Clean Air Act,[60] Denver became one of the first five areas to be designated as a federal air quality control region. The others were the Chicago, New York, Philadelphia, and District of Columbia areas.[61] In 1968, based on this federal designation, the existence of air pollution throughout the state, and the lack of local funding and personnel, the highly respected League of Women Voters of Colorado called for the creation of a statewide pollution control authority with the power to implement uniform air pollution control and to enforce and supervise the construction of new air pollution sources.[62]

At the close of the 1960s, the need for comprehensive state and federal control of stationary and mobile sources of pollution was as clear as Colorado skies were filthy. Denver could not go it alone, despite the adoption of city ordinances to cut smokestack emissions in half and the enforcement against smoking vehicles.[63] Discussion began about reducing automobile use through mass transit.

> Taking action against the automobile...is only one aspect of the assault on air pollution. A great deal must be done also to clean up stationary

---

[56] Gordon G. Gauss, *Suburbs Prohibit Burning of Trash*, ROCKY MTN. NEWS, Jan. 2, 1968, at 10.
[57] *Id.*; *Incinerator Ban Begins in Area*, DENV. POST, Jan. 4, 1968, at 26.
[58] *See Incinerators Still Smoking at Springs*, ROCKY MTN. NEWS, Jan. 4, 1968, at 31.
[59] Air Pollution Control Act, ch. 357, sec. 2, § 5(4)(c), 1967 Colo. Sess. Laws 756, 756 (codified at COLO. REV. STAT. § 66-29-5(4)(c) (Perm. Cum. Supp. 1967)).
[60] Air Quality Act of 1967, Pub. L. No. 90-148, 81 Stat 485 (codified as amended at 42 U.S.C. § 1857-1857l (1967)).
[61] LEAGUE OF WOMEN VOTERS OF COLORADO, AIR POLLUTION CONTROL IN COLORADO—1968, at 1 (1968).
[62] *Id.* at 2.
[63] Don Lyle, *Council Ends '69 Session With Pollution Curb Okay*, ROCKY MTN. NEWS, Dec. 30, 1969, at 8.

sources of pollution and to develop mass transit systems that reduce automobile use.

Denver will need all the help it can get from the state and the federal government to win the battle for clean air.[64]

In the crucial arena of public opinion, the stage was now set for strong state and federal air quality regulation.

II. VISIBLE PROGRESS, THE 1970S

The decade of the 1970s blew strongly across the face of America, fundamentally revamping pro-settlement laws affecting the environment. No place felt the effect of these laws more significantly than the West, which for over a century had depended on natural resource extractive and manufacturing industries to fuel its growth, including mining, smelting, steel-making, power production, lumber milling and waste burning. A healthy and enjoyable environment for people, plants, and animals became both an article of faith and a political platform for a new generation of office holders and seekers. State and federal air pollution control acts hammered out the way—all because citizen voters could see and smell how bad the problem really was.

A. Colorado Air Commission Established

Nineteen seventy was the state and national air-shed year for air quality legislation. The Colorado General Assembly and the United States Congress adopted comprehensive, interlocking statutes for controlling air pollution.[65] The genius of the federal law was that it set national goals for air pollution control and strong back-up measures to achieve them, but also allowed the states to shape and enforce their own laws, which could be more stringent than the federal requirements. While the 1970 CAA focused primarily on public health and welfare protection,[66] Colorado's 1970 Air Pollution Control Act also included a mandate to protect the enjoyment of "nature and scenery" throughout the state.[67]

---

[64] Editorial, *Denver Needs Help in Smog Battle*, DENV. POST, Dec. 18, 1969, at 22.

[65] Air Pollution Control Act of 1970, ch. 64, § 1, 1970 Colo. Sess. Laws 220 (codified at COLO. REV. STAT. § 66-31-1 to -26 (Perm. Cum. Supp. 1971) (current version at COLO. REV. STAT. §§ 25-7-101 to -1309 (2003))); Clean Air Amendments of 1970, Pub. L. No. 91-604, 84 Stat 1676 (codified at 42 U.S.C. §§ 1857 to 1857b-1 (1971) (current version at 42 U.S.C. §§ 7401-7671(q) (2003))).

[66] *See* Clean Air Amendments of 1970, Pub. L. No. 91-604, 84 Stat 1676. *See also* Whitman v. Am. Trucking Ass'ns., 531 U.S. 457, 465 (2001) (stating that section 109(b)(1), 42 U.S.C. § 7409 (b)(1), "instructs the EPA to set primary ambient air quality standards 'the attainment and maintenance of which...are requisite to protect public health with and adequate margin of safety'" and the costs of achieving these standards are set without regard to the costs of achieving them).

[67] 1970 Colo. Sess. Laws 220 (codified at COLO. REV. STAT. § 66-31-1 to -26 (Perm. Cum. Supp. 1971) (current version at COLO. REV. STAT. § 25-7-102 (2003))).

[I]t is hereby declared to be the policy of the state to achieve the maximum practical degree of air purity in every portion of the state. To that end, it is the purpose of this article to require the use of all available practical methods to reduce, prevent, and control air pollution throughout the entire state of Colorado....[68]

The Colorado air act created a nine-member citizen Air Pollution Control Commission with "maximum flexibility" to adopt a "comprehensive program for...control of emissions from all significant sources of air pollution, and...ambient air goals for every portion of the state."[69] The General Assembly directed the Commission to receive and decide all applications for hearings on violations or applications for variances, or to assign them to the Variance Board for hearing and decision.[70]

The Commission's primary job was to adopt air contaminant emission control regulations for an impressive, illustrative, but not all-inclusive list of health-threatening, visibility-threatening, and nuisance-causing pollutants. These included particulates, sulfur oxides, sulfuric acids, hydrogen sulfide, nitrogen oxides, carbon oxides, hydrocarbons, fluorides, other chemical substances, odors, open burning of all types, organic solvents, photochemical substances, and toxic gases.[71]

The General Assembly also catalogued a breath-inspiring, non-inclusive list of air pollution sources for the Air Commission to control, including incinerators, the storage and transfer of petroleum products and other volatile sources, construction and demolition operations, the operation of parking lots, fuel additives, wigwam waste burners, pulp mills, alfalfa dehydrators, asphalt plants, industrial process equipment, industrial spraying operations, the reduction of animal matter, motor vehicles and airplanes, diesel-powered machines, engines, equipment, storage, the transfer of toxic gases, and any other industrial or commercial activity which tends to emit air contaminants.[72]

In other words, virtually every aspect of Colorado commerce and life activity causing air pollution became subject to the state's air quality restoration program. The

---

[68] 1970 Colo. Sess. Laws 220, 220 (codified at Colo. Rev. Stat. § 66-31-2 (Perm. Cum. Supp. 1971) (current version at Colo. Rev. Stat. § 25-7-102 (2003))).

[69] 1970 Colo. Sess. Laws 220, 222-23 (codified at Colo. Rev. Stat. §§ 66-31-5(1), -6(1)(a) (Perm. Cum. Supp. 1971) (current version at Colo. Rev. Stat. § 25-7-109(1)(a) (2003))). See § 66-31-3(5) (defining ambient air as "the surrounding or outside air").

[70] 1970 Colo. Sess. Laws 210, 223 (codified at Colo. Rev. Stat. § 66-31-5(7) (Perm. Cum. Supp. 1971)).

[71] 1970 Colo. Sess. Laws 210, 225 (codified at Colo. Rev. Stat. § 66-31-8(2)(a)-(i) (Perm. Cum. Supp. 1971) (current version at Colo. Rev. Stat. § 25-7-109(2) (2003))).

[72] 1970 Colo. Sess. Laws 210, 225-26 (codified at Colo. Rev. Stat. § 66-31-8(3)(a)-(l) (Perm. Cum. Supp. 1971) (current version at Colo. Rev. Stat. § 25-7-109(3) (2003))).

General Assembly assigned important responsibilities to the Air Pollution Control Division, including monitoring the air, identifying air pollution sources, recommending emission control regulations and ambient air quality standards to the Commission, staffing the hearings of the Commission and the Variance Board,[73] and obtaining compliance with Commission-adopted regulations.[74]

B. The Air Division Gets Active

The 1970 Colorado air act also established a permit system in the Air Division to control new and modified air pollution sources prior to the start-up of their operations, and required polluters to file emission notices disclosing emission type and quantity.[75] These key provisions of the state act, like its federal counterpart, front-loaded the air quality priority into the way Coloradans conducted business.

Based on a pre-existing Health Board standard, the first emission control regulation adopted by the Commission—led by its Administrator Joe Palomba—was directly aimed at controlling visible air pollution. Its trigger mechanism was an opacity standard that regulated the degree to which a smoke plume could mask the vision of a person attempting to look through it.

Trained "smoke readers" had used the Ringelmann Chart for years as a means of gauging the offensiveness of smoke plumes. To read black smoke, the inspector would hold the chart at arm's length, look through the hole in the chart's upper center, and compare the shade or density of the smoke with the shades printed on the chart.[76] To read white smoke, inspectors employed an equivalent opacity test learned at a state certification course.[77] Because fine particulates in smoke plumes cause both visibility restriction and health effects, an opacity standard aims to reduce particulate loading into the air by requiring installation of control equipment or cessation of the pollutant-causing activity, with resulting health and visibility benefits.

The pioneering federal and state air statutes set the framework for visible progress to control air pollution, but enforcement of those laws in the face of skeptical and uncooperative businesses became necessary.

C. Colorado Attorney General Takes a Lead Role

It takes the devoted attention of public law enforcement officers to translate statutes into court decisions and constructive advice for decision makers. In the

---

[73] COLO. REV. STAT. § 66-31-14 (Perm. Cum. Supp. 1971) (current version at COLO. REV. STAT. § 25-7-111 (2003))).
[74] §§ 66-31-10, -13 (current version at COLO. REV. STAT. § 25-7-111 (2003)).
[75] § 66-31-12 (current version at COLO. REV. STAT. §§ 25-7-114 to -114.4 (2003)).
[76] Bob Jain, *Denver's (and Your) Air Pollution Problem*, DENV. POST, Jan. 21, 1962, (Empire Magazine), at 4.
[77] *Lloyd A. Fry Roofing Co. v. Air Pollution Variance Bd.*, 553 P.2d 800, 806-07 (Colo. 1976).

1970s, the Colorado Attorney General's office emerged on the front line of the air pollution control fight.

1. The First *Fry* Case

Manufacturing industries—one example of an initially uncooperative industry—were accustomed to using the public's air resource as a dumping space. Some business owners could not believe the government could force them to change their pre-existing practices and cost them money they did not choose to spend. The Fry Roofing Company in Commerce City, for one, refused to comply. It challenged the constitutionality of the act's sweeping grant of authority to the Air Commission, particularly the air purity goal and the act's alleged illegal retroactive application against pre-existing practices.

Fry Roofing cooked roofing oils in its Adams County plant, which was one of 24 plants it operated nationwide for making asphalt shingles. "Old man Fry," as the irreverent young regulators began to call him, said he'd go all the way to the Colorado Supreme Court to prove his point. He did. Twice. In October of 1969, the Health Department issued an order directing Fry to cease emitting air pollutants from its plant. At a July 16 hearing, the Variance Board denied Mr. Fry's request for a variance because he repeatedly refused to submit a control plan. Newly constituted under the state's 1970 air act, the Air Commission refused to exercise its discretionary review authority over the Variance Board's decision. On July 31, 1972, the Colorado Supreme Court rejected Fry's challenge to the constitutionality of the air act, affirming the Adams County District Court.[78]

Fry argued to the Supreme Court its theory of unlawful legislative delegation to an administrative agency due to an asserted lack of standards for controlling the agency's exercise of discretion. Commenting on the ineffectiveness of air pollution control efforts and laws prior to the 1970 act, the Colorado Supreme Court rejected Fry's contention. It determined: (1) the term "air pollution" itself constitutes a sufficient standard for rulemaking; (2) the General Assembly directed the Commission and Health Department to develop and maintain a "comprehensive program" for air pollution prevention and control throughout the state; and (3) the General Assembly had provided sufficient guidelines for the Air Commission to do the job.

> The scope and guidelines to be followed by the commission in discharging its duties and responsibilities are those which are necessary or appropriate to foster the health, peace, safely, general welfare, convenience and comfort of the people of the state, and which facilitate the enjoyment of nature, scenery, and other resources of the state.[79]

---

[78] *Lloyd A. Fry Roofing Co. v. Air Pollution Variance Bd.*, 499 P.2d 1176, 1176-77 (Colo. 1972).
[79] *Id.* at 1179.

Fry also complained that the statute was so vague that no business could determine what conduct was necessary to avoid an injunction and the civil penalty sanctions of the air act.[80] In response, the Colorado Supreme Court pointed to the extensive procedural protections the legislature had provided—cease and desist orders giving notice of the alleged violations; administrative and judicial review appeal rights; opportunities for stay of enforcement pending appeal; and prohibition on civil and injunctive remedies until the cease and desist order became final.[81]

Rejecting Fry's illegal retroactivity argument, the Colorado Supreme Court held that the air act dealt only with "*future* conduct," in the form of a violation of a final cease and desist order.[82] The Colorado Supreme Court refused to reverse the variance denial. Examining the hearing record, the court upheld the Variance Board's finding that technology existed to control emissions at the Fry plant, and that Fry had presented no definite plan for the installation of the control equipment—"a condition upon which the variance board relies to insure compliance in the reasonably foreseeable future...."[83]

Fry also asked the court to rule that four citizen groups had no right to be heard in the administrative proceedings. The court held that the Variance Board and the Commission have "unfettered and sole discretion" to grant intervention to citizen groups.[84]

Early in the life of the 1970 Colorado air act, no clearer legislative and judicial blessing for Colorado's fresh air program could have seemed possible. But Mr. Fry was obstinate and decided not to comply, despite citizen outcry and the Colorado Supreme Court's ruling.

2. The Western Alfalfa Case

Enter into office, January of 1975, Governor Dick Lamm and Attorney General J.D. MacFarlane. Pollution control was among their highest priorities. MacFarlane, through his Deputy Attorney General, Jean Dubofsky, assembled an initial team of young lawyers to take office with him. They included an EPA water quality enforcement attorney and an air quality enforcement attorney,[85] who became the nucleus of the new Natural Resources Section that MacFarlane created in the Attorney General's Office.

The air enforcement program faced challenges early in 1975 not only from Fry, but also from Western Alfalfa Corporation, operator of three agricultural hay dryers in

---

[80] *Id.* at 1180.
[81] *Id.*
[82] *Id.* at 1180-82.
[83] *Id.* at 1181.
[84] *Id.*
[85] David W. Robbins and the author.

northern Colorado. In 1969, a Health Department inspector made air pollution observations at the three plants, resulting in cease and desist orders for violation of the then-applicable forty percent opacity standard.[86]

In a challenge brought by Western Alfalfa in 1973, both the state District Court and the Court of Appeals ruled that these inspections constituted warrantless searches in violation of the Fourth Amendment to the United States Constitution.[87] The Court of Appeals reasoned that the company had suffered infringement of its confrontation rights in the administrative hearings.[88] Not having learned of the inspector's presence until the receipt of the cease and desist orders two weeks after the alleged violation day, the company

> could not effectively rebut the evidence against it since it had no representative present at the time the test was administered.... Since violations of the Act can be based upon emissions aggregating three minutes or more during any hour and since the evidence by its very nature is continually dissipating, we conclude that it is constitutionally mandatory in this type of case that the party accused be aware of the taking of tests and measurements on its premises at the time they are made.[89]

This 1973 Court of Appeals ruling caused alarm to enforcement personnel in Colorado and throughout the United States. Announcing the presence of an air pollution inspector, some feared, could simply result in the suspected offender shutting down the polluting activity until the inspectors departed.

The Colorado Supreme Court denied certiorari and the case then went to the United States Supreme Court in 1974.[90] In support of the state of Colorado, California's Attorney General's Office—aided by an EPA regional enforcement attorney based in Colorado—wrote a brief joined by 34 other state Attorneys General, asking the Supreme Court to reverse the Colorado Court of Appeals.[91]

Because the air pollution inspector "had sighted what anyone in the city who was near the plant could see in the sky—plumes of smoke," the United States Supreme Court unanimously applied the "open fields" plain view exception to the Fourth

---

[86] Leland P. Anderson, Comment, *Requirement of Notice in Visual Opacity Readings*, 51 DENV. L.J. 603, 613 (1974).
[87] *W. Alfalfa Corp. v. Air Pollution Variance Bd.*, 510 P.2d 907, 907-08 (Colo. App. 1973).
[88] *Id.* at 909-10.
[89] *Id.* at 910 (citations omitted).
[90] *Air Pollution Variance Bd. v. W. Alfalfa Corp.*, 416 U.S. 861 (1974).
[91] *Id.* The EPA was not a party to the appeal and did not enter an amicus appearance. But, the Enforcement Director for EPA Region VIII, Irv Dickstein, lent the author's brief-writing services to the California Assistant Attorney General in charge of preparing the states' amicus curiae brief, Daniel Taaffe, because opacity readings were a mainstay of federal and state air enforcement throughout the country.

Amendment, thereby reversing the Colorado Court of Appeals.[92] On the due process issue raised by Western Alfalfa—that the "secret nature of the investigation"[93] deprived the company of its ability to put on any rebuttal evidence—the Court remanded the case for further decision because it was unsure of whether the Colorado Court of Appeals had based its decision on state or federal constitutional grounds.

On remand in 1975, the Colorado Court of Appeals—relying on both the state and federal constitutional due process guarantees—continued to require notice to the company "that evidence is being gathered and be afforded a reasonable opportunity to be present...."[94] The court's opinion implied a potential alternative to notice so long as the company "otherwise be provided with an adequate opportunity to gather similar probative evidence," but then receded from this suggestion by holding that constitutional due process gave the company a right to have "contemporary knowledge" of inspection tests "being made."[95]

The Court of Appeals announced its decision against the State one week before Colorado Attorney General MacFarlane took office. Explaining the state's decision to file an appeal with the Colorado Supreme Court, the new Assistant Attorney General for air enforcement, recently hired from the EPA regional office, observed, "If you go to inspect a polluter and tell him why you're there, he can shut down and go to lunch."[96] He added that "notifying a polluter right after an inspection is all that is required by state law."[97] Following the Court of Appeals decision, upon the advice of the Attorney General's Office, the Air Division changed its inspection practice to include reasonably prompt notice to companies of opacity readings after the inspector made them.

---

[92] *Id.* at 865. Discounting the presence of the inspector on the company's outside grounds as having constitutional significance, the Court's opinion pointed out that

> [t]he EPA regulation for conducting an opacity test requires the inspector to stand at a distance equivalent to approximately two stack heights away but not more than a quarter of a mile from the base of the stack with the sun to his back from a vantage point perpendicular to the plume; and he must take at least 25 readings, recording the data at 15- to 30-second intervals.

Id.

[93] *Id.* at 865-66.

[94] *W. Alfalfa Corp. v. Air Pollution Variance Bd.*, 534 P.2d 796, 801 (1975).

[95] *Id.*

[96] *Pollution Ruling to Be Appealed*, Rocky Mtn. News, Feb. 27, 1975, at 38.

[97] *Id. See also* Anderson, *supra* note 86, at 618 (suggesting that when allowing leeway for the enforcement inspection, but also providing the alleged polluter a meaningful opportunity to gather its own evidence, "notice must be given...only within a reasonably short period of time thereafter so as not to deprive the party of his right to a fair trial.").

3. Attorney General Takes On The Air Commission

The stakes in *Western Alfalfa* and *Fry* were enormous. Prior to Attorney General MacFarlane taking office, Law review commentaries had severely questioned (1) whether the 1970 Colorado air act contained sufficient authority for the Commission, Variance Board, and Air Division to obtain air pollution clean-up,[98] (2) whether these agencies could resist industry arguments and delay tactics,[99] and (3) why the Assistant Attorney General assigned to the Variance Board—which was frequently suspending enforcement of air regulations—was making fewer and fewer appearances at Board hearings.[100]

The Air Commission's ability and will to implement effective emission control regulations soon became an issue between the Attorney General and the Commission. In March of 1975, the Commission voted to relax its previously adopted standards to control power plant sulfur dioxide emissions for seven more years.[101]

Instead of proposing a revised regulation for this relaxation of regulation, the Commission simply attached its existing regulation to the notice of hearing and invited public comment. Attorney General MacFarlane informed the Commission that its notice of hearing was defective and its ensuing revision of the rule illegal, based on insufficient public notice. Nevertheless, the Commission voted to put the relaxed regulation into effect.[102]

The Attorney General responded that he would have to "confess error" should the Commission's action be challenged in court.[103] Environmental groups, including the Colorado chapter of the Sierra Club, had opposed the weaker regulations during the public hearing. Ultimately, the Commission rescinded its vote to publish the revised regulation and ordered new hearings.[104]

---

[98] *See, e.g.*, Jan G. Laitos, *Institutional Response to an Environmental Crisis: The Failure of State Air Pollution Control*, 48 DENV. L. J. 519, 533-35 (1972); COLO. REV. STAT. § 25-7-116 (Supp. 1971). The Air Pollution Variance Board became the Air Quality Hearings Board in 1979, then the General Assembly abolished it in 1984. *See* Air Quality Control Program, ch. 211, 1984 Colo. Sess. Laws 768 (current version at COLO. REV. STAT. §§ 25-7-101 to -139 (2003)).

[99] Jan G. Laitos, *The Limits of the Law: Functional Failures of the Air Pollution Variance Board*, 44 U. COLO. L. REV. 513, 521 (1973) (stating, based on case examples before the Variance Board, that "[v]ariances are increasingly becoming licenses to pollute.").

[100] *Id.* at 527.

[101] Ken Gepfert, *MacFarlane to Challenge Weakened Air Regulations*, ROCKY MTN. NEWS, May 23, 1975, at 6.

[102] *Id.*

[103] *Id.*

[104] Steve Wynkoop, *New Hearings Ordered on Oxide Rules*, DENV. POST, June 13, 1975, at 3.

4. The Second *Fry* Case

The Fry Roofing penalty and injunction enforcement case went to an eight-day trial in June of 1975 before a jury in Adams County District Court. The jury found that Fry had violated Regulation No. 1's opacity standard (ratcheted down from 40 to 20 percent opacity) 83 times since 1971.[105] Judge Clifford Gobble assessed a $41,500 civil penalty and, adopting the jury's findings as his own, issued an injunction preventing the plant from violating the 20 percent opacity standard. The judge stayed execution of the injunction for three months to give Fry the opportunity to make a "genuine" effort to comply with the law.[106]

Instead of ordering and installing control equipment, Fry appealed. Seven years after the Division had issued Fry the first cease and desist order, the Colorado Supreme Court upheld the injunction against further violation, but ordered the trial court to reduce the amount of civil penalties[107] to reflect its decision in *Western Alfalfa* on the issue of reasonable notice of inspection.[108] The court also decided that air cases do not require a jury trial—though one had been impaneled in this case as a precaution should the court hold a jury trial to be necessary.

In *Western Alfalfa*, announced the same day as *Fry*,[109] the Colorado Supreme Court upheld the validity of the visible emission standard. It found the standard technically sound, and the Air Division opacity readings accurately performed. The court explicitly recognized the link between opacity standards and the reduction of particulate loading into the air. Reciting that "public enjoyment of the air resources of this state" is an explicit legislative objective of the state's air act,[110] the court held that standards for visual clarity were enforceable. On the issue of whether due process required prior, contemporaneous, or reasonable after-the-fact notice of inspection to the company, the court held for requiring notice of inspection results within a reasonably short time following the inspection, because the deterrent force of a potential surprise inspection is an effective compliance tool.

> Due process contemplates that notice should be given of a visual opacity reading by the Department of Health within a reasonably short period

---

[105] Howard Pankratz, *Fry Roofing Co. Guilty in Colo. Air Pollution*, Denv. Post, June 27, 1975, at 20. The EPA provided key expert testimony at the trial, and Assistant Attorneys General Gene Lucero and the author tried the state's case. Michael Gilbert represented the citizens group during the long struggle to obtain Fry Roofing's compliance. After the Supreme Court's second Fry decision against him, Fry sold his roofing company to the Owens Corning Co., which promptly installed the needed air pollution control equipment.

[106] *Firm Penalized on Clean-Air Violation*, Denv. Post, July 10, 1975, at 25.

[107] *Lloyd A. Fry Roofing Co. v. Air Pollution Variance Bd.*, 553 P.2d 800, 810 (Colo. 1976).

[108] *Air Pollution Variance Bd. v. W. Alfalfa Corp.*, 553 P.2d 811 (Colo. 1976).

[109] *Lloyd A. Fry Roofing Co. v. Air Pollution Variance Bd.*, 553 P.2d 800, 810 (Colo. 1976); *Air Pollution Variance Bd. v. W. Alfalfa Corp.*, 553 P.2d 811 (Colo. 1976). The author had the privilege of arguing both cases to the Colorado Supreme Court.

[110] *W. Alfalfa*, 553 P.2d at 814.

of time following the completion of the inspection. Because surprise may play a crucial role in the course of some inspections, we do not require prior or contemporary notice of the inspection. Basic fairness is achieved...by delivering actual notice to a plant manager or officer or agent thereof within a short period of time following the inspection.[111]

In *Fry*, the Colorado Supreme Court upheld the injunction based on six opacity readings reporting violations, accompanied by reasonably short notice thereafter,[112] and ruled that the state need not make a showing of irreparable injury because the statute provided for an injunction to prevent future violations of the final cease and desist order. The court affirmed the Court of Appeals decision in *Western Alfalfa* to suppress the inspection tests because the Air Division inspectors had provided none of the opacity readings to the company within a reasonable period of time after taking them.

August 23, 1976, the day the Colorado Supreme Court announced its decision in both cases, was a great day for Colorado air enforcement. The state Air Division and the Attorney General's Office proved that the quality laws were not only visionary; they had teeth and could bite into long-practiced habits of doing business. Attention now focused on two state agencies, the Air Commission and the Variance Board, which would have much to say about whether the state would adopt and enforce control regulations capable of cleaning up the air.

D. Stationary Source Control

The 1970 CAA provided for Colorado and the other states to adopt and enforce an implementation plan[113] for attainment and maintenance of the national ambient air health standards.[114] When submitted by the state and approved by the EPA, the state emission control regulations in the plan became federally enforceable.[115] With strong state and federal control laws in effect, the public's expectation and investment in air pollution control began to produce returns. A sense of public mission began to pervade legislative halls, citizen board and commissions, environmental organizations, and the agencies charged with making pollution control plans work.

But progress was slow in the first decade of the new air laws because air pollution was so immense and the necessity of businesses to make the needed expenditures so great. State agencies in many instances had to plead with polluters to submit plans for cleaning up their operations and seemed captive to counterpleas that strict

---

[111] *Id.* at 816.
[112] *Fry*, 553 P.2d at 810.
[113] 42 U.S.C. § 7410 (1977); Clean Air Amendments of 1970, Pub. L. No. 91-604, 84 Stat 1676.
[114] 42 U.S.C. § 7409.
[115] 42 U.S.C. § 7413.

enforcement would shut business down causing people to lose their jobs. Indeed, the General Assembly had established Colorado's air pollution Variance Board for the very purpose of relaxing the Commission's regulations for as long as companies might need.

1. Controlling the Power and Steel Plants, The Commission Gets Active

Inevitably, the backup federal enforcement power had to come into play. In July of 1976, the EPA filed a lawsuit in the U.S. District Court for Colorado to enforce the state's opacity standard at the CF&I Steel Plant in Pueblo. Previously, the EPA had issued timetables for CF&I to correct its furnace shop and coke plant emissions, which CF&I failed to meet.[116] Frustrated with unsuccessful attempts to obtain CF&I compliance and not wanting to cede air quality decision making to the EPA, the Variance Board began denying variance applications for plant activities for which control techniques were available, rejecting the company's arguments that air pollution control would cost too much.[117]

Also in 1976, the Air Division began to issue permits requiring new Colorado-Ute[118] and Public Service Company[119] coal-fired power plants to install sulfur-dioxide scrubbers to prevent state ambient air quality standard violations. Holding regulation development and permit review hearings in the local areas, the Commission received much citizen comment in favor of the pollution controls.[120]

Industry lawyers challenged the Commission's authority to condition permits on compliance with state ambient air standards.[121] Ambient standards address the allowable concentration of pollutants in the outside air. Emission control regulations apply at the source from which pollutants are emitted. The companies argued that the Commission only had authority to adopt emission control regulations and that it could not include compliance with state ambient air standards as a condition of construction permits.[122] The Air Division initiated this controversy by including in the Public Service Pawnee Power Plant permit a condition that would trigger the

---

[116] Claire Cooper, *1st Federal Clean-Air Suit Filed Against CF&I Corp.*, ROCKY MTN. NEWS, July 3, 1976, at 6.

[117] *Id.*

[118] Steve Wynkoop, *Air 'Scrubbers' Decreed for Yampa Power Units*, DENV. POST, Aug. 29, 1976, at 29; *Install 'Scrubber' Units, Ute Power Plant Ordered*, ROCKY MTN. NEWS, Aug. 29, 1976, at 13.

[119] Al Nakkula, *Pollution Control Unit Allows Public Service Pawnee Plant*, ROCKY MTN. NEWS, July 23, 1976, at 5.

[120] Bob Jain, *Pawnee Plant for Morgan Stirs Up Verbal Dust*, DENV. POST, May 9, 1976, at 18.

[121] Steve Wynkoop, *PSC Trying to Avert Air Controls on Pawnee Plant*, DENV. POST, Aug. 22, 1976, at 20.

[122] Steve Lang, *Industries Challenge Pollution Standards*, ROCKY MTN. NEWS, Aug. 26, 1976, at 6.

installation of control equipment if air pollution receptors, placed in farmers' corn fields, detected a violation of ambient air standards.[123]

Looking to preserve rural and mountain vistas, the Commission agreed with the Division. It read Colorado's air act to include the protection of good ambient air against avoidable deterioration. It made no sense to commence the clean-up of existing sources while allowing new or modified sources to escape installing and operating the best available pollution control devices.

The power industry was arguing that burning "low-sulfur Western coal" should be a form of control.[124] The Commission's counter-position—to protect good air areas by requiring the installation of control technology or the denial of construction permits—presaged the subsequent federal prevention of significant deterioration program ("PSD") that Congress mandated in the 1977 CAA amendments.[125]

AMAX Coal Company, a division of AMAX Inc., intervened in the Pawnee Power Plant proceedings to claim a trade secret privilege for certain information relating to its coal supply contract with PSCo. The Commission responded that Colorado's air act required public disclosure of "emission data," so that interested citizens could participate in permit hearings. At issue were the sulfur dioxide emissions that could result from burning the coal. While the Commissioners, the Air Division staff, and the expert for the Environmental Defense Fund viewed the contract and coal data under a protective order procedure, AMAX filed suit in Fort Morgan and Denver District courts to prevent public disclosure of its claimed-to-be privileged-information.

Granting review under its original writ jurisdiction, the Colorado Supreme Court read Colorado's air act to provide that the local district court has review venue over any issues associated with a particular air pollution source.[126] In contrast, judicial review of Commission rulemaking resides in the Denver District Court.[127] The Air Division, Environmental Defense Fund, and AMAX settled the suit by a stipulation in Morgan County District Court that made the sulfur dioxide emission

---

[123] *See* Richard J. Schneider, *Pawnee Power Plant Construction OK'd, but PSC Objects to Some Terms*, ROCKY MTN. NEWS, Feb. 12, 1976, at 5; *see also* Steve Lang, *PSC's Request to Build Plant Runs into Snag*, ROCKY MTN. NEWS, Mar. 4, 1976, at 5.

[124] Schneider, *supra* note 123.

[125] Richard L. Griffith, *The Colorado Prevention of Significant Deterioration of Air Quality Program*, 12 COLO. LAW. 1927, 1983-86 (Dec. 1983); *see Envtl. Def. Fund v. Colorado Dep't of Health*, 731 P.2d 773, 775 (Colo. App. 1986).

[126] *Air Pollution Control Comm'n v. Denver County Dist. Court*, 563 P.2d 351, 354 (Colo. 1977).

[127] Diane L. Burkhardt, *A Practitioner's Guide to the Colorado Air Quality Control Commission*, 16 COLO. LAW. 1347, 1405, 1407 (Aug. 1987).

data public and withheld privileged commercial and financial information from disclosure.[128]

In the Colorado-Ute permit matter, the company did not seek judicial review of the permit condition requiring its Craig plant to meet the state ambient air standards. Nevertheless, it later challenged the Commission's use of those standards in reviewing and conditioning permit applications to require SO_2 scrubbers, including those in the Craig station permit. In a suit Public Service Company initially joined, but later dropped out of, the Colorado Court of Appeals invalidated the state ambient air permit condition that Colorado-Ute had not originally taken to judicial review.[129]

The controversy about the use of state ambient standards as an enforcement condition in stationary source permits produced a legislative change. Based on 1979 changes to Colorado's air act,[130] the Commission amended its new or modified source regulation in 1980.[131] Compliance with State ambient air quality standards would now appear as a permit condition only in the absence of an applicable federal ambient standard.

Accordingly, the Colorado Supreme Court vacated the Court of Appeals decision, finding Colorado-Ute's generic challenge to use of state ambient air standards as a permit condition to be moot because the Commission's revised regulation reserved state ambient standards for application only when no counterpart national ambient standard existed. And, the court held Colorado-Ute to compliance with the state ambient air standard condition in the Craig station permit because the company had not timely filed for judicial review under the State Administrative Procedure Act.[132]

In another industry-filed case, the Colorado Supreme Court recognized the standing of affected businesses to seek pre-enforcement judicial review of Commission decisions.[133] Litigation by CF&I resulted in the Court of Appeals invalidating the Commission's fugitive dust regulation for its vagueness and its

---

[128] Stipulation dated Feb. 7, 1978 (on file with author). David C. Mastbaum represented EDF and a citizen's group calling itself Information Please, Inc., an association of concerned farmers and individuals in the power plant's vicinity. Charles W. Newcom of Dawson, Nagel, Sherman & Howard represented AMAX Coal Company. Hubert Farbes and the author represented Colorado at the Air Commission hearings and in court.

[129] *Colorado-Ute Electric Ass'n v. Air Pollution Control Comm'n*, 648 P.2d 150, 153 (Colo. App. 1982).

[130] Colorado Air Quality Control Act, ch. 266, 1979 Colo. Sess. Laws 1017, 1030-31 (codified at COLO. REV. STAT. § 25-7-114(4)(b) (Repl. Vol. 1973, as amended)).

[131] 5 COLO. CODE REGS. § 1001-5 (2002).

[132] *Air Pollution Control Comm'n v. Colorado-Ute Electric Ass'n*, 672 P.2d 993, 997 (Colo. 1983).

[133] *CF&I Steel Corp. v. Colorado Air Pollution Control Comm'n*, 610 P.2d 85, 92 (Colo.1980).

discriminatory treatment of private versus public sources.[134] The Court of Appeals criticized the regulation because it failed to differentiate between wind-blown dust and dust-stirring caused by machinery. The Court of Appeals balked at the use of the opacity method for observing dust violations because the emissions were not from a discrete point. Particularly scathing was the Court of Appeals's rejection of the Commission's rationale that private companies could more readily afford to control unpaved roads than public agencies. After the Colorado Supreme Court granted certiorari, it then dismissed the appeal at the parties' request—in effect, the Commission conceded defeat on this one.[135]

2. Commission Collaborative Rulemaking

In response to this string of industry-instituted litigation against Commission regulations, causing delay and uncertainty to an effective control program, the Commission successfully turned to a subcommittee format for formulating proposed regulations.[136] With one or more of the Commissioners presiding, these informal sessions with Air Division staff allowed business representatives and citizens to participate in regulation development at an early stage.

The formality of the rulemaking hearing had not lent itself to talking out loud about scientific, technical, and policy agreements and disagreements. This new process allowed the airing of issues and differences preliminarily. Often, these interchanges resulted in the Air Division being dispatched to return with additional data and analysis that regulated businesses, the EPA, or other state pollution control agencies would supply.[137] Then proposed regulations would be shaped and proposed for public hearing.

The General Assembly spurred on the Commission's turn to a more collaborative rulemaking approach. In 1979, it adopted revisions to Colorado's air act that established legislative review of state implementation plan measures that the

---

[134] *CF&I Steel Corp. v. Colorado Air Pollution Control Comm'n*, 640 P.2d 238, 241-42 (Colo. App. 1981).

[135] *Colorado Air Quality Control Comm'n v. CF&I Steel Corp.*, 662 P.2d 488, 489 (Colo. 1983). One who has been so involved on the public regulation side of the air quality effort, such as the author, can overlook or ignore the contributions made by those who represented business concerns in the many hearings, court cases, and legislative committee meetings from the 1970s to the 1990s. Here I acknowledge the dedicated work for their clients of Jim Sanderson and Don Cawelti for PSCo; Bill Robb and David Furgason for CF&I; Ira Rothgerber and Bob Slosky for Fry Roofing Company; and Girts Krumins for Colorado-Ute.

[136] Burkhardt, *supra* note 127, at 1408.

[137] The Commission has prepared a helpful flow chart for the formal rule-making process. *See* GUIDEBOOK TO THE AIR QUALITY CONTROL COMMISSION'S RULE-MAKING PROCESS, at app. A, 22 (Mar. 11, 1999).

Commission intended to submit to the EPA for approval.[138] The General Assembly required the federally enforceable plan to include only those cost effective measures necessary to comply with federal law. More stringent state requirements would be reserved for state enforcement only.

Through the work of the Air Commission, the Division, and the Attorney General's Office—combined with the EPA's backup enforcement authority, technical assistance, and state program funding grants—stationary source control was well under way by the end of the 1970s.

The Commission's effort to keep already clean air clean bore fruit. In 1979, The General Assembly approved the Commission's 1977 designation of Colorado category 1 areas for the protection of national parks, monuments, and wilderness areas from sulfur dioxide emissions resulting mainly from power plants. These areas included Rocky Mountain and Mesa Verde national parks, the Great Sand Dunes, Dinosaur and the Black Canyon of the Gunnison national monuments, and the Weminuche, West Elk, Mount Zirkel, Flattops, Eagles Nest, and Maroon Bells wilderness areas.[139]

Under the 1977 CAA Amendments, the PSD[140] built upon Colorado's pre-existing Category 1 designation of national parks and wilderness areas. The PSD permit program is designed to protect air that is cleaner than the national ambient air quality standards. It includes a highly protective limit for sulfur dioxide emissions that could impact federal Class I areas. In Colorado, these areas, of course, include the Flat Tops Wilderness, which is only 50 miles downwind from the vast oil shale deposits in the Pieceance Basin.

Soon after the 1977 federal amendments, President Jimmy Carter's campaign for America's energy independence spurred a flurry of hopeful oil shale development projects. The Bureau of Land Management (BLM) conducted an air quality assessment as part of its proposed oil shale leasing program. Early permits submitted by project developers proposed installing pollution control technology that would control oil shale SO_2 emissions in the 50 to 70 percent range. The BLM's assessment showed that a much higher degree of control would be required. Accordingly, when the EPA issued the first PSD permit, for Texaco's project, it set the required level of control at 90 percent. This shocked the industry because it projected project costs could increase as much as 15 to 20 percent as a result of the

---

[138] *See* Act of June 20, 1979, ch. 406, 1979 Colo. Sess. Laws 1539, 1552 (codified at COLO. REV. STAT. § 25-7-133 (Repl. Vol. 1973, as amended) (current version at COLO. REV. STAT. § 25-7-133 (2003))).

[139] Colorado Air Quality Control Act, ch. 266, 1979 Colo. Sess. Laws 1017, 1054-55 (codified at COLO. REV. STAT. § 25-7-209 (Repl. Vol. 1973, as amended) (current version at COLO. REV. STAT. § 25-7-209 (2003))).

[140] 42 U.S.C. §§ 7470-7491 (2003).

stringent limit.[141] As it turned out, the market price of oil dropped far below the price that would support oil shale development. The oil shale bust, a recurrent theme in Colorado history, had come back round again.

East of the Continental Divide, bad air data in the mid-1970s indicated the need for far more control of existing air pollution and this produced a great deal of contention about what should be done and what it would cost to do it. Front Range growth and automobile emissions came into focus as a huge source of air pollution. The beloved car, a very visible sign of American freedom that propelled a significant part of the American economy and gave the average Americans the ability to see and enjoy this magnificent country, needed a major tune up. A large part of Colorado's air problems rolled directly out of Henry Ford's invention.

III. MOBILE SOURCES AND THE BROWN CLOUD, THE 1980S

The motor vehicle, highway construction, and homebuilding industries that drove America's post-World War II economic expansion contributed greatly to dirty air because the internal combustion engine that turned the wheels emitted carbon monoxide, particulates, volatile hydrocarbons, and nitrogen oxides in prodigious amounts.

A. *The Dirty Beloved Automobile*

As stationary sources were being controlled, finger pointing turned to the pollution-causing activities of citizens and their cars. The Colorado Air Commission's 1978 Report to the Public stated that "existing *controlled* stationary source emissions of particulates, carbon monoxide, and hydrocarbons account for only 10 percent, 6 percent, and 5 percent, respectively, of the total emissions of each of those pollutants in the Denver Region."[142] Additional stationary source controls could only achieve substantial gains in the control of nitrogen oxide emissions.[143]

As with eliminating backyard trash burning, citizens found it hard to change their pollution-causing habits. To Coloradans and other American westerners, freedom and the car were synonymous. Add to this the fact that convenient public transportation was virtually non-existent.

> While the public is increasingly aware of the automobile as a major polluter, there is no evidence that drivers are willing to abandon the car for other forms of transportation.
>
> . . .

---

[141] E-mail from Bob Yuhnke, Attorney, to author (Mar. 11, 2004, 11:05:00 MDT) (on file with author). Yuhnke represented the Environmental Defense Fund in discussions about the best available control technology necessary to protect the Flat Tops Wilderness Area.
[142] AIR POLLUTION CONTROL COMM'N, 2 REPORT TO THE PUBLIC 59 (1978).
[143] *Id.* at 61.

A comparison of states' legislative initiatives to meet the federal requirements as set forth by the 1970 Amendments to the Clean Air Act shows that, in the western states, the problems of dealing with the automobile are of foremost importance. Individual strategies for restricting automobile use, relating land use to this restriction, and taking steps to increase mass transit are just in the discussion stages.[144]

Of course, Colorado and other states depended on the promulgation and enforcement of federal motor vehicle emission control standards for new cars. Rampant auto pollution in cities across the United States spurred standards requiring the development of clean air technologies for new cars. Because of its high elevation and the lower oxygen content in its air, Colorado air pollution control strategies had to focus on cleaner cars, emission control repairs, and fuels that burned cleanly at high altitudes.

B. Vehicle Inspection and Maintenance

Keeping the emission control devices working properly through a vehicle inspection-maintenance program was a necessary and early measure adopted by the Commission and Air Division. In 1977, the General Assembly authorized planning for such a program.[145] This new statute assigned the Air Commission the job of adopting exhaust gas emissions standards and motor vehicle inspection regulations. The proposed standards would be subject to legislative review before they would go into effect, and the Department of Revenue was to oversee the licensing of inspection stations.[146]

However, the 1978 session produced H.B. 1209, a bill that would have deprived the Air Commission of its authority to set mobile source emission standards, assigning this power instead to the Executive Director of the Department of Revenue and transferring all Air Division mobile sources personnel to that department.[147] Also, enactment of this bill would have required the Commission to obtain Legislative Council review of any state implementation plan measure before it was submitted to the EPA.[148]

Calling attention to the public's concern about the Brown Cloud, Governor Lamm vetoed H.B. 1209. In doing so, he rebuked the General Assembly for undercutting the state's ability to develop its own state implementation plan to come into compliance with the national health standards.

---

[144] *Id.* at 174.
[145] Act of June, 30, 1977, ch. 564, 1977 Colo. Sess. Laws 1901, 1901-12 (codified as amended at COLO. REV. STAT. §§ 42-4-301 to -315 (Repl. Vol. 1974, as amended)).
[146] 1977 Colo. Sess. Laws 1902, 1902-04 (codified at COLO. REV. STAT. §§ 42-4-308 to -309 (Repl. Vol. 1974, as amended)).
[147] H.R. 1209, 51st Gen. Assem., 2d Reg. Sess., at 15-17, 35, 37 (Colo. 1978).
[148] H.R. 1209, at 5-7 (current version at COLO. REV. STAT. § 25-7-133 (2003)).

It is tragic that in a year when the public has recognized the Brown Cloud for the threat that it is, and has been urging strong action to fight this menace, that the Legislature has produced a bill that is actually a *step backward* in the fight towards cleaning our air.

Four months ago I asked this Legislature to make air pollution control the number one priority for this legislative session.

. . .

A memorandum of law prepared by the Attorney General concludes that if HB 1209 was allowed to become law, it would "make it impossible for this state to assert that it has the requisite enabling authority and administrative capacity to comply with the Federal Clean Air Act."[149]

Propelled by the 1977 CAA,[150] in 1979, the General Assembly adopted the revised Colorado Air Quality Control Act.[151] Among other things, it required the Department of Health and the Department of Revenue to develop a pilot program to test "various vehicle emission control alternatives which may include emission testing and maintenance, air pollution control tune-up, and vehicle modification alternatives as determined by the commission."[152]

In 1980, the General Assembly ultimately adopted the "Automobile Inspection and Readjustment program," otherwise known as the "AIR Program," which required motorists to obtain an emission compliance windshield sticker for their cars.[153] The Air Commission had adopted standards and procedures for the inspection and maintenance of motor vehicle model years 1968 to 1981.[154] This law allowed certified mechanics at neighborhood garages to perform emission testing to see that cars conformed with these standards and regulations. The General Assembly required the Commission to adopt new standards annually for each succeeding model year.[155] It assigned to the Department of Revenue the job of

---

[149] Veto Message of Gov. Lamm, H.R. 1209, 51st Gen. Assem., 2d Reg. Sess., H.J. 1004, at 44-54; H.J. 1005, at 31-37 (May 8, 1978).

[150] Clean Air Act Amendments of 1977, Pub. L. No. 95-95, § 105, 91 Stat. 685, 689 (current version at 42 U.S.C. § 7408 (2003)).

[151] Colorado Air Quality Control Act, ch. 266, 1979 Colo. Sess. Laws 1017, 1017-1061 (codified as amended at COLO. REV. STAT. § 25-7-101 to -305 (Repl. Vol. 1973, as amended)).

[152] 1979 Colo. Sess. Laws at 1049 (codified at COLO. REV. STAT. §§ 25-7-130(2)(a) (Repl. Vol. 1973, as amended)); *see also* 1979 Colo. Sess. Laws at 1049-50 (codified at COLO. REV. STAT. § 25-7-131 (Repl. Vol. 1973, as amended) (current version at COLO. REV. STAT. §§ 25-7-130, 131 (2003)).

[153] Act of May 23, 1980, ch. 169, 1980 Colo. Sess. Laws 757, 757-74 (codified at COLO. REV. STAT. §§ 42-4-306.5, -307 to -316 (Repl. Vol. 1973, as amended)).

[154] § 4, 1980 Colo. Sess. Laws at 761-64.

[155] § 4, 1980 Colo. Sess. Laws at 762.

licensing inspection stations and mechanics to perform repairs on cars that did not pass.[156]

Concerned about negative public reaction to the program because of the time and cost required for obtaining inspections and performing needed repairs, the General Assembly required the Air Division to maintain a telephone answering service and to report yearly on the status of the AIR program.[157] For motor vehicles model year 1981 or newer, the legislature capped the cost of required repairs at $100. After spending this amount, a certificate of emissions adjustment would be issued.[158] Under the aegis of Air Division Director, Dr. Jim Lents, the program went into operation.[159]

In reaction to the 1990 CAA amendments,[160] the General Assembly in 1992 adopted provisions presaging an enhanced inspection and maintenance program with centralized inspection stations in the six county Denver Metropolitan Area.[161] The Assembly enacted such a program the next year under threat of federal sanctions that included the loss of highway funds. The 1993 legislation authorized a "loaded mode" test, which tested emission levels as the engine was running at various speeds.[162] The enhanced program went into effect as a condition to vehicle registration because of the Denver Metropolitan Area's non-attainment status.[163]

C. Oxygenated Fuels

Because the inspection/maintenance program was an insufficient motor vehicle control strategy because it only served to check for the deterioration or disconnection of motor vehicle emission control devices in individual vehicles, the Commission in 1987 began requiring the use of oxygenated gasoline during wintertime to reduce carbon monoxide emissions in Colorado's worst air regions.[164]

The newly-emerging alternative fuels industry vigorously campaigned for approval of an oxygenate standard so high that only ethanol or methanol would pass. Denver Conoco Refinery spokespersons testified in favor of setting a standard that would allow the gasoline producers and the ethanol producers to compete in providing air

---

[156] §§ 3 & 5, 1980 Colo. Sess. Laws at 759-60, 764-65.

[157] § 5, 1980 Colo. Sess. Laws at 764.

[158] § 8, 1980 Colo. Sess. Laws at 767.

[159] DENVER METRO AIR QUALITY, *supra* note 18.

[160] Act of Nov. 15, 1990, Pub. L. No. 101-549, 104 Stat. 2399, 2433-34 (codified at 42 U.S.C. § 7511a(c)(3)(B)-(C) (2003)).

[161] *See* Act of May 27, 1992, ch. 179, 1992 Colo. Sess. Laws 1163, 1171 (codified at COLO. REV. STAT. § 25-7-105(13)(a) (2003)).

[162] *See* Act of June 8, 1993, ch. 321, 1993 Colo. Sess. Laws 1922, 1925-26, 1931-32 (codified at COLO. REV. STAT. §§ 42-4-306.5, -307(Repl. Vol. 1993)). *See* COLO. REV. STAT. § 25-7-105(13)(a) (2003).

[163] *See* 42 U.S.C. § 7511a(c)(3) (2003).

[164] *See* COLO. REV. STAT. § 25-7-106(1)(e) (2003); 5 COLO. CODE REGS. § 1001-16 (2003).

quality benefits. This was a refreshing development in a very contentious rulemaking proceeding. While many of the major gasoline producers opposed any "oxyfuels" program, they grudgingly conceded the viability of a regulation that would allow them to compete against the "gasohol" industry by means of a petroleum-based additive.

The Denver Chamber of Commerce supported the oxy-fuels program at the Commission's hearings. This evidenced an important change in the business community. Large manufacturing operations had been the long-time mainstay of commerce in Colorado. That had given way to an economy based on new home and office construction required to serve the new and growing populace, who expected and demanded better air.

As a result of its hearings, the Commission adopted a gasoline oxygenate level that allowed the use of methyl tertiary butyl ether ("MTBE"). Ironically, the federal government and the Commission later banned MTBE when it began to show up as a toxic pollutant in ground water.[165]

What the oxy-fuels experience proved was that fuel improvements could reap pollution reduction benefits, and competition between fuel suppliers for "clean fuels" would benefit the public at a moderately increased cost—about $2.90 per household during the 1987–88 winter Better Air Campaign season, which was far less than the $7.00 per car that one major oil company had predicted.[166]

Testimony at the Commission's oxy-fuels hearings included an oil industry claim that the program wouldn't work and that women and children would die in the streets because cars would literally stop running.[167] But cars continued to run, and cleaner motor vehicle fuels in use today include compressed natural gas, propane, and electricity.[168]

D. Transportation, Land Use, and Air Quality Planning

It wasn't magic—but it was magical—that Colorado's historical preference for deferring hard matters to local governments actually produced a new generation of city council persons and mayors who took on the challenges handed to them. They campaigned for urban-suburban air quality, land use, and transportation plans. In the 1980s, the Commission, Denver officials, and air quality citizen groups focused their attention on sky-rocketing auto use and the huge contribution motor vehicle use was making to Colorado air pollution. Air

---

[165] *See* COLO. REV. STAT. § 25-7-139 (2003); 5 COLO. CODE REGS. § 1001-16 at 1(I)(D)(2) (2003).

[166] Lou Chapman, *Oxy-Fuel Project Cost Drivers Less Money Than Predicted*, DENV. POST, Apr. 22, 1988, at 4B.

[167] Dick Cooper & Jeffrey A. Roberts, *Mixed Signals Sent on Air Pollution*, DENV. POST, Jan. 27, 1989, at 1B.

[168] *Id.*

pollution control planning led to community planning and reinvigorated Denver's entrepreneurial role.

1. Imagine a Great City

A change in Denver mayoral politics in 1982 resulted in the election of a strong air quality advocate, Federico Peña. His "Imagine a Great City" was a clarion call for change.[169] It included seeing the mountains clearly and breathing healthy air.

Cut off from annexing additional land because of the Poundstone Amendment,[170] choked with air pollution, and confronted with suburban competition for attractive retail and residential development, Denver pressed to revitalize its historic role as the entrepreneurial, cultural, and political core of Colorado opportunity.[171]

Degraded air was the most visible symbol of Denver's leadership slide, and the citizenry, business community, and media were ready for revival. During 1983, his first year in office, Mayor Peña presented to the Air Commission a commitment by city workers to commence a ride-sharing program that would extend area-wide the next year.[172] On bad air days during the winter, citizens chosen based on their license plate number would be asked to participate in voluntary no-drive days. On the worst days, the plan would request that drivers cancel non-essential trips.

Comprised of 42 different towns and cities in the Metropolitan Area, the Denver Regional Council of Governments ("DRCOG") rejected the ride-share proposal. In adopting it anyway, the Commission appealed to DRCOG to reconsider its opposition "because air pollution is a problem that needs area-wide cooperation."[173] Downtown Denver, Inc. appeared before the Commission to endorse the

---

[169] *See* CAROL ABBOTT ET AL., COLORADO: A HISTORY OF THE CENTENNIAL STATE 341 (3d ed. 1994).

[170] COLO. CONST. art. XX, § 1 (1974). This 1974 initiated amendment to the Colorado Constitution required voter approval by the electorate of an area Denver proposed to annex. Adopted largely in reaction to the desegregation decision of the federal District Court, this amendment to preserve the suburbs resulted in Denver's later ability to hold its water supply for the primary use of the core city. *See Bennett Bear Creek Water Dist. v. City & County of Denver*, 928 P.2d 1254, 1272 n.27 (Colo. 1996); CARL UBBELOHDE ET AL., A COLORADO HISTORY 349 (8th ed. 2001).

[171] An early example of this entrepreneurial spirit occurred after the Civil War, when General William Tecumseh Sherman was assigned military jurisdiction over the West. He decided he needed to see what was there. He traveled up the Platte Trail; then came down the Front Range from Fort Laramie. He most looked forward to seeing and being in the Rocky Mountains. He was a private person. He hated receptions and having to make speeches, but the civic leaders of Denver came out to see him and invite him to a reception and give a speech. Their motivation was to get the Army to build forts in Colorado so Denver merchants could sell them supplies. *See* ROBERT G. ATHEARN, WILLIAM TECUMSEH SHERMAN AND THE SETTLEMENT OF THE WEST 75 (1956).

[172] Sandy Graham, *City Workers to Spearhead Denver Car-Pool Program*, ROCKY MTN. NEWS, Nov. 11, 1983, at 11.

[173] *Id.* (quoting the author).

ride-sharing plan. Moderating its position in response to the Commission's appeal, DRCOG became the regional coordinator of a matching carpool service.

2. Metropolitan Air Quality Council and Transportation Roundtable

To spur local air quality advocacy and planning, Governor Lamm and Mayor Peña organized the Metropolitan Air Quality Council in 1985,[174] which Steve Howards and Patti Shwayder staffed. Under the Chairmanship of Michael Shonbrun, the Council met at National Jewish Hospital, internationally known for its respiratory health expertise, and Council members became publicly vocal about the need to "move people, not cars."[175]

The MAQC, as it was called, endorsed clustered housing, mandatory shuttles to bus stops, land use controls to reduce vehicle miles traveled, wood burning bans, extensive use of oxygenated fuels, conversion of Public Service power plants to natural gas, and emission tests for diesel cars and trucks.[176]

Confronted with a divisive mass transit debate pitting suburban beltway advocates against those who were pushing core area redevelopment, Governor Roy Romer and Senator David Wattenberg formed the Transportation Roundtable in June of 1988. Late in the summer, Governor Romer endorsed mass transit for Denver's southeast and southwest corridors. Mayor Peña had warned the Roundtable that "the city will die unless future transportation needs are met by rapid transit, instead of additional automobile lanes. Widening highways will destroy neighborhoods."[177]

The Governor's trial balloon called for funding mass transit through beltway tolls and it prompted skepticism.[178] Beltway supporters opposed the siphoning off of their revenues while MAQC members feared the E-470 and W-470 beltway proposals would "throw the metro area even further out of compliance with federal air quality standards by encouraging private automobile use."[179]

The Governor's Transportation Roundtable ultimately recommended fixing road and transit priorities based on the consideration of three factors: air quality,

---

[174] *See* Rebecca Cantwell, *Hazy Days for Air Council*, ROCKY MTN. NEWS, July 16, 1990, at 7 (story on new Regional Air Quality Council referring to predecessor Metropolitan Air Quality Council).

[175] Editorial, *A Transportation Superfund*, DENV. POST, Sept. 15, 1988, at 6B.

[176] Lou Chapman, *Improving Land Use Smog War's Next Goal*, DENV. POST, May 16, 1988, at 1A.

[177] Berny Morson, *Romer Backs Rail Lines for Southern Corridors*, ROCKY MTN. NEWS, Sept. 3, 1988, at 30.

[178] Terry Kliewer, *Panel Cool to Using Beltway Tolls for Rapid Transit, Roads*, DENV. POST, July 26, 1988, at 2B.

[179] *Id.*; Bill McBean, *E-470 Growth Key: Downtown v. Suburbs*, DENV. POST, Nov. 2, 1988, at B1; *see* Vincent Carroll, *Urban Sprawl Would Ignore Red Light on E-470*, Nov. 4, 1988, at 65.

mobility, and safety.[180] Amidst speculation that mandatory no-driving restrictions would be necessary in order for the Denver Metropolitan area to meet the national health standards for carbon monoxide and particulates,[181] voters in Adams, Boulder, and Jefferson County defeated the proposed W-470 beltway[182] portion of a comprehensive Metro beltway by a 5-to-1 edge.[183] Nevertheless, the electorate in the E-470 area voted to proceed with that portion of the beltway as a toll road.

Air quality advocates read the defeat of the W-470 proposal as a citizen call to elected officials saying, "Get your act together and have a plan that makes sense."[184] The MAQC supported DRCOG's 2010 transportation plan proposal for developing a rapid-transit system radiating from downtown Denver,[185] but opposed its proposal to complete the Denver metro beltway.

DRCOG's 2010 transportation plan was the first in Colorado to undergo a comprehensive air quality analysis. Mayor Federico Peña was committed to building Denver International Airport east of downtown, with the possibility of a rail link into the city. The air quality analysis done in connection with the environmental impact statement for the airport demonstrated that DRCOG's plan, along with the E-470 beltway, would cause future violations of the national health standards for particulates and ozone. Concerned about violating the health standards and jeopardizing federal funding, Governor Romer defined the role of the Transportation Roundtable to include transit funding and additional air quality measures.[186]

The Transportation Roundtable and the General Assembly's Legislative Review Committee ultimately endorsed three priorities for the metropolitan area: "[c]ost effective measures for making better use of existing transportation systems[, i]mprovements necessary for safety and air quality[, and b]uilding a transit system parallel with beltway construction."[187]

In the 1989 legislative session, General Assembly leaders Dave Wattenberg, Al Meiklejohn, Don Ament, Danny Williams, and Norma Anderson all helped to

---

[180] Vincent Carroll, *Traffic Puzzle Planners Caught Between Moving More People While Polluting Less*, ROCKY MTN. NEWS, Jan. 15, 1989, at 57.

[181] Thomas Graf, *Specter of Driving Bans Raised, Strategies Offered to Fight Area's Top Environmental Concerns*, DENV. POST, Jan. 27, 1989, at 3B.

[182] *See* Terry Kliewer, *W-470 Hailed as Vital to Growth, Assailed as Brown-Cloud Harbinger*, DENV. POST, Jan. 25, 1989, at 3B.

[183] Terry Kliewer, *W-470 Fee Suffers Resounding Defeat*, DENV. POST, Feb. 8, 1989, at 1A.

[184] Jim Kirksey & Jay Grelen, *Highway's Foes Say Voters Want Data, Better Planning*, DENV. POST, Feb. 8, 1989, at 10A.

[185] Leroy Williams, Jr., *Planning Against Pollution*, ROCKY MTN. NEWS, May 23, 1989, at 8.

[186] E-mail from Robert Yuhnke to author (Mar. 6, 2004, 08:43:00 MDT) (on file with author). Yuhnke represented the Environmental Defense Fund in Colorado air quality matters, as well as being a member of the MAQC and the RAQC.

[187] Greg Hobbs, *Legislature Gridlocks on Transportation*, DENV. POST, May 1, 1989, at 7B.

craft bills setting forth a comprehensive air quality/transportation framework. Political, business, and community leaders supported these bills,[188] but the bills died near the end of the session. Governor Romer then called a special session that resulted in creation of the Metropolitan Transportation Development Commission.[189]

3. The Metropolitan Transportation Development Commission

The MTDC's job was to submit a metropolitan transportation plan to the General Assembly no later than January 31, 1990, and to consider among other proposals "[t]he parallel buildout of mass transit and regional roadways, transportation systems management, and air quality issues."[190] Governor Romer appointed the members of the Commission in August of 1989, and they went to work soon after.[191]

Also in the summer of 1989, Governor Romer replaced the Metropolitan Air Quality Council with the Regional Air Quality Council. The Denver Regional Council of Governments appointed fifteen of the thirty members of the newly-formed RAQC, which started work on August 9, 1989, as the lead air quality planning group for the Denver Metropolitan area.[192] In light of the adverse air quality impacts projected for DRCOG'S 2010 Plan, MAQC members appointed to RAQC continued to question that plan, which projected that vehicle miles traveled would double but did not commit to offsetting air quality strategies. One member said,

> 'That kind of scenario will wipe out the gains we've made from wood burning restrictions, offset the reductions in carbon monoxide through better fuels and emission systems and increase the brown cloud.'[193]

Observing that the metro area did not comply with federal clean-air standards for carbon monoxide and fine particulates and that a state implementation plan to

---

[188] *See id.*
[189] Act of July 11, 1989, ch. 10, 1989 Colo. Sess. Laws 69, 69-72 (codified at COLO. REV. STAT. § 43-2-148 (Repl. Vol. 1984, as amended)).
[190] 1989 Colo. Sess. Laws at 70 (codified at COLO. REV. STAT. § 43-4-148(3) (1984 Repl. Vol., as amended)).
[191] Dick Cooper & Terry Kliewer, *Romer Names Metro Transport Commission*, DENV. POST, Aug. 2, 1989, at 3B. The members were former state Representative Bud Hover, Denver Mayor Federico Peña, Jim Smith of U.S. West Communications, Boulder County Commissioner Ron Stewart, state highway commissioner Tom Strickland, Aurora Mayor Paul Tauer, Tom Thomas of the Regional Transportation District Board, Morrison Town board member John Thomasson, Adams County Commissioner Elaine Valente, and Greg Hobbs as Regional Air Quality Council representative. The Commission selected Tom Strickland as its chair.
[192] *See* Thomas Graf, *Air Quality Council Looking for Director with Superhero Traits*, DENV. POST, Aug. 10, 1989, at 8B.
[193] Thomas Graf, *Clean Air Drive 'Not Tough Enough'*, DENV. POST, Oct. 16, 1989, at 10A.

achieve compliance was due the next year, the EPA warned that mandatory measures would be required and only a program with a proven track record would be credited under the federal CAA.[194]

Surveys conducted in 1989 by the Metropolitan Transportation Development Commission ("MTDC") revealed that metro-area residents loved their cars but hated the Brown Cloud, as the Front Range pollution soup came to be known.[195] They favored a rail system to reduce pollution and congestion.[196] Kicking off the Clean Air Colorado program—a year-round voluntary effort to encourage carpooling and driving reductions on high pollution days—Governor Romer credited the oxy-fuels program for reducing carbon monoxide by 10 to 12 percent; however, he said, more needed to be done in every area, including transit.[197]

The MTDC endorsed the construction of light rail in three Denver corridors and the completion of the E-470 beltway. When the MTDC took its vote to send the proposal to public hearing, a Jefferson County Commissioner who supported building W-470 grumbled from the audience audibly, "[N]obody is going to use it."[198] The public weighed in at the hearings with both fervent supporters and adamant detractors arguing their viewpoints.[199]

In two successive years, the General Assembly considered bills to refer the MTDC recommended Metropolitan Transportation Plan to the voters for approval. The 1990 and 1991 sessions defeated both of these bills in close votes in the Senate after House passage, in part due to rural fears that an independent source of transportation funding for Denver might isolate the West Slope's quest for the funding it needed. Western Slope leaders have long viewed transportation dollars as an economic lifeline and have depended on a statewide approach to building and maintaining Colorado's transport network.

---

[194] *Id.* Near the close of the 1980s, former Chair of the Air Commission Carol Sullivan found good news in the "considerable progress" made towards carbon monoxide control, but also warned. "The mountains will disappear...if we continue at our current pace. In fact, the Rockies already now fade away some days into a grey-brown blur." Carol Sullivan, *Will Pollution Hide Our Mountains in 2100?*, DENV. POST, July 22, 1989, at 7B.

[195] Thomas Graf, *Commuters Love Cars but Hate Brown Cloud*, DENV. POST, Oct. 29, 1989, at 4B. Joe Palomba, who later became the Air Commission's first administrator, had written a report for the Colorado Department of Health in 1961 describing Denver's bad air as a "brownish-blackish cloud." By the 1980s, the "Brown Cloud" had become the proper name for a very improper and unpopular condition of pollution. Gary Massaro, *The Guy Who Gave Brown Cloud a Name*, ROCKY MTN. NEWS, Oct. 31, 1999, at 40A.

[196] *Id.*; *Freedom From the Road: Public Support is Swinging Toward Light-Rail System*, ROCKY MTN. NEWS, Nov.19, 1989, at 74.

[197] Graf, *supra* note 195.

[198] Berny Morson, *Light Rail May Figure in Area Transport Plan*, ROCKY MTN. NEWS, Nov. 20, 1989, at 8.

[199] Mary George, *Public Takes Swipes at Metro Transportation Plan*, DENV. POST, Dec. 3, 1990, at 1B.

The MTDC's 1990 report to the General Assembly[200] called for a 20-year transportation plan that included:

- A two-track light rail system...from downtown Denver to the southeast Metro area along I-25 to the Tech Center.

- A light-rail spur...along I-225 connecting Aurora to both downtown Denver and the Tech Center.

- A two-track light rail system...from downtown Denver southwest along Santa Fe to Mineral Avenue.

- A fourth rapid transit corridor [linking] downtown Denver with Jefferson County, running parallel to Colfax Avenue.

- A dedicated busway...along U.S. 36, connecting Boulder with the...I-25 North [busway].

- [A] dedicated busway...[from] I-25 North...from U.S. 36 to 120th Avenue.

- [A] transit corridor linking downtown Denver, Stapleton Airport...and the new Denver International Airport.

- [A] downtown Denver "crossmall" [linking] transit...from the north and south as well as passenger traffic from the 16th Street Mall....

- [A] system of bikeways and pedestrian walkways.

- [S]pecial transit programs [for the elderly and disabled].

- [C]onver[sion of]...motor fleets to alternative fuels, such as methanol, compressed natural gas and propane.

- [C]onstruction of sound barriers.

- [Improvements of]...major traffic corridor[s]...including Wadsworth, Santa Fe, State Highway 287, U.S. 36, 120th Avenue, Colorado Blvd., Colfax Avenue, Havana, Parker Road and Hampden Ave.

- [Construction of] the E-470 toll toad.

- Traffic system management improvements, [such as] traffic signalization, ramp metering, extra turn lanes, bus pull-offs, and electronic signage [for motorist advisories].[201]

---

[200] METRO. TRANS. DEV. COMM'N, A REGIONAL SOLUTION TO METROPOLITAN TRANSPORTATION: FINAL RECOMMENDATIONS TO THE COLORADO GENERAL ASSEMBLY (Jan. 1990).
[201] *Id.* at 15-17.

The funding package would include a five percent sales tax on car rentals, a five cent per gallon motor fuel tax, a .4 percent sales tax, and a $10.00 vehicle registration fee increase. General sales tax revenues from the package would fund rapid transit and other special projects because rapid transit was seen to benefit the community as a whole. Roadway improvements would be funded by the motor fuel, vehicle registration, and car rental taxes specified in the package. A new Metropolitan Transportation Authority would be created to oversee implementation of the plan.[202]

After the 1990 defeat, the MTDC submitted a revised plan to the 1991 legislature.[203] The 1991 plan proposed a 50-50 split between rapid transit improvements and road improvements. Reacting to criticism of the 1990 plan, the MTDC now proposed that the Metropolitan Transportation Authority would serve only as a financing and priority setting entity and would not build and operate the system. DRCOG would retain its role in transportation planning as the designated Metropolitan Planning Organization under the federal air act. The Regional Transportation District ("RTD") would construct and operate the rail lines. A Northwest Parkway linking E-470 and C-470 would be built.

The rapid transit, special project, and road improvements contained in the 1990 plan were re-proposed in the 1991 plan. In the reconfigured financing proposal, the General Assembly would specify the funding mechanism and any increase in the gas tax would be put to a statewide vote and, if approved, would benefit projects around the state.

This second referendum bill again failed by a close vote in the Senate and the opportunity for early completion of a comprehensive, well-funded, multi-modal, transportation system for the Metro area evaporated. Instead of a 1992 referendum on a coordinated transportation plan, the public received Doug Bruce's tax and revenue limitation proposal, which it approved.[204]

Consequently, RTD was on its own in starting a rapid transit system from downtown Denver, north to Five Points and southwest to Littleton, funded by a combination of the tax revenues that it raised and federal grants. The electorate did not approve RTD's "Guide the Ride" extension of the budding light rail network. Not until 1999 was the public given the opportunity to vote upon and approve a new funding mechanism for light rail as well as the highway improvements Governor Bill Owens had campaigned for.[205] The result is the now-commenced

---

[202] *Id.* at 26-29.
[203] METRO. TRANS. DEV. COMM'N, CONSENSUS '91: A REPORT ON THE DEVELOPMENT OF THE TRANSPORTATION SYSTEM IN THE DENVER METROPOLITAN AREA (Jan. 1991).
[204] COLO. CONST. art. X, § 20 (1992).
[205] Act of June 2, 1999, ch. 280, 1999 Colo. Sess. Laws 1108, 1108-20 (codified as amended at COLO. REV. STAT. §§ 43-4-701 to -715 (2003)).

construction of the southeast rail connection and the I-25 road expansion between the Denver Tech Center and downtown. This delayed vote reaped increased costs and achieved fewer improvements than the MTDC plan would have provided had the General Assembly referred the original measure and had the voters approved it.

Despite the loss of the MTDC proposal, the need for a multi-modal transportation system in the Metro area responsive to air quality criteria has remained a paramount public priority. The 1990 CAA amendments required each state to develop a transportation-air quality planning process for the development and implementation of measures necessary to demonstrate and maintain attainment of national ambient air quality standards. This reform included the "conformity amendment," which conditions a state's receipt of federal funding on its demonstrating that the transportation plan for its metro areas will achieve the level the state had set for motor vehicle emissions in its air quality implementation plan.[206] As the Metropolitan Planning Organization for Denver area transportation, DRCOG now, for the first time, had a great incentive to cooperate with RAQC and the Air Quality Commission.[207]

Though it failed to achieve its financing and construction goals, the MTDC effort helped develop a better working relationship among the transportation agencies. As the MTDC was still in the process of trying to obtain legislative approval to put a referendum to the voters to build the beltway/rapid transit infrastructure, Governor Romer and Senate President Ted Strickland formed the 37-member Strategic Planning Task Force on Statewide Transportation. The Task Force was called on to make recommendations on the development of a plan for making Colorado a "transportation hub" for the United States.

The Task Force's final report to the General Assembly's Highway Legislation Review Committee recommended a statewide plan for a network of highways, a rail system, airports, and alternate modes of transit in the metropolitan areas. It also recommended the creation of a State Department of Transportation with authority

---

[206] Act of Nov. 15, 1990, Pub. L. No. 101-549, 104 Stat. 2399, 2435 (codified as amended at 42 U.S.C. §§ 7408(e) & (f), 7506(c). *See* COLO. REV. STAT. §25-7-105(1) (2003). Bob Yuhnke of the Environmental Defense Fund, a member of the MAQC and the RAQC, was the author of the conformity amendment which required the transportation planning agency in a metropolitan area to design a regional transportation system that would achieve the levels of vehicle emissions required for attainment of air quality standards. Yuhnke organized the national coalition of transit agencies, metropolitan planning organizations and state air agencies that won enactment of the conformity provision. *See* Notes & Comment, *The Conformity Coalition*, ENVTL. F., Sept.-Oct. 1992, at 8-9. A nationwide expert in the requirements of transportation and air quality planning, Yuhnke aided the discussion of many such strategies in Colorado.

[207] David Pampu of the DRCOG staff was a constant participant in transportation/air quality planning for many years, patiently attending seemingly endless meetings and debates.

to implement the system.[208] The report contained findings and recommendations from the Environmental Focus group to "encourage the growth of well-planned and livable communities that place a premium on parks, open space, bikeways, walkways, and alternative forms of transportation including bus, rail, and high occupancy vehicle lanes."[209]

In 1991, a bi-partisan bill co-sponsored by a long list of Colorado legislators created the state's Department of Transportation, giving it power to "address the statewide transportation problems faced by Colorado; and...obtain federal funds by responding to federal mandates for multi-modal transportation planning."[210] This incredibly important statute brought into being a Colorado agency that, along with the Air Commission and the RTD, has the authority to mobilize citizen aspirations for a livable Colorado.

Citizen approval for the needed funds is crucial to fulfilling these aspirations. RTD is currently planning to ask the voters in the seven-county Denver Metropolitan Area to approve a plan for a transit network that essentially mirrors and improves upon the plan the MTDC recommended 15 years ago.

If approved by the voters, new commuter rail lines will run from downtown Denver to the Jefferson County courts in Golden, to Ward Road in Arvada, to Boulder and Longmont north along the I-25 corridor to 160th Avenue, to the Denver International Airport, with connecting links along the I-225 corridor to serve Aurora's new city center and the Fitzsimmons medical complex. There will be rail extensions to Highlands Ranch and Lone Tree, and suburb-to-suburb bus service would be increased.[211]

E. Plans to Bust the Brown Cloud

While progress was being made in the mid-1980s toward meeting the national health standards through the control of invisible gaseous emissions, like carbon monoxide from motor vehicles, Coloradans still faced foul-looking air. Citizen advocacy was reaching a crescendo. The MAQC's call in the spring of 1987 for Public Service Company's three Denver Metro power plants to switch permanently from coal to natural gas—met by PSCo's prompt rejection—prompted Governor

---

[208] STRATEGIC PLANNING TASK FORCE ON STATEWIDE TRANSP., A STRATEGIC PLAN FOR TRANSPORTATION DEVELOPMENT IN COLORADO, REPORT TO THE HIGHWAY LEGISLATION REVIEW COMMITTEE OF THE GENERAL ASSEMBLY 4-13 (1990).

[209] *Id.* at 56.

[210] COLO. REV. STAT. §43-1-101(1)(d) & (e) (2003). *See* 1991 Colo. Sess. Laws, ch. 188, at 1019-1138. Co-sponsors included Senator Tom Norton, who later became Senate President and then Executive Director of the Colorado Department of Transportation, as well as Representatives Norma Anderson and Lew Entz (now Senators) and Senator Tillie Bishop of the Western Slope.

[211] Jeffrey Leib, *FasTracks Vote Likely in '04*, DENV. POST, Nov. 5, 2003, at 1B.

Romer to organize a major study of possible cures for the Brown Cloud.[212] The Air Commission and EPA Region 8 had long wanted a complete source apportionment study of Front Range air pollution.

1. The First Brown Cloud Study

Interested in practical measures to control pollution and understand its causes, Governor Romer called on the private sector, and in particular PSCo, its coal supplier Cyprus Minerals Company, and its natural gas supplier Colorado Interstate Gas Company, to help fund the study.[213] They agreed. Regional Administrator Jim Scherer added the EPA's full support. The Greater Denver Chamber of Commerce, headed by Richard Fleming,[214] stepped forward to coordinate this unprecedented scientific and socio-economic study.[215]

Ben Byan of the Chamber, Joel Kohn of the Governor's Office, and Irv Dickstein, Director of the EPA's regional enforcement branch, incorporated the non-profit Metro Denver Brown Cloud Study, Inc. to receive and administer funds for the study. They engaged Dr. John Watson as the Principal Investigator. Administered by Carol Lyons, the work geared up in the 1987–88 winter season. An extensive network of air quality monitoring devices was installed to track and record emissions. PSCo volunteered to burn natural gas for 45 days to test the effectiveness of fuel switching.

Through source characterization, ambient air pollution sampling and analysis, visibility and optical monitoring, meteorological monitoring, and data analysis and computer modeling, this study documented the complex interaction of primary and secondary particles. Both were contributing to the Metro Area's visible air pollution.

Primary particles include combustion-produced carbon from mobile sources, industrial operations, wood burning stoves and fireplaces, and geological dust from roadways, vacant lots, river banks, and agricultural areas. The invisible gases that combine to form the secondary particles are "precursor emissions" including sulfur dioxide, nitrogen oxides, hydrocarbons, and ammonia emitted by motor vehicles, power plants, oil refineries, and other industrial processes. Ammonia comes from agricultural operations, sewage treatment plants, and other biological sources. The secondary particles formed from these gases are ammonium nitrate, ammonium sulfate, and organics.[216]

---

[212] 1987-88 METRO DENVER BROWN CLOUD STUDY, PROJECT SUMMARY 1 (Oct. 1988).
[213] This remarkable public/private partnership demonstrated how far Colorado's air restoration efforts had come since the days of back yard trash burning and uncontrolled industrial smoke.
[214] *See* REGIONAL AIR QUALITY COUNCIL, *supra* note 18, at 2.
[215] 1987-88 METRO DENVER BROWN CLOUD STUDY, *supra* note 212, at 6.
[216] *See id.* at 14, 16.

2. Brown Cloud Study Conclusions

The Brown Cloud study concluded that, during the worst episodes, pollution migrates down the South Platte River Valley as far as 60 miles to the northeast and then returns as "aged" pollution. During this transport process, urban pollution combines with the invisible gases emitted by agricultural operations in the Platte River valley to form secondary particles that return and mix with primary particles continually-emitted in the metropolitan area.

"Sewer of the air"—that '60s term used by the press—turned out to be an apt description of this mess. The Brown Cloud included a witches' brew:

> [Twenty-five percent]—primary fine particle emissions from mobile sources and from residential wood burning, [and vegetative burning]. [Half of the primary particulate motor vehicle emissions were from diesel engines.].... Dust contributes an average of approximately ten percent of the visibility impairment. The contribution of dust to the brown cloud increases [significantly] after the roads are sanded.[217]

Nearly all the remainder—secondary particulates caused by the interaction of invisible gases, ammonium nitrate particles—constituted about 25 percent of the Brown Cloud, with ammonium sulfate particles constituting about ten percent.[218] As to the precursor gases, half of the nitrogen oxides came from mobile sources and half from coal-fired power plants.[219] Half of the sulfur dioxide came from coal-fired power plants, the rest from refineries, diesel trucks, and cement plants.[220]

The PSCo natural gas burning experiment significantly reduced sulfur dioxide and nitrogen oxide emissions,[221] but did not lead to visibility improvements during the natural gas-burning days, so the report said. Because of the complex interactions leading to the formation of secondary particulates from urban and agricultural emissions, the Brown Cloud staffers could not correlate emission reduction directly to visibility improvement. They recommended a future effort to monitor coal-burning conditions for a comparison with gas-burning data.[222] This recommendation later produced a second Brown Cloud study.

The Brown Cloud report's conclusion was that no one control strategy could deliver the air pollution knock-out punch. Emission reductions would have to come from many different particulate and gaseous sources.[223]

---

[217] *Id.* at 19.
[218] *Id.*
[219] *Id.*
[220] *Id.*
[221] *Id.* at 60.
[222] *Id.* at 63.
[223] *Id.*

3. Brown Cloud Control Strategies

Perhaps the most significant practical aspect of the Brown Cloud report was its identification of possible clean air strategies, all of which have since been adopted in some form:

- Implementation of mass transit.
- Coal to gas conversion for industrial and power plant boilers.
- Post combustion cleanup for industrial and power plant boilers. [Clean coal burning technology including] sodium based dry sorbent injection system....
- Alternative fuels [to replace] diesel vehicles.
- Reduction of residential wood burning emissions.
- [Control of] oil, gas, and chemical processing facilities [particularly refineries].
- Low sulfur diesel fuel standards for fuel sold in Colorado.
- More stringent emission inspection and maintenance (I/M) program for gasoline powered vehicles.
- Reduction of airborne reentrained dust [such as road sanding controls].[224]

Governor Romer called a press conference to hail completion of the Brown Cloud study. He pressed for implementation of all the listed control measures, except for the coal to natural gas fuel switch.[225] He said power plants were "insignificant contributors" to the Brown Cloud and the projected loss of 870 coal mining jobs on the Western Slope was unacceptable, although the study estimated the offsetting creation of 840 natural gas jobs in northeastern Colorado. The Governor preferred use of cleaner-burning coal technology. Coal and power companies lauded him for this.[226]

Despite MAQC member criticism about eliminating the fuel-switching option,[227] the Denver press was behind putting more air pollution controls in place, whatever

---

[224] *Id.* app. 2, at 70, 72-75. Air pollution alerts to trigger emission reduction strategies was also suggested.

[225] *See* Governor Roy Romer, Statement on the 1987-88 Metro Denver Brown Cloud Study (Oct. 7, 1988).

[226] Katherine Corcoran, *Romer Defends Coal-Burning Plants*, DENV. POST, Oct. 8, 1988, at 1A.

[227] A soon-appearing *Westword* article displayed Governor Romer on its front page, wearing a crown of smoke stacks. Interviews with MAQC members, Denver officials, and scientists questioned the clean bill for the power plants. Bryan Abbas, *Romer's Cloud Control, What Did a Million-Dollar Study Buy? More Dirty Air*, WESTWORD, Nov. 16-22, 1988, at 12.

they might be.[228] PSCo blunted the coal/natural gas controversy by converting its non-operable, nuclear-powered St. Vrain plant to natural gas. Prodded by the Public Utilities Commission and citizen watchdogs, PSCo announced inclusion of conservation and alternative cleaner energy measures as part of its power supply agenda.

F. Regional Air Quality Council Established

Viewing the MAQC as too narrowly-based to achieve the air pollution control consensus he envisioned, Governor Romer in June of 1989 replaced it with a thirty-member Regional Air Quality Council ("RAQC") consisting of many local Denver government officials and chaired by Harris Sherman. The Council chose Ken Lloyd as its Executive Director.[229]

Though the DRCOG had lobbied hard for the position of lead regional air quality planning agency, as well as lead transportation planning agency, Governor Romer refused to acquiesce. He elected to go forward with an independent air quality planning agency, as his predecessor Governor Lamm had when he constituted MAQC.[230] Rather than ignoring and isolating all of his MAQC critics, Governor Romer appointed a number of them to RAQC.

The Governor also created the Colorado Environment 2000 Citizens Committee. Among other recommendations, its final report endorsed the Brown Cloud control strategies and MTDC's call for a twenty-first century metropolitan transportation control plan featuring mass transit.[231]

In 1989, the General Assembly directed the Air Commission to establish a visibility standard for Front Range air, the nation's first such standard for an urban area.[232] It also enacted legislation, proposed by MAQC, to authorize the Commission's adoption of regulations limiting the use of wood burning stoves and fireplaces during high pollution days.[233] Despite the legislature's fairly frequent salvos to the Air Commission about sticking to cost-effective control measures, the General

---

[228] Editorial, *Going After the Brown Cloud*, DENV. POST, Oct. 9, 1988, at 4D; Editorial, *Public Service May Do Even Better than Switch to Gas*, ROCKY MTN. NEWS, Dec. 9, 1988, at 78 (quoting a member of the MAQC as saying, "If we can burn coal and get the same emissions reductions (we would get) from burning natural gas, then we ought to be all for it.").

[229] Rebecca Cantwell, *Hazy Days for Air Council*, ROCKY MTN. NEWS, July 16, 1990, at 7.

[230] Thomas Graf, *Details on Proposed Air Quality Group Given*, DENV. POST, Apr. 27, 1989, at 2B.

[231] Thomas Graf, *Threats to State Environment Cataloged, Polluted Skies, Fouled Water, Vanishing Wetlands, Pesticides Top Report of 31 Problems*, DENV. POST, Jan. 11, 1990, at 1B.

[232] Act of May 26, 1989, ch. 235, § 4, 1989 Colo. Sess. Laws 1155, 1156-57 (codified at COLO. REV. STAT. § 25-7-106.1 (Rep. Vol. 1982, as amended) (repealed 1996)); DENVER METRO AIR QUALITY, *supra* note 18, at 2.

[233] 1989 Colo. Sess. Laws at 1157 (codified at COLO. REV. STAT. § 25-7-106.3 (Repl. Vol. 1982, as amended)).

Assembly endorsed a visibility standard, plainly responding to wide-spread citizen disgust about not seeing their beloved mountains.

The business community's interest in the economic development potential of restoring world-class vistas was persuasive. Air quality control had turned into a bi-partisan public effort, and the cost of pollution technology installation was being spread among all citizens in the form of higher power rates and product prices. In survey after survey, the public stated its willingness to pay to restore the brightening air.

IV. HEALTH STANDARD ATTAINMENT AND MAINTENANCE, THE 1990S

It turns out that restoring and maintaining Colorado's air resource is a yardstick of Colorado's leadership capability. Just as many stepped forward in the beginning of the fight against the Brown Cloud, many have continued to step up for clean air.

A. Clean Air Leadership

Through many a contentious episode, a way was forged by the start of the 1990s to bring Colorado into compliance with national ambient air quality standards and to reduce the Brown Cloud substantially. To make this possible, Governor Romer, the General Assembly, the Air Commission, RAQC, and Denver Mayors Federico Peña and Wellington Webb, joined together with local air quality planning agencies and many local government officials, citizen activists, and business leaders across the state.[234]

Commending its commitment to air quality restoration, the U.S. Conference of Mayors bestowed upon Denver the 1990 national "City Livability Award." The ever-vigilant media hailed Mayor Peña's receipt of the award as being on behalf of the entire Metro area, and called for the "battle to improve air quality" to continue.[235]

Inexorably, as a new motor vehicle fleet rode into Colorado, as businesses came to see clean and healthy air as a valuable community asset, as the state's tourist industry emerged as a strong economic factor, and, most importantly, as citizens counted good air restoration and maintenance among their highest priorities, Colorado managed to come into compliance with the national health standards by the start of the twenty-first century.

---

[234] Denver had the vigorous and able assistance of Tony Massaro and Theresa Donahue. Governor Romer had Joel Kohn, Cole Finegan, Wade Buchanan, and Patti Shwayder, formerly of the MAQC staff, who he appointed to head the Colorado Department of Health and the Environment.

[235] Jeffrey Leib, *Air Award May Open Eyes to City*, DENV. POST, June 19, 1990, at 1B; Editorial, *Livable City Award Deserved*, DENV. POST, June 19, 1990, at 6B.

B. The Second Brown Cloud Study and New Initiatives

Metro Denver Brown Cloud Study, Inc. contracted to produce a second study in the early 1990s. This was a modeling effort aimed at analyzing the secondary particulate problem. It was staffed by Paulette Middleton, Principal Investigator, Skip Spensley, Administrator, and Warner Reeser, Technical Advisor. Their analysis reaffirmed that the Brown Cloud is comprised mainly of tiny solid particles and aerosols, which become suspended in the atmosphere.[236] They named wood burning, street-sanding, mobile sources and power plants as significant contributors to the Brown Cloud.[237]

Changes Congress made to the CAA in 1990 played a major role in Colorado's clean air restoration. Borrowing from the Clean Water Act's design for periodically renewable discharge permits, the new federal act required the state to (1) maintain a current emissions inventory for the six national health standard pollutants and a multitude of hazardous substances, and (2) institute an operating permit program for large stationary sources—to include compliance with any new standards or regulations adopted after issuance of the permits.[238] As a result, the Air Commission extensively revised its Regulation No. 3 to comply with the federal requirements, requiring permit renewal applications every five years.[239]

Amidst new research by the Webb-Waring Lung Institute, which was investigating a wide variety of health injuries resulting from bad air, including heart attacks, strokes, arthritis, tumors, Alzheimer's disease and lung disease,[240] the Air Commission and the General Assembly adopted many new measures, including mandatory wood-burning controls, enhanced inspection/maintenance of motor vehicles, operating permits for stationary sources, alternative de-icing agents to

---

[236] BROWN CLOUD II: THE DENVER AIR QUALITY MODELING STUDY, FINAL SUMMARY REPORT 1 (Dec. 1993).

[237] The metropolitan brown cloud study effort raised $1.2 million dollars for the first study and 1.0 million for the second study, with 45% donated by coal interests, 45% from gas interests, and the remaining from interest groups such as the Wood Smoke Alliance and the Automobile Manufacturers. E-mail from Ben Bryan, Denver Chamber of Commerce, to author (Jan. 8, 2004) (on file with author). Enron Gas Processing Company and Enron Oil Trading & Transportation Company—by agreement between them and Metro Denver Brown Cloud Study, Inc.—contributed $278,358 to the study derived from a settlement agreement reached with the EPA in another matter. The author represented the Enron Companies in fashioning these agreements. The Enron penalty funds were earmarked for additional studies that the Regional Air Quality Council identified. *Id.*

[238] Jefferson V. Houpt, *Colorado's New Clean Air Program*, 22 COLO. LAW. 541, 541-42 (Mar. 1993).

[239] Thomas Morris, *Colorado's Clean Air Act Amendments Regulations*, 23 COLO. LAW. 861-62 (Apr. 1994); *see* COLO. REV. STAT. § 25-7-114.3 (2003).

[240] Kris Newcomer, *Researchers Study Polluted Air as Trigger for Disease*, ROCKY MTN. NEWS, Oct. 28, 1990, at 8.

eliminate the particles emitted from re-entrained street sand, and a variety of other air pollution reduction requirements.[241]

In 1994, the General Assembly created the Visibility and Air Quality Related Values Task Force, and charged it with recommending ways to protect federal class one areas (national parks and wilderness areas) from visibility impairment and acid deposition.[242] The National Park Service and the Forest Service were especially concerned about the effects power plant and automobile emissions were having on the plants, animals, soil, and water in Rocky Mountain National Park and the Indian Peaks Wilderness—where high rates of acid and nitrate deposition threatened water quality in pristine high altitude watersheds.

With a legislatively-prescribed life of only one year, and in the context of the by-now-familiar but tiresome standoff between the coal and power companies, on one side, and the natural gas and air quality advocates on the other side, this task force was unable to reach agreement on what particular control measures it should propose. But it did recommend new legislation enabling the Air Commission to address air quality-related values in national parks and wilderness areas. Air quality-related values include odor, flora, fauna, soil, water, geological features, and cultural resources. The General Assembly agreed. In 1996, it adopted amendments to Colorado's air act, assigning the Commission this responsibility.[243]

An environmental law suit aimed at PSCo's Hayden power plant in the Yampa River Valley also produced tangible results. Concerned that the Hayden Plant was contributing to acid deposition in the Mt. Zirkel Wilderness Area and causing health and visibility impairments, the Sierra Club—represented by Reed Zars—sued the company in Colorado Federal District Court for air pollution violations. This suit resulted in a $2 million fine to the company. PSCo agreed to donate $2.25 million to conservation projects in the Steamboat Springs area and invest $150 million for air pollution controls at the Hayden Plant.[244]

As part of his clean air work, Mayor Wellington Webb in 1994 prevailed upon the Air Commission to rescind its approval—given just a month before—for a metro air quality plan that would have increased the allowable particulate emissions ("PM_{10}") mobile source emissions budget from 44 tons per day to 60 tons per day. A press report hailed the perspicacity of Webb's leadership, as the less stringent limit would have "diminished downtown's status as the economic capital of

---

[241] Rebecca Cantwell, *Cleaning Up our Dirty Air: The Fallout, Tighter Curbs Will Crimp Wood-Burning*, ROCKY MTN. NEWS, Oct. 28, 1990, at 8.

[242] Act of May 25, 1994, ch. 246, § 4, 1994 Colo. Sess. Laws 1390, 1393 (codified at COLO. REV. STAT. § 25-7-213 (Repl. Vol. 1989, as amended) (repealed 1995).

[243] COLO. REV. STAT. §§ 25-7-1001 to -1008 (2003).

[244] Berny Morson, *Public Service to Pay Huge Fine*, ROCKY MTN. NEWS, May 23, 1996, at 5A.

Colorado...with a single shrewd political move, Webb found a way to improve his city's environment and economy."[245]

At stake from Denver's point of view was the health of metro citizens and the possibility that suburban roads would be built at the cost of a transit plan for the central area. Using its power to review portions of the Air Commission-adopted state implementation plan prior to its submission to the EPA, the General Assembly directed that the 60 ton per day level, not the tighter limit, be used for transportation conformity purposes in connection with federal funding requests.[246] At the same time, the Assembly preserved the tighter limit as a regulation adopted under the state's reserved authority, apparently allowing RAQC and the Air Commission to design Brown Cloud reduction measures to meet the stricter particulate limits.

Plainly seeing the need for a long-range air quality plan, RAQC in 1996 launched the Blueprint for Clean Air, a comprehensive evaluation of the strategies needed to maintain air quality over the next 20 years.[247] As a result, Xcel Energy (formerly Public Service Company) agreed to reduce its sulfur dioxide emissions by 70 percent and its nitrogen oxide emissions by 40 percent at its coal-fired Metro area power plants.[248] A bill passed by the General Assembly in 1998 allowed the utility company to pass along the costs of the cleanup, estimated at $211 million dollars, to consumers.[249] Governor Romer had called for such reductions when he announced the results of the Brown Cloud study in October of 1988.[250]

Progress kept coming. The Air Commission adopted more stringent emission requirements for motor fuels.[251] DRCOG placed a high priority on a Metro Vision 2020 land use and transportation plan that included urban growth boundaries.[252] With the active support of the General Assembly and Governor Bill Owens, voters overwhelmingly approved a General Assembly referendum that proposed financing

---

[245] Mark Obmascik, *Webb's Vision Clear in Urging Tougher Air Pollution Fight*, DENV. POST, Nov. 19, 1994, at B1.

[246] Act of May 31, 1995, ch. 227, sec. 1, § 25-7-105(1)(a)(III), 1995 Colo. Sess. Laws 1149, 1149-50.

[247] DENVER METRO AIR QUALITY, *supra* note 18, at 3.

[248] Regional Air Quality Council, *Update on the Blueprint for Clean Air, supra* note 22, at 1. The RAQC and air quality advocates were catalysts for this result. Jim Martin of the Environmental Defense Fund, for example, had long been active in negotiations with PSCo to achieve power plant controls in the metro area. As part of this effort, in 1998, the General Assembly adopted provisions for regulatory assurances to stationary sources against Air Commission further requirements in a 15-year period, if they would commit to significant voluntary emission reduction measures. *See* COLO. REV. STAT. § 25-7-1201 to -1208 (2003).

[249] Act of May 27, 1998, ch. 267, sec. 3, § 40-3.2-101 to -102, 1998 Colo. Sess. Laws 1044, 1050-51. *See* Fred Brown, *Clean-Air Strategy Unveiled, Regional Commission Targets Brown Cloud in 7-Step Program*, DENV. POST, July 10, 1998, at A1.

[250] Romer, *supra* note 222, at 7.

[251] *Id.*

[252] *Id.*

for the widening of I-25 as well as light rail construction along the corridor in the south Denver Metro area, with a spur along I-225 to Parker road in Aurora.[253]

DRCOG's 2025 Transportation Plan now calls for 93 centerline miles of rail or high occupancy vehicle lanes, with rail to Golden and the Denver International Airport, radiating out of a revitalized Union Station. The rail system is expected to make about 158,000 passenger trips per day.[254]

C. Demonstrable Achievement

By the close of the 1990s, the Denver Metropolitan region had gone 13 years without violating the one-hour ozone standard and eight years without any violations of the 24-hour PM_{10} particulate standard.[255] Governor Bill Owens submitted Colorado's request for attainment and maintenance designation for these pollutants and for carbon monoxide, which the EPA subsequently approved.[256]

In its 2001–02 Report to the Public, the Air Commission was privileged to tell Colorado citizens that "Colorado maintained compliance with all federal health-based standards in fiscal year 2002."[257] As new cars get cleaner, the inspection maintenance program contributes a diminishing percentage of air pollution benefit. Currently, only seven percent of cars inspected fail the test. As a result, the state has introduced a Rapid Screen program to sort out cars that do not need a full-scale emissions test. Vehicles owners who drive by the sensor and pass the test receive a postcard notification that they do not need the complete inspection.[258]

V. FUTURE CHALLENGES, 2000 AND BEYOND

Is clean air restoration an interim respite in a surge of growth-spurred pollution? The Air Commission and the EPA are warning citizens of the need for renewed vigilance. The Front Range is having trouble with maintaining the ozone

---

[253] *Id.* at 2.
[254] DENVER REG'L COUNCIL OF GOV'TS, METRO VISION 2025 INTERIM REGIONAL TRANSPORTATION PLAN 55 (2002).
[255] Regional Air Quality Council, *Maintenance Plans Adopted for Ozone and PM_{10}*, AIR EXCH. 1 (Summer 2001), *available at* http://www.raqc.org/newsletters/AirExchange/summer2001.pdf.
[256] *Denver Breathes Easy with EPA's Blessings*, ROCKY MTN. NEWS, Aug. 10, 2002, at 19A. Governor Owens had the help of State Transportation Executive Director Tom Norton, Department of Health and Environment Executive Director Jane Norton (now the state's Lieutenant Governor) and Doug Benevento, who succeeded Jane Norton as Health and Environment Director.
[257] COLORADO AIR QUALITY CONTROL COMM'N, REPORT TO THE PUBLIC 2001-2002 at 1 (Oct. 1, 2002), *available at* http://www.cdphe.state.co.us/ap/down/01-02finalreport.pdf [hereinafter COLO. AIR QUALITY CONTROL COMM'N].
[258] Todd Hartman, *Emissions Tests Barely Worked*, ROCKY MTN. NEWS, Nov. 29, 2003, at 4A.

standard,[259] and the metropolitan area has the third-worst traffic congestion in the nation after Los Angeles and San Francisco.[260] The state visibility standards were violated 55 times during the 2001–02 winter.[261] Regional haze continues to interfere with citizen enjoyment of our national parks and wilderness areas.[262]

In talking to Colorado residents, one may find that they still complain about the dirt in Colorado's air and fear health problems.[263] The Air Commission set the state's visibility standard based on the results of extensive citizen surveys designed to ascertain the vista-viewing the public deems acceptable. The visibility standard is exceeded if 7.6 percent or more of the light in a kilometer of air is blocked over a four-hour average from eight a.m. to four p.m.[264]

It has become obvious that attaining and maintaining health standards alone is not enough and can still leave Colorado with levels of visibility impairment that citizens don't like. They place a high premium on being able to see and enjoy their magnificent surroundings.

James Michener, a lover of Colorado's mountains, plains, and rivers, wrote sadly in the early 1970s about Front Range smog. His *Centennial* country—even while he was writing that great book celebrating the eons of Colorado and its civilizing contemporary experience—was suffering terribly from air pollution:

> Denver must certainly be one of the most civilized places on earth, with a bright new art museum, a good orchestra, one of the world's best natural history museums, and a recreation area including twoscore mountain peaks over fourteen thousand feet high. It also has one of America's

---

[259] During the summer of 2003, the Denver Metropolitan region violated EPA's new eight-hour ozone standard, based on the three-year average. E-mail from Ken Lloyd, RAQC Director, to author (Dec. 19, 2003) (on file with author). Because of the Early Action Compact Colorado previously entered into with the EPA, nonattainment designation because of this violation will be delayed if Colorado puts additional measures in place to assure attainment. *See* REGIONAL AIR QUALITY COUNCIL, OZONE EARLY ACTION COMPACT, *available at* http://www.raqc.org/ozone/EAC/ozone-eac.htm; *see also* COLORADO STATE UNIVERSITY, NORTHERN FRONT RANGE AIR QUALITY STUDY, *available at* http://www.nfraqs.colostate.edu/nfraqs/index2.html (last visited Feb. 12, 2004).

[260] John Rebchook, *Panelist: FasTracks Will Create Jobs*, ROCKY MTN. NEWS, Mar. 13, 2004, at 16C.

[261] COLO. AIR QUALITY CONTROL COMM'N, *supra* note 257, at 2.

[262] *Id.* at 8. *See* Air Pollution Control Div., *Issue Paper: Colorado's Regional Haze SIP Development Process, Presentation of Options to the Colorado Department of Public Health and Environment* (approved Apr. 18, 2002).

[263] On March 12, 2004, the Air Commission adopted additional measures to meet the national health standards for ozone; new controls would address thousands of oil and gas pumping and storage facilities and require gasoline producers to sell fuel with slightly lower volatility levels. The General Assembly will be reviewing these additions to Colorado's state implementation plan. *Board OKs Tougher Plan to Fight Smog*, ROCKY MTN. NEWS, Mar. 13, 2004, at 24A.

[264] *Id.*

worst pollution problems, for air from the prairies backs up against that wall of mountains, producing a smog that makes the one in Los Angeles look like a summer haze.[265]

Come back, James Michener! Air quality control has a lasting place in this state's agenda to protect people, plants, animals, and our economic well-being. It's about community. From wherever they come to be here, Coloradans of this and every future generation—like the Native Americans and Hispanos who preceded us before the founding of the Colorado Territory—will always lift their hearts to the peaks of the Divide and join in the public discourse so necessary to keeping the air clean.

Our poetic love affair with the West and all its possibilities inspires what we can and will do. The great twentieth-century Irish poet W.B. Yeats extols the beauty of the brightening air in these stanzas from the *Song of Wandering Aengus:*

> I went out to the hazel wood,
> Because a fire was in my head,
> And cut and peeled a hazel wand,
> And hooked a berry to a thread;
> And when white moths were on the wing,
> And moth-like stars were flickering out,
> I dropped the berry in a stream
> And caught a little silver trout.
>
> When I had laid it on the floor
> I went to blow the fire aflame,
> But something rustled on the floor,
> And some one called me by my name:
> It had become a glimmering girl
> With apple blossom in her hair
> Who called me by my name and ran
> And faded through the brightening air.[266]

The hazel wand is our dedication to community. The glimmering girl is Colorado.

---

[265] JAMES A. MICHENER, ABOUT CENTENNIAL, SOME NOTES ON THE NOVEL 41 (Random House 1974).
[266] W.B. YEATS, THE COLLECTED POEMS OF W. B. YEATS 57 (definitive ed., final rev. 1965).

Surely, there is more work to do, but today's Brown Cloud is a shadow of the 1950s version that caused citizens to experience mucked-up vision and wheezing lungs. The public debate about growth, transportation, land use, increased automobile traffic, and air quality must produce solutions, or Colorado will find a half-century of progress evaporated to a blip of light in a returning smog-filled twilight.[267]

Through many a political and economic thicket has streamed the hope and the glory of restoring our air. May each generation breathe well, see clearly, and carry on Colorado's clean air heritage.

---

[267] *See* Joey Bunch, *On the Road to Dirtier Skies?*, DENV. POST, Dec. 28, 2003, at 1A.

Lawyers & Judges Trail Guides & Mapmakers

TURNING FORWARD

Earth turns for a reason,
night and day, day and night,
equilibrium.

Death is the absence of seasons,
but death, too, will have
its season.

To the whirling Orb, gravity
holds us—children, parents,
friends.

Graceful moves, one at a time,
require seasoning.

On Starting Law School
(Letter to his daughter)
August 1997

Emily,

Tomorrow you begin law school. May you have the joy of learning, the gift of questioning, zest for debating the alternatives, a sense for the fair and practical answer, the desire to help others, a strong feeling of confidence in yourself, the humility of the searcher.

This is the profession most dedicated to questioning. Thomas Jefferson, who preceded you as a lawyer, said that free inquiry is the only way to avoid error. When doubtful, ask another question. Trust the instincts of your heart. Answers will appear through scholarship, reason, and instinct.

Being a fine person in community with problem-solving ability is what good lawyering is about. You can do this because you know what the fight for your own voice really means and costs. So you can help others find theirs, so they may be treated fairly.

Emily Dickinson's dad was a lawyer. Did he ever sense that his lawyerly success would pale in light of her ability to ask the universal question, enjoy the debate, and find the answer in the nows of the celebration of each day in the home of her own heart?

624

> Forever—is composed of Nows—
> 'Tis not a different time—
> Except for Infiniteness—
> And Latitude of Home—

> From this—experienced Here—
> Remove the Dates—to These—
> Let Months dissolve in further Months—
> And Years—exhale in Years—
>
> Without Debate—or Pause—
> Or Celebrated Days—
> No different Our Years would be
> From Anno Domini's—
>
> > Emily Dickinson, in *The Complete Poems of Emily Dickinson,*
> > Thomas H. Johnson, Ed. (Little, Brown and Company, 1960).

You're an Emily. I'm glad to be your Dad.

The River Trip of Your Life
To the University of Denver Law School Entering Class
August 18, 2000

Get ready for the river trip of your life. You are called to this. A calling is the signal your heart and mind receives from your premonitions and gives back to your prophecies. Sometimes the signal will not prove to be the one you ultimately act on. But no opportunity taken is a waste of your time or energy.

Get ready for the river trip of your life. A river takes shape from its tributaries. You will know when you're on the mainstream of your calling—it will bring you joy in the journeying. If there is no joy in the journeying when you've tried your premonitions and your prophecies now lead you in a different direction, then act on that which gives you joy and serves community; in this way you find yourself.

Get ready for the river trip of your life. Each of us has a call, whether or not we complete a law degree or become a licensed attorney. Every citizen has a calling to learn something of the law, for law is the instrument of service. Every citizen has a call to justice, for justice is the instrument of community. Every citizen has a call to love, for love is the instrument of peace.

When you're on the river trip of your life, you're on the way of service, community, and peace. You get to love yourself because you can hold yourself to the mirror each morning and evening and say, "I have this day been a worthy instrument."

I wrote this poem for my daughter on her graduation from this school this past May:

GRADUATION

> Law is the instrument of service,
> serve well your clients,
> number among them
> those who cannot repay,
> except by gratitude.

> Justice is the instrument of community,
> work for justice with all the eloquence
> you can muster, among your gifts
> array justice for others as
> you would yourself.
>
> Love is the instrument of peace,
> draw your strength from
> the peace that passes understanding,
> among the rewards you shall receive,
> the joy of loving who you are.

Get ready for the river trip of your life. A person trained in the law can choose to exalt his or her interests over those of clients and community. When this happens, the instrument of the law is bent to self-service. When your choice is to serve clients and community, you become a self-fulfilling instrument. Nothing we do is accomplished totally in isolation. What we accomplish by our energy and initiative comes to pass only in community. Opportunity for accomplishment is presented to us by the needs of others.

Get ready for the river trip of your life. Humility, hard work, collegiality—these are the lights that light your way, that accompany the exaltation for victory well-won. Arrogance, bad temper, expediency—these are tools of inevitable self-defeat; although it may seem that you have momentarily triumphed by sweeping others away, how you bullied others will not be forgotten.

Get ready for the river trip of your life. Swear yourself as a student of the law, here and now, to humility, hard work, and collegiality. Swear yourself to patience and to truth-telling. Truth-telling is a habit of mind and heart. The truth-telling I am talking about is one that can keep the confidentiality of the lawyer-client relationship when you have earned this privilege by graduation and licensing. The truth-telling I'm talking about involves not only the avoidance of lies but also the avoidance of the semblance of lies, which masquerades as half-truth and induces others to rely on your unreliable half-lie, whether of conduct, speech, or silence.

Get ready for the river trip of your life. If you make a mistake, own it as yours. Use it as the instrument for righting yourself. If what you have said in earnest belief proves to be wrong and others have relied on it, do not let those people assume they have donned a life vest when what you have handed them is not equipped with straps and will fail to sustain them in the rapids if they are spilled. Correct what you have said by what you have subsequently learned. Own up to not knowing it all.

Get ready for the river trip of your life. Doing well is important, but doing well can only be really accomplished in community. Your professors, your fellow students, the cases you shall analyze and discuss, the vigor of free and open discussion all are at the heart of schooling in this calling to the law, justice, and love, service, community, and peace. Mark well that the impression you will make on others is measured by the mark you make on yourself. Will you mark yourself as selfish, self-serving, a bully? Or will you mark yourself as one to whom others turn for thoughtful discussion and presentation? Let the joy of learning permeate all the long and lonely hours of puzzling, puzzling, puzzling. Counselor you shall be called when others shall begin to rely upon you.

Get ready for the river trip of your life. Take hold of the oars; be sure your baggage is stowed; experience the slow water and the fast water with others. They will help you see sucker holes and constellations you may not have seen. Think of yourself as a global positioning device. Triangulation has always been the key to mapmaking. You need more than one landmark. Pick out several. Who and what shall be your landmarks? Believe me: solitude can renew you. Take for yourself the time apart you need. But remember that the journey cannot be pursued over the long haul in isolation from others. You will need their help. Earn it by helping them.

Get ready for the river trip of your life. The canyons, plains, and mountains, mesas, vistas—Colorado calls you home. Seek out the urban and rural meanderings that refresh you. Often your best thoughts occur on the walking, climbing, biking, or boating path after you've set the book down.

Get ready for the river trip of your life. The law and the facts and the judgment decision-makers express on the law and the facts: this is the triangulation of every case you shall study and of every case that you shall help to shape as a lawyer. Get your bearings. Hope greatly. Do not despair. Every person who is called is tempted to lay the burden down. That's when a true calling will bump you along into persevering.

Get ready for the river trip of your life. The wonderful teachers of the law school are your river guides. You have chosen well. You feel a little insecure on the boat? Engage your guides in the art of questioning that is their basic tool. Orient yourself, pick yourself one or two non-academic interests you can pursue, service to the law school community, service to the community of local, state, and country which shall be your lifelong calling. Learn how to problem solve and to test your proposed solution or solutions by interchange with those you learn to trust, because they too have engaged in the research and thought to which you should become accustomed. Don't be afraid to seem stupid to others; what is important is the discipline of seeking understanding.

Get ready for the river trip of your life. Many interesting navigational subjects will you learn: Contracts—how the law is made by agreement with another party; Torts—how the duty of reasonable care governs relationships; Criminal Law and Procedure—how the government bears the burden of persuading citizens that the accused has committed the crime and how the perpetrators of crime are called to account by legal means; Property—how the rights of freedom include ownership rights that can be regulated in the public good and are owed the government's protection; and Civil Procedure—how courts obtain jurisdiction and process cases to a conclusion.

Here's a poem I wrote for Lucy Marsh, one of your future teachers, to introduce civil procedure as a practicing attorney might see it:

LUCY'S CIVIL PROCEDURE

Plaintiff, defendant,
cross-claim, counter-claim,
third-party claim,
surely someone is to blame!

Personal jurisdiction,
subject matter jurisdiction,
if you don't got both,
it don't matter all the same!

Summons and complaint,
answer and defense,
cause for relief?
Motion to dismiss!

Plead the facts,
follow the law,
the law and the facts,
baby, that's what it's all about!

You discover me,
I'll discover you,
you get my interrogatory,
I get to see what you've got!

Admit, deny, say you don't know,
duty of disclosure,
case management,
time well spent is time well earned!

If the material facts are uncontested,
no need to have a trial,
get the judge to say the law,
summary judgment's a dandy out!

The facts may be this,
the facts may be that,
you still with me?
It's time for trial management!

Trial to the jury,
trial to the bench,
grab your suspenders,
hope you've got evidence!

Somebody's going to win,
somebody's going to lose,
let's hiney-ho to the hall
and have us a settlement!

Client says no,
there's a principle at stake,

try the very best you can,
the truth ain't no mistake!

So you got a raw deal?
you can post a bond,
then you get to sing
appeal, appeal, appeal!

  Before you stretches the river trip of your life. Launch! And may your journey bring you joy.

Ethics and the Law for Water and Environmental Lawyers
Water and Environmental Sections, Colorado Bar Association
November 1996

Over the past decade, dear friends and colleagues of our generation have been lost to us: John Carlson, Chuck Woodruff, Charles Eliot, and John Land. They were known to us as fine lawyers and fine people. As we make our own passage, may we remember them and the gift of being here with each other.

So in considering your invitation to speak of ethics, lawyers, and the law, I am drawn to think of those basic elements we are privileged to work with: the land, the air, the water, the fire of our intellects, the people and the community we serve, all that moves and floats and flies. Becoming fine lawyers and fine people in family and community in this magnificent place, Colorado—what an ethical calling we have engaged! What a quest we share.

In volume three of *The Lord of the Rings*, Sam, believing that Frodo is dead from the mighty sting of the monster Shelob, has taken up the dreaded ring of power and faces three momentous choices: (1) he can fulfill his Master's quest and take the ring to Mount Doom, where it was forged, and cast the thing to destruction so the Dark Lord can't rule evilly with it; (2) he can take the ring for himself and attempt to wield its power over all creation; or (3) he can stay with his friend to whatever end may befall them both.

How to make the choice?

> In that hour of trial it was the love of his master that helped most to hold him firm; but also down in him lived still unconquered his plain hobbit-sense: he knew in the core of his heart that he was not large enough to bear such a burden, even if such visions were not a mere cheat to betray him. The one small garden of a free gardener was all his need and due, not a garden swollen to a realm; his own hands to use, not the hands of others to command.
> J.R.R. Tolkien, *The Lord of the Rings*, Vol. 3, Bk. VI, Chap. 1.

Sam chooses to return to his fallen friend and, by using Frodo's sword Sting just in time, rescues him from the death-dealing blow of an orc. You see, Frodo was not dead, only paralyzed for a time. Now awake, he demands back the ring, succumbing momentarily to its power to possess and corrupt. Sam hands back the ring. Then the befogging surge of greed and jealousy that Frodo felt dissipates, and he beholds his savior/friend standing true, brave, and uncorrupted. Cries

Frodo to Sam: "Forgive me" and then, "I must carry the burden to the end." Replies Sam: "But I can still help, can't I."

So unto Mount Doom march these two only, as the world smolders about them. They fulfill their quest, destroy the glittering evil. From the Grey Havens unto the West sails Frodo—and for Sam, the honor most treasured, he may now return to his beloved garden.

Of course J.R.R. Tolkien was writing about lawyers, the law, and ethical practices.

The law may be wielded as a sword in defense of justice and the defenseless, or worn as a corrupting ring of power. Lawyers may be poisoned by the twin monsters of arrogance and greed, fall into a deep sleep, or be rescued by a true and honest friend—humility and common sense. It's a long struggle, this day-by-day getting up, and we can't answer the call on our own. The strength to carry on takes some company. We need to get our hands into the soil. Gardening is the practice of sanity and the cultivation of all that grows lovely.

Gardening brings us back to the earth and our roots. The seasons of our lives hold power by which to grow or be impaired. "The force that through the green fuse drives the flower/Drives my green age; that blasts the roots of trees/Is my destroyer." Dylan Thomas, from "The Force that Through the Green Fuse Drives the Flower," *Complete Poems of Dylan Thomas* (Daniel Thomas, Ed., 1971).

Wendell Berry writes of the sowing:

SOWING

In the stilled place that once was a road going down
from the town to the river, and where the lives of marriages
   grew
a house, cistern and barn, flowers, the tilted stone of borders,
and the deeds of their lives ran to neglect, and honeysuckle
and then the fire overgrew it all, I walk heavy
with seed, spreading on the cleared hill the beginnings
of green, clover and grass to be pasture. Between
history's death upon the place and the trees that would have
   come
I claim, and act, and am mingled in the fate of the world.

Wendell Berry, "Sowing," Farming: A Handbook,
Poems by Wendell Berry (1970).

A world historical act resides each day in us—even when our powers have seemingly fallen to ruin—when we draw upon the power of our renewable youth.

Hear From Ecclesiastes (II:7-10, 12:1):

> Rejoice, O young man, O young woman, while
>   you are young
> And let your heart be glad in
>   the days of your youth.
> Follow the ways of your heart,
>   the vision of your eyes;
> Yet understand that as regards
>   all this
> God will bring you to
>   judgment
> Ward off grief from your heart
>   and put away trouble
> From your presence,
>   though the dawn of youth is
> Fleeting.
> Remember your Creator in
>   the days of your youth,
> Before the evil days come
> And the years approach of
>   which you will say,
> I have no pleasure in them.

Of course, Dylan Thomas, Wendell Berry, and the prophets were speaking of lawyers, the law, and ethical practices.

In the days of our youth, we wander the hills and the valleys, the creeks, or the seashore always thinking of what may be. We watch our fathers plant and our mothers store up the preserves we carry on the shelves of our memory. We turn the pages of our studies, take the oath of the lawyer's office, start our own families. We argue vigorously, take this position and that, answer to superiors, discover the very few whose performance, grace, and sagacity we would hope to emulate, get smacked by what we did not anticipate, learn the difference between bombast and effective advocacy, and find that we are sought by clients and community for what we can do for others. We earn the appellation "counselor."

On days when the conflict wears us down and the blue funk settles in, the geography of our youth, those bell jars shelved to the recesses of our hearts, can be summoned forth.

Recall if you will that particular place in creation you call upon when the stress and the noise seem unbearable, your head rattles, your hand, eye, and tongue seem caught in gibberish. Reflect that location: sea grass and the lapping tide with your sand castle toes in the water? A creek with bed of russet leaves and blessed hum while you lie back on the bank amidst the towering hardwoods? The top of a hill with row on row of other hills for roaming? Back porch in summer, going nowhere you swing in an arc, and locusts play their exotic fiddles into evening? Mary Jane on a glistening ski day and you're flying off the mountain!

Emily Dickinson was 12 years old when Thomas Cole painted his ecstatic four-piece work "The Voyage of Life"—depicting "Childhood," "Youth," "Manhood," and "Old Age." Out of a cavern into the dawn on a small canoe, angel at the stern, emerges the child; along a bright and broadly flowing river the angel, from the bank, bids the youth on toward the castle shimmering in the air; down the cataract swirls the adult while the angel watches anxiously from above; onto the bay of the ocean floats the old man, his angel leading him into the glowing rays of sundown. From the East unto the West, in our singular canoe, do we navigate the waters of our destiny with the aid of those who care for us.

Emily Dickinson never wandered from her garden, though she journeyed far and wide through her powerful mind. Death, the God who suffered the death of children—being a creative woman in a male-dominated religious and civic society with no ear for her voice—these were Emily Dickinson's trials. Her spirit persevered, and I am pleased this day to voice her song:

254

Hope is the thing with feathers
That perches in the soul,
And sings the tune without the words,
And never stops at all,

And sweetest in the gale is heard;
And sore must be the storm
That could abash the little bird
That kept so many warm.

I've heard it in the chillest land,
And on the strangest sea;
Yet, never, in extremity,
It asked a crumb of me.

Emily Dickinson, in *The Complete Poems of Emily Dickinson*, Thomas H. Johnson, Ed. (Little, Brown and Company, 1960).

In our own time, Terry Tempest Williams, setting out peeled oranges, calls upon the birds and the western landscape to help her through the impending cancer death of her mother:

> Peeling an orange is a good thing to do in the mountains. It slows you down.
> You bite into the tart rind, pull it back with
> your teeth and then let your fingers undress the citrus.
> Nothing else exists beyond or before this task. The naked fruit is
> in your hands waiting for sections to be separated. Halves.
> Quarters. And then the delicacy of breaking the orange down to
> its smallest smile. I lay out these ten sections on the flat granite rock
> I am sitting on.
> The sun threatens to dry them. But I wait for the birds.
> Within minutes, Clark's nutcrackers and gray jays join me. I
> suck on oranges as the mountains begin to work on me.
> This is why I always return. This is why I can always go home.
>
> Terry Tempest Williams, *Refuge: An Unnatural History of Family and Place*, (Vintage Books, 1992) at 160.

The land, the rivers, they hold and extend to us many treasures when we borrow of them well. Replant we must. When all seems barren, the waters of our enthusiasm bathe and heal. Our lungs and thoughts require the fire of inspiration. We journey through strange and familiar geographies—the latitudes and longitudes of our choices inform our view. William Stafford:

LOOKING FOR GOLD

> A flavor like wild honey begins
> when you cross the river. On a sandbar
> sunlight stretches out its limbs, or is it
> a sycamore, so brazen, so clean and bold?
> You forget about gold. You stare—and a flavor
> is rising all the time from the trees.
> Back from the river, over by a thick
> forest, you feel the tide of wild honey
> flooding your plans, flooding the hours
> till they waver forward looking back. They can't
> return: that river divides more than
> two sides of your life. The only way
> is farther, breathing that country, becoming
> wise in its flavor, a native of the sun.
>
> William Stafford, *The Way It Is, New and Selected Poems by William Stafford* (1998).

Of course Thomas Cole, Emily Dickinson, Terry Tempest Williams, and William Stafford were thinking about lawyers, the law, and ethical practices.

We are that part of creation given of the gift of intelligence to find in our own nature the ability to respond to the beauty of nature and find, amidst all our trials, our own way. When we touch and convey a truth honestly to a decision-maker through the oft-honed skill of our written and oral translation, we may obtain justice for our client and the personal satisfaction of professional achievement.

Thomas Jefferson was a lawyer, thinker, writer, inventor, politician, architect, outdoorsman, negotiator, mentor, and gardener. Said Jefferson: "Reason and free inquiry are the only effectual agents against error. Give a loose to them...". Bernard Mayo, *Jefferson Himself*, at 81.

Jefferson welcomed disputation. If our ideas and ideals cannot withstand scrutiny, they do not tap what's best in us. To argue convincingly is to alter another's viewpoint by appealing to a shared experience or aspiration, to summon up something forgotten, to realize a new synthesis, to engage in professional conflict that illuminates the inquiry without resort to bullying tactics.

Our heritage is this: to engage each other firmly and fairly. We are of Jefferson's and Lincoln's profession. We live in a time and place of remarkable beauty and energy. We took, each of us, the Colorado oath, a call to public duty and service through personal excellence and achievement. We swore to represent our clients faithfully, to help those without the resources to help themselves, to work for justice, and to abide by the law.

We pledged faith, we lawyers, to the law and to ethical practices. We honor our mentors; let us mentor others.

Recall now with me that Colorado lawyer's oath you took, so that with hobbit sense/horse sense/common sense each day you wake, you may accomplish a daily choice that works to fulfill that oath. One handiwork a day to mark each our personal and professional lives, what tapestries we might together shape. All the colors of our talent, all the fibers of our strength!

Colorado Attorney's Oath of Admission

I DO SOLEMNLY SWEA.R by the Everliving God (OR AFFIRM) that I will support the Constitution of the United States and the Constitution of the State of Colorado; I will maintain the respect due to Courts and judicial officers; I will employ only such means as are consistent with truth and honor; I will treat all persons whom I encounter through my practice of law with fairness, courtesy, respect and honesty; I will use my knowledge of the law for the betterment of society and the improvement of the legal system; I will never reject, from any consideration personal to myself the cause of the defenseless or oppressed; I will at all times faithfully and diligently adhere to the Colorado Rules of Professional Conduct.

Taking Our Constitutional
Ethics Committee, Colorado Bar Association
Snowmass, Colorado
July 18, 1998

Thank you! Bobbie and I took our constitutional this morning. We walked up the summer road through the columbine and rose hips. A fat robin was having a worm breakfast. A cloudless Colorado morning. We passed a string of condominiums and some gorgeous houses being built for inclusion in future issues of *Architectural Digest*. The sun beat fiercely on us.

We thought of turning back. But there, tied to a tree, was a cooler of water and paper cups—a ski area's version of the well of Jericho—a blessing to thirsty summer walkers. So we went a little farther up and found the cool of the aspen. A wetland seep appeared from within the mountain. A rivulet ran.

Grasses and cat tails. We felt a whole lot better. As Colorado does so often—and so well with elevation—vistas opened up. We could see the Roaring Fork Valley and, on the other side, Snowmass Creek bearing its way—down and away—from the snow capped peaks.

I cannot ever get close to the Continental Divide without remembering that the apparent geographical and political divisions of "East Slope" and "West Slope" yield to the common merging at the higher elevations. The land teaches us.

. . .

Can there be a better place than the West and Colorado in which to practice ethics? You will answer, "It must be so in every place!" Yes, but our starting and our homing place is here, between the crags and the wildflowers. And, after the long climb and the gaining of the pass, when we set to pushing sundown back on golden ripples of the lake, as Thomas Hornsby Ferril asked, who can tell which ocean we shall blunder to?

We must first know our own location. Finding one's location involves triangulation. In producing the first topographical map of Colorado, the Hayden Survey mapped 1,000 peaks in three field seasons of the early 1870s. So, too, with personal landscape. You and a couple of landmarks must intersect: three basic points of intersection: you, family, and community.

This fixing of one's position by reference to the surrounding human and natural circumstance—identifying the duties owed to each for living within community, this landscape of nature and of the soul—we call the contemplation and the practice of this art "ethics." It's the daily stuff of living and starts with your morning constitution.

We recognize the boundaries of the jurisdiction we travel within. We recognize the landmarks and navigate by them. When in doubt, we seek the help of navigational aids and the good will of others. Judgment always comes to play in finding our way.

. . .

We are engaged in a great service profession, we lawyers and judges, we spouses of lawyers and judges, we clients, we citizens, we the community who depend upon the practice of the art of justice. Tying words to thought to invoke the image and the reality of justice is our daily work. Having been sworn to the cause of justice, we must speak and act against bias and prejudice, especially in our workplace and in the organizations to which we belong. This work starts with your morning constitution and extends up the side of the mountain and back again.

This morning, you the members of the ethics committee debated how to serve your fellow citizens by providing them—and this is the great contradiction and dilemma—with less than full representation in litigation matters.

This is a tough concept. Litigation has been the province of lawyers and judges, standing wig-to-wig in the Inns of the courts of England. Now in our county and our district courts of the state, nearly one-half of the matters are being conducted by persons who appear before the decision-maker without an attorney. In many instances, they must contest with a party who is represented by an attorney.

How has this come to be, that a profession trained for the courtroom appears in the courtroom less and less in proportion to the growing number of disputants? Two main factors, perhaps, lack of money and lack of trust.

The purchase of our analytical and rhetorical art costs too much for many persons. A growing number of citizens think they can do better, do not have confidence in us, or, quite simply, have no choice.

So you wrestle with a new way of providing access to the courts: access by a client you represent in a limited capacity, one who appears in court without your presence but armed with the words and the thoughts you have helped him or her put to a pleading the court will utilize in decision making.

In the past, courts have depended on the veracity and diligence of attorneys in preparing pleadings. The concept is that an attorney will aid the court in making a just decision, not mislead it, and, at the same time, will safeguard the interests and confidences of the client.

If we are to contemplate using attorneys for litigation purposes without them signing pleadings or entering appearances, don't we need a change to the Colorado Rules of Civil Procedure and pertinent Rules of Professional Conduct? Rule 11 currently provides for only the all-or-nothing scenario of the historic litigation paradigm. If a lawyer represents a client who is involved in litigation, he or she must sign the pleadings and make an entry of appearance until the litigation is completed or the court allows the attorney to withdraw.

Thus, Rule 11 appears to presume currently that a *pro se* party who signs the pleading himself or herself is not being represented. Limited representation is foreign to the litigation practice yet appears to be in demand—a way that lawyers can serve their fellow citizens without undertaking the full responsibility of representation.

But limited representation is, nevertheless, representation, and the attorney continues to bear professional responsibility and owes a degree of diligence and candor to the court that must hear and decide the case. So I commend you and the Civil Rules Committee and other members of the bench and bar to the work of re-bundling the unbundling concept, which it seems should include identifying the duties and rights of the *pro se* litigant—and the role and responsibilities of the attorney who provides limited litigation representation—in the context of the judicial forum.

We drink from our past traditions, the well of Jericho, and also the contemporary cooler on the mountain, as we travel paths not previously or personally known to us. In finding our way (as individuals and a society) we bring our personalities, our various cultural, professional, and personal backgrounds and expertise, our differences and our agreements—rich, diverse, capable of resolution by way of exercising informed judgment—to this important and humbling work. Our generation—all persons in this room—we are called upon to provide more straightforward and effective access to justice in a complicated and legalistic society implicating persons of unequal education and economic means, of different viewpoints and persuasions.

The framework that guarantees our liberties is the law. The law is the reflection of a civilized society seeking to find its way in the course of time, and on any given day, utilizing the compass of fair play, when there is no clear or easy passage. Rules of procedure are meant to provide stability and are subject to considered change.

The new jury reform rules are intended to allow the jurors more participation in the matters they are called upon to decide. They may keep notes, take their notebooks into the jury room containing the instructions of the court and key documents, propose questions for the judge to ask to witnesses, and engage in pre-deliberation discussion perhaps. It's like turning the altar around so that the congregation can better participate in the communion they are called upon to witness.

The new attorney discipline rules are intended to resolve problems or potential problems between attorneys and clients before they become intractable episodes requiring and deserving discipline. The advertising rules adopted last year are intended to bring information to the community regarding the availability of lawyers and legal services without false advertising regarding capability or potential results.

The new pro bono aspirational rule adopts a target of at least 50 hours of free legal service by each attorney, every year, for those who cannot afford to pay.

All of these changes involve and require re-triangulation. Hearing your discussion of this morning—particularly all the energy and enthusiasm and experience you bring to the disputation in formulating your recommendation to the court—reminds me once again of the great resource Coloradans bring to bear on the challenges of achieving justice in contemporary America.

DO NOT SHY

Do not shy from conflict,
friction is the match head,
the rubber on the road
encountering resistance,
igniting forward progress.

But only an instrument.
the wheel turns, the fire
burns to move and forge
differences into resolution
of the coming conflict.

You go forward in the finest tradition of our profession. Thank you!

Light Bearers
Law Education Committee, Colorado Bar Association
Vail, Colorado
September 24, 1999

Good morning! Thanks for your invitation. What a glorious fall day yesterday was, the mountains blazing with aspen, the full moon arcing through the sky over the Vail Valley. Every day we wake to Colorado is a day worth living. And consider this, we rejoice in the coming of the winter snows. Can the citizens of many states claim that for fun and economic health? Yet, for peace of heart and promise of the future, our winter hopes turn to the glory of spring along the prairie creeks and in the mountain wildflower meadows. We wake to the dream of now and live by the fire lit by this land, the community in which we live, and the family we love.

Our fine western poet, William Stafford, described this quickening:

THE DREAM OF NOW

When you wake to the dream of now
from night and its other dream,
you carry day out of the dark
like a flame.

When spring comes north, and flowers
unfold from earth and its even sleep,
you lift summer on with your breath
lest it be lost ever so deep.

Your life you live by the light you find
and follow it on as well as you can,
carrying through darkness wherever you go
your one little fire that will start again.
William Stafford, *The Way It Is: New and Selected Poems* (1998).

We lawyers and judges, at our professional best, are light bearers. At our professional worst, we can't get the fire started. When the storm's coming on, the skill of the mountain man or woman is to find the dry kindling, then strike the spark that holds the flame to the wood to cook the meal.

Legal services are the kindling wood of citizenship. Without the aid they offer, our fellow citizens struggle in the dark when the storm of conflict is bearing down on them. You help show your clients how to start the fire and keep it going. You teach them how to gather together the pine needles of the facts, how to add the branches of the law patiently, how not to smother the nascent flame by loading on the heavy stuff all at once, how to tell one's story effectively by keeping it simple and making it interesting.

Teacher, counselor, experienced outfitter, you prepare them; you don't make the journey for them. You point them west and let them make their own discoveries.

Again, William Stafford:

WEST OF HERE

The road goes down. It stops at the sea.
The sea goes on. It stops at the sky.
The sky goes on.

At the end of the road—picnickers,
rocks. We stand and look out:

Another sky where this one ends?
And another sea?
And a world, and a road?

And what about you?
And what about me?

William Stafford, *The Way It Is: New and Selected Poems* (1998).

A Former Water Lawyer's View of Torts
Colorado Trial Lawyers Association and Colorado Bar Association
February 9, 2000

Well, thanks for being here. However, I thought I was addressing the Colorado Trail Users Association. I'm somewhat confused about the notion of a Trial Lawyer's Association. I thought, after graduation from law school, you either passed the bar and got admitted or you joined the F.B.I. I didn't know you had to keep on trying.

How long must you maintain this trial status? Is it like being cast into the sixth circle of Dante's Inferno without a glass of lemonade?

I practiced water law for 21 years before assuming the bench. During that time my partner, Bob Trout—you can tell a good water lawyer by his name—once had to do a trial. I asked him how it was. He said that condemnation was a whole lot of fun. I agreed with him. I'd been in a Roman Catholic Seminary for a year during college.

Trout said you had to have evidence. This surprised me. Torquemoda usually did without. Using a whole lot of water normally did the trick. First they trussed you up with a whole lot of rope and a whole lot of iron gadgets. If you sunk and drowned you were innocent. If you survived, they'd kill you because you must have gotten help from the devil. Things got a whole lot better when the Pope got into the business of tort reform. He went to a play by an English writer and got stuck on the line, "The first thing you do is kill all the lawyers!"

Trout said his trial was actually before three commissioners. I felt better about that. If I recall correctly, the inquisitors normally traveled around the countryside in groups of three looking for deep lakes and fast rivers.

That's a curious notion, isn't it, "assuming the bench." I thought when you became a judge, you didn't have to assume anything. You either had evidence that the bench actually existed or you granted the defendant's motion for mistrial.

The idea of having plaintiffs is disturbing. What is it they're crying about? My mother always told me to be happy. "Don't look plaintiff all the time!" she'd say. My dad told me not to worry. "You'll be a man before your mother yet," he said. I really admired my father for all the encouragement he gave me. He was a civil engineer. He once asked me what I was going to do with a history degree. I told him I didn't know but the Spanish were up to some interesting things in the Dark Ages.

Tort law, on the other hand, is a somewhat modern development I've come to understand since assuming the bench. It apparently grew out of some difficulties the French kings were having with dessert. Even today, when you travel to France they'll bring you a whole tray of "torts" so you can have your choice.

The distinction between an intentional tort and a negligent tort is also quite interesting. An intentional tort involves a whole lot of batter. The negligent tort just kind of happens when the cook isn't looking.

A tort gives rise to damages. For example, when you return from France none of your pants fit.

France is a civilized country. The judge conducts the investigation, conducts the trial, and weighs down the defendant with a whole lot of ropes and iron gadgets. It's called the Civil Code. In contrast, the English have the common law. What's common about it is that no one can understand what it is. That's why the English invented the jury. It takes 12 people to help decide what the facts were.

I think the history profession has the right idea. It takes only one of them and a publisher to decide what the facts are. Up at the University of Colorado, they're specializing in revisionist history. Patricia Limerick, for example, is saying the American West involved problems with a whole lot of bad men.

My grandmother was Irish. Although she wasn't from County Limerick, she could recite a number of them from memory. Memory is a good thing. It's the entire basis of the common law. I wish my Dad were still alive. I could tell him history turns out to be a very useful thing.

The revisionist historians don't like Colorado's water doctrine of prior appropriation. They think that taking all the water out of the streams to grow corn in the desert can interfere with the flow of the river. My former partner, Trout, must have had a mother like mine. "I wish they'd stop being so plaintiff," he'd say. "They ought to take a good look at the Grand River Ditch," he'd say. "It sure looks a whole lot like a river."

The Grand River Ditch is surely a grand thing to see, I agree. The Colorado River used to be called the Grand River until the west slope congressman Ed Taylor thought the Colorado River ought to be in Colorado. So he moved it from Utah. Then the people on the eastern slope figured out how to put it in a ditch and run it around the mountain at the top of the Divide so you could grow corn in the desert, proving that Stephen Long didn't know what he was talking about and proving Colorado boomers like Governor Gilpin absolutely right. All you need is revision and plenty of west slope water to make the desert bloom.

So Colorado's water doctrine is first in time, first in right—use it or lose it! We call the people who came up with that one "pioneers." The revisionist historians think that pioneers included a whole lot of bad men doing bad things. Water lawyers like to argue they got tired of a whole bunch of French and English and Spanish kings and made the desert bloom, and what's the west slope going to do with all that water anyway?

Tort law involves a former water lawyer getting used to a very different notion of breach. A really big flood can breach a dam. Take, for example, the Castlewood Dam that blew out in the thirties and left only a canyon in its place. This was truly a disaster because you can lose your water right by abandonment if you don't store and use your water because your client can't afford to rebuild it. Without water clients, water lawyers tend to be abandoned, which is worse than any natural disaster could be.

This is the advantage in being a tort lawyer. Every disaster helps business. If a duty's breached, there's either a retainer from an insurance company to keep the defense bar going or a contingent fee that will ultimately be paid by the insurance company to keep the plaintiff bar going. So what's there to cry about in this?

Duty, breach, causation, damages, collection of fees. The common law is beautiful. The jury returns a verdict. Having a verdict usually means that someone wins. When someone wins, that encourages another disaster. On the other hand, legislators are enamored of tort reform. Every year there's another bill to do away with disasters....

I know how you trial lawyers must feel about this. The revisionist historians think that Colorado has too many water lawyers and they're bad for the natural environment that was here before four million people and Californians decided that Colorado should become the next California. I think the trial lawyers ought to join the water lawyers association and the water lawyers ought to join the trial lawyers association. This would accomplish a whole lot of understanding about different ways of looking at breaches.

Water lawyers have a whole lot to learn about insurance companies, for example. Apparently, an insurance company is a group of investors who take a whole lot of money to make a whole lot of money to pay a smaller amount of money in the event of disasters they hope won't occur but know from the law of averages will occur but hopefully not in the actuarial lifetime of a whole lot of policy holders who pay a whole lot of money because they're afraid of disasters. The job of an insurance company is to take claims and sit on them awhile so the money eventually necessary to pay the claim—especially the added claim for bad faith denial of coverage—can earn a little more interest on the insurance company's bad investments.

When you think about it, water law is not a whole lot different. The water lawyer files a water claim on behalf of a client and hopes the good Lord will make it rain. Trial lawyers and water lawyers like to associate themselves with rainmakers. That Bulldog Guy is a good example!

When I assumed the bench, the trial lawyers association told me they were going to give me a hornbook on torts. I thought this was a good idea because my wife is a gourmet cook and we'd always talked about going to France some day. I also thought that having a hornbook would be fun. I've always been fascinated with railroads.

Many of my water clients also had cows with horns. One of my clients took me aside one day when I was on my way to do my first trial after being a water lawyer for 20 years. He said, "Now I want you to know before you go in to talk to that guy in the robe who assumed the bench how to tell the difference between a cow and bull."

The best thing about having a client is having one. This is another thing that the newly formed trial water lawyers association could have a CLE conference on. That one about "How To Gang Up On Allstate" may not get credit next year after the legislature runs another insurance company bill.

. . .

After this talk I'm thinking about calling my mother and some revisionist historians and confessing to bad thoughts and bad deeds, the kind of things that are good for the law business but that legislators want to do away with and newspapers like to plaintiff about.

Well, that just about does it for "A Former Water Lawyer's View of Torts." Well, maybe not. I would like to provide you trial lawyers with the definition of a "well" straight out of Colorado's water statutes: "'Well' means any structure or device used for the purpose or with the effect of obtaining groundwater for beneficial use from an aquifer." Even cooler about this definition is what is not "well":

> "Well" does not include a naturally flowing spring or springs where the natural spring discharge is captured or concentrated by installation of a near-surface structure or device less than ten feet in depth located at or within fifty feet of the spring or springs' natural discharge point and the water is conveyed directly by gravity flow or into a separate sump or storage, if the owner obtains a water right for such structure or device as a spring pursuant to article 92 of this title.
>
> C.R.S. § 37-90-103(21)(a) and (b).

Some of you trial lawyers might be thinking that whoever thought up this sunken definition and pumped it up for a legislator to carry the water of whatever lobbyist trucked it in to the capitol committed a tort. But, being a former water lawyer who assumed the bench, I don't think it looks a whole lot different than a lot of tendered or actually delivered jury instructions.

Who really believes a jury understands those instructions anyway? A jury usually uses common sense. That's why there's a right to have real people make the important decisions about compensation to innocent victims who have suffered injury and the protection of defendants, and insurance companies against undeserved recoveries.

Thanks for your indulgence today. I learned in the seminary that indulgences can keep you out of Dante's Inferno. By the way, you owe the state one credit for listening to me bull you about two liquid assets that are very precious to the legal profession, water and money.

Note: It is possible, in preparing this talk, that Justice Hobbs had an ex parte conversation with the Firm of Belushi, Sellers, Chase, Martin & Murray.

Tribute to Clyde O. Martz*
20th Anniversary Celebration of the University of Colorado
Natural Resources Law Center
Denver, Colorado
October 26, 2002

It's a great privilege to speak about Clyde Martz, citizen of Colorado, citizen of the United States, teacher, scholar, advocate, writer, counselor, government official, a lawyer's lawyer, a judge's lawyer, law firm partner, natural resources expert, mentor, friend, husband to Ann, a man of his times, an exemplary man, a man who has endowed those who follow him by practicing excellence in public and in private life, Clyde Martz.

Aristotle, speaking of ethics, said that three kinds of life stand out: the life of enjoyment, the life spent in public affairs, and the life of contemplation. *Ethics*, Book 1, at 289 (in Bambrough 1963, *The Philosophy of Aristotle*).

So we pass the centuries from Aristotle's birth in 384 to the life of Clyde Martz bridging the twentieth and twenty-first centuries.

We here assembled proudly claim Clyde Martz as our western kinsman, a man of optimism, practicality, contemplation, hard work, excellence, and dedication to the private and the public good. We have witnessed his enthusiasm; we have winced at the force of his critique; we have recognized the truth of his criticism and the truth of his intellect and the truth of his uncompromising belief in our ability to air our differences in community, with good will and with fortitude.

Jim Martin, Director of the Natural Resources Law Center, asked me to speak of the role Clyde Martz plays in the past, present, and future of natural resources law. I do so gladly, with that sense of historical perspective that Clyde's writings manifested from his earliest career days.

I hold up to you Clyde O. Martz, Associate Professor of Law, University of Colorado, author of *Cases and Materials on the Law of Natural Resources*, which deals with water rights and mineral rights. The opening sentence reads like the

---

* Quotes in this speech from previously published materials are reprinted by permission of Clyde O. Martz.

closing sentence of an opening and closing argument in favor of historical perspective for the respect of public and private rights in the natural resources:

> Natural Resource Law is concerned with the techniques by which private interests in the water, minerals and land of the public domain or in *publici juris* are acquired; the nature of these interests; and the common law and statutory responsibilities that individuals who exploit the resources of the country owe to others who hold like interest and to the public.

Teddy Roosevelt, the progressive conservationist, would call that a bully platform! Clyde Martz is no bully, but he knows how a good platform is made and endures, through careful analysis, respect for precedent, getting off the high horse to see if the platform really holds up to scrutiny and will support the weight of present and future community need.

Jack Little, who worked in the Interior Solicitor's Office with Clyde, recalled fondly to me this past week that he still consults his notes of Clyde's remarks in class, notes Jack made as he heard the wisdom embodied in the natural resources casebook take wing through Clyde's teachings. These teachings provided the orientation of many future practitioners and government officials who owe their love of this oh-so-special field of western endeavor to Clyde, as he moved from venue to venue in pursuit of common sense and scholarship.

I hold up to you Volume VI-A of the 1954 *American Law of Property* and its 1997 supplement, Clyde Martz addressing rights incident to possession of land and water rights. Between 1954 and 1977 there occurred significant—though not entirely satisfactory—advances in the integration of surface water and tributary groundwater in water rights law and administration.

In the 1977 supplement to the *American Law of Property*, at 1083, Clyde reiterates two great principles of United States and western water law: that (1) all non-navigable waters of the public domain became *publici juris* subject to the plenary control of the states with the right in each to determine for itself to what extent the rule of appropriation or the common law rule of riparian law for surface waters and *cujus est solum maxim* for groundwater should apply; and (2) that the patentee of land out of the public domain is entitled only to such water rights as are recognized by local customs and state laws.

Clyde observed then what the drought of 2002 has made a truism: "Increasing scarcity of water in the arid Western states, coupled with technological awareness of the hydraulic interaction between alluvium groundwaters and waters of flowing streams, has led to expanded legislative and administrative control over groundwater diversion and use."

Clyde has been particularly interested in the government's fiduciary role over the management and administration of the water resource and its protection of property rights to the use of water. Citing the Mining Act of 1866 and Article XVI, Section 5, of the Colorado Constitution, Clyde identifies a trustee responsibility for water administration. Every word of his formulation is carefully crafted on the platform of precedent and of the need to respect public and private rights and responsibilities over the conservation and use of the public's water resource:

> Colorado declared that all of the waters of natural streams are the property of the public and dedicated to public use. By such declaration with respect to waters in which it had no proprietary interest, the state assumed a trusteeship role to administer the waters of the state for the benefit of the public. As such, it became responsible not only for minimal administrative functions but also for administration of the kind a trustee owes to the beneficiary of the trust. Its responsibilities include, first and foremost, the conservation of the estate and avoidance of waste; second, the promotion of beneficial use by assisting the appropriator in achieving use objectives to the maximum extent feasible; third, the representation of beneficiaries in a *parens patriae* capacity and maintaining the use regimen on the river system; and fourth, the promotion of efficiency and prudence of the kind expected of a trustee."

Clyde O. Martz and Bennett W. Raley, "Administering Colorado's Water: A Critique of the Present Approach," in *Tradition, Innovation and Conflict: Perspectives on Colorado Water Law* 41, 42 (MacDonnell, Ed., Natural Resources Law Center, 1986).

Clyde has been persistent in criticizing Colorado for its preference for adjudication of water rights and changes of water rights over a system that would allow State Engineer Determination subject to limited Administrative Procedure Act review. *Id.* at 55-58. He calls for a regime of water management that would identify wasteful diversions and water use practices behind the headgate, with authority in the State Engineer to inspect and order an appropriate duty of water allocation to the holder and user of the water right. *Id.* at 53-54.

Clyde has been persistently critical of Colorado's groundwater law, blaming inconsistent delegation of authority and responsibility over designated groundwater, Denver Basin groundwater, and non-tributary groundwater on special interest groups and "certain self-serving legislative representatives" acting for the advantage of "a particular group of water users." *Id.* at 57.

He has written that Colorado's groundwater resources are "abundant, economically accessible, and terribly important to the long-range economic development of the state." Clyde O. Martz, "The Groundwater Resource," in *Water and the American West, Essays in Honor of Raphael J. Moses* 92 (Getches, Ed., Natural Resources Law Center, 1988). He suggests a program of optimum use to increase the development of groundwater consistent with the protection of senior water rights.

Clyde's indictment of special interest influence on water law and policy is not restricted to certain water user interests; he had choice words for what he terms the "Environmental Overreach Period":

> This period is characterized by a total subordination of natural resource development to environmental and wildlife absolutes with frightening decision making authority vested in private, politically oriented self-interest groups.

Clyde O. Martz, "Natural Resources Law: An Historical Perspective," in *Natural Resources Policy and Law, Trends and Directions* 36 (MacDonnell and Bates, Ed., Natural Resources Law Center, 1993).

Clyde urges a historical perspective in natural resource legislative, administrative, and judicial decision-making based on facts, not perception; use, not over-regulation; conservation and balance for optimum economic social and economic returns, not absolutist dogma. *Id.* at 47-48.

I hold up to you a list of 109 published case decisions in state and federal courts, including the United States Supreme Court, wherein Clyde O. Martz appeared as counsel. He has had some famous wins, for example, *Leo Sheep Company v. United States*, 440 U.S. 668 (1979) in the United States Supreme Court, and *Fellhauer v. People*, 167 Colo. 320, 447 P.2d 986 (Colo. 1968) in the Colorado Supreme Court.

Leo Sheep contains a very interesting historical account of the Railroad Acts and the checkerboard land ownership patterns of the United States retaining the even numbered sections of land while the railroad received the odd-numbered sections along the route to promote railroad construction. *Fellhauer* contains an extensive discussion of groundwater hydrology and the need for the State Engineer to adopt rules and regulations to allow groundwater pumping without injury to senior surface rights.

I think the opinions of Justice Rehnquist and Justice Groves in those cases likely reflect the scholarship and inspiration Clyde O. Martz brought to the briefs and oral arguments (John Sayre on the oral argument for Clyde in the *Fellhauer* case due to Clyde's departure for service in the United States Department of Justice). Judges like being part of the long, well-informed view.

Clyde has had some famous losses too, for example, the *United States v. District Court in and for Eagle County*, 169 Colo. 555, 458 P.2d 760 (1969) McCarran Amendment case when he was in Lyndon Johnson's Justice Department. Justice Groves held that the United States was subject to adjudication of its federal reserved water rights in Colorado courts.

Clyde also lost his amicus argument in *Southeastern Colorado Water Conservancy District v. Shelton Farms*, 187 Colo. 181, 529 P.2d 1321 (1974). Justice Groves ruled that cutting down water-loving trees couldn't be used as credit in augmentation plans. Advocacy doesn't always produce the result your client hoped for, but if you do it well, like Clyde did, you still participate in how the law continues to perform in community.

Clyde authored some notable Solicitor's Opinions when he served as President Carter's Interior Solicitor. For example, he opined that the United States had no claim for a federal appropriative water right under the Federal Land Management and Policy Act and the Taylor Grazing Act. This opinion states that federal agencies should, as a matter of policy, acquire water rights in accordance with the substantive and procedural provisions of state law, with limited exceptions. 88 I.D. 253, January 16, 1981.

Throughout his career, Clyde has viewed the public interest as serving the interests of individuals, businesses, and the community. Throughout his life, he has demonstrated excellence. That great treatise, the *American Law of Mining*, contains his work and comprehensive insight into the mining law. More significantly, the work is dedicated to him as "the one individual [who] stands out above all others." Clyde was probably embarrassed by this, as he is tonight, for humility is also one of his great virtues.

Aristotle went on to say in his work Ethics that "the good for man proves to be activity of soul in conformity with excellence...[this] requires a complete lifetime." *Ethics, id.*, at 293.

Clyde, I help to deliver the personal testimony of those assembled here and those who wish they could be here. You have lived three lives in one, the life of enjoyment, the life of public affairs, and the life of contemplation. You have excelled in the art of excellence. We your students, your colleagues, your beneficiaries, do remember, shall remember.

Persuading the Decision-Maker*
The Colorado Lawyer, Judges' Corner
September 2000

We belong to a profession that specializes in the tongue being tied to the brain, in judgment being informed by common sense and scholarship. We have the opportunity to help shape the affairs of community or to hinder them, to forward justice in the ongoing dialectic between the rights of the individual and the rights of the public or to decline any notion of responsibility except that of single-minded devotion to advancing our own careers.

This link between the tongue and the brain extends to the hand. What you write is committed to decision-makers in the expectation that it will aid in solving a problem. As you commit your thoughts to the screen or the yellow tablet, the words you find to express your research and your logic, whether drafting a pleading or a transactional document, are intended to explain, instruct, and problem-solve. You are both a translator and a guide. When you set yourself to the task of persuasive and logical presentation, your skill, your anxiety, your expectations of yourself, your client's expectations of you—all of these are at work.

Bearing the client's burden can be weighty. Sometimes it may seem you carry that weight all alone. Yet, if the joy of helping to solve the problem goes out of the work, the inevitable stress of taking responsibility for the work may translate into a seizure of fear: fear of inadequacy, fear of being wrong, fear of losing. Fear can lead to intimidating others in the mistaken belief that one might storm away those who get in the way. On the other hand, fear of not getting it as right as you can may spur that form of creative tension that leads to re-examining the initial premise, resulting in an unexpected solution.

Being either destructive or creative is common to the profession. You can be on the defensive or attack, in which case the decision-maker may start to wonder whether the sword you brandish or the flag you wave so righteously may not be a diversion for your lack of support troops and the absence of a well-conceived campaign and an ample supply train.

But here I am writing about battle when what I really want to say is, *relax!* You have many decisions to make and much strategy to consider, but you are not responsible for the final decision. Under our method of justice, the ultimate decision is not within your control; it belongs to another who must hear from

---

* Reproduced by permission of the Colorado Bar Association from Volume 29, September 2000, p. 63, © Colorado Bar Association 2004. All rights reserved.

someone else—or many someone else's—as well. It belongs to someone who has been freed from the responsibility of advocacy, so that he or she might apply professional skill, perception, and experience in making this judgment and moving on to the next.

You help the decision-maker orient to the geography of the case—law and facts and, most important, the law applied to the facts through reasoned expression. Your words are not graffiti thrown against a wall in self-indulgent display. You are drawing a trail map for others to follow who will enjoy the challenge and sights along the way. It contains a vision of where you're taking those who have committed themselves to your guidance. Call this vision the theory of your case. Use significant signposts to mark the way. Remember what it's like to be turned loose by an inexperienced guide who leaves you without a compass when the whiteout is blowing in.

You provide the structure, the framework, of the journey. You orient the decision-makers at the outset. You describe what they will see when they get to the fishing hole. You supply them with brightly-colored flies. You teach them how to read the waters.

Of course, there's another professional guide at work. She's on the opposite bank, got there by a different route, and sees the water differently. You don't want your fisher people wandering upstream or downstream without you, so you have to be effective in keeping them centered with their lines in the water. My father told me you don't catch any fish when the line is snagged up in the spool or the fishing rod is reclining comfortably against a tree.

The art of effective advocacy resides in telling a good story that strikes true and holds firm. It is about experiencing the right way to go because it makes sense from where your listeners have been, where they would like to go, and where they may go, with your help. It's about handing the responsibility over to the decision-maker to land a judgment, having located the fishing hole.

EASY ON THE WATER

>Easy on the water
>flip a fly
>so from underneath
>a graceful flight
>appears
>worth a closer look,
>no artifice must seem.
>Slap a pool
>with plated flashy spoon

>and slackened line
>only sends a school
>to scattering
>a reel's worth of winding.
>Easy on the water!

Decision-makers want to believe that what they do is important. You help them match this belief to the mirror of your case. Does it make sense? Does it track the law? Is it just?

Think well, write well, explain well. Erect the trail markers that lead the travelers along. Please don't forget that none of this is possible without the hopelessly inarticulate first draft. If you don't have one or two or three of these along the way, you've probably extinguished the emergence of some of your best work. No painter starts with the masterpiece. You have to mount the scaffold, lie on your back, stare up at the plaster and start to paint—a finger, then a toe, then the glow and the face of God.

Hone your skills of observation, your sense of humility, the confidence of your intuition, the logic of honest talk. Would you be convinced if you heard or read your argument? Don't hesitate to share it with someone who helps you see the landscape better. Ask this, let others ask this of you: If you were the decision-maker, would you be convinced that the way you have shown is the way to take? Is the way you suggest worth recording for the future guidance of others who face the problem of choosing which way to go?

Because you are writing for the decision-makers who must themselves write, you can benefit from consulting trail maps they have written. You'll find them in P.2d or F.3d or U.S. Reports. There's a little piece of explained geography on every page. I like to think about writing an opinion by considering the direction a horse takes to best. The horse goes forward best; backing up causes it to rear and buck. So write in the active voice. Don't write in the passive voice. The horse goes forward. The worst professional writing, particularly in the law, is that which obscures rather than exposes, that which exalts dogma and undermines common sense, that which speaks *ex cathedra* but lacks authority because it does not root the law and the facts to justice in the case.

Clarity and simplicity are hard won. They're born of humility and hard work. Enjoy telling your story of the case! Then leave the rest of the work to your interested listeners.

Gregory J. Hobbs, Jr. is a Justice of the Colorado Supreme Court This article is based on previous presentations to the firm of Davis, Graham & Stubbs, the Environmental Defense Fund, and the Conference of the National Association of Attorney Generals.

Book Review: *Thinking Like a Writer**
The Colorado Lawyer
December 2003

Book review of Stephen V. Armstrong and Timothy P. Terrell, *Thinking Like a Writer: A Lawyer's Guide to Writing and Editing* (New York, NY: Practicing Law Institute, 2003).

This is the writing book judges use. Lawyers who write for judges will use this book, too.

I first met Professor Tim Terrell of Emory University School of Law at the New York University new appellate judges' school in 1997. A prerequisite for attending was that every judge must have routinely published really badly written opinions, for at least a year—thinking they were really well-written.

Imagine my embarrassment on learning what the written page had done to me! (That's passive voice for not taking responsibility, a typical writing ploy of judges, advocates, and law professors. It just happened to them! Or him! Or me! Nobody knows who did it or how or why.)

It's not pretty when Professor Terrell holds your writing hand and eye to the mirror. But the result is satisfying when you start to think and look like a writer. Thinking and looking like a writer takes "Transforming western Colorado into Kansas by imposing 'super-clarity' on even the most technical convoluted material," and "Addressing your readers' needs specifically enough to make the document a sharp scalpel, not a blunt instrument, for the operation they want to perform."

I get squeamish about becoming a Kansan through elective surgery. But the point is salutary. You can lose and hurt your readers in the land of The Great Divide. Map the territory well, and they'll find their way (with your expert guidance), and thank you for the trip.

I'm going to reveal three basic secrets the authors disclose openly: (1) the law is so complex it needs your clear and concise explanation—this is what you can do best for decision-makers; (2) if your reader can't understand what you are

---

* Reproduced by permission of the Colorado Bar Association from Volume 32, December 2003, p. 60, © Colorado Bar Association 2004. All rights reserved.

saying, you probably don't understand it either; and (3) decision-makers will blame you for poor writing that wastes their time. On the other hand, control of the subject matter and its presentation lends authority to your teaching, encourages trust, and invites reliance. Let the reader know at all times where you are going, deliver on those promises by taking the reader there, and sum up the highlights of the journey.

Armstrong and Terrell will walk you through the principles and techniques of becoming a good legal writer. Clarity, organization, focus, flow, and emphasis—marshaled from the standpoint of your reader's perspective—these are the signal marks of persuasive writing. Make the structure of your presentation explicit, and deliver accordingly. When you promise that the important legal principles are three—and you discuss four, two, or who knows how many—the reader gets confused, and you look silly. When you get beyond 12 words without punctuation, you've dunked your charge into the swamp.

Lead with a punch. A carefully selected topic sentence serves, simultaneously, as rear-view mirror and full-view front window. You look both ways through them. You bridge the preceding point to the next and the next. Soon, you and your reader will pass important mile-markers together.

After you make your point simply and directly—stop. Announce the itinerary up front. Signpost the important junctions. It takes a land bridge to enter Kansas from western Colorado across The Great Divide. Detours are mess-ups. The purpose of the writer is to help the reader through the maze. Navigating side-by-side with the decision-maker, talking the theme and details of the story as you move on, is the advocate's art. Good briefs and good opinions open and close with portals to understanding. The facts, the law, the judgment to be made from applying the law to the facts—this is the way that lawyers and judges move through well-written briefs and opinions.

"Start Me Up!" shout the Rolling Stones. There's really no substitute. Because we were trained in law school, we usually start backwards. Then, because the process of straightening ourselves out is so painful, we want to dump the whole explanation—you know, how we saw the light and found the way—on the reader. The horse doesn't care how you slaved all day to bring in the hay. The horse wants to eat. But you must begin with the haying. Lay it out there, edit out the chaff, bundle it up, then hold it out. Thoroughbreds will be feeding out of your hands.

The authors of *Thinking Like a Writer: A Lawyer's Guide to Writing and Editing* teach that good legal writing has grace, vitality, and character—an energetic rhythm—that engage the reader, serve the message well, and enhance your credibility. True to promised form, at the end as in the beginning, Armstrong and Terrell summarize the steps you will take again and again in thinking like a writer. It's fun to see how privileged you and your readers are when you write well.

Swearing in New Attorneys
October 20, 2003

I write this on a day I have the privilege—with six colleagues of the Colorado Supreme Court—to preside over the swearing in of new Colorado attorneys. A day of celebration, all the hard work and worry ends with commencement, the starting forth.

These new lawyers join a stressed and stressful profession, in community, to serve their fellow citizens who desperately need wise and affordable counsel. The profession of Jefferson and Lincoln is a call to serve, with scholarship and common sense, the workings of justice—incident by incident, matter by matter, case by case, in community.

Every generation has an opportunity for renewal. The great idea of progress in history is to share with friends and strangers, at the scarce and genuine watering hole, the drinking gourd of justice—a sip at a time.

Renewal stems from realizing one's time and place through every pursuit men and women have the opportunity to undertake. In a just society, renewal often arises from a pack of lies set straight by conflict, dialogue, understanding, and informed decision making.

We become holders in due course of the commitment our ancestors made to us when we negotiate in good faith—when we wake up in the morning to the land that Black Elk, a Native American, recalls when he intones this powerful message-song:

> A thunder being nation I am, I have said.
> A thunder being nation I am, I have said.
> You shall live.
> You shall live.
> You shall live.
> You shall live.
>
> John G. Neihardt, *Black Elk Speaks: Being the Life Story of a Holy Man of the Oglala Sioux* at 258 (1932).

In this time and place we together share, our powerful blessings include the First Amendment—that delicious, ribald fruit of the most awful tyrannies humans have experienced. Our heritage is the separation of church and state and the diverse speaking of tongues devoted to community decision making.

History, poetry, legislating, judging—these, together with every other endeavor—teach this: we must practice the discipline of reflective remembering and the skill of responsible speaking.

As a Justice, I have the privilege of public speaking and writing. Fellow citizens often call upon me to keynote their conference, or celebrate their marriage, or write about the law, history, and ethics.

As an ode lends itself, I find that praise comes closer to hitting the mark as a motivator that is far more powerful than fear. Optimism is a trait of westerners, born of a sudden storm and a clearing sky that are frequently visible at the same time.

The tables we turn best are the ones we wait upon and sit around. Humility comes of learning just how hard it is to remember to thank those who make, in any way, our day possible.

TABLES

Praise
to the person who assembles the
table from cherry oak and maple
who lend their hearts and grain,
                      praise be.

Praise
to the person who sets the table,
serves the food, who cleans and
sweeps and puts away utensils,
                      praise be.

> Praise
> to the person who joins discourse
> round the table, who listens patient
> for reply of elders, children, guests,
> > praise be.
>
> Praise
> to the person who spreads upon
> the table paper pen and book, who
> place enacts contemplation's nook,
> > praise be.
>
> Praise
> to the person who may decide the
> table's extension, who re-chooses
> each and every for an honored seat.
> > praise be.

Self-governance has a long and contemporary history. It occurs whenever men and women forge conflict into resolution, struggle against the land into living within it and with each other, respectfully.

POLIS

"Polis" is an ancient word for self-governed community.

The Greek City State,

The Greeley Colony,

Family, girl or boy scout troop, farm lot, schoolroom, athletic field, feed lot, bank board, water board, trout pool, the open range,

Plains or mountain campfire.

A time and place for gathering round a source of light and warmth and dinner sizzle-cooked of fish filet or rib aroma on the wind,

For gathering round the bard, the story-teller, the gentle politician—
motivator, statesman, prophet—

He or she who stirs glowing embers for the sparks to rise,
as though ascending fireflies

Are winging to all degrees and possibilities
a compass may point to.

Ideas born of campfires are glimmering fireflies,

To stir them really good for wing-taking takes some really good Heartwood, a firm
and kindly touch, visions that stir in the heart

So to part the dark, so we might see on through the shadows
confidently—whomever's heart we may touch.

Congratulations to my law clerks this year, Nikki Patterick and Joslyn Wilschek, in joining this momentous profession. May you praise this day many years in the future, and keep your fires burning!

Fishing
   and the
   Supreme Court

OUT THE WINDOW

Some days I look
out the window
and get nothing done
but the looking,

I see the bird lady
feeding pigeons
in Civic Center Park,
I see citizens waving

Multi-colored signs
at the Capitol
or at each other,
I see the naked trees

And when their raiment's full,
growing in the open space
between the monuments,
I see the southern end

Of Rocky Mountain Park,
and all the while I dream
of hiking trips
through the streets

To the Confluence,
to Wild Basin,
to Streams
I cannot see.

**Fishing and the Supreme Court—
Making the Transition from Private Practice***
The Colorado Lawyer, Judges' Corner
December 1996

I appreciate the invitation to write about the transition from law practice to the Colorado Supreme Court. I am thankful for the 25 years of lawyering that preceded my first day with the Court: 18 years in private practice, four years with the Colorado Attorney General's Office, two years with the United States Environmental Protection Agency, and one year as law clerk to Tenth Circuit Judge William E. Doyle. I am very pleased to be serving the people of the State of Colorado once again.

The well-wishing and the expectations that accompanied my nomination by the citizen commission, and appointment by Governor Roy Romer, will long sing in my ears:

I STAND TO THE WATERFALL

>I stand to the waterfall
>your hope outpours.
>I am bathed
>
>Your voices roaring wet
>rainbow ferns. I
>feel like
>
>Dancing.

Thank you. I expect to earn your confidence. Colorado judges—Municipal, County, District, Court of Appeals, Supreme Court—I've always admired them. I'm glad to continue my career by joining them.

Each morning I pass a photograph of Judge Doyle on the way to my new office. He served on the Colorado Supreme Court in the early 1960s when I was

---

* Reproduced by permission of the Colorado Bar Association from Volume 25, December 1996, p. 31, © Colorado Bar Association 2004. All rights reserved.

in high school (wish he'd been alive to share the joy of my swearing-in day). I greet my three law clerks, look southwest to the glorious spine of the continent, and settle down in front of my Gateway 2000 computer.

> The phone almost never rings.
> I don't get any faxes.
> I've got no clients.
> The unending supply of Oreo cookies
> stocked by the Office Manager—
>
> Gone!
>
> At least I'm familiar with the Gateway 2000.
> Legal argument and lawyering.
> I've briefed and argued cases before every one of my six new colleagues.
> I can stock the Oreos!
>
> I am welcomed warmly.

The Court is holding oral arguments my first day, May 1, 1996. We hear six cases. Each justice has read every brief in preparation for hearing oral argument, as well as the certiorari memorandum which was prepared by the assigned justice and law clerk when the court was considering whether to review a Court of Appeals decision in whole or part.

The interchange during oral argument between Court and counsel is very active. Each justice has a vote and comment sheet with the briefs on the bench. Long sharpened pencils with erasers are provided and utilized. Lawyers have a very important role to play in the outcome of the case.

You listen to the questions asked by the other justices. Answers are given. You gain a sense of the geography of the case. Insurance, contracts, torts, crimes, sovereign immunity, family law, and water. "Egad!" (as Judge Doyle used to say). This is the general practice of law and it's fascinating.

In conference, just before lunch, we vote on the three morning cases. The Chief Justice calls on me to recite how the case should be decided and why. Around the table, junior to senior, each justice has his or her say. The Chief recites last, then assigns the drafting of a proposed majority opinion to one of the six, or himself.

The afternoon proceeds in the same way. We hear 35 cases in six days. The Chief is fairly even in distributing the work. Each of us receives five opinions to draft. This will happen again in three months.

I learn that proposed opinions must be circulated by 5:00 p.m. on a Thursday. The protocol of the Court calls for each proposed opinion to reflect a thorough reading of the record and the applicable cases. Each proposal is to be of a quality suitable for future deliberation. A special concurrence or dissent, if any, is due by 5:00 p.m. on Tuesday. The final vote on the case occurs on Thursday morning at the weekly decisional conference.

Between Thursday and Thursday, the authoring justice visits with other justices who have questions or suggestions about a proposed opinion. The discussion is rigorous and collegial. Changes may be made in the proposed majority, concurring, or dissenting opinions, or the authoring justice may decide to adhere to the proposal and see how the final vote turns out at conference. A dissent may capture the majority and become the opinion of the Court, or be withdrawn.

Any justice, including the authoring justice, may request that a proposed opinion be passed until the next conference for further consideration. As a result of the consultation process of the Court, an announced opinion may have been revised three or more times by the authoring justice before its adoption and release by the Court.

In Thursday conference we also consider and vote, junior to senior, on cases submitted on the briefs, original petitions, grievances, certiorari petitions, civil and criminal rule changes, motions, and matters involving governance of the Judicial Branch of Colorado government. It's a mountain of reading. Assignments for written opinions on these matters and the other work of the Court are made by the Chief, adding to those assignments from cases submitted on oral argument.

The decision to review a court of appeals decision is guided by Appellate Rule 49 and is based upon the memorandum prepared in random rotation by the assigned justice and law clerk, who make a recommendation to the full court. Since receiving a matter on certiorari is within the sound discretion of the court, which issue or issues to take, if any, turns upon the apparent significance of the matters raised by the cert petition and how the Court of Appeals addressed them. Three votes are necessary to grant the taking of an issue.

We go to lunch after the Thursday conference, so the tough and sometimes divisive work of the day can be followed by respectful camaraderie.

The opinions of the Court are announced on Monday. Modifications to opinions may or may not be made, based on rehearing petitions, at the next conference. On Friday we turn to the next batch of proposed opinions submitted by the other chambers, and we continue to write on our own assignments.

The intellectual joy of a fine lawyerly discussion with partners and associates at a law firm is the best way I can describe what goes on between the justices, and between a justice and his or her law clerks. As with new colleagues in a law firm, mentoring of the law clerks is important to the work of the court and their professional development and satisfaction. (Thank you, Judge Doyle.)

What's really different from law practice is having a vote. At least four of us must agree. We must explain the result to those who bring each case and to the people of Colorado. We are yoked together, week by week, each of us attuned to every matter that comes before the Court. What an investment the people of Colorado have made in commanding this much resource to individual matters.

We realize we likely are the final opportunity for justice in the case. Reaching the right result for the right reason is a continuing and humbling effort.

Most satisfying is to author an opinion of the Court. It's like pulling a native trout from the stream, holding it up to the light for a snapshot, releasing it back to the stream, walking upriver to the next pool hearing the waters sing.

POOL

What about a pool
attracts? Peace of it,
danger of falling in,
bugs?

A pool looks back,
You see your self
within, above,
behind...

You desire rocks to throw
you think you see a fish,
cloud fleet passes
over you...you Disappear.

The waters look different in every case. I'm thinking that the art of judicial practice must include a feel for the interplay between past case experience and the current live one. Good legal writing is hard work. An apparent distinction from law practice is more time for this kind of reflective fishing between phone calls.

Greg Hobbs is a graduate of Boalt Hall, University of California Berkeley (J.D., 1971) and the University of Notre Dame (B.A. History, 1966). He practiced water and environmental law before his appointment to the Colorado Supreme Court on April 18, 1996, including as a shareholder of Hobbs, Trout & Raley, P.C. and a partner of Davis, Graham & Stubbs.

Protocols of the Colorado Supreme Court*
The Colorado Lawyer
March 1998 (updated here as of publication)

Note: A 1982 article by Justice William H. Erickson summarizes the Supreme Court's internal operating procedures as they then existed [see 11 *The Colorado Lawyer* 356 (Feb. 1982)]. A 1996 article describes the workings of the court from a new justice's perspective [see 25 *The Colorado Lawyer* 31 (Dec. 1996)]. This article, which first appeared in the Judges' Corner feature of *The Colorado Lawyer*, summarizes protocols of the current court (the periodically updated text of this article appears on the Colorado Supreme Court Homepage at www.courts.state.co.us/supct/supct.htm).

Membership of the Court

The current members of the Colorado Supreme Court are Chief Justice Mary J. Mullarkey; Justice Rebecca Love Kourlis; Justice Gregory J. Hobbs, Jr.; Justice Alex J. Martinez; Justice Michael L. Bender; Justice Nancy E. Rice; and Justice Nathan "Ben" Coats.

The Role of the Chief Justice and Staff to the Justices

The Chief Justice is the executive head of the Colorado Judicial Branch and is the leader in its administration. The State Court Administrator, who is appointed by the court, reports directly to the Chief Justice and oversees an administrative staff.

The Chief Justice is elected by the justices and serves at the pleasure of the court. In addition to administrative responsibility for the entire court system, the Chief Justice presides over all conferences, oral arguments, and hearings of the court; assigns all opinions for authorship; and designates in consultation with the court which justice or justices shall serve as liaison to the various committees and special committees of the court. These committees include the Commission on Families in the Colorado Courts, Civil and Appellate Rules Committees, Criminal Rules Committee, Attorney Regulation Advisory Committee, Board of Law Examiners, Gender and Justice Committee, Access to Justice Commission, and Judicial Advisory Council, among others.

---

* Reproduced by permission of the Colorado Bar Association from Volume 27, March 1998, p. 21, © Colorado Bar Association 2004. All rights reserved.

The Chief Justice has authority, in consultation with the full court, to issue Chief Justice Directives pertaining to matters of judicial administration.

The court works collegially. During the typical week, there is much visitation and informal discussion among the justices on all matters pending for decision. Each justice has three full-time positions: two law clerks and a judicial assistant.

Each chambers has a personal computer for each justice and employee. The computers are networked to tie the seven chambers and the Clerk's office together. The Supreme Court Library is available to the judiciary, the legal profession, and the public for legal research. In addition, the judiciary has a master contract for electronic research.

The court uses the Supreme Court home page to post matters of interest to the public and the bar on the Internet, such as rule changes, Chief Justice Directives, certiorari grant or denial announcements, and opinions of the court (www.courts.state.co.us/supct/supct.htm). On Fridays from September through June, the Web page contains an announcement of the names of the cases for which opinions will be issued the following Monday morning.

Case Decisions and Other Matters

Approximately 64 percent of the court's caseload represents appeals from the Colorado Court of Appeals. The court receives and reviews nearly 900 certiorari petitions each year concerning decisions rendered by the Court of Appeals. The court has no set number of certiorari petitions it will grant, but generally averages a grant of approximately one out of 14 certiorari petitions. Under C.A.R. 50, the court may grant certiorari in a case that is pending but has not gone to decision in the Court of Appeals. This power is rarely exercised.

The court also reviews original proceeding petitions under C.A.R. 21; petitions for *habeas corpus* review; interlocutory appeals by the prosecution from suppression orders in criminal cases; ballot title submissions; attorney discipline cases; certified questions from the federal courts; and direct appeals, such as water cases, Public Utility Commission cases, and capital punishment cases that bypass the Court of Appeals by law. In FY 2003, the court issued 84 opinions, all published. In addition, the court disposed of 1,354 other matters, primarily through denial of certiorari and Rule 21 petitions.

Oral Argument and Case Assignment

The court has a 12-month work year. However, during July and August, the court does not hold weekly conferences or issue opinions. During this time, the justices write proposed opinions they have not yet presented to the court for review; attend educational conferences; take their vacations; and vote by written vote sheet on pending certiorari petitions and original proceedings. From September to June, except during a two-week Christmas break and in the midst of oral argument, the justices meet each Thursday in conference to decide all pending matters that are ready for vote.

Oral arguments are held approximately seven times a year for two or three days during the period of September through June. Oral arguments are open to the public. The Chief Justice makes opinion-drafting assignments based on the preliminary vote in the case, which is taken after the oral arguments in the morning and, again, when the afternoon arguments have been concluded.

The court sits *en banc*. Four votes are required to decide any matter coming before the court, except for the grant of a certiorari petition, which requires three votes.

Twice a year the court convenes at a high school for oral argument in two cases. Members of the bar association meet with teachers to help prepare the students in advance for the arguments they will witness. Justices return after oral argument to answer questions, except questions concerning the merits of the cases just argued or other matters pending for decision before the court.

Thursday Decisional Conference

The court's weekly decisional conference (September through June) is called to order at 9:00 a.m. each Thursday morning. Each justice is expected to attend or, if absent, must leave a vote sheet for all pending matters ready for decision. The Chief Justice presides and votes are taken, proceeding from junior to senior justice, with the Chief Justice voting last. When rendering the vote, each justice recites his or her reasons therefore. Any justice may request a matter to be passed to the next conference for a vote, and the present conference may be used for discussion of the case instead. Passing a matter is a courtesy asked by one justice of the others; a justice's request to pass the case for vote at a future conference is always honored.

The order of business at the Thursday conference is as follows: proposed opinions; petitions for rehearing on issued opinions; voting on, and assignment for opinion, of cases submitted on the briefs without oral argument; certiorari petitions; original proceedings requesting a Rule to Show Cause; attorney discipline cases for assignment and preparation of an opinion; and administrative matters, including rule changes and any other matter concerning governance of the court or the Judicial Branch. Sometimes, the court acts to dismiss a matter as "improvidently granted" because the court, on reflection, determines not to issue an opinion in the matter and to let the lower court decision stand.

Decisions of the court on cases and certiorari petitions are announced the Monday following the Thursday decisional conference by means of an announcement sheet and issued opinions, all of which are made available at the Clerk's Office in hard copy. While the full text of opinions is posted on the Web site on Mondays, the case numbers and case captions of opinions to be issued on Mondays are posted the preceding Friday. The newly issued announcements and opinions are available on the Internet at the Supreme Court's home page, www.courts.state.co.us/supct/supct.htm, and the Colorado Bar Association home page, www.cobar.org/coappcts/scndx.htm.

Ad Hoc Conferences on Original Petitions/Duty Judge

Original petitions under C.A.R. 21 are assigned to each of the seven chambers in rotation by the Clerk of the Court. The assigned justice reports on the matter, with his or her recommendation, at the regular Thursday decisional conference, by internal e-mail communication to all of the other justices, or a justice may call an in-person ad hoc conference of the court if the petition merits immediate action. At least four justices must agree in order to take a Rule 21 matter. An individual justice may issue a short-term stay or other temporary order pending the court's decision on the petition.

There is a monthly Duty Judge assigned by the Chief Justice, in rotation, to rule on matters brought to that justice by the Clerk of the Court, such as motions for *amicus curiae* appearance, extensions of time, or extended-page briefing. The Duty Judge may act on any matter requiring immediate attention when the other justices are not available.

Certiorari Petitions

Based on the briefs and issues raised and the guidelines set forth in C.A.R. 49, approximately half of the certiorari petitions for circulation and decision go to the seven justices without preparation of a certiorari memorandum ("non-memo certs"). Each justice reviews the Court of Appeals decision (whether published or not published), together with the certiorari petition and any response thereto, and may request preparation of a certiorari memorandum before a vote is taken. The justices vote on these non-memo cert petitions by means of vote sheets maintained in the Clerk's Office.

The other certiorari petitions and those extracted from non-memo consideration by any justice are delivered in random rotation by the Clerk of the Court, Susan Festag, to the seven chambers. The assigned justice in turn assigns a law clerk to prepare a certiorari memorandum on the case. The assigned justice reviews the certiorari petition, any response thereto, and the memorandum, makes any desired change to the memorandum, and circulates the memorandum and the Court of Appeals opinion to the other six justices, noting on the face of the memorandum the recommendation of the assigned justice regarding which issues, if any, should be taken on certiorari.

Votes of three justices are required to grant any issue by way of certiorari. When certiorari is granted on one or more issues in a case, the certiorari memorandum usually serves as the bench memorandum for oral argument. Pending certiorari petitions are decided at the weekly Thursday decisional conference, except during July and August when each justice's vote is entered on a written vote sheet kept in the Clerk's Office.

Proposed Opinions

Proposed majority opinions must be circulated by the authoring justice to the other six justices by 5:00 p.m. Thursday. Any justice has until the following Tuesday at 5:00 p.m. to propose a written concurrence or dissent. Generally, before a justice presents a concurrence at a decisional vote conference, that justice confers with the authoring justice regarding potential revisions in the proposed majority opinion to accommodate the concurring view, if possible. The vote on the proposed majority opinion and concurring or dissenting opinions, if any, occurs on the following Thursday. Any justice, including the authoring justice, may request that the vote be passed to the next week's conference in favor of a discussion of the matter at the pending conference, or because the justice needs more time to consider the matter or to write a concurring or dissenting opinion.

A justice may determine not to participate in an opinion, under the Code of Judicial Conduct, for a conflict or the appearance of a conflict. An opinion or order of the court will identify any justice who is not participating.

Each justice works to review the proposed opinions of the other justices as a first priority in dealing with pending work. When disagreement between justices occurs on any matter, it is becoming the practice that the justices will confer concerning the disagreement, to the extent possible, before conference. Every change to a proposed opinion must be circulated to the other six chambers.

A majority opinion that has received at least four votes at the weekly decisional conference is prepared in final slip opinion form, together with any concurring or dissenting opinion, by Friday noon. The authoring justice's law clerk or judicial assistant is responsible for copying and assembling the required copies for the Clerk's Office by Friday noon for distribution upon announcement Monday morning. Each issued opinion is accompanied by a cover page synopsis of the case prepared by the authoring justice.

Governance of the Judicial Department/Community Outreach

The court is responsible for governance of the Judicial Department, and each justice is active, by assignment by the court, on various committees and in bar association activities. In addition, each justice engages in discretionary community activities subject to the Judicial Canons. All members of the court are engaged in educational activities of their choosing.

Conclusion

The court's work lies not only in deciding cases, but also in the overall administration of justice and the judicial system in Colorado. Each justice plays a direct role in all decisions of the court, unless the justice has determined that he or she should not participate in a proceeding because of the standards set forth in Canon 3(C) of the Code of Judicial Conduct.

May Day Anniversary: On Being an Imminent Jurist*
The Colorado Lawyer, Judges' Corner
September 2001

On May 1, 2001, I celebrated my fifth anniversary in the judicial corner. I have several refractions regarding this experience, which I dislike unburdening you with.

Imminent Jurist

In an article in the June 2001 issue of *The Colorado Lawyer* praising John Sayre, Brooke Wunnicke (who after a long career with the District Attorney and a prominent 17th Street law firm now refers to herself as a "girl reporter") recused me of being an "eminent jurist." I thank her for thinking I am jurist trying to do my best.

Brooke's encouragement is like my father's. He often said to me, "Just pretend you are jurist trying to do your best"; also, "You gave it a lick and a promise." I have applied these compliments in choosing dogs as lifetime companions that died every thirteen years.

Sitting Softly

I should tell you that being on the bench is not as hard as you might think. Although the lawyers can't see over the elevated hardwood that separates them from us, I like to dissemble to them in appellate practice seminars for CLE credit that we actually sit softly on their cases. Some of us bring in a cushion or two, so we can be ready for oral arguments and overlook the hardwood for the time clock.

The Chief Justice is in charge of the time clock. Each attorney must stop in mid-thought when his or her time runs out. This is an important point in each attorney's life, so I consider lawyer last words to be valuable in deciding how to vote.

Lawyer Last Words

Some of the most profound revelations I've misperceived as an imminent jurist are lawyer last words. For example, this one from a tortious attorney, who whispered with a sort of a moan: "negligence." Timely insight! I too had discovered while eating at La Fiesta the day before that prudence is not often modeled in the back 30 pages of *Westword*.

---

* Reproduced by permission of the Colorado Bar Association from Volume 30, September 2001, p. 61, © Colorado Bar Association 2004. All rights reserved.

Another memorable lawyer last word occurred when a ligation specialist blurted out, "Fifty-nine!" just as the Chief Justice was cutting him off. Rightfully so! I considered his remark rude. I was humbled to learn later that he was referring to post-trial relief. I didn't realize there was any such thing. One of my law clerks, having studied at Harvard Law School with several of their prominent columnists, pointed out my ignorance—which I promptly utilized in several subsequent opinions.

Northern Exposure

As an imminent jurist for five years, I have differentiated the diffidence the common law distinguishes to a statue. This appeared because I moved from the south side of the State Court Judicial Building to the north side. Based on seniority from the north, I see the space between the City and County Building and the State Capitol. A whole lot of things get in between: a pointed obelisk, the Ten Commandments, the Liberty Bell, pigeons, people, and police cars following them on the grass at a respectful distance of five to ten feet. In America, we hold our statues in common. Dopey and his six colleagues stand on a pedestal high above a corporate headquarters in L.A.

Poetic License

One of the benefits of being an imminent jurist is being poetry-slammed. The Rocky Mountain News and the Denver Post periodically produce "poetry slams" in their Saturday editions. A columnist applauded Governor Romer's departure from office for appointing "poets" and "Peace Corps Volunteers" to the Colorado Supreme Court. As an imminent jurist, unable to respond to the press, I unnaturally took no offense to this remark because of resume resemblance.

The First Amendment grants the media poetic license to use strict construction of statues as a cannon.

Thank You

I am looking forward to the next five years of being an imminent jurist. I thank Governor Romer for sending me back to school to discontinue miscorrecting my malaprops. He disliked pedestals. I hope the L.A. schools aren't prepared for him.

> Talk about a fix,
> Dopey and the Six
> have feet of stone,

Can't speak or write
about their differences
or hear what others say,

Can't see the difference
between a wrong and
bending to a better way.

Greg Hobbs is a Justice of the Colorado Supreme Court. His first "Judges' Corner" article, on transition from private practice to the bench, appeared in the December 1996 issue of The Colorado Lawyer. Five years later, adopting the tongue-in-cheek style of the Denver Bar Association's Annual April 1st issue of The Docket, he offers some injudicious thoughts on being an imminent jurist.

Two of a Piece*
The Colorado Lawyer, Judges' Corner
April 2003

Lawyers and judges are literate people. They master words and their nuances. They explain the law and justice clearly and concisely to decision makers and the community.

Until they start writing! Then the glop plops back on the page.

When this happens to me—like every time I start to write—I try to re-convince myself, "I can do this!" "Back to the basics," I remind myself. "Two of a piece, sound and sense."

I think being a good writer takes being a good sign reader and a good mapmaker. Words are signs we post to map the understanding we have assimilated for the purpose of mapping others to a better understanding. Good brief or opinion writing is hard work. And great fun. The fun's in looking back at the path you smoothed through the swamp.

Sound and sense, sign reading and mapmaking, two of a piece.

The Privilege of Being a Sign Reader

Words will leave imprints on the blank page, like snow prints in the forest a woodsman can make in stamping out the way. Whether for pleasing and intelligent effect is for the reader to test when trying to follow along. Words leave echoes.

At the start of a connecting thought, listen for associations to what has come before. The strap of the boot to the walking device makes the meaning of the next step possible. To go the distance, your reader will need the feel of a clean and comfortable fit.

---

* Reproduced by permission of the Colorado Bar Association from Volume 32, April 2003, p. 39, © Colorado Bar Association 2004. All rights reserved.

Shelter your charge from a fester of blisters. Let the rub of your encounter—raw with the cluster of confusing possibilities—be your own secret. Progressive friction hews to the true of the argument's steady progress.

Pack your knapsack with no-doze snacks. Ideas are power bars—nuts to crack, reasons to chew on. Ration them well. Loose your reader to the well of discovery that community well-being imparts to the law.

Justice is not a vaporous ideal. It's the thirst for searching out the water hole. To smell the oasis and then, unerringly, to humble on the path that leads some other there—and they to others. There's the privilege in the discipline of being a sign reader.

MUSTER

> Muster scholarship and common sense,
> the law finds its way in the work of cyclical illumination,
> let your flashlight shine, then convey it away.
> Be the herald of a natural light.
> In the night and day episodes of cause and effect,
> in re-sorting the risk of retrying the why,
> retie the binding that worthies the journey.

Mapping the Way, Notes to Law Clerks and Brief Writers

I prepared the following notes to assist in the orientation of new law clerks. I hope brief writers will find something of note here also.

Welcome! I look forward to working with you.

You have entered a community of service to the people of Colorado. In the time we have together, let's do the very best research, analysis, thinking, and writing we can. I expect your loyalty to the exercise of common sense and the articulation of good judgments.

Opinion writing is our primary obligation and privilege.[1] The other two branches of government need not explain their decisions. We must. We do so publicly. Opinions of the court are governance instruments. They should reflect scholarship and community experience.

The published opinion must reflect the landscape of the case—its story (the operative facts), its fishing hole (the law), and its catch (the law applied to the facts resulting in the holding).

At the opinion's outset is a trailhead announcement, an introduction that contains a short statement of the following:

> Where we've been,
> Where we're going,
> Where we are.

From this roadmap, the opinion proceeds and varies not from it. Signposts appear at critical junctions. Horses and hikers move forward. No surprises. Here's where we've been. Here's where we're going. Here's where we are. Vision, revision, judgment.

The opinion has three parts that follow its trailhead announcement:
    I. Facts and Procedural History;
    II. Statement of the holding, followed by exposition of
        A. The procedural and substantive law applicable to the case,
        B. Discussion of the facts, law, and judgment of the case;
    III. The court's order disposing of the case.

Easy Strides

Clarity begins immediately and never ceases—active tense, active sense. Topic sentences at the beginning of each paragraph look backward/look forward. They are the glue; they hold your teachings between. Read the topic sentences front to back. Your travelogue's in them. Do they stand for linked understanding?

Good writing is good thinking, good execution. The fox continuously re-walks her territory. The English language lends itself to this: No Cigar Spit.

EASY STRIDES

> To write in legal simple
> is most difficult,
> bad legal writing
> is cigar spit,

> Break the congealment
> into chunks and cores,
> let the reader breathe
> naturally, pose, repose
>
> Experience: Here's where
> we've been, Here's where
> we're going, Here we are!
> Vision, Revision, Judgment.
>
> The fox continually re-walks
> her territory, nose to the wind,
> ear to the ground, alert to
> purpose, easy strides.

Chunks and Cores

You don't want your reader flopping on glop. More than eight to twelve words, unpunctuated, is a swamp. You'll lose your company. The reader's eye and the writer's idea should coincide. The object is understanding. You are an educator, a storyteller.

A storyteller walks the reader through the up and down to the trail's ending. The pace you set varies. At the core of every sentence is the principal thought. Appendages to the core—the "chunks"—are arms and legs; they must have utility. Rhythm helps the body dance.

Good judgments do not dwell in ether. They are windows on Colorado's experience. To serve as precedent, published judgments must walk off from you on their own: strong, confident, and coherent.

JUST DESSERTS

> Judges enjoy the last word
> by keeping their mouths shut
> after their judgments are in.
> Whether it's a good judgment

> Does not depend on who says
> what about them, but whether
> they speak experience accurately.
> Peoples and principles are Wilderness—
>
> Shaped. Holding court's a session
> in dutch-oven cooking, citizens stir
> ingredients, what they do, what they say.
> Just desserts merit savoring.

You're going to enjoy this work, so let's begin working through it together.[2] Welcome!

NOTES

[1] Thanks to Professor Tim Terrell of Emory University for his short course to the Justices of the Colorado Supreme Court, entitled *Judicial Opinion Writing: Beyond Logic to Coherence and Strength* (April 2002).

[2] For an opinion that's mapped like this, see *Stewart v. Rice*, 47 P.3d 316 (2002).

State Water Politics Versus an Independent Judiciary: The Colorado and Idaho Experiences†

University of Denver Water Law Review, reprinted with permission
Fall 2001

I. INTRODUCTION

A great privilege of being a state supreme court justice is the opportunity to author an important water opinion. It could also be one's last important opinion. Especially if the case involves a close, split decision of your court and you are up for reelection in a contested race.

In May of 2000, Justice Cathy Silak lost reelection to the Idaho Supreme Court. In November of 1954, Chief Justice Mortimer Stone lost reelection to the Colorado Supreme Court. The unifying element of both defeats: each justice authored a decision with a one-vote-margin in favor of the United States in a highly contested water case.

Chief Justice Stone's four-to-three opinion held that the downstream Colorado-Big Thompson Reclamation Project of the Bureau of Reclamation on the Blue River had storage rights and direct flow hydropower rights senior to the Denver Water Board's upstream municipal diversions on the same river.[1] Justice Silak's three-to-two opinion held that congressional designation of three downstream Idaho wilderness areas included federal reserved water rights with seniority over upstream agricultural, municipal, and commercial diversions.[2]

---

† 5 U. DENV. WATER L. REV. 122 (2001). © University of Denver Water Law Review 2001.
Justice Hobbs was appointed by Governor Roy Romer to the Colorado Supreme Court on April 18, 1996, and was retained for a ten-year term by the Colorado voters in November of 1998. He has an A.B. in History from the University of Notre Dame. After graduation with a J.D. from Boalt Hall, University of California, Berkeley, in 1971, he served as law clerk to Tenth Circuit Judge William E. Doyle, then practiced as an EPA enforcement attorney for two years and a Colorado Assistant Attorney General for four years. He was a partner with the law firms of Davis, Graham & Stubbs, as well as Hobbs, Trout & Raley before becoming a justice. For the 17 years of his private practice, he represented the Northern Colorado Water Conservancy District, among other water, environmental, land use, and transportation clients. While in private practice, he represented the Colorado Water Congress in the wilderness water rights litigation in Colorado federal courts on behalf of water interests opposing the Sierra Club's assertions that wilderness area designation creates implied reserved water rights.

[1] *See City and County of Denver v. N. Colo. Water Conservancy Dist.*, 276 P.2d 992 (Colo. 1954).
[2] *See In re SRBA*, No. 24546, 1999 Idaho LEXIS 119, at *1 (Idaho Oct. 1, 1999), *superseded on rehearing by Potlatch Corp. v. United States*, 12 P.3d 1260 (Idaho 2000).

In both instances, Colorado and Idaho state law provided for contested elections of supreme court justices.[3] During the campaigns, media attention focused on assertions that the decision would deprive present and future state water users who depended on upstream sources of supply of water. While it does not appear that the litigating parties or their attorneys orchestrated public reaction to the court decisions, the cases were still pending before the two supreme courts as the judicial election contests unfolded. Underlying the press reports on the rehearing petitions were the suggestions that the pending election might lead the authoring justice to reconsider, the concurring justices to reconsider, or that defeat of the authoring justice would bring in a new justice favorable to reversing the one vote outcome of the case. This situation created speculation that politics might have motivated the court's original decisions, and any reconsideration of them. In both instances, the justices authoring the majority decisions overwhelmingly lost reelection. Their opponents assumed office under a cloud of partisan controversy.

In the case of Justice Silak, the court granted a rehearing in which a member of the court's initial majority switched her vote, so that the dissenting position became the majority. Justice Silak voted for rehearing, but on rehearing maintained her earlier position and became the author of a two member dissent. The court announced its new decision reversing the old, while she was serving out her term.

It appears from the press attention in both decisions, and to the election races following them, that each justice lost largely because of one opinion they authored, despite the many they were responsible for during their judicial service. Many members of the bar held each justice in high regard for his and her prior judicial performance. Nevertheless, given the initial outcry over the decisions, the public reaction took on a life of its own, eclipsing the merits of both the besieged justices and the justices' opponents.

The Colorado and Idaho experiences, forty-five years apart, invoke the ability and commitment of the western states to provide fair state proceedings in the ongoing McCarran Amendment[4] adjudications. State commitment to fair judicial proceedings underpins the exercise of jurisdiction under the McCarran Amendment. Through this amendment, Congress waived the sovereign immunity of the United States to suit in state court for determination of federal agency and tribal water rights claims. This article first addresses the landscape of the McCarran proceedings and the intersection of state water politics as viewed through the

---

[3] In 1966, Colorado voters approved a constitutional amendment requiring the Governor to appoint judges and justices from a list of two or three nominees forwarded by the nominating commissions. The appointed judge or justice serves for two years before standing at the next general election for retention, on a yes or no basis, for a specified term of years. COLO. CONST. art. VI, §§ 20, 24, 25.

[4] 43 U.S.C. § 666 (1994).

Colorado and Idaho experiences. These experiences illustrate the need for state judiciaries, the water bar, and state officials to recommit to maintain the appearance and the reality of fairness in state water proceedings for all parties, regardless of whether their claims are based on state or federal law.

II. The McCarran Landscape

ASK ME

Some time when the river is ice ask me
mistakes I have made. Ask me whether
what I have done is my life. Others
have come in their slow way into
my thought, and some have tried to help
or to hurt: ask me what difference
their strongest love or hate has made.

I will listen to what you say.
You and I can turn and look
at the silent river and wait. We know
the current is there, hidden; and there
are comings and goings from miles away
that hold the stillness exactly before us.
What the river says, that is what I say.

William Stafford[5]

A. Creation of Use Rights in Water, A Public Resource

Congress carved the states west of the continental divide out of the public domain from lands it acquired through the 1803 Louisiana Purchase, the 1846 Oregon Compromise, and the 1848 Treaty of Guadalupe Hidalgo.[6] While the discovery of gold and silver jump-started the entire region's settlement, public land and water have been the most enduring treasures of the West, along with its magnificent

---

[5] William Stafford, *Ask Me, in* The Way It Is: New and Selected Poems by William Stafford 56 (1998).
[6] Loren L. Mall, Public Land and Mining Law 7-8 (3d ed. 1981).

landforms and vistas. Reducing public land and water to possession and ownership has been a preoccupation of state and territorial law from the outset.[7]

Congress created wealth in the western states by making the public land and water available for ownership and use. The Homestead Act of 1862,[8] the Railroad Acts of 1862 and 1864,[9] and other significant statutes resulted in the disposition of two-thirds of the West's surface acreage into state and private ownership.[10] The other one-third remains in federal ownership,[11] principally comprised of lands managed by the Forest Service and the Bureau of Land Management govern.[12] They include the critical watersheds the states depend upon for water supply. On them, through them, and from them exist the reservoirs, rights-of-way, ditches, and pipelines necessary to store and convey water to farms, cities, and businesses.

Congress early decided to separate legal interests in land and water. Through federal statutes, it authorized conveyance of patents to land without interests in water. Water remained a public resource subject to disposition through the operation of state and federal law. This was most notable through the 1866 Mining Act[13] and the 1877 Desert Lands Act.[14] Congress (1) conceded to the states and territories jurisdiction to create property interests in the use of all available unappropriated waters on the public domain, subject to the right of the government, at anytime in the future, to reserve then-unappropriated waters for federal purposes; and (2) provided for water users to have occupancy of retained federal land for the purpose of constructing and maintaining storage and conveyance works necessary to place the water to use for state and private purposes.[15] The Public Land Law Review Commission, in 1970, reported that federal lands comprised "the source of most of the water in the [eleven] coterminous western states, providing approximately 61 percent of the total natural runoff occurring in the region."[16]

---

[7] For example, Colorado defined "any right to occupy, possess and enjoy any portion of the public domain" as "a chattel real *possessing the legal character of real estate*." This was a departure from the common law concept of "naked possession," that the Colorado Supreme Court termed "remarkable." *Gillett v. Gaffney*, 3 Colo. 351, 358 (1877); *see Bd. of County Comm'rs v. Vail Ass'n*, 19 P.3d 1263, 1269 n.8 (Colo. 2001).

[8] Homestead Act of 1862, ch. 75, 12 Stat. 392.

[9] Railroad Act of 1862, ch. 120, § 3, 12 Stat. 489, 492, *amended by* Railroad Act of 1864, ch. 206, § 4, 13 Stat. 356, 358; *see McCormick v. Union Pac. Res. Co.*, 14 P.3d 346, 352-53 (Colo. 2000).

[10] For a review of the public land laws, see Mall, *supra* note 6; BENJAMIN HORACE HIBBARD, A HISTORY OF THE PUBLIC LAND POLICIES (1965).

[11] PUBLIC LAND LAW REVIEW COMMISSION, ONE THIRD OF THE NATION'S LAND: A REPORT TO THE PRESIDENT AND TO THE CONGRESS 27-28 (1970) [hereinafter ONE THIRD OF THE NATION'S LAND].

[12] National Forest Management Act of 1976, 16 U.S.C. §§ 1600-1687 (1994); Federal Land Policy and Management Act, 43 U.S.C. §§ 1701-1784 (2001).

[13] The Mining Act of 1866, ch. 262, 14 Stat. 251.

[14] The Desert Lands Act of 1877, ch. 107, 19 Stat. 377.

[15] *California Oregon Power Co. v. Beaver Portland Cement Co.*, 295 U.S. 142, 163-65 (1935).

[16] ONE THIRD OF THE NATION'S LAND, *supra* note 11, at 141.

Most western states adopted the custom of appropriation—first in time of use, first in right for the amount of water placed from the natural streams to beneficial use—to administer their water resources.[17] California, however, recognized pre-existing riparian rights.[18] Each state adopted its own water allocation mechanism, confirming uses solely through judicial proceedings, as in Colorado's instance,[19] or through a combination of administrative and judicial proceedings in the other western states.[20]

The western states universally recognize waters of the natural stream as a public resource. Private rights therein arise only by use of unappropriated waters, in the amount of the appropriation taken at an identified point of diversion, for a beneficial use, in order of priority from the available source of supply, subject to the exercise of prior uses.[21] Primarily, a water right functions to afford legal protection for its owner to intercept water in priority at the point of the right's operation, wherever that is in the watershed within the state. Thus, a senior water right located downstream commands the passage of the needed water past the upstream junior users. Historically, large downstream agricultural rights have exercised this control, requiring municipal and other later evolving demands for water to either take the risk of shortage or develop alternative sources of supply.

From their inception, the western territories and states proceeded without interruption to create property rights in water under territorial and state law. Four significant events that altered the states' presumed sole possession of the field occurred at the turn of the nineteenth century. First, the federal forest reservations came into being under the 1897 Forest Organic Act, which included a state and federal water law savings provision.[22] Second, with the passage of the 1902 Reclamation Act,[23] which directed that federal projects obtain water rights in accordance with state law, the United States began to construct and manage those projects both for the benefit of state and local sponsors, and to achieve ancillary federal purposes, such as recreation, flood control, and power production. Third, in 1908, the United States Supreme Court, in a case involving a tribal

---

[17] *See, e.g., Coffin v. Left Hand Ditch Co.*, 6 Colo. 443, 447-49 (1882).
[18] JOSEPH L. SAX ET AL., LEGAL CONTROL OF WATER RESOURCES: CASES AND MATERIALS 295-97 (3d ed. 2000).
[19] *See* Gregory J. Hobbs, Jr., *Colorado's 1969 Adjudication and Administration Act: Settling In*, 3 U. DENV. WATER L. REV. 1, 19 (1999).
[20] *See* John E. Thorson, *State Watershed Adjudications: Approaches and Alternatives*, 42 ROCKY MTN. MIN. L. INST. §§ 22-01, 22-06 to 22-08 (1996); SAX ET AL., *supra* note 18, at 183-87.
[21] *See generally* SAX ET AL., *supra* note 18, at 280-309; *see, e.g., Santa Fe Trail Ranches Prop. Owners Ass'n v. Simpson*, 990 P.2d 46, 53-54 (Colo. 1999) (holding that diversions made pursuant to a decreed water right, when not used for decreed uses, do not establish historical use for the purposes of a change of water right proceeding).
[22] National Forest Organic Act of 1897, 16 U.S.C. § 481 (1994).
[23] Reclamation Act of 1902, 43 U.S.C. § 383 (1994).

reservation,[24] determined that federal reservations—in the absence of an express reservation of water—carry with them an implied reservation of sufficient, unappropriated water necessary to prevent defeat of the reservation's primary purposes.[25] Finally, the Supreme Court, in 1907, first exercised its original jurisdiction to resolve water allocation disputes between states, fashioning the law of equitable apportionment of interstate streams.[26] This, in turn, gave rise to a fifth major occurrence; creation of interstate water compacts, which Congress approved in the Compact Clause of the United States Constitution in the 1920s.[27]

Hence, from the earliest part of the twentieth century, the states have known of the existence of retained congressional authority to reserve unappropriated waters for federal purposes. An 1899 Supreme Court case presaged the *Winters* doctrine,[28] and the year before the enactment of the 1964 Wilderness Act, the Supreme Court applied the reserved rights doctrine not only to Native American reservations, but also to certain recreation and wildlife areas, and a national forest as well.[29] The states themselves encouraged the federal government to have a significant role concerning intrastate and interstate streams, primarily to secure federal funding for water projects they could not afford or did not choose to finance themselves. In regard to the reclamation program, the states understood that the Bureau of Reclamation would hold water rights appropriated under state law, originally for the benefit of agricultural users, later extended to a variety of purposes, including municipal, industrial, power production, flood control, fish and recreation, and water compact deliveries.[30] The tribal rights[31] and agency rights for the primary purpose of federal reservations, however, were another matter. They arose out of federal law, in particular congressional exercise of the property clause.[32]

---

[24] *Winters v. United States*, 207 U.S. 564 (1908).

[25] *Id.* at 577.

[26] *Kansas v. Colorado*, 206 U.S. 46, 117-18 (1907).

[27] U.S. CONST. art. I, § 10, cl. 3; *see e.g.*, Colorado River Compact, 1923 Colo. Sess. Laws 684; COLO. REV. STAT. § 37-61-101 (2001) (Boulder Canyon Project Act ratifying the Colorado River Compact, 43 U.S.C. § 617 (1994)).

[28] *United States v. Rio Grande Dam & Irrigation Co.*, 174 U.S. 690, 703 (1899).

[29] *Arizona v. California*, 373 U.S. 546, 601 (1963). *See also California v. United States*, 438 U.S. 645, 662 (1978) ("except where the reserved rights or navigation servitude of the United States are invoked, the State has total authority over its internal waters"); *Federal Power Comm'n v. Oregon,* 349 U.S. 435, 444-45 (1955) (upholding authority of Federal Power Commission to license power projects on reserved lands, subject to prior vested rights).

[30] *Bd. of County Comm'rs v. Crystal Creek Homeowners' Ass'n*, 14 P.3d 325, 329-40, 342 (Colo. 2000).

[31] Susan M. Williams, *The Winters Doctrine On Water Administration*, 36 ROCKY MTN. MIN. L. INST. §§ 24-1, 24-6 to 24-8 (1990).

[32] U.S. CONST. art. IV, § 3, cl. 2.

B. The Interest of the States in Adjudicating Federal Claims

The immunity of the United States to compelled appearance in state court proceedings became an increasing problem as the states continued to exercise their congressionally conferred and repeatedly recognized authority to create water rights in unappropriated public waters. Whether state law based, as with reclamation projects, or federal law based, as with tribal and federal land reservations, state forums did not determine the United States' water rights. Whatever litigation occurred to determine federally held water rights occurred in federal court, while the states proceeded on a separate track as to state based claims not owned by the United States government.

The situation became intolerable to the western states.[33] The security and dependability of water rights turn on the enforceability of their priority in times of short river supply.[34] The right to divert a certain amount of water from the available natural stream supply at a specific location, to the exclusion of all others not then in priority, is the essence of a water right. The reason for adjudicating a federal reserved water right is the same as all other rights to the use of water—to realize the value and expectations that enforcement of that right's priority secure.[35] In times of short supply, water users depend on the state to exercise its police power to curtail junior uses in favor of senior uses, regardless of the identity of the owner of the right, state or federal. To accomplish this, managers must determine the amount and priority of rights drawing on the watershed.

Because the states could not haul the federal agencies and tribes into state court, they were unable to secure reliability for state-created water rights and meet future needs due to uncertainty about the nature, extent, and priority of federal water rights. In sum, administration of rights within the watershed, who gets to divert, and who does not, cannot occur in the absence of comprehensive identification and adjudication of all rights, state or federal.

Accordingly, after a prolonged effort and over the resistance of the Justice Department and federal agencies, Congress passed the 1952 McCarran Amendment permitting state joinder of the United States and Indian tribes in state court water adjudications.[36] In order to assert this jurisdiction, states relying primarily on administrative mechanisms commenced comprehensive adjudications to determine the rights of all users, including federal entities.

---

[33] Thorson, *supra* note 20, §§ 22-16 to 22-24.
[34] *Empire Lodge Homeowners' Assoc. v. Moyer*, No. 00SA211, 2001 Colo. LEXIS 1061 (Colo. Dec. 17, 2001).
[35] *Navajo Dev. Co. v. Sanderson*, 655 P.2d 1374, 1380 (Colo. 1982).
[36] Bennett W. Raley, *Chaos in the Making: The Consequences of Failure to Integrate Federal Environmental Statutes with McCarran Amendment Water Adjudications*, 41 Rocky Mtn. Min. L. Inst. §§ 24-04 (1995).

Three Colorado cases that the United States Supreme Court ultimately decided established that federal courts and state courts, under the McCarran legislation, have concurrent jurisdiction to determine federal rights. However, when a McCarran proceeding begins in the state court, the federal court should defer to the state judicial determination of the federal rights, whether or not the federal litigation preceded the state litigation.[37]

Implicit in the refusal of federal courts to exercise their concurrent jurisdiction is that federal agencies and tribes have equal access to fair state judicial forums, along with state and private claimants. As Justice Brennan wrote for the Court in *Colorado River Water Conservation Dist. v. United States*,[38] which recognized the authority of the states to join tribal claims under McCarran:

> We emphasize, however, that we do not overlook the heavy obligation [of the federal courts] to exercise jurisdiction. We need not decide, for example, whether, despite the McCarran Amendment, dismissal would be warranted if more extensive proceedings had occurred in the District Court prior to dismissal, if the involvement of state water rights were less extensive than it is here, or if the state proceeding were in some respect inadequate to resolve the federal claims.[39]

Additionally, when a state joins the United States in a McCarran proceeding, the United States must assert all federal claims to water rights; if not, the court may concede the priority of the federal rights, including both reserved and appropriative rights, to intervening state and private junior rights.[40] In turn, this has compelled federal agencies and tribes to participate in litigation they might otherwise have postponed or foregone entirely.

Congressional adoption of a plethora of environmental laws, starting in the 1960s, has caused federal agencies to manage their lands with greater attention to values other than resource extraction, such as recreation, fish and wildlife, wild and scenic rivers, national parks, and wilderness area preservation, among others. Members of the water bar have pointed out that failure of the United States to claim state or federal appropriative water rights for environmental purposes, such as endangered species protection, defeats the purposes of the McCarran Amendment and the federal environmental laws, since reserved water rights either will not exist or will be uncertain. The argument is that a secure water right, administered in

---

[37] The Colorado Trilogy: *Colo. River Water Conservation Dist. v. United States*, 424 U.S. 800, 810, 820 (1976); *United States v. Dist. Court*, 401 U.S. 527, 530 (1971); *United States v. Dist. Court*, 401 U.S. 520, 525 (1971).
[38] *Colo. River Water Conservation Dist.*, 424 U.S. at 800.
[39] *Id.* at 820.
[40] *United States v. Bell*, 724 P.2d 631 (Colo. 1986).

priority vis-à-vis other water rights, is the most rational and consistent way to accommodate important state and federal interests in water. Resorting to regulatory mechanisms on an ad hoc basis, such as by-pass flows the Forest Service can impose as a condition for right-of-way permit renewal, diminishes the yield of pre-existing water rights, undermines reliability, promotes disorder, intensifies hostility, leads to takings actions, and generally favors chaos over law.[41]

In short, whether for a traditional type of consumptive use, such as agricultural or municipal, a non-consumptive use, such as hydropower, flood control, or environmental uses, federal officials and agencies who do not assert federal water rights claims in the McCarran proceedings may be in dereliction of their congressionally assigned public duties. When these claims are asserted, state judges must give them fair consideration and uphold federal ownership of rights that have a basis in either state or federal law, regardless of political controversy within the state over the filing, existence, nature, or extent of the claims.

McCarran adjudications are underway in the state courts of Arizona, California, Colorado, Idaho, Montana, New Mexico, Nevada, Oregon, Utah, Washington, and Wyoming, with Texas already having completed a comprehensive adjudication.[42] The United States Constitution vests the authority in state judges to apply both state and federal law. Pursuant to the Supremacy Clause, they must uphold federal law when there is federal preemption.[43] The experiences of Colorado and Idaho, sparked by the majority opinions of Justices Stone and Silak, demonstrate the magnitude of the legal and governmental issues involved, and go straight to the heart of federalism, separation of powers, and the ability of judges to refrain from political influence in making decisions.

---

[41] Raley, *supra* note 36, § 24-06. The problem for federal agencies with this approach is that such claims provoke intense state political reaction and litigation, as the federal filings in Idaho's Snake River Basin adjudication illustrate. The right of the United States to obtain appropriative rights under federal law, in contradistinction to state law, has also been highly controversial and, although the western states, except for New Mexico, have state law mechanisms for instream flow water rights, they typically hold these in state ownership and do not allow federal agencies or others to appropriate or hold them.

[42] Thorson, *supra* note 20, § 22-05. For example, the Arizona proceedings involve 77,000 water right claims, and the Idaho Snake River proceedings involve 185,000 claims. *Id.*

[43] U.S. CONST. art. VI, cl. 2.

III. The Colorado Experience

> I tell you, gentlemen, you are piling up
> a heritage of conflict and litigation
> over water rights, for there is not
> sufficient water to supply these lands.
>
> John Wesley Powell[44]

In October of 1954, the Colorado Supreme Court issued its opinion in the Blue River case, pitting Denver's claims for municipal supply against a United States reclamation project.[45] At that time, Colorado law provided for contested election of judges. The author of the four-to-three decision, Chief Justice Mortimer Stone, was up for reelection in November. He had drawn a ballot challenger.

The case was highly significant. It involved the water right priorities of the City and County of Denver, the City of Colorado Springs, seven counties of northeastern Colorado, and fifteen counties of Colorado's western slope, which encompasses most of Colorado's future demand for surface water. The principal focus was the relative priorities of Dillon Reservoir and Green Mountain Reservoir, which is situated not far downstream from Dillon on the same river.[46]

Congress had authorized Green Mountain Reservoir as part of the Colorado-Big Thompson Project ("C-BT"). The Bureau of Reclamation administered the project, designed to provide 100,000 acre-feet of water per year for future uses on the western slope of Colorado's continental divide, and 240,000 acre-feet of water per year to the seven-county area of northeastern Colorado for agricultural, municipal, and industrial uses. The project authorized construction of a trans-mountain diversion tunnel running west to east under the surface of Rocky Mountain National Park.[47]

Green Mountain Reservoir would store an additional 52,000-acre feet of water to provide replacement water for senior uses on the western slope drawing on Colorado River water, thereby allowing out-of-priority diversions to northeastern Colorado. Power production at the Green Mountain site would help repay the

---

[44] JOHN WESLEY POWELL, OFFICIAL REPORT OF THE INTERNATIONAL IRRIGATION CONGRESS 109, 112 (1893), *quoted in* DONALD WORSTER, A RIVER RUNNING WEST: THE LIFE OF JOHN WESLEY POWELL 529 (2001).

[45] *See generally City and County of Denver v. N. Colo. Water Conservancy Dist.*, 276 P.2d 992, 1012 (Colo. 1954) (holding that, following the Act of 1877, all nonnavigable waters, then a part of the public domain, became *publici juris*, subject to the plenary control of designated states).

[46] *Id.* at 995-97.

[47] *See generally* DANIEL TYLER, THE LAST WATER HOLE IN THE WEST: THE COLORADO-BIG THOMPSON PROJECT AND THE NORTHERN COLORADO WATER CONSERVANCY DISTRICT (1992).

United States for C-BT construction costs, along with project power features on the eastern slope, and the repayment obligations of the Northern Colorado Water Conservancy District ("Northern District"), the project's northeastern Colorado sponsor. The water users of the 15 county Colorado River Water Conservation District ("River District") were the primary beneficiaries of Green Mountain Reservoir.[48]

The agreement between northeastern Colorado and the western slope water interests was an elevated achievement. Colorado is the state of the Great Divide, hydrologically and politically. Eighty percent of the average annual precipitation arises on the western slope; 80 percent of the population and much of the irrigable acreage of the state lies on the eastern slope. The River District and the Northern District, both established in 1937, safeguard the water interests of their regions.[49] The authorizing legislation for formation of the Northern District required mitigation to the western slope for trans-mountain diversions from the natural basin of the Colorado River within the state.[50] Congressman Ed Taylor of the western slope had successfully insisted on provisions in the congressional authorization requiring construction of the Green Mountain Reservoir, the western slope protective feature, before any of the features designed to benefit the eastern slope.[51]

The Bureau of Reclamation proceeded with construction of the C-BT Project commencing with Green Mountain Reservoir, as Congress had directed, however, litigation over water rights priorities was inevitable.[52] The City and County of Denver, proceeding with its own financial resources and free of any state or federal legislative provisions, planned on constructing Dillon Reservoir to divert Blue River waters through its own trans-mountain tunnels for use in the City and County and its service areas in the mushrooming metropolitan area.[53]

Although a water right arises only from actual application of water to a beneficial use, Colorado law allows for relating the priority date of the water right back to the date when the claimant took its first act evidencing the intent to appropriate a certain amount of available unappropriated water at a specific location for beneficial use, provided that construction of the project proceeds with reasonable diligence.[54] The relation back doctrine thereby permits the appropriator the time required to engineer, finance, and construct the water works necessary to use the water.

---

[48] *Id.*
[49] *Id.*
[50] *Id.*
[51] *Id.*
[52] Tyler, *supra* note 47, at 205-15.
[53] *Id.*
[54] *Sieber v. Frink*, 2 P. 901, 903 (Colo. 1884).

Relying on an appropriation date of 1935 for the Colorado-Big Thompson Project, the two districts—allied as they were in the construction and operation of the federal reclamation project—claimed that Denver had not been diligent in pursuing its Blue River claims. Denver had asserted a 1921 date for Dillon Reservoir based on its overall planning for a comprehensive water system along the eastern and western slope sources.[55] Refusing to appear in the state court suit pre-McCarran, the United States filed a parallel suit in the Colorado Federal District Court.

The Colorado Supreme Court's decision provided a date of 1946 based on Denver starting work on the Montezuma trans-mountain tunnel that year.[56] Concluding that Denver had not been diligent in pursuing its Blue River claims, the court postponed the City and County's asserted earlier priority in favor of the federally held priority for the C-BT Project.[57] The dissent—signed by the only three judges from the Denver metropolitan area—declared that because of Denver's work on its comprehensive water system, the City and County had been diligent and was entitled to the earlier date.[58]

Denver newspapers proclaimed calamity and sided with the dissent. Denver faced a dry future because the majority, through Justice Stone, had turned control of the Blue River over to the United States. The *Denver Post* started its coverage on October 19, 1954, in an article reporting a rumor that the Colorado Supreme Court was close to ruling against Denver in the proposed Blue River diversion case.[59] The rumored outcome was four-to-three against Denver. The *Post* said there were "reports that attempts were being made by the state Republican high command to hold up the decision until after the election because of jolting political aspects."[60] Attorneys told the *Post* that the decision "means that Denver has no legal right to 177,000 acre-feet of water" sought from the Blue River.[61]

The court issued its opinion late in the afternoon of the day the *Post's* morning edition had broken the story. The next day, October 20, the *Post* reported that the priority date awarded to Denver of June 24, 1946, would "entitle Denver only to a little surplus flood water in wet years."[62] Justice Stone had "doomed" Denver's future. A "Denver spokesman," commenting on the decision, said, "the city will make no attempt to divert the 788 second-feet permitted, declaring that

---

[55] *See generally* TYLER, *supra* note 47.
[56] *Id.*
[57] *Id.*
[58] *Id.*
[59] Bert Hanna & Nello Cassai, *4-3 Decision Against City, Lawyers Told*, DENV. POST, Oct. 18, 1954, at 1.
[60] *Id.*
[61] *Id.*
[62] *City Failed to Establish Claim, Jurist Says*, DENV. POST, Oct. 19, 1954, at 2.

such diversion would not be financially feasible."[63] An accompanying editorial asserted that "[t]he effect of the decision is to award virtually the entire flow of the Blue [R]iver to Green Mountain reservoir, a part of the Colorado-Big Thompson project, and to the Green Mountain hydro plant where the government generates electricity."[64]

On October 26, the *Denver Post* endorsed Justice Stone's opponent, Henry S. Lindsley, stating: "Justice Stone wrote the recent majority opinion of the state supreme court which constituted a serious blow to Denver's plans for increasing its dwindling water supply by tapping the Blue River."[65] The *Post* acknowledged that "Justice Stone has been a distinguished jurist..."[66] Discounting political motivations of its own, the *Post* nevertheless said that Justice Stone should go, maintaining that although judges should not base decisions on politics, "it is important, however, that younger men be elected to the court whenever younger men of demonstrated knowledge, understanding and character are offered as candidates."[67] Justice Stone was 72; his opponent, 51.

Denver filed for rehearing and a series of *Post* stories and columns up to election day speculated on the severe damage dealt to Denver and the chances of a rehearing—and reversal—if Justice Stone's opponent was elected. Newspapers in northeastern Colorado and on the western slope countered with articles, columns, and editorials in favor of Justice Stone's decision and his retention.

On the first Tuesday of November 1954, a flood of Denver metropolitan votes took Justice Stone down.[68] The Denver Water Board filed successive rehearing petitions, including one after Justice Lindsley had taken his place on the court. Justice Lindsley refused to vote for rehearing;[69] as a result, Justice Stone's opinion stood.

The Colorado Supreme Court's decision produced a settlement in the federal court case the next year. In return for a power interference agreement, that would store and divert water otherwise required to run through the turbines at Green

---

[63] *Id.*
[64] Editorial, *The Supreme Court vs. a Growing City*, DENV. POST, Oct. 20, 1954, at 16.
[65] Editorial, *On Selecting Judges*, Denv. Post, Oct. 26, 1954, at 16.
[66] *Id.*
[67] *Id.*
[68] Bert Hanna, *Denver's Vote Decisive in Supreme Court Race*, DENV. POST, Nov. 3, 1954, at 23.
[69] Justice Holland, one of the dissenting justices, explained that he and his fellow dissenters and the new member of the court, Justice Lindsley, "unhesitatingly participated in the matter of the denial of the last of the subsequent motions [for rehearing] as proper procedure to establish finality as is proper in this, as well as other litigated cases," despite the dissent of the three and the arrival of a new judge who had not participated in the majority's decision. *See City and County of Denver v. N. Colo. Water Conservancy Dist.*, 276 P.2d 992, 1023 (Colo. 1954) (Holland, J., dissenting).

Mountain dam downstream of Dillon Reservoir, in 1955, Denver stipulated to the senior priority of the Colorado-Big Thompson Project. Today, Denver operates Dillon Reservoir as its premier water storage reservoir; the C-BT Project has a long record of service to Northeastern Colorado; and the 100,000 acre-feet of water in Green Mountain Reservoir is fully subscribed for western slope uses, mainly providing replacement water for junior out-of-priority diversions on the western slope subject to curtailment otherwise.[70]

In 1966, Colorado voters approved a state constitutional amendment abolishing contested judicial races, in favor of citizen-commission nomination of trial court and appellate court candidates, followed by gubernatorial appointment, and a retention/non-retention vote for a term of years after two years of service. Upon Justice Stone's death, the Colorado Supreme Court presided over a eulogy to his excellence as a justice and the example his reelection defeat has set for a better way of selecting and retaining judges. Said Leonard Campbell, a leader of the Colorado Bar Association, on this occasion:

> I listened and remembered well when Alden Hill spoke about the election of 1954 when Mortimer Stone was defeated, improperly defeated in the election held that year. Perhaps it's somewhat fitting as a Denverite born here, somewhat related on occasion to the Water Department, that we acknowledge what has been acknowledged countless times, that never was there an election for any judge of this Supreme Court that was more discussed after the election in which the judge gained in stature; he gained in stature every time that it was discussed; and never was it more clearly demonstrated that there was a deficiency in the elective process that did not return him to office.[71]

After his defeat, Justice Stone went on to serve as a referee with the National Railroad Adjustment Board and Mediation Board, deciding dockets of disputes between railroads and their employees. He died 24 years after his election defeat at the age of 95.

---

[70] Every one of these water features helps to put Colorado's entitlement under the Colorado River Compact to use within the state, while serving important recreational and environmental needs. *Krupp v. Breckenridge Sanitation Dist.*, 19 P.3d 687, 690 (Colo. 2001). Particularly in the headwater counties of Grand, Summit, and Eagle, home to ski area, summer resort, and residential development, the western slope's recreational and residential economy is largely possible because of replacement releases from Green Mountain Reservoir, permitting out-of-priority diversions. *In re Application of Denver*, 935 F.2d 1143, 1146 (10th Cir. 1991).

[71] *See* Proceedings in the Supreme Court of Colorado, Friday, April 14, 1978, to honor the memory of the late Honorable Mortimer Stone as a Justice and Chief Justice of the Court, *in* unpaginated preface to 195 Colo. (1978).

IV. THE IDAHO EXPERIENCE

Ideals and actions do not automatically coincide. Given the history of Idaho's irrigated landscape, a corollary might be added to this basic observation. A belief that humans should conquer and exploit the environment does not necessarily mean that they will actually achieve their objectives. As the irrigated landscape showed, nature often eluded ideals: a conquest myth did not produce a conquered land.[72]

In October 1999, the Idaho Supreme Court issued its opinion on wilderness water rights in the Snake River Basin McCarran adjudication.[73] Idaho provides for the contested election of judges but without party identification. If a candidate in the primary does not obtain a majority vote, a run-off election occurs as part of the general election. The author of the three-to-two decision, Justice Cathy Silak, was up for reelection. The controversy over her opinion drew a ballot opponent who defeated her overwhelmingly.

Inconclusive Colorado litigation had preceded this case. The Idaho case involved the United States Forest Service assertion of implied federal reserved water rights for three wilderness areas, some of which were downstream of agricultural, municipal, and mining areas. Although the Sierra Club had brought federal litigation against the Forest Service in Colorado seeking to compel it to claim wilderness water rights, the Tenth Circuit Court of Appeals refused to do so, and found the case hypothetical and nonreviewable.[74] The Colorado Federal District Court had ruled in favor of the theory of such rights, but stated its inability to order the Forest Service to adjudicate them. Instead, it ordered the Forest Service to devise a plan to protect wilderness water resources in the absence of obtaining water rights for them.[75] Because the Tenth Circuit found the case not ripe for decision, it vacated the district court's holding.

Colorado water user interests had intervened in the Sierra Club litigation with an eye towards the proposed designation of downstream wilderness areas on forest

---

[72] MARK FIEGE, IRRIGATED EDEN, THE MAKING OF AN AGRICULTURAL LANDSCAPE IN THE AMERICAN WEST 207-08 (1999).

[73] *See generally In re SRBA*, No. 24546, 1999 Idaho LEXIS 119, at *1 (Idaho Oct. 1, 1999) (affirming the district court's order granting the United States's reserved water rights for the Frank Church River of No Return, the Selway-Bitter Root, and the Gospel-Hump Wilderness Areas).

[74] *Sierra Club v. Yeutter*, 911 F.2d 1405, 1421 (10th Cir. 1990).

[75] *Sierra Club v. Lyng*, 661 F. Supp. 1490, 1503-04 (D. Colo. 1987); *Sierra Club v. Block*, 622 F. Supp. 842, 866-67 (D. Colo. 1985).

lands in the state. In these instances, reservation of a wilderness water right could block future upstream water development on non-wilderness lands.[76]

In Idaho, the designation of wilderness areas downstream of developing lands had already occurred. The Forest Service, therefore, undertook in Idaho's McCarran proceedings to meet its perceived responsibility for asserting the existence of federal reserved water rights for wilderness areas, where such rights could make a difference in protecting wilderness water resources. Namely, for the Selway-Bitterroot (designated by Congress in 1964),[77] the Gospel-Hump (designated by Congress in 1978)[78] and the Frank Church River of No Return (designated by Congress in 1980)[79] wilderness areas.

The wilderness water rights claims were highly controversial from the outset. Cities, irrigation districts, and mining and timber companies contested them both in the trial court and on appeal. The state district court judge, conducting the comprehensive Snake River Basin Adjudication, ruled in favor of the federal wilderness water rights claims, as well as those for national recreation areas and wild and scenic rivers in Idaho.

Idaho water users filed a brief arguing that the doctrine of implied reserved water rights is an anachronism. They argued that when Congress raises and debates the water issue, then fails to resolve it, as with the Wilderness Act, the courts should refuse to act to imply a reserved water right, for this would violate separation of powers. In such a circumstance, they asserted, the *New Mexico* doctrine of deference to state water law should apply to the case rather than the *Winters* doctrine. In *United States v. New Mexico*,[80] the United States Supreme Court held that instream flows for fish and wildlife, recreation, and other multiple uses of forest lands, were secondary purposes of national forest designation, the primary purposes being timber production and water production for western settlers.[81] Accordingly, the water users contended that implied reserved water rights do not exist for wilderness designations.

A majority of the Idaho Supreme Court justices agreed with the adjudication court. Justice Silak's opinion relied on the *Winters* doctrine, as other United States

---

[76] The subsequent 1993 Colorado Wilderness Act—mostly headwaters areas, but including three downstream segments—disclaimed the creation of wilderness reserved water rights as a result of that particular designation, while preserving any pre-existing federal rights in the areas. Colorado Wilderness Act of 1993, § 8, Pub. L. No. 103-77, 107 Stat. 756, 762-64.
[77] *See* Wilderness Act of 1964, Pub. L. No. 88-577, 78 Stat. 890.
[78] Act of Feb. 24, 1978, Pub. L. No. 95-237, 92 Stat. 43.
[79] Act of July 23, 1980, Pub. L. No. 96-312, 94 Stat. 948.
[80] *United States v. New Mexico*, 438 U.S. 696 (1978).
[81] *Id.* at 710. Applying *New Mexico*, the Idaho Supreme Court unanimously decided in another case that the Multiple Use and Sustained Yield Act of 1960 did not create an express or implied reservation of water. *United States v. City of Challis*, 988 P.2d 1199, 1207 (Idaho 1999).

Supreme Court decisions have interpreted it, spelling out the doctrine of implied reserved water rights to prevent defeat of the primary purposes of federal reservations.[82]

As Judge John Kane had done in his vacated Colorado Federal District Court decision, the Idaho Supreme Court determined that congressional designation of wilderness areas on forest lands is a new reservation overlaid on an existing one, the primary purpose of which is to protect the wilderness values existing as of the date of designation.[83] Because water is an essential attribute of wilderness, a federal water right is necessary to prevent its impairment. Justice Silak wrote:

> Through the Wilderness Act, Congress established a new category of federal lands—the national Wilderness Preservation System. Unlike the MUSYA [Multiple Use and Sustained Yield Act], the Wilderness Act prescribes a unique management scheme that clearly aims to preserve the wilderness character of the designated lands. The designation of the Wilderness Areas at issue in this case continued the withdrawal of these areas from the public domain. Moreover, it is also clear that the Wilderness Areas were established for the purpose of wilderness preservation. Therefore, we conclude that the congressional designations of the Wilderness Areas are reservations of land established for the primary purpose of wilderness protection and preservation.[84]

Citing the opaque language of the 1964 Wilderness Act regarding water rights, "'nothing in this Act shall constitute an express or implied claim or denial on the part of the Federal Government as to exemption from the [s]tate water laws',"[85] the majority concluded that wilderness designation did not create an express federal reserved water right.[86] It then undertook to determine the existence of an implied reserved water right.[87]

The majority opinion focused on the central function of Idaho water law—to provide for the future appropriation of unappropriated, unreserved water—versus the forceful language of Congress regarding its intent to preserve the wilderness areas as they were at the time of their designation:

> Idaho law provides that all non-reserved, unappropriated water within the state is subject to appropriation to further domestic and economic

---

[82] *Cappaert v. United States*, 426 U.S. 128, 138-39 (1976); *Arizona v. California*, 373 U.S. 546, 600 (1963).
[83] *In re SRBA*, No. 24546, 1999 Idaho LEXIS 119, at *19-20 (Idaho Oct. 1, 1999).
[84] *Id.*
[85] *Id.* at *20.
[86] *Id.*
[87] *Id.* at *20-24.

development...A review of the Wilderness Act demonstrates that the prior appropriation doctrine is inconsistent with congressional intent to preserve the wilderness character of the Wilderness Areas.[88]

The three-member majority determined that the wilderness water reservation was for all the water:

> As discussed above, the appropriation of water from within the Wilderness Areas would defeat Congress's [sic] primary purpose of preserving the unimpaired wilderness character of the areas. The Wilderness Act makes clear Congress' intention that the Wilderness Areas "be administered...in such manner as will leave them unimpaired for future use and enjoyment as wilderness, and so as to provide for...the preservation of their wilderness character."...Congress defined wilderness as "an area of undeveloped Federal land retaining its primeval character and influence, without permanent improvements or human habitation, which is protected and managed so as to preserve its natural conditions."...Water is required to effectuate the purpose of maintaining wilderness in its pristine natural condition. Because removing water necessarily impairs the natural state of the wilderness lands, Congress must have intended to reserve all unappropriated water....Therefore, we hold that the SRBA district court correctly concluded that the entire unappropriated amount of water within the Wilderness Areas is necessary to accomplish the purposes of wilderness preservation and protection.[89]

The majority did not address the water users' argument that the implied reserved water right doctrine is an anachronism and creates separation of powers problems if applied to wilderness designations. This problem arising because courts cannot legislate to create a water right when Congress has raised the issue but has declined to resolve it.

The dissent wrote that implied reserved water rights cannot exist when it is clear that Congress has taken up the water issue and has not expressly reserved unappropriated water.[90] The language no claim/no denial of exemption from state water law, it said, meant Congress intended no claim for wilderness water rights.[91] The dissent also concluded that wilderness designation is a management directive to the administering agency, not a reservation overlying original Forest reservation.[92]

---

[88] *In re SRBA*, 1999 Idaho LEXIS 119, at *24.
[89] *Id.* at *27-28.
[90] *Id.* at *38 (Kidwell, J., dissenting).
[91] *Id.* at *41.
[92] *Id.* at *47.

Reacting to a torrent of immediate and widespread adverse reaction to the decision across Idaho that took on a life of its own, *The Idaho Statesman* editorialized on October 14, 1999, for Justice Silak's reelection defeat:

> Through the hand-wringing over Idaho's water rights, there is one quick-fix solution available to voters: elect a new Supreme Court justice. Justice Cathy Silak, who on Oct. 1 wrote the explosive opinion that turns over water rights in wilderness areas to the federal government, is up for re-election in May. Hers is the only seat that will be available. That leaves an opening for anybody who thinks she was in error in assuming the intent of Congress to give the federal government rights over Idaho's wilderness water.[93]

The editors went on to opine that Silak "should be well aware" that not a single Idaho politician in the last thirty-plus years, "Democrat or Republican," would dare run on a platform allowing the federal government "to control every drop of water in designated areas of the state."[94] While the editorial said it was too early to tell whether an opponent could defeat her based on one decision, the "controversial ruling was approved on a [three-to-two] vote, so all it takes is one change on the [s]upreme [c]ourt—one individual who demonstrates a greater sensitivity to what's at stake, which is Idaho's water sovereignty."[95]

The Statesman proclaimed that "[s]ome state leaders warn that thousands of Idaho water users, including Treasure Valley residents, could lose their right to use water for drinking, farming, and making microchips. Farmers are especially worried about their livelihoods coming to an end and fields turning to sagebrush."[96] The trial attorney for the United States was reported as saying it was not the government's aim to claim every drop of water allocated since 1980. The editorial concluded that "[i]f Silak wants to help her cause, she could push for a rehearing on this case and be open to changing her mind. Her future on the Idaho Supreme Court may depend on what she does on this issue."[97]

Shortly after this editorial appeared, the court granted a rehearing. Justice Silak voted to oppose rehearing. A state district judge filed his candidacy to run against her. On March 13, 2000, *The Statesman* reported that Justice Silak's adversary had recused himself from further proceedings at the trial court level in a

---

[93] Editorial, *Idahoans Could Place Water Rights Issue In Their Hands*, IDAHO STATESMAN, Oct. 14, 1999, at 6b. The author thanks reporter Dan Popkey of the Idaho Statesman for the courtesy of providing articles and editorials of that newspaper appearing over the course of the election controversy.
[94] *Id.*
[95] *Id.*
[96] *Id.*
[97] *Id.*

controversial school finance case because, in his view, the Idaho Supreme Court had rewritten the Idaho Constitution, and for him to implement the court's decision would be to violate his oath of office.[98] *The Statesman* also quoted a state republican legislator as saying, "'Three strikes against this court, and especially against Cathy Silak. She's out....We have to send that message. If we can't do it legislatively, by tying their hands, then we've got to send a message by replacing her.'"[99] The article said, "Critics, including virtually every elected official in Idaho, contend the court misinterpreted congressional intent on reserved water rights in the 1964 Wilderness Act."[100]

Justice Silak attempted to respond by pointing to her record. *The Statesman*, on April 29, 2000, quoted the Boise attorney chairing Justice Silak's reelection campaign as saying that the court's five justices issued unanimous rulings in 74 of 88 cases before them and Justice Silak had filed only three dissents.[101] Asked to respond, Justice Silak's opponent pointed to her vote in the school funding and water rights decisions as indicative of her disregard for the law.[102]

Within days of the upcoming election, *The Statesman*—reviewing the judicial record and statements of both candidates—reversed its initial editorial suggestion that voters should oust Justice Silak from office. It endorsed her reelection:

> Silak's record shows no evidence of judicial activism. Last year, she sided with the court's majority in 93 out of 96 published opinions; this is hardly the record of a maverick. Silak declined to answer the same religious questionnaire [her opponent] answered, saying it would be unethical to discuss her opinion. She's right.[103]

The editorial pointed out that Justice Silak's opponent had:

> answered an endorsement questionnaire from a religious group, where he discussed his evangelism, opposition to abortion and deeply held belief in creationism and his conviction that the Bible is the source of our moral law.... Revealing religious and moral views for a political

---

[98] Mark Warbis, *Tempers Run Hot Over High Court's Recent Rulings*, IDAHO STATESMAN, Mar. 13, 2000, at 1b.

[99] *Id*. The reference to three strikes was to a case where the Idaho Supreme Court had overruled a lower-court decision absolving St. Alphonsus Regional Medical Center of an employee's molestation of a minor, the public schools case where the court determined that the state had a constitutional obligation to ensure that students can attend public schools that provide "a safe environment, conducive to learning," and the wilderness water rights case. Id.

[100] *Id.*

[101] *Candidate Takes on Justice Silak's Record of Rulings*, IDAHO STATESMAN, Apr. 29, 2000, at 1b.

[102] *Id.*

[103] Editorial, *Justice Silak Has Experience and Judicial Temperament*, IDAHO STATESMAN, May 21, 2000, at 10b.

endorsement leaves the public to question [his] detachment and erode confidence in his decisions."[104]

Justice Silak fell to overwhelming defeat on May 23. Although she attributed her defeat to "partisanship" and not necessarily her water opinion,[105] *The Statesman* on May 27, 2000, quoted a political analyst as saying that her vote in support of federal water rights was the likely cause.[106] "Water rights is the third rail of Idaho politics....Because of that decision, most of the focus was on her. Even though there was a lot of good reporting on [her opponent's] missteps, the focus was on water rights."[107] The election campaign cost both candidates a total of $290,000, with Justice Silak slightly outspending her successful opponent.[108]

On October 27, 2000, with the election five months behind, the Idaho Supreme Court reversed directions, determining that no implied federal reserved water rights existed for the three wilderness areas.[109] The lead opinion for the new majority stated that "[t]he language of the Wilderness Act indicates that it sets aside land and prohibits its development, nothing more."[110] Accordingly, the wilderness designation has no extraterritorial effect on water development outside of wilderness boundaries. "A clear indication of the creation of implied water rights as claimed by the United States does not exist in the language of the Wilderness Act or in its legislative history."[111]

Specially concurring, the chief justice questioned the continued viability of the *Winters* doctrine. "Where, as in this case, Congress has chosen for whatever reason, not to create an express water right despite its knowledge of a potential conflict, I believe it can no longer be inferred that such a right is necessary to fulfill the purposes of the reservation."[112] She said to *The Statesman* on October 28, 2000, that "the suggestion that she had made a political rather than legal decision

---

[104] *Id.*

[105] Ken Miller, *Silak Blames Partisanship for Loss More than Water Rights Ruling*, IDAHO STATESMAN, May 27, 2000, at 6a. Idaho's system of scheduling judicial elections at the time of the party primaries may accentuate former party affiliations, although the judicial election is theoretically non-partisan. Media coverage regarding the Idaho election continuously reported that a Democratic Governor had appointed Justice Silak, and she had been active in Democratic politics before taking office. Approximately 86 percent of the total votes cast in the primary election were Republican.

[106] Ken Miller, *Politics Under Scrutiny After Court Election*, IDAHO STATESMAN, May 27, 2000, at 1a.

[107] *Id.*

[108] *Supreme Court Race Was Most Costly Ever*, IDAHO STATESMAN, June 23, 2000, at 1b.

[109] *Potlatch Corp. v. United States*, 12 P.3d 1260, 1266 (Idaho 2000).

[110] *Id.*

[111] *Id.* at 1268.

[112] *Id.* at 1271.

[was] 'insulting'."[113] Acknowledging that, "'You're asking a question that's fair game'," the chief justice explained that she had changed her mind based on the briefs and the oral argument on rehearing, lengthy discussion, and her own lengthy restudy of the applicable law.[114]

The *Times-News* issue of October 28, 2000, quoted Idaho's Governor as saying the "[s]upreme [c]ourt made the right call," and the Idaho Deputy Attorney General's office as saying the new ruling "'reaffirmed the long-standing principle of primacy of state water law.'"[115] Pointing to the existence of more than 150,000 water rights claims in 38 counties involved in the pending Snake River Basin adjudication, the Speaker of Idaho's House of Representatives proclaimed, "[i]t gets us to where we can, in the negotiations and the mediations, proceed from a position of strength rather than a defensive posture."[116]

In light of the Idaho experience, *The Statesman* editorialized on October 31, 2000, that the state should reexamine its method of selecting judges through contested elections. "Until there is change in the system, challengers in [s]upreme [c]ourt contests will continue to press the political envelope."[117]

V. FEDERALISM, AN ENDURING HERITAGE

That open space that fills your vision and lifts your heart when you drive across the West is federal open space, most of it. Federally owned, protected, managed, federally kept open to almost any sort of reasonable public use. If it brings some irritations from hordes of tourists, it also fills the local treasury, and it gives a large part of the spaciousness and satisfaction to western living. As for wilderness areas, if we had had to depend on the states for their protection, there would pretty clearly be none.... If the West is going to be saved in anything like its present state, it will not be by the states or the oligarchs who dominate most western capitals. It will be accomplished, if at all, by the greatest cooperation possible between state and federal, private and federal, private and state, business and agriculture.

Wallace Stegner[118]

---

[113] Rocky Barker, *Water Ruling Reversed*, IDAHO STATESMAN, Oct. 28, 2000, at A 01.
[114] *Id.*
[115] N.S. Nokkentved, *Justices Reverse Water Ruling*, TIMES-NEWS, Oct. 28, 2000, at A1.
[116] *Id.*
[117] Editorial, *Our View*, IDAHO STATESMAN, Oct. 31, 2000, at B 08.
[118] WALLACE STEGNER, *Land: America's History Teacher*, *in* MARKING THE SPARROW'S FALL: WALLACE STEGNER'S AMERICAN WEST 274, 276 (Page Stegner ed., 1998).

The Idaho election result reverberated across the United States. The Georgetown University Law Center's Environmental Policy Project urged environmental interests nationwide to take an active role in future state judicial elections.[119] In light of national news reports, those interested in preserving judicial independence and resisting political influences on judges questioned whether the Idaho Supreme Court, particularly its chief justice, had found itself in a political firestorm, the intensity of which it had not foreseen and did not withstand.

The impact of the Idaho experience on western state McCarran adjudications remains to be seen. Additionally, the states differ in their methods for selecting state judges and their political climates. While fed-supplicating and fed-denigrating may be a stock-in-trade of water politics—raising the fervor and the fever of water lawyers—a state judge takes an oath of office to uphold the constitution and the laws of the United States and the state. In instances of preemptive conflict, federal law prevails. In addition, judicial ethics require judges to reach reasoned decisions and not alter the conclusions they reach based on political considerations.

Evidence that state water politics is poisoning the well of fair hearings has its remedy in the exercise of federal court concurrent jurisdiction over the claims of the federal agencies and the tribes. The split of the Idaho Supreme Court on the issue of wilderness water rights dramatizes the toll federalism can take on state judges, as they grapple with strongly advocated, inherently adversarial positions with political content and implications.

Scholarship, deference to legislative intent, and straightforward exposition of the court's reasoning—this is the judicial ideal. The judicial ideal should be the expected norm.

Justice Silak's opinion in favor of wilderness water rights, like Judge Kane's before it in Colorado, was based on the forceful declarations Congress made in legislation favoring wilderness preservation. Her opinion was principled, not outlandish. It relied on the words of the statutes, the evident intent of Congress, leaving to legislators the evident policy issues.

The dissent to Justice Silak's opinion was also principled. It pointed out that neither the 1964 Wilderness Act, nor the individual Idaho wilderness designations created an express reserved water right.[120] The language of no claim/no denial of exemption from state water law was patently the product of compromise designed

---

[119] ENVIRONMENTAL POLICY PROJECT, GEORGETOWN UNIVERSITY LAW CENTER, CHANGING THE RULES BY CHANGING THE PLAYERS: THE ENVIRONMENTAL ISSUE IN STATE JUDICIAL ELECTIONS 48 (2000).
[120] *In re SRBA*, No. 24546, 1999 Idaho LEXIS 119, at *41 (Idaho Oct. 1, 1999) (Kidwell, J., dissenting).

to sidestep the issue. However, because the intent of Congress is determinative and Congress raised the very issue and then declined to resolve it, any court could logically conclude that Congress was not concerned with the creation of reserved water rights for wilderness areas, leaving the *New Mexico* doctrine applicable, as opposed to the *Winters* doctrine.

The Idaho Supreme Court majority and dissenting opinions—both sets of them—are well joined. The strength of the court's combined exposition, together with the evident need for final resolution, would seem to have made the Idaho case a logical candidate for United States Supreme Court review, but the government did not pursue a petition for certiorari. Congress and/or the Supreme Court has yet to resolve the polar opposites of wilderness water rights advocacy, the not-one-drop-shall-you-take from a wilderness area position versus the thou-shalt-not-tred-on-me state water law position.

The dilemma the Idaho Supreme Court faced is a study for other state supreme courts. Justice Silak's reelection bid, like Justice Stone's before it, became a political crucible, overshadowing the role of courts in the separation of powers and the merits of those serving in judicial office. Unlike Justice Stone's instance, where the Colorado Supreme Court refused to grant rehearing, the Idaho Supreme Court granted rehearing and reversed the outcome when the chief justice, who had concurred with Justice Silak's opinion, agreed with the two dissenters to deny the wilderness water claims. The rehearing process extended through Justice Silak's defeat.

While a judge should vote for rehearing if he or she may have misapprehended the facts or the law of the case, a rehearing and the substitution of an opposite opinion, is rare, in contrast with modifying the decision to make corrections while maintaining the same outcome and denying the rehearing petition. The essence of appellate deliberation is to test the strength of the proposed opinion, intellectually and practically. The appellate process is deliberate enough to allow thorough study and consideration before the court's final vote and release of a majority opinion. Non-authoring justices have a choice between two proposed opinions—to choose one or the other, or to author yet a third opinion, for the purpose of gaining a clearer majority or sharpening the court's analysis.

Significant questions deserve doubled efforts at consensus building among the justices whenever possible. Because justices must work in isolation, rather than the consultation in which the officials of the legislative and executive branches are free to engage in, they always owe to each other the courtesy of well-expressed critique, thoughtful insight, and prudent foresight.

The Idaho Supreme Court's switched outcome is likely to be the source of continued speculation. Did the court engage in politics in reaching its first decision, in granting the rehearing, in reversing itself on rehearing amidst a public outcry?

Or did the majority justices simply get it wrong, with the authoring justice bearing the ultimate responsibility?

Lost in the Idaho controversy is the fact that the Idaho Supreme Court, despite denying the wilderness water rights claims on rehearing, nevertheless determined that congressional legislation designating certain Idaho national recreation areas and wild and scenic rivers carried with them expressly reserved water rights, the amount thereof to be quantified on remand.[121] Idaho water users also strongly contested the existence of these rights, and the Idaho Supreme Court decisions in this regard. Others like it, arising from the McCarran proceedings, are candidates for United States Supreme Court review as well.

Thus, despite the surrounding political rhetoric of state primacy and sovereignty in water matters, it is clear that the Idaho Supreme Court did not take Justice Silak's defeat as a reason to retreat to an unmitigated application of state water law, in the face of the Constitution and laws of the United States. And in rulings by the Arizona Supreme Court in adjudication of tribal water rights,[122] McCarran decisions in Idaho's Snake River Basin Adjudication bode well for the ability of western state courts to go about the judicial business of resolving state and federal water claims.

The role of settlement in these complex adjudications is also important. Subordination of federal claims to present and reasonable future needs of the state is a possibility, in return for recognition of enforceable rights for protection of environmental values. Those committed to absolutist positions on both sides of the equation always have difficulty with such proposals, but significant differences can make for significant settlement achievements, accommodating important interests. Surely, Congress has delivered severely contrasting mixed messages through its traditional deference to state law and its strong environmental protection statutes.

Water users of all stripes, including those favoring environmental uses, are bound—in the system of water use property rights that Congress and the states have fostered—to the fundamental precept that juniors must stand aside while seniors exercise their rights, when there is not enough to supply all uses. Ignoring this in favor of passionate commitment to one's own point of view and interest

---

[121] *Potlatch Corp. v. United States*, 12 P.3d 1260, 1268-69 (Idaho 2000); *Potlatch Corp. v. United States*, 12 P.3d 1256, 1258-59 (Idaho 2000). The court refused to recognize the reserved water rights claims for certain recreation areas and national wildlife refuges in the state, applying the *New Mexico* doctrine. *United States v. Idaho*, 23 P.3d 117 (Idaho 2001); *State v. United States*, 12 P.3d 1284, 1290-91 (Idaho 2000).

[122] *In re General Adjudication of All Rights to Use Water in the Gila River System and Source*, No. WC-90-001-IR, 2001 Ariz. LEXIS 205 (Ariz. Nov. 26, 2001); *In re General Adjudication of All Rights to Use Water in the Gila River System and Source*, 989 P.2d 739 (Ariz. 1999).

mistakenly ignores the operative principle that water remains a public resource committed to disposition and use in priority.

Undoubtedly, the Idaho Water Bar will look both to the boundaries of its advocacy role and to its role in fostering a continuously independent and fair judiciary. So will the water bars of the other western states, in light of the Colorado and Idaho experiences. Fair judges conducting fair hearings must be the norm. Judicial political decision-making has no place in the separation of powers. That would undermine public confidence even more surely than a handful of controversial decisions.

The media also plays a very important role. Through reporting and editorializing, it can stand watch on the maturation and well being of each state's community. Operating in the community requires good scholarship, common sense, an eye to history, attention to detail, and well considered premonitions of future possibilities. If judges must run against opponents for election and raise funds, can they really focus on the merits of the cases before them? In light of the recent experience, the Idaho press began to engage in reflective deliberation on the important issues of government, natural resource use and preservation, and the federal relationships involved. Such public inquiry has a way of spilling into public policy.

The two chambers of the western heart, the two lobes of the western mind, are beneficial use and preservation. Growth and glorious natural habitat, this is the heritage of the public domain. Our rapidly urbanizing western experience—bridled by our love for the vistas, rivers, and all life, our natural optimism, our need for each other—in all of this our western place, so prized by the entire country, shall carry us forward.

Water and the West

ONE BODY, ONE SPIRIT, MANY FUTURES

Those who came before—yes,
they are with us still.
We know them by their names:
Need, Conflict, Confusion, Good
Will. They made—as best they could—
a compact, a basic apportionment,
based on the lay of the land
and the need of the people.

The idea is this: fifty-fifty,
the upper, the lower, head-to-toe,
joined at the gut and the hip—
mountains, the great Grand Canyon,
the vast Southwest—always
the River at the heart of all
possibility. And, so, we go
one body, one spirit, many futures.

Historical Perspective on Western Land and Water Law
Colorado River Compact Symposium, Water Education Foundation
Santa Fe, New Mexico
May 30, 1997

The call of freedom and the call of the river are strong and synonymous in the myth of our western New World. Walt Whitman sang it so:

> Carrying my knapsack and gun, or a miner in
> California, or rude in my home in Dakotas's
> woods, my diet meat, my drink from the spring
> ...aware of the fresh free giver the flowing
> Missouri...solitary, singing in the West, I
> strike up for a New World.
>
> Walt Whitman, "Starting From Paumanok," in
Leaves of Grass, 1891-1892 Edition (Random House, Inc.).

Said Jefferson to Meriwether Lewis: "The object of your mission is single, the direct water communication from sea to sea formed by the bed of the Missouri & perhaps the Oregon." Stephen E. Ambrose, *Undaunted Courage, Meriwether Lewis, Thomas Jefferson, and the Opening of the American West* (Simon & Schuster, 1996) at 116 (Quoting Letter of Jefferson to Lewis).

"The direct water communication from sea to sea...perhaps"!!!

Myth, reality, and the inevitable challenge of reconciling the two by discovery and hard work—Jefferson posed and predicted so well the western dilemma and experience.

If Walt Whitman were alive today, would his song turn towards a wistful lament?

> Carrying my REI water bottle and my Salt River field
> glasses, or a yuppie in California redwoods, or crude
> in my seat in Mile High Stadium, my diet corn dogs,
> my drink from a thousand shot glasses at the MGM Grand
> ...aware that nothing's free at Bullfrog Marina...in

> a crowd at La Fonda, groaning for a ticket to
> whatever's happening, solitary, talking to myself,
> I strike out at the New World.

Eighty-five percent of us who now live in the West dwell in cities for our daily work, but our spirit belongs to the mountains, mesas, deserts, canyons, and rivers. No other place seems like home, and to be away is disorienting.

Wallace Stegner, the author of that stupendous biography of John Wesley Powell, *Beyond the Hundredth Meridian*, said this of the American western experience:

> Our very virtues as a pioneering people, the very genius of our industrial civilization, drove us to act as we did. God and Manifest Destiny spoke with one voice urging us to "conquer" or "win" the West; and there was no voice of comparable authority to remind us of Mary Austin's quiet but profound truth, that "the manner of the country makes the usage of life there, and the land will not be lived in except in its own fashion."
>
> Wallace Stegner, *Where the Bluebird Sings to the Lemonade Springs* (Random House, 1992) at 87.

Each new generation rediscovers the West. On the top of Flattop Mountain at the crest of the Divide (in what is now Rocky Mountain National Park), the Eureka Ditch was cut by farmers in the nineteenth century to divert a small flow of water from the Pacific side to the Atlantic side of the mountain for use in northeastern Colorado. Operation of the ditch was grandfathered as a use when the park was created, and it was later acquired by the City of Loveland. Two years ago the City agreed with the Park Service to abandon the ditch in exchange for an equal amount of water yield from the Colorado-Big Thompson Reclamation Project out of the park's share of project waters.

. . .

Off the top of Flattop Mountain to the west the Colorado River gathers in the snowmelt of May and falls precipitously into the Colorado-Big Thompson

Project at the base of Rocky Mountain National Park. The Project's four flat water bodies are a National Recreation Area. And so the river runs and pools from the Rockies to the All American Canal, delight of fishermen and boaters, inspiration of photographers, painters, and writers, engine of farms and cities, hope and despair of planners and reformers, habitat of many lives besides human which depend upon the way we act, or restrain ourselves from acting, for maintenance of their place.

We've done our best and worst and a lot of average work in settling this, our western place. From the 1860s to the 1960s, federal policy favored the development of the West on a predominantly utilitarian note. Notable exceptions were the creation of national parks and monuments that fired the imagination of Easterners and Westerners alike: Yellowstone, Yosemite, the Grand Canyon, and a host of other parks and monuments, smaller, less known, every bit a part of the western heartland. Thomas Moran, in his great painting "The Chasm of the Colorado" (1873-74), depicted rock, storm, abyss, and far away river as a metaphor of wilderness and the promise of human redemption:

> ...the storm is essential to the meaning of the painting. The shower with its rainbow and the giant depression into which it pours are inseparable. Each requires the other for definition and completion, both in Moran's painting, where the two elements interact compositionally and symbolically, and in the land itself—the Grand Canyon and throughout the Southwest—where water is the very stuff of life...The juxtaposition of these opposing elements, the rock and rain, hole and rainbow, and their complex interactive symbology form the central ambiguity and meaning of Moran's painting. The conjunction of these forms in the picture is parallel to the conflict of positive and negative forces in the Grand Canyon itself...Moran's sensitivity to the subtleties of the opposing elements of rock and water in his visual expression of the place suggest a close relationship to the controversies in the early 1870s about the arability of the desert Southwest and points to Moran's personal relationship with John Wesley Powell, the principal proponent of the debate...[Powell] refers to the water as "degrading," "disintegrating," and "dissolving" the rock, all terms connoting destruction, but elsewhere he refers to irrigation water's potential to "redeem" the land, a

creative and sacred act of renewal.... Powell saw the philosophical aspects of the land as inseparable from their practical application; the two approaches were inextricably intertwined.

Joni Louise Kinsey, *Thomas Moran and the Surveying of the American West* (Smithsonian Institution Press, 1992) at 98-99, 108.

The selling of the West by development interests often included selling the magnificence of the West as promotional backdrop. Jackson's photograph of the Mount of the Holy Cross, followed by Moran's painting of the same, illustrated how God had blessed America by carving the face of the wilderness with a Christian symbol. A manifest destiny, unnecessarily exclusionary, view of divine providence, certainly. But strangely right enough too! Every cirque and mountain peak, every rivulet and gaining river, bears the mark of miracle.

Only in the last half of the twentieth century have we turned to preserving the last vestiges of wild America as wilderness. Now, we are reclaiming our waterways from our trashways for walking paths and wildlife preserves. We hear the music of running water and see the heron stand on a sandbar in the midst of our most urban environments. Amusement parks are built along such waterways. But riding the roller coaster at Denver's Elitch Gardens is nothing like running Westwater Canyon through the red rock country of the Colorado River.

Perhaps, in the midst of the increasing urbanization of the West, we may begin to feel that sense of awe that Native Americans experienced when they consumed animals and other natural resources with gratitude and acknowledgment of the power conferred on one through borrowing the other's substance and spirit. A great joy of opening a farm headgate and running water onto a field is to see a row of melons take shape or the corn to sprout, and give thanks to the river.

Thomas Hornsby Ferril wrote of the need to hold our romanticism to the firm grip of everyday life and thereby sound our reality in the concrete form of poetry:

> [L]andscape such as ours cannot be ignored. It is an integral part of our emotional experience. A mountain range is forever a blue wall behind which something is happening. Being an emotional person, it is difficult for me to turn from those glorious ranges and say to myself: more water, better tilth, more straw needed for bedding, earlier decomposition of

manure, higher yields of grain, alfalfa, sugar beets, yet this is the road to poetry: men in action, the transitoriness of life, memory, desire, agony, ecstasy.

James C. Work, Ed., *Prose and Poetry of the American West* (University of Nebraska Press, 1990) at 391.

My wife Bobbie and I own, with our son Dan and daughter-in-law Alison, a 25-acre farm in New Mexico along the Pecos River outside of Anton Chico. In April, we helped clean out the laterals below the farm headgate and enjoyed the irrigation water singing sweetly to the garlic and the apricot we had planted. Working that farm reminds us of what Aldo Leopold said: "We abuse land because we regard it as a commodity belonging to us. When we see land as a community to which we belong, we may begin to use it with love and respect." Erik Bruun and Robin Getzen (Eds.), *The Book of American Values and Virtues* (Black Dog & Leventhal Publishers, Inc., 1996) at 238.

Our neighbor farm owners are Hispanic Northern New Mexicans. They could not love, respect, or live upon this land without their 1844 water rights. 1844 predates Kearney's claim of this land for the United States in defiance of Mexico. The State of New Mexico's role in defending its share of the Pecos River Compact with Texas is essential to its cultural and community interest.

It takes some being away from the West to remind ourselves that water rights are a unique characteristic of our heritage.

The soldiers, mapmakers, and explorer/scientists who went west after the Civil War informed Congress that the Homestead Act of 1862 would have little effect in settling the West without storage and a water law suitable for the arid lands. In his pioneering report, "Lands of the Arid Region of the United States," John Wesley Powell spoke about a new law and practice of water that was arising from western necessity. He spoke of a "natural right to the use of water":

> The ancient principles of common law applying to the use of natural streams, so wise and equitable in a humid region, would, if applied to the Arid Region, practically prohibit the growth of its most important industries. Thus it is that a custom is springing up in the Arid Region which may or may not have the color of authority in statutory or common law...certain it is that water rights are practically being severed from the natural channels of the streams; and this must be done.... Perhaps

an amplification by the courts of what has been designated as the *natural right* to the use of water may be made to cover the practices now obtaining; but it hardly seems wise to imperil interests so great intrusting them to the possibility of some future court made law.

John Wesley Powell, *Lands of the Arid Region of the United States*
(Facsimile of the 1879 Edition, the Harvard Common Press, 1983) at 42-43.

We now know from archaeology that ancient peoples of the Southwest practiced irrigation. A Zuni emergence myth relates the power of water, the growth of crops, and the holy bonding of the two in the fruitful corn that men and women consume for sustenance:

> These plumes, with prayers and offerings, they planted in the valleys...Lo! for eight days and nights it rained and there were thick mists; and the waters from the mountains poured down bringing new soil and spreading it over the valleys where the plumed sticks had been planted. "See!" said the fathers of the seed clan, "water and new earth bring we by our supplications."

James C. Work, Ed., *Prose and Poetry of the American West*
(University of Nebraska Press, 1990) at 19.

As Powell suggested, the western states did not leave the formation of water law and the creation of water rights to the courts to sort out without guidance; rather, state constitutions and statutes provided for the protection of water rights as property rights. Invoking the recognition that the United States Constitution extends to property rights vested under state law, the Congress through the Mining Act, the Desert Lands Act, the National Forest Organic Act, and other statutes provided states with the ability to continuously allocate unappropriated water, vest water rights, and divert water in the course thereof from the streams on federal as well as non-federal lands within the boundaries of each state.

In the post-Civil War era, conservation concerns grew as unbridled economic impetus showed what despoliation can mean. We have an anti-eastern arrogance about us, we westerners, equaled only by the arrogance of those who are not from here! Some of the greatest shapers of the West were westward-looking easterners: John Wesley Powell of Ohio, and Teddy Roosevelt and Gifford Pinchot of New York and the Potomac. They and their fellow Progressive Conservationists believed in human achievement and fulfillment through a healthy physical environment, personal democracy, and the possibility of individual economic advancement. They detested monopolies and advocated that the remaining federal lands should be withdrawn from settlement under the Homestead Act and dedicated to the efficient and sustained use of the West's natural wealth through scientific and technological means of resource conservation.

The other conservation movement that existed when Theodore Roosevelt entered the White House in 1901 was led, ironically, by a westerner who desired to halt the use of the western public domain entirely, John Muir. He advocated land reservations as a means to perpetually preserve them as wilderness for the benefit of a "tired, nerve-shaken, over-civilized people." A prototype rugged individualist, Muir fought for non-use and was detested, or ignored, by westerners, while the patricians, Roosevelt and Pinchot, received support by western cities and farmers who depended upon the forested watersheds for a long-term supply of water. In his fine book about the conservation conflict in Colorado and the West at the turn of the nineteenth century, Michael McCarthy observes:

> The attitude of Coloradans toward Roosevelt and Pinchot clearly illustrated the divergence of opinion that existed in the state over the conservation issue. For while the two men were accorded widespread contempt in the Colorado backwoods, they also commanded a large following all across the state. Roosevelt's support came primarily from urban centers, plains cities such as Denver, Colorado Springs, and Pueblo and Western Slope settlements like Delta and Montrose, areas dependent on the preservation of mountain watersheds for irrigation and water supplies.
>
> G. Michael McCarthy, Hour of Trial, *The Conservation Conflict in Colorado and the West 1891-1907* (University of Oklahoma Press, 1977) at 88.

Senator Henry Teller of Colorado had screamed, with all the fury of a stump speaker denouncing the hated federal autocrat, that the remaining public lands within the state should be handed over wholesale to private enterprise; instead, with the support of Coloradans, 14 million acres were reserved as National Forest land. Today, under the 1964 National Wilderness Preservation Act—the heritage of Muir's respect for the unique West—three million of those acres are now preserved as designated wilderness.

The guarantee that the National Forests would remain available for access to the settlement of water rights under state law and the operation of waterworks on and through the forest reservations won the day for the federal land presence, which continues to be the indispensable stitching of our fabric. *United States v. New Mexico*, 438 U.S. 696, 712 (1978). Go East, old man, if you want to be hemmed out by private land! If you want to take a good long walk and smell the ponderosa, try a National Forest in any of our western states.

In taking that walk, we should not forget the western water law heritage that led to the designation of these alluring canopies of green between the barren crags and the browning prairie. Congress provided in the 1897 Forest Organic Act that:

> All waters within the boundaries of national forests may be used for domestic, mining, milling, or irrigation purposes, under the laws of the State wherein such national forests are situated, or under the laws of the United States and the rules and regulations established thereunder.
>
> 16 U.S.C. § 481 (1994).

But individual state law does not exclusively govern the creation of water rights. The notion that all water flowing within a state had been deeded to that state, upon its admission to the Union, for disposition solely under its own constitution and laws was profoundly disturbed by two early twentieth-century holdings of the United States Supreme Court. In *Winters v. United States*, 207 U.S. 564 (1908), the Court held that the United States, in connection with creating land reservations for the Native Americans, had reserved water rights to carry out the primary purposes of those reservations out of then-unappropriated waters within the States wherein the reservations were located.

In *Kansas v. Colorado*, 206 U.S. 46, 92-94, 117 (1907), the Court announced that each state can choose its own water law, whether riparian or prior appropriation, but no state can impose its choice of law on another state. The national government's interest in reclamation of arid lands could not supplant the water law selection of either state, and an equitable apportionment of the interstate water body can be ordered by the Court, subject to revisions from time to time, in the exercise of the Court's original jurisdiction. This was a classic border war. Colorado had claimed all the waters arising within its boundaries under its constitutional doctrine of prior appropriation; Kansas asserted that its riparian system should prevail because the Colorado Territory had been carved out of the 1854 Kansas Territory in 1861. Both states, as a result of the enunciation of the doctrine of equitable apportionment on a case-by-case basis, were left with the possibility of continuous litigation in the Supreme Court to determine from time to time what an equitable apportionment might be.

The Supreme Court's next equitable apportionment decision, *Wyoming v. Colorado*, 259 U.S. 419 (1922), involved two prior appropriation states, and much to the horror of the upstream state, the Court allowed the senior priorities within the downstream state to control. Even the most ardent proponents of western prior appropriation law were thunderstruck with the nerve-shattering implications of a "first in time, first in right" state anchoring the interstate river and controlling the destiny of its elevated neighbors.

A compact is both state and federal law. It is meant to govern interstate water allocation and replace exercise of the original jurisdiction of the United States Supreme Court, except with regard to enforcement of the compact. Ratification of a compact may be seen as the exercise by Congress of its power to consent to interstate commerce limitations inherent in fulfillment of the compact's purpose. *Simpson v. Highland Irrigation Company*, 917 P.2d 1242, 1249, n.8 (Colo. 1996). A state may create and vest water rights as property, but only with regard to its allocated share of the interstate waters. *Hinderlider v. La Plata River & Cherry Creek Ditch Co.*, 304 U.S. 92, 106 (1938).

The basic guarantee of the Colorado River Compact is that beneficial water uses within the Upper Basin and Lower Basin states may be allowed to deplete the waters of the Colorado River each year in the amount of 7,500,000 acre-feet each basin, each year. The Lower Basin's allocation has largely been developed through federal financial assistance during the Reclamation era. The Upper Basin states have not experienced the same level of commitment. Nevertheless, a principal reason for the Colorado River Compact, and its most enduring aspect for the Upper Basin states, is the Congressional authorization for continuing creation of property rights in its citizens by a signatory state with regard to its unconsumed allocated share of the river's waters. After all, this is what the architects of the Compact wished to preserve perpetually to the states within the constitutional framework of compact federalism, realizing that full use of each state's share might prove to be a long-term proposition.

We've done our best and worst (and a lot of average work) in settling this, our western place. Powell's irrigation survey and the 1902 Reclamation Act, a product of western irrigation boosterism and progressive Conservationism, led to the possibility of the Colorado River Compact and its implementation as America began to re-prize its natural heritage. The great guarantors and equalizers of the Compact allocation, Lakes Powell and Mead, hold between them that most awesome of the American preserves.

Could the Major have foreseen that the quiet river turns and hanging gardens he floated past in Glen Canyon would be transformed into 2,200 miles of shoreline around an immense inland sea of human creation, with over two million boaters a year playing above the stretch of river where his few gathered strength for the plunge into the gut of the primordial chasm?

The fight for preservation of the Grand Canyon and Echo Park far upstream produced their preservation and the inundation of Glen Canyon, which, in a consequential way, led to the 1964 Wilderness Act and the 1969 National Environmental Policy Act. Our resource use and preservation heritage lies mightily in this river, which begins off the top of Flattop Mountain in Rocky Mountain National Park and runs and pools its way to the All American Canal before entering Mexico.

Water is a public resource that can be put to private uses. Today cities and public districts are the predominant actors in the arena of water use. They can be expected to reflect their citizen constituencies. As this constituency rediscovers the beauty and economic value of restoring water to dried-up stream stretches for wildlife habitat and recreational purposes, the value of water rights as property acquired and held in the public sector through enduring investment will compete in the market to attract water rights formerly utilized in irrigation. The West's water and land heritage, its respect for property rights, and its individualism practiced in community will continue to serve its future.

Donald Pisani has written that "The study of the West must begin from the ground up, rather than from the top down: the parts must be understood before sense can be made of the whole...to appreciate the region's diversity." Donald J. Pisani, *To Reclaim a Divided West* (1992) at 332.

The new, growing, and changing civilization of our beloved West is more potentially fruitful than ever. Along with Native American and Anglo peoples, Hispanic, Asian-American, and African-American populations, whose ancestral muscle helped to build our nation's infrastructure, will increasingly take leadership roles in the impetus for a just society of opportunity and optimism, hallmarks of our western makeup. Let us not contest that the true destiny of America was not manifest destiny, but it genius—amidst struggle and transition—for attracting peoples and cultures of the world to inclusion in its citizenship and, by reason of that inclusion, to work for the rights of man and woman.

I opened with Wallace Stegner, speaking of the western experience, so shall I close:

<blockquote>
Wanted

A True Civilization

Not a Ruthless Occupation

Disguised As Romantic Myth.
</blockquote>

Machu Picchu*

University of Denver Water Law Review, reprinted with permission
Fall 2002

Book Review of Kenneth R. Wright and Alfredo Valencia Zegarra, *Machu Picchu: A Civil Engineering Marvel* (American Society of Civil Engineers, Reston, Va., 2000),
and
Ruth M. Wright and Alfredo Valencia Zegarra, *The Machu Picchu Guidebook: A Self-Guided Tour*, (with Archeological Map of Macho Picchu), (Johnson Books, Boulder, Colo. 2001).

Coloradans Ken and Ruth Wright have teamed with Peruvian archeologist Alfredo Valencia to place back in working order the 16 fountains of Machu Picchu. You can see for yourself.

The Inca were master water handlers. They chose Machu Picchu as a ceremonial center because the mountains and the river spoke to them of life-giving power. The Urubamba River, far below, snakes triangular around the base of Machu Picchu and Huayna Picchu mountains. A saddle between these peaks cradles the temples, the rock shrines, the dwelling places, and the agricultural terraces that dance between the clouds in early morning and emerge to sunlight by noon.

Water is at the center of it all. Wright and Valencia's paleohydrologic studies reveal how the Inca predicated the design and construction of Machu Picchu upon the flow of a spring. From high on the side of Machu Picchu Mountain, a canal brings water across an agricultural terrace to the first fountain just above the Temple of the Sun. From there, 16 fountains splash, spout, and sing down a staircase to the Temple of the Condor.

Study the foldout archeological map of Machu Picchu inside Ruth's and Alfredo's *Machu Picchu Guidebook*. See how the Inca trail leads into the upper and lower agricultural terraces. Notice how the Inca Canal cuts across the drainage moat to bisect the western and eastern urban sectors. Spot the Sacred Rock at the start of the Huayna Picchu trail, where Quechua families still hug the visible manifestation of Pachamama, the earth mother.

---

* 6 U. DENV. WATER L. REV. 137 (2002). © University of Denver Water Law Review 2002.

Now you are ready for your self-guided tour. Just inside the entrance gate, climb to the Guardhouse. Pause to see how the water supply canal passes right by food storehouses. Cross the Inca trail coming in from Cusco and stand beside the Guardhouse. Below you stretch the whole of this incredible cradle of civilization; the lovely green of the main plaza feeding llama and alpaca; the Inca stones rising on either side to form the ceremonial and residential edifices; and the crop-growing terraces on the flanks of the cradle falling away to the Urubamba River.

Step-by-step, Ruth and Alfredo talk you, by the printed page, through these wonders. Plan on spending several days there. You will have the joy of misty mornings and sun-streaked afternoons. The day-train trippers will be gone. Wind through the Rock Quarry. Pause in the quiet of the Unfinished Temple. You can take the time to side hike to the Sun Gate, Machu Picchu Mountain, the Inca Drawbridge, and Huayna Picchu Mountain. Talk with other visitors. The world is here for good reason.

Ruth and Alfredo immensely aid the visitor's Machu Picchu experience. They bring new information to old understandings:

> There are many different ways to experience Machu Picchu. We hope this guidebook will give you the tools to do it in your own way. In the last several decades, much has been learned about the Inca in general and Machu Picchu in particular. Since the Inca had no written language, scientists have had to "read" their artifacts, their stones, their temples, and their mummies to establish their place in history. Recent information and new analyses of earlier findings are shedding additional light on these truly remarkable people and their culture.

The *Machu Picchu Guidebook* starts with an introduction to the history and topography of Machu Picchu. Chapters follow dedicated to the Guardhouse and the Terrace of the Ceremonial Rock; the Western Urban Sector; the Eastern Urban Sector; Various Sites on the Way Out; and Side Trips. Marvelous detail attends every page. The accompanying photographs are many and well shot. They draw your attention to the features described in the text.

Pay particular attention to the numerous huacas. These are the Inca sacred places, typically consisting of naturally situated or human placed rocks cut to the shape of surrounding peaks. These people loved their mountains.

Don't be afraid to make some wrong turns as you orient yourself. The structure of the *Machu Picchu Guidebook* divides Machu Picchu into hemispheres. You start by going down from the Guardhouse to the Main Gate to the Temple of the Sun; then you turn laterally to the residence of the Inca and back through the Western Urban Sector up to the Rock Quarry, the Sacred Plaza, and the Intiwantana. Then you proceed clockwise past the Sacred Rock and Unfinished Temple into the Eastern Urban Sector, finishing at the Temple of the Condor.

Making the walk in this way takes you away from the staircase of the 16 fountains early on. You encounter the staircase and the fountains again when you reach the Temple of the Condor much later. Sometime during your multi-day visit to Machu Picchu, you will want to follow the staircase in one continuous movement down from the Main Gate to see, feel, and hear the fountains flow sinuously.

The May 2002, issue of *National Geographic Magazine* contains yet another map of Machu Picchu derived from the Wright-Valencia partnership. This map shows how magnificent Machu Picchu must have looked with its thatched roofs uplifted to the condor sky.

Underneath your feet at every turn is the invisible 60 percent of Machu Picchu. In their *Civil Engineering Marvel*, Ken and Alfredo describe the genius of Machu Picchu's foundational structure. The Inca edifices and agricultural terraces stand the test of time because of careful drainage and methodical trench work. The visible 40 percent of Machu Picchu rests on mountain bedrock and the skill of people who learned through ancestral experience how to counter earthquake and erosion's despoiling effect.

Ken and Alfredo deduce from their studies that the Inca did not irrigate the agricultural terraces at Machu Picchu, though they did elsewhere. Here, the rainy season and supplemental importation of agricultural products met the needs of the small resident population and the influx of those attending rituals. The Inca ruler Pachacuti began Machu Picchu as a ceremonial retreat in A.D. 1450. It likely ceased normal operation by A.D. 1540 due to the collapse of the Inca Empire under Spanish invasion.

Ken and Alfredo explain that Machu Picchu's durability stems from high quality professional workmanship:

> Machu Picchu's technical planning is surely the key to the site's longevity and functionality. The Inca's careful use of hydraulic, drainage, and construction techniques ensured that the retreat was not reduced to

rubble during its many years of abandonment. These techniques, combined with a strong knowledge of hydrology, were what made it a grand and operational retreat high in the most rugged of terrain.

The *Civil Engineering Marvel* is easily readable, yet contains much study and analysis of Machu Picchu's structural accomplishment. Ken and Alfredo devote chapters to (1) setting, geology, climate, and site selection; (2) city planning and engineering infrastructure; (3) hydrogeology, collection works, water requirements, and water supplies; (4) hydraulic engineering, water supply canal, and fountains; (5) drainage infrastructure, surface runoff and drainage criteria, agricultural terraces, and urban sector; (6) agriculture, hand-placed soil, crop water needs, and adequacy of nutrient production; (7) building foundations and stone walls; (8) construction methods, rock quarry, transporting and lifting rocks, using wood and vegetation, roof structures, canal stones, floors and plaster, bridges, and tools of the trade; (9) cultural background and Inca heritage; and (10) a walking tour of the engineering works (Ruth's contribution).

Dr. Gordon McEwan, excavator of Pikillacta and Chokepukio, illuminates the cultural background of the Inca in a fine chapter he contributes to the *Civil Engineering Marvel* (chapter 9). He further explains in a June 2002 *National Geographic Magazine* article how the Inca culture built upon the Wari culture (A.D. 600-1000). At Pikillacta, the Wari relied on an aqueduct whose portals also served as their gateways and guard ways to the Cusco Valley. Before the Wari, dating from B.C. 200, the Pukara and the Tiwanaku peoples conducted water for pragmatic and religious purposes.

The Inca were religious and practical people. They revered the earth, the mountains, and the sky, as their descendants the Quechua still do. On mountain torsos, they saw visages of the serpent, the puma, and the condor. Rocks and dead ancestors were equally alive to inform and inspire the Inca by daily consultation in community. They were expert engineers, architects, and water workers. Joseph and Pharaoh-like, they dreamed of drought and famine; so, they stored the plentiful crop against the certitude of impending scarcity. The Inca exacted a tax in the form of labor. In return, the community benefited from stored food and ritual celebrations.

In the third summer of a North American western drought (A.D.2002), with the published work of Ken, Ruth, and Alfredo in hand—I could see it too—how water works at Machu Picchu for domestic water supply, aesthetic, and spiritual needs. The Inca water containment and delivery structures join those of the Mayans at Tikal, the Anasazi at Mesa Verde, and the Hopi at their mesas in a centuries-old mosaic of water use in the Western Hemisphere.

In scarcity lies the opportunity for community. The native peoples of the Americas practiced the art of water works construction out of ingenuity and necessity, praying to the gods for rain to fill their earth-constructed hope against despair. The native peoples also demonstrated that water supply planning and infrastructure is a core responsibility of those who would govern in the public interest. Westerners always come round to the practical and symbolic value of water for people and the environment.

I especially like the fountains.

SIXTEEN FOUNTAINS

Down a granite staircase sixteen
Fountains carry the spring
Falling from the Sungate, high on
Machu Picchu mountain

You can hear the mountain—singing
Hands of master craftsmen
Scoring stone with hammer rock and
Praying Pachamama

To the temple of the arcing
Sun, jetting water out
When water runs for rock and men
And all is feminine.

To Ken and Ruth Wright and Alfredo Valencia.

Gregory Hobbs is a Justice of the Colorado Supreme Court. Ken Wright is Principal Engineer of Wright Water Engineers, Inc, Denver, Colorado. Ruth Wright, a former member of the Colorado General Assembly, is a Board Member of the Northern Colorado Water Conservancy District. Alfredo Valencia is a Professor of Archaeology at the Universidad de San Antonio Abad in Cusco, Peru.

The Role of Climate in Shaping Western Water Institutions†
University of Denver Water Law Review, reprinted with permission
Fall 2003

ULYSSES' TALE, DANTE, THE INFERNO

[A]nd turning our stern toward morning, our bow toward night,
we bore southwest out of the world of man;
we made wings of our oars for our fool's flight.
. . . .
Five times since we had dipped our bending oars
beyond the world, the light beneath the moon
had waxed and waned, when dead upon our course

we sighted, dark in space, a peak so tall
I doubted any man had seen the like.[1]

THE ASCENT FROM HELL, DANTE, THE INFERNO

[A]nd it may be that moved by that same fear,
the one peak that still rises on this side
fled upward leaving this great cavern here.
Down there, beginning at the further bound
of Beelzebub's dim tomb, there is a space
not known by sight, but only by the sound
of a little stream descending through the hollow
it has eroded from the massive stone
in its endlessly entwining lazy flow.

---

† 7 U. DENV. WATER L. REV. 1 (2003). © University of Denver Water Law Review 2003. Justice Hobbs of the Colorado Supreme Court is the author of the *Citizen's Guide to Colorado Water Law*, which the Colorado Foundation for Water Education published in 2003. He is co-convenor of *Dividing the Waters*, an educational project of the western water judges. This article was first prepared as a talk for the Natural Resources Law Center of the University of Colorado, June 2003.

[1] DANTE ALIGHIERI, THE INFERNO, Ulysses' Tale, Canto XXVI, Circle 8, *Bolgia* 8:115-17, 121-25 (John Ciardi trans., New American Library 1954) (1306-21).

> My Guide and I crossed over and began
> to mount that little known and lightless road
> to ascend into the shining world again.[2]

A. Explorers

Ulysses—traveling west—spotted a peak so tall no man had seen the like. The poet and his guide climbed out of hell through a hollow that a little stream—discovered only by its sound—had bored, into the lighted upper world.

As westerners, we recognize this immediately: Dante's tales are the story of the Great Western Journey. We feel the joy and awe of Zebulon Pike and Major Stephen H. Long (1806 and 1820) in sighting the Great Divide, rising out of a scorched and blasted desert plain and ascending up a freshet of mountain water.[3] Traveling with Long, botanist Edwin James observed:

> The images of pools of water, which we saw in the deserts of the Platte, appeared to us similar to those mentioned by Elphinstone, likewise to those observed by Nieburgh in Arabia, where inverted images were seen.[4]
>
> . . . .
>
> They ascended a primitive mountain which seemed to be of superior elevation, in order to overlook the western ranges, but they here found their horizon bounded by the succeeding mountain, towering majestically above them. To the east, over the tops of a few inferior elevations, lay expanded, like an ocean, the vast interminable prairie, over which we had so long held our monotonous march.[5]

Aridity. That's why the vistas shine so. And why the noses of our best western writers twitch so dryly.

---

[2] DANTE ALIGHIERI, THE INFERNO, The Ascent From Hell, Canto XXXIV, Circle 9, *Round* 4: 127-38 (John Ciardi trans., New American Library 1954) (130-21).
[3] FROM PITTSBURGH TO THE ROCKY MOUNTAINS: MAJOR STEPHEN LONG'S EXPEDITION 1819-1820, at ii, viii-ix (Maxine Benson ed., 1988).
[4] *Id.* at 195.
[5] *Id.* at 210.

B. Writers

DROUTH—1824

> Hear how the wagons crack
> In the copper drouth of the prairie,
> The pitch that boils from the seams
> Is not yet chilled by the moonrise,
> The great wheels groan like slaves,
> Under the loads they carry,
> The wheels are shrunken and spiked
> With wedges to keep them from breaking.[6]

REPORT ON THE LANDS OF THE ARID REGION OF THE UNITED STATES

The Arid Region is...something more than four-tenths of the whole country, excluding Alaska.

. . . .

... During the fall and winter the streams are small; in late spring and early summer they are very large. A day's flow at flood time is greater than a month's flow at low water time. During the first part of the irrigating season less water is needed, but during that same time the supply is greatest. The chief increase will come from the storage of this excess of water in the early part of the irrigating season.

. . . .

... All the waters of all the arid lands will eventually be taken from their natural channels, and they can be utilized only to the extent to which they are thus removed, and water rights must of necessity be severed from the natural channels.[7]

LIVING DRY, WALLACE STEGNER'A AMERICAN WEST

Adaptation is the covenant that all successful organisms sign with the dry country.... [W]ater is safety, home, life, place. All around those

---

[6] Thomas Hornsby Ferril, *Drought—1824*, in THOMAS HORNSBY FERRIL AND THE AMERICAN WEST 16, Robert C. Baron, Stephen J. Leonard, and Thomas J. Noel. eds., (Fulcrum Publishing, Golden, Colorado and the Center of the American West, University of Colorado at Boulder, 1996).

[7] JOHN WESLEY POWELL, REPORT ON THE LANDS OF THE ARID REGION OF THE UNITED STATES 5-6, 13-14, 42 (facsimile reprint, Harvard Common Press 1983) (2d ed. 1879).

precious watered places, forbidding and unlivable, is only space, what one must travel through between places of safety.[8]

The Southwest

As a result of these three drying agents—sun, wind, and transpiration—all but the highest mountains suffer from what agronomists call "moisture deficiency." In many places this deficiency exceeds twenty inches. This means that no matter how excellent the soil or how free of frost the nights, unless irrigation water equal in amount to twenty or more inches of rain is spread at appropriate intervals on the fields, crops cannot be grown.[9]

Colorado, A History of the Centennial State

[P]eriods of abundant rainfall and drought have occurred in regular cycles on the plains. The years from 1865 to 1872 were dry; those from 1873 to 1885 were wet. Droughts then came in cycles of twenty-one years, with the driest years occurring in 1892, 1912, 1934, and 1953. Total rainfall in the bad years dropped 15 to 25 percent below normal, with most of the reduction during the July and August growing seasons.[10]

The Land of Little Rain

Not the law, but the land sets the limit. Desert is the name it wears upon the maps.... Void of life it never is, however dry the air and villainous the soil.[11]

Water and the West, The Colorado River Compact and the Politics of Water in the American West

No area of the world is more aware of the current water crisis than western America, a vast arid and semiarid region embracing nearly half the continent of North America. Except for a strip along the north Pacific coast and isolated areas in the high mountains, the West is a region of sparse rainfall and few rivers. The implications of these facts of geography have been enormous. From the time of the first settlers to

---

[8] Wallace Stegner, *Living Dry, in* Marking the Sparrow's Fall 213, 226-27 (Page Stegner ed., 1998).
[9] David Lavender, The Southwest 20 (1980).
[10] Carl Abbott et al., Colorado: A History of the Centennial State 173 (3rd ed. 1994).
[11] Mary Austin, The Land of Little Rain 1 (1950).

the present, few westerners have failed to comprehend that control of the West's water means control of the West itself—its industry; agriculture; population distribution; and, withal, the direction of the future.[12]

We have learned from the relatively new science of paleohydrology not to be so arrogant or dismissive about the origins and reasons for mid-nineteenth century western water development. Native Americans, followed by Hispanic Americans, were working the waters of the Americas long before the Oregon Trail, from the ocean-like prairie to the waves of mountains blue to the western shores, opened for the Overlanders a way west.

C. Native American Water Uses

1. Puebloans of Mesa Verde

William H. Jackson, photographer and artist, accompanied the mapmakers.[13] As a member of Ferdinand V. Hayden's Survey of Colorado in 1874-75, Jackson described the Pueblo ruins of the Puebloans (Anasazi) in the Mesa Verde region.[14] High up on the side of a southeast-facing cliff, he spotted ruins of ancient homes up a series of weathered steps perched—almost impossibly—on sheer vertical space ledges.[15] Opposite one of the rooms was "a large reservoir, or cistern, the upper walls of which came nearly to the top of the window."[16]

In 1893, the archaeologist G. Nordenskiold found what he called "conclusive evidence that the cliff-dwellers had to contend with the same dry climate and the same scarcity of water as now obtain in these regions."[17] He described an ancient reservoir—enclosed by a circular wall, with a ditch running into it—that he found on Chapin Mesa.[18] Nearby were the ruins of a considerable village.[19] Referring to the ruins of ancient irrigation works found in Northern Arizona, Nordenskiold conjectured, "It is not at all improbable that irrigation by artificial means was in use even among the prehistoric inhabitants of the Mesa Verde."[20]

---

[12] NORRIS HUNDLEY, JR., WATER AND THE WEST: THE COLORADO RIVER COMPACT AND THE POLITICS OF WATER IN THE AMERICAN WEST, at ix (1975).

[13] *See* W. H. Jackson, *Ancient Ruins in Southwestern Colorado*, in 1 BULLETIN OF THE UNITED STATES GEOLOGICAL AND GEOGRAPHICAL SURVEY OF THE TERRITORIES, 1874 AND 1875, at 17 (Washington, D.C., Gov't Printing Office 1875).

[14] *Id.* at 17-38.

[15] *Id.* at 20-21.

[16] *Id.* at 21.

[17] G. NORDENSKIOLD, THE CLIFF DWELLERS OF THE MESA VERDE 73 (Mesa Verde Museum Association, Inc. 1990) (1893).

[18] *Id.* at 74.

[19] *Id.*

[20] *Id.*

In 1985, reporting on the University of Colorado's survey of Mesa Verde National Park, which took place between 1971 and 1977, archeologist Jack E. Smith reported the existence of two possible ancient reservoirs. The first is known as Mummy Lake (Far View Reservoir, probably the reservoir Nordenskiold had described) and is located on Chapin Mesa, the second is in Morefield Canyon.[21]

Recent survey, engineering, and archeological work by teams of the Wright Paleohydrological Institute—in cooperation with the National Park Service and the Colorado Historical Society—has confirmed the existence of four ancient Mesa Verde reservoirs.[22] Examination of sedimentation samples, soil and pollen testing, and broken pottery and other cultural artifacts, have produced estimates of the operational life of these reservoirs:

- Morefield Reservoir in Morefield Canyon (AD 750-1100)

- Far View Reservoir (also known as Mummy Lake) on Chapin Mesa (AD 950-1180)

- Sagebrush Reservoir on an unnamed mesa west of Chapin Mesa (AD 950-1100)

- Box Elder Reservoir in Prater Canyon (AD 800-950).[23]

Ken and Ruth Wright, with the help of Jack Smith and others from the Wright Paleohydrological Institute, conducted field investigations of the Morefield Reservoir in October 1995, May 1996, and May 1997, excavating an exploratory trench with a permit from the Park Service.[24] The Morefield reservoir mound is 220 feet in diameter, rises 16 feet above the valley floor, is 21 feet deep, and has a long berm-looking structure extending north from the reservoir up the valley floor to intercept the intermittent stream channel.[25]

---

[21] JACK E. SMITH, MESAS, CLIFFS, AND CANYONS: THE UNIVERSITY OF COLORADO SURVEY OF MESA VERDE NATIONAL PARK 1971-1977, at 14-15, 21 (1986).

[22] The following Reports by Wright Paleohydrological Institute each discuss one of the four ancient reservoirs: DAVID A. BRETERNITZ, THE 1969 MUMMY LAKE EXCAVATIONS: SITE 5MV833, at 27 (1999); JACK E. SMITH & EZRA ZUBROW, 1967 EXCAVATIONS AT SITE 5MV1931, MOREFIELD CANYON, MESA VERDE NATIONAL PARK, COLORADO 35 (1993); KENNETH R. WRIGHT, MESA VERDE PALEOHYDROLOGY, SAGEBRUSH RESERVOIR SITE 5MV1936, at 74 (2002); see WRIGHT WATER ENGINEERS, FINAL REPORT: MOREFIELD CANYON RESERVOIR PALEOHYDROLOGY, MESA VERDE NATIONAL PARK; SITE 5MV1931, PROJECT # 96-02-090 (1998); WRIGHT PALEOHYDROLOGICAL INST., MUMMY LAKE PALEOHYDROLOGY STUDY 48 (2000).

[23] RUTH WRIGHT, PREHISTORIC COLORADO RESERVOIRS AT MESA VERDE NATIONAL PARK 1 (2003).

[24] WRIGHT WATER ENGINEERS, supra note 22, at iii, 15.

[25] KENNETH R. WRIGHT, WATER FOR THE ANASAZI: HOW THE ANCIENTS OF MESA VERDE ENGINEERED PUBLIC WORKS 19, 26 (2003). I had the privilege in May of 2003 to be part of a Wright/National Park Service/Colorado Historical Society survey team for the Box Elder Reservoir in Prater Canyon.

The entire structure looks like an inverted frying pan.[26] Sediment samples showed that clay and sand were carried into the reservoir from the stream channel; the clay helped to seal the reservoir from leaking.[27] The Puebloans mucked out the sediment as best they could, throwing the material onto a growing embankment.[28] The mound rose over the centuries from sedimentation. What probably began as a hole dug into the channel to intercept shallow groundwater became an off—channel reservoir as the intermittent stream routed itself around a rising embankment.[29]

Potsherds in the Morefield Reservoir trench were evidence that the people dipped water out of the reservoir and carried it away in water jars.[30] They used deer antlers, sticks, and baskets to muck out the reservoir.[31]

The Puebloans used a feeder ditch or canal to divert water into the reservoir.[32] There are numerous large stones—the size of a large cowboy hat, and larger—lying at the surface of the dike that extends from the reservoir north.[33] The rocks are aligned and clearly appear to have been placed there, not washed in. This is evidence of the ditch or canal structure cutting northward to intercept the stream channel, 1,400 feet of it![34]

Apparently, the Puebloans used the four reservoirs for a drinking water supply. At Mesa Verde, they were dry land farmers, growing corn and storing it in nearby granaries they built of rock.[35] They knew of droughts; in fact, they tried to keep up to two years of corn in storage.[36]

There's a great kiva near the Morefield Reservoir.[37] House ruins in the vicinity show a population of nearly 500 people.[38] They must have been proud of their reservoir, and very worried that it took so much work to muck out the reservoir and lengthen the canal. As the berm grew, they had to shift their diversion point

---

[26] WRIGHT WATER ENGINEERS, *supra* note 22, at 1.
[27] KENNETH R. WRIGHT, *supra* note 25, at 26.
[28] *Id.* at 21.
[29] *Id.* at 19-21.
[30] WRIGHT WATER ENGINEERS, *supra* note 22, at 21.
[31] *Id.* at 22.
[32] *Id.*
[33] *Id.* at 23.
[34] *Id.* at 22.
[35] There is evidence that Native Americans grew maize in the center of the Colorado Plateau 3000 years ago. R.G. MATSON, THE ORIGINS OF SOUTHWESTERN AGRICULTURE 258 (1991).
[36] Richard G. Milo, *Corn Production on Chapin Mesa: Growing Season Variability, Field Rotation, and Settlement Shifts, in* PROCEEDINGS OF THE ANASAZI SYMPOSIUM, 1991, at 35, 39-40 (Art Hutchinson & Jack E. Smith eds., 1991).
[37] KENNETH R. WRIGHT, *supra* note 25, at 19.
[38] WRIGHT WATER ENGINEERS, *supra* note 22, at 13.

again and again to intercept the shifting stream channel.[39] They must have prayed for the rain to come and the water to enter the canal without washing it out.

The Wright Final Report on the Morefield Reservoir Investigation has a chart of tree ring data that show an annual average precipitation of eighteen inches per year from AD 800 to AD 1100—not much different from today in the Mesa Verde region, but there were good wet years and recurring droughts.[40] The Anasazi farmers, like today's, remained perched between a sudden flood and enduring scarcity.

PUEBLO PEOPLE OF MESA VERDE

> You want to know where water's precious,
> Where every scoop of dirt's a prayer of life;
> And tomorrow's blessing—carried in a pot
>
> Of clay is a source of wonder up a slope
> A thousand years away—perch upon
> A buried kiva's rim and take within the
>
> Arcing southeast sun this light they saw—
> You see—and may you keep this light
> Within and speak it openly;
>
> They worked and loved, like we, this
> Land, this calling, this Mesa Verde.[41]

The Wrights credit the ancestral Puebloans with having good organizational capabilities and considerable skill in building and maintaining large public works with rudimentary tools in a harsh climate:

> Long before Columbus sailed for America, the ancestral Puebloans, people that we refer to as the Anasazi, were thriving at Mesa Verde, even though the winters were harsh and water supplies were limited. They had no written language; they did not have bronze, iron, or steel; and they did not use the wheel. As a result, our American history books tend to underrate them in terms of technical capabilities and social organization. However, the Anasazi had rudimentary knowledge of hydrological

---

[39] KENNETH R. WRIGHT, *supra* note 25, at 21.
[40] WRIGHT WATER ENGINEERS, *supra* note 22, at 11-12.
[41] Gregory Hobbs, May 2-4, 2003.

phenomena, water transport, and storage. To build reservoirs, they also had good organizational capabilities; otherwise, their large public works efforts requiring major and continuous operation and maintenance work would not have been possible. They were able to plan, build, and operate reservoir projects in southwestern Colorado more than one thousand years ago. The evidence that they left behind has provided ample proof of their civil engineering achievements that spanned hundreds of years.[42]

The four Mesa Verde reservoirs captured water only during storm events from runoff in the canyons and on top of the mesas.[43] The two mesa-top reservoirs lacked natural drainage basins.[44] Nevertheless, well-traveled paths, the environs of pueblos, and upslope agricultural fields created runoffs from even small rainfalls.[45]

Extended droughts periodically occurred.[46] One of these in the 800s, resulted in depopulation for a time,[47] although the so called "Great Drought of 1276-1299" in the region may have been the reason why the Pueblo people abandoned Mesa Verde by 1300.[48] Why they left is still a mystery the archeologists have not solved. Perhaps, the combined factors of a shortage of wood for construction and fuel, depletion of soil nutrients, and the rise of the Pueblo culture in New Mexico and Arizona attracted them to move to the "big city" to join others already there![49]

---

[42] RUTH WRIGHT, *supra* note 23, at 1.

[43] *Id.* at 3.

[44] *Id.*

[45] *Id.*

[46] Jeffrey S. Dean & Carla R. van West, *Environment-Behavior Relationships in Southwestern Colorado, in* SEEKING THE CENTER PLACE: ARCHAEOLOGY AND ANCIENT COMMUNITIES IN THE MESA VERDE REGION 81, 87 (Mark D. Varien & Richard H. Wilshusen eds., 2002) (From tree ring studies, droughts of 15 or more years' durations are evident for AD 990-1015, 1030-1050, and 1276-1299.).

[47] Eric Blinman, *Adjusting The Pueblo I Chronology: Implications For Culture Change At Dolores and In The Mesa Verde Region At Large, in* PROCEEDINGS OF THE ANASAZI SYMPOSIUM, 1991, at 51, 55 (Art Hutchinson & Jack E. Smith eds., 1991) "A major series of droughts hit the Mesa Verde region in the AD 805-825 period, probably terminating the early villages as viable farming communities...." *Id. See also* Richard H. Wilshusen, *Estimating Population in the Central Mesa Verda Region, in* SEEKING THE CENTER PLACE, ARCHAEOLOGY AND ANCIENT COMMUNITIES IN THE MESA VERDE REGION 101, 107, 111, 119-120 (Mark D. Varien & Richard H. Wilshusen eds., 2002) (A substantial reduction in the population of the area may have occurred between AD 880 and AD 940, with population increases between AD 950 and AD 1200, for a total population of 11,000 to 14,000 persons, one-sixth of whom were at Mesa Verde, the rest located on the Great Sage Plain and Dolores areas of Southwestern Colorado; by AD 1200, total migration occurred, not, apparently, in response solely to drought as populations had persisted in the area throughout prior droughts).

[48] Carla R. van West, *Reconstructing Prehistoric Climatic Variability And Agricultural Production In Southwestern Colorado, A.D. 901-1300: A GIS Approach, in* PROCEEDINGS OF THE ANASAZI SYMPOSIUM, 1991, at 25, 28-31 (Art Hutchinson & Jack E. Smith eds., 1991).

[49] *Id.* at 30-31.

For example, groups may have moved to the Hopi villages on their mesas and the Rio Grande Pueblos.[50]

2. The Hopi

Lieutenant Joseph C. Ives of the United States Corps of Topographical Engineers encountered the Hopi (called Moqui then) in 1857 during the expedition when he wrecked the steamboat—emblazoned "Explorer" on its wheel house—at Black Rocks, where Boulder Canyon Dam now stands.[51] Proceeding on foot and mule overland, he arrived at the South Rim of the Grand Canyon.[52] Acrophobic at seeing that astounding chasm, Ives uttered one of history's most ironic false prophecies:

> The region last explored is, of course, altogether valueless. It can be approached only from the south, and after entering it there is nothing to do but to leave. Ours has been the first, and will doubtless be the last, party of whites to visit this profitless locality. It seems intended by nature that the Colorado River, along the greater portion of its lonely and majestic way, shall be forever unvisited and undisturbed.[53]

Following the drainage of the Little Colorado River, Ives found the Hopis on their mesas.[54] He described how at several of the villages—by a system of upper and lower reservoirs, intake ditches, and irrigation ditches—the Hopi stored, conveyed, and used drinking, irrigation, and stock water:

> The face of the bluff, upon the summit of which the town was perched, was cut up and irregular. We were led through a passage that wound along some low hillocks of sand and rock that extended half-way to the top. Large flocks of sheep were passed; all but one or two were jet black, presenting, when together, a singular appearance. It did not seem possible, while ascending through the sand-hills, that a spring could be found in such a dry looking place, but presently a crowd was seen collected upon a mound before a small plateau, in the centre of which was a circular reservoir, fifty feet in diameter, lined with masonry, and filled with pure cold water. The basin was fed from a pipe connecting with some source of supply upon the summit of the mesa. The Moquis looked amiably on while the mules were quenching their thirst, and then my guide informed me that he would conduct us to a grazing camp. Continuing to ascend we came to another reservoir, smaller but of more elaborate construction and finish. From this, the guide said,

---

[50] *Id.* at 31.
[51] JOSEPH C. IVES, CORPS OF TOPOGRAPHICAL ENGINEERS, 36TH CONG., REPORT UPON THE COLORADO RIVER OF THE WEST, EXPLORED IN 1857 AND 1858, at 81-82, 119-20 (1st Sess. 1861).
[52] *Id.* at 98-99.
[53] *Id.* at 110.
[54] *Id.* at 119.

they got their drinking water, the other reservoir being intended for animals. Between the two the face of the bluff had been ingeniously converted into terraces. These were faced with neat masonry, and contained gardens, each surrounded with a raised edge so as to retain water upon the surface. Pipes from the reservoirs permitted them at any time to be irrigated.

Peach trees were growing upon the terraces and in the hollows below. A long flight of stone steps, with sharp turns that could easily be defended, was built into the face of the precipice, and led from the upper reservoir to the foot of the town.[55]

Ives, an engineer, admired the engineering skill of the Hopi:

The whole reflected great credit upon the Moquis' ingenuity and skill in the department of engineering. The walls of the terraces and reservoirs were of partially dressed stone, well and strongly built, and the irrigating pipes conveniently arranged. The little gardens were neatly laid out.[56]

Ives depended on Native American guides to lead him to other water holes as he trekked back out of what appeared to him as an appalling, exotic, bone-dry, except-for-a-few human-created-garden-spots landscape.[57]

3. Early Spanish Explorer Reports

The Spanish explorer Francisco Vasquez de Coronado—looking for mineral treasure his culture coveted—reported that the Native Americans of the Southwest worshipped water: "So far as I can find out, the water is what these Indians worship, because they say that it makes the corn grow and sustains their life, and that the only reason they know is because their ancestors did so."[58] The Maya practiced water religion by means of the "most elaborate New World water cult," and like many Native Americans, particularly in the desert southwest, "[b]ecause of its cardinal role in the daily struggle for survival [water] was also afforded a telling reverence in southwestern religion, mythology, and lore."[59]

---

[55] *Id.* at 120 (describing water works at Mooshahneh).
[56] *Id.* at 124 (describing water works at Oraybe).
[57] *Id.* at 125-131.
[58] IRA G. CLARK, WATER IN NEW MEXICO 1 (1987) (quoting letter of Coronado to Mendoza written on 3 Aug. 1540). The Hohokam understood the importance of laying out the canal with good gradient for water flow, and may have plastered the bottom of canals with adobe to prevent leakage. MICHAEL C. MEYER, WATER IN THE HISPANIC SOUTHWEST, A SOCIAL AND LEGAL HISTORY, 1550-1850, at 12 (1984).
[59] MEYER, *supra* note 58, at 8-9.

In 1697, Padre Kino and co-explorer, Captain Juan Mateo Manje, reported seeing ruins of waterworks built by the Hohokam in the Arizona Salt and Gila river drainages.[60] Archaeological investigations in the nineteenth and twentieth centuries revealed an estimated total of 135 to 150 miles of canals in the Salt River Valley alone by AD 800.[61] Some of the irrigation works may have existed as early as 300 B.C.[62]

Complicated water systems flourished among Mexico's high aboriginal cultures:

> In Yucatán, Oaxaca, and the Central Valley of Mexico complicated water systems flourished. Sophisticated irrigation agriculture allowed the food surplus which, in turn, made the development of urban civilization possible. Throughout the constellation of civilizations in central and southern Mexico one could find diversion and check dams, dikes, canals, sluices, aqueducts, deep wells, reservoirs, tanks, and irrigation ditches with technologically advanced headgates and lateral channels.[63]

D. Hispanic Water Uses

For nine years, from 1831-1840, Josiah Gregg crossed and re-crossed the plains by means of the Santa Fe Trail.[64] In *Commerce of the Prairies* he describes the acequia system by which the Hispanic settlers irrigated long, narrow parcels abutting the stream from a mother ditch feeding smaller laterals to five or six-acre fields.[65] Operation and maintenance of the acequias was a common enterprise for the benefit of the community. Three hundred or more acequias were operating in New Mexico by the 1800s.[66]

The *Siete partidas* (1265), *Política indiana* (1647), *Recopilación* (1681), and *Novísima recopilación* (1805), and specific ordinances and royal decrees were a basic source of Spanish and Colonial law, including the law of water use.[67] The Plan de Pitic (1783) set forth a mechanism for the assignment of land and irrigation water rights.[68] A special commissioner in the locality was to divide the water "in such a way that all the land subject to irrigation (that portion previously

---

[60] CLARK, *supra* note 58, at 1.
[61] *Id*. at 2.
[62] *Id*.
[63] MEYER, *supra* note 58, at 16-17.
[64] JOSIAH GREGG, COMMERCE OF THE PRAIRIES xix (Max L. Moorhead ed., 1954).
[65] *Id*. at 107-08.
[66] New Mexico State Engineer's Office, Acequias (July 1997), *available at* http://www.seo.state.nm.us/water-info/acequias/acequias-ditches.html (last modified Oct. 29, 1998).
[67] MEYER, *supra* note 58, at 106-11.
[68] *Id*. at 157-58.

designated as subject to irrigation) would receive its benefits, especially during the spring and summer, the season most crucial to a successful harvest."[69]

The construction of an irrigation system for the new communities began even before the houses, public buildings, and churches were finished.[70] "[I]t was crucial to have the ditches in place before the first sowing."[71] The water official (alcalde) assigned and supervised the irrigation schedule of each farmer.[72]

Beneficial use and priority of use, along with cooperation in community, were important principles in the New Mexico water system, which derived from Moorish and Spanish laws and customs. Settlers were to respect the amount of water the Native Americans had long used for drinking water and irrigation.[73] However, conflicts between neighboring landowners, and between Native Americans and the Hispanic settlers, inevitably occurred because land with a reliable and permanent water source was scarce.[74]

The New Mexico acequia tradition influenced Colorado in two direct ways. First, the oldest continuous water right in existence today is for the 1852 San Luis People's Ditch diverting from Culebra Creek.[75] It was built to irrigate the fields of Hispanic settlers on the Sangre de Cristo Grant, an 1844 Mexican land grant.[76]

Second, when Benjamin Eaton—later, a Colorado governor—became disillusioned with gold mining as one of the Colorado 1859ers, he learned to work acequia water on the Maxwell Land Grant outside of Cimarron, New Mexico.[77] Returning to homestead in Colorado Territory in 1864, he dug his own irrigation ditch and helped to construct the Union Colony No. 2 Canal in the early 1870s and, later, both the Larimer and Weld Canal in northern Colorado and the High Line Canal in the Denver basin.[78] As a member of the territorial legislature, constitutional convention, and state legislature, he worked to shape the prior appropriation provisions of the Colorado Constitution and early statehood water statutes, including the Adjudication Acts of 1879 and 1881.[79]

---

[69] *Id.* at 36.
[70] *Id.* at 37.
[71] *Id.*
[72] *Id.* at 36.
[73] CLARK, *supra* note 58, at 17.
[74] MEYER, *supra* note 58, at 47-49.
[75] JANE E. NORRIS & LEE G. NORRIS, WRITTEN IN WATER: THE LIFE OF BENJAMIN HARRISON EATON 24 (1990).
[76] *Lobato v. Taylor*, 71 P.3d 938, 943 (Colo. 2002).
[77] NORRIS, *supra* note 75, at 32, 220-22.
[78] *Id.* at 94, 221-22.
[79] *Id.* at 94, 104, 122, 139, 140, 146, 214.

E. Climate and the Water Laws

1. The Western Movement

The western movement was more than seeking the material goal of working lush farmlands in Oregon, like Ulysses venturing west: "It was Manifest Destiny made visible in wheel tracks. It was, as Thoreau recognized, a culmination of Occidental man's age-old instinct to follow the setting sun to the blessed isles, to the gardens of the Hesperides."[80] But the emigrants into the West had to go through the arid lands to get there. U.S. Army Captain Randolph Marcy's 1859 guide to the Overland Trail warns of "long stretches where grass and water are scarce."[81]

Walter Prescott Webb observed that settlers coming into contact with strange and new conditions can become innovators. Sometimes, their way of coping is a radical break from the past:

> In the development of institutions there is always a conflict between custom and necessity. Through custom people cling to old traditions and try to perpetuate them by adapting them to new conditions, but necessity argues the case on its merit without much regard for precedent. Out of the conflict comes a compromise in which the old is modified and adapted. Since the frontier was ever in contact with strange and new conditions, the frontiersman became an innovator and therefore sometimes a radical.[82]

Sharp departure from prior customs may result in new laws that institutionalize the change. This happened in the American West, because of climate. Colorado's experience is an excellent example.

2. Droughts Give Rise to Prior Appropriation Law

The years from 1865 to 1872 were dry.[83] In 1872, the Colorado Territorial Supreme Court issued its first water decision, *Yunker v. Nichols*.[84] The reality of settling into the arid lands, long known to the Native and Hispanic Americans by hard experience—that water is a scarce and precious community resource needed to grow crops—produced a radical break from the pre-existing English and American common law, which the Territorial Supreme Court encapsulated as the ruling principle of Colorado water law:

---

[80] DAVID LAVENDER, WESTWARD VISION: THE STORY OF THE OREGON TRAIL 27 (1963).
[81] RANDOLPH B. MARCY, THE PRAIRIE TRAVELER: A HAND-BOOK FOR OVERLAND EXPEDITIONS 45 (Harper & Brothers 1959) (1859).
[82] WALTER PRESCOTT WEBB, THE GREAT PLAINS 385 (1931).
[83] ABBOT ET AL., *supra* note 10, at 157.
[84] 1 Colo. 551 (1872).

> [R]ules respecting the tenure of property must yield to the physical laws of nature, whenever such laws exert a controlling influence.
>
> In a dry and thirsty land it is necessary to divert the waters of streams from their natural channels, in order to obtain the fruits of the soil, and this necessity is so universal and imperious that it claims recognition of the law.[85]

The law of water scarcity and need—so the court declared—imposed a servitude across private and public lands for the building of ditches to divert and carry water to its place of beneficial use for irrigation, wherever that might be.[86] The pre-existing English and American common law assigned the right to use the waters of the stream only to those who held land adjoining the stream, limited the amount to de minimus consumption, and required the landowner's consent for any crossing of property or the construction of facilities on the lands of another.[87] *Yunker v. Nichols* abrogated all three of these pre-existing property right formulations in favor of public water ownership and the establishment of use rights therein by private individuals and public agencies.[88]

Although the court based its decision in part on a statute of the first territorial legislature in 1861,[89] it baldly proclaimed that the necessity of water use in the arid climes prevented the legislature from repealing the fundamental right of the people to access and use the scarce public water supply:

> I conceive that, with us, the right of every proprietor to have a way over the lands intervening between his possessions and the neighboring stream for the passage of water for the irrigation of so much of his land as may be actually cultivated, is well sustained by force of the necessity arising from local peculiarities of climate....
>
> It seems to me, therefore, that the right springs out of the necessity, and existed before the statute was enacted, and would still survive though the statute were repealed.

---

[85] *Id.* at 553.

[86] Colorado law initially focused exclusively on irrigation, despite the stereotypical belief that mining produced the water law. Not until 1903 did Colorado adopt an adjudication act that provided for decreeing the priority dates of all beneficial uses, not just irrigation. *See* Gregory J. Hobbs, Jr., *Colorado's 1969 Adjudication and Administration Act: Settling In*, 3 U. Denv. Water L. Rev. 1, 9 (1999).

[87] *Yunker*, 1 Colo. at 552-53.

[88] *Id.* at 556, 559.

[89] Act of Nov. 5, 1861, §1-6, 1861 Colo. Sess. Laws 67-68 (protecting and regulating the irrigation of lands).

If we say that the statute confers the right, then the statute may take it away, which cannot be admitted.[90]

The 1876 Colorado Constitution ratified the principles of *Yunker v. Nichols*, establishing prior appropriation for beneficial use as the governing precept for the waters of the natural stream, and providing for a right of private condemnation across the lands of another to build the necessary water works for beneficial use.[91] In 2002, the Colorado Supreme Court, citing the court's 1872 decision, reiterated the Colorado Doctrine as follows:

> Advancing the national agenda of settling the public domain required abandonment of the pre-existing common-law rules of property ownership in regard to water and water use rights. Reducing the public land and water to possession and ownership was a preoccupation of territorial and state law from the outset. A new law of custom and usage in regard to water use rights and land ownership rights, the "Colorado Doctrine," arose from "imperative necessity" in the western region. This new doctrine established that: (1) water is a public resource, dedicated to the beneficial use of public agencies and private persons wherever they might make beneficial use of the water under use rights established as prescribed by law; (2) the right of water use includes the right to cross the lands of others to place water into, occupy and convey water through, and withdraw water from the natural water bearing formations within the state in the exercise of a water use right; and (3) the natural water bearing formations may be used for the transport and retention of appropriated water. This new common law established a property-rights-based allocation and administration system which promotes multiple use of a finite resource for beneficial purposes.[92]

The water provisions of Colorado's 1876 constitution and Adjudication Act of 1879 directly resulted from upstream/downstream junior/senior disputes over water scarcity.[93] The 1870 Union Colony—downstream, near the confluence of the Cache la Poudre and South Platte Rivers—built and began to operate their irrigation canals, only to find in 1874 that diversions by a new, upstream ditch near old Fort Collins had reduced the Cache la Poudre's flow to a trickle.[94] Clearly, the priority system and its enforcement—prior reliance on turning the water to beneficial use and protecting that use—had to be institutionalized within the three branches of Colorado government for the benefit of the citizens. Therefore, the

---

[90] *Yunker*, 1 Colo. at 570 (Wells, J., concurring).
[91] COLO. CONST. art. XVI (1876).
[92] *Bd. of County Comm'rs v. Park County Sportsmen's Ranch*, 45 P.3d 693, 706 (Colo. 2002).
[93] COLO. CONST. art. XVI (1876); Act of Feb. 19, 1879, 1879 Colo. Sess. Laws 94.
[94] ROBERT G. DUNBAR, FORGING NEW RIGHTS IN WESTERN WATERS 88-89 (1983).

Colorado General Assembly assigned the state's judiciary to decree water rights priorities, and the state and division engineers and water commissioners to enforce them.[95]

The pitch of water scarcity resounds repeatedly along the channel of the water law.

1882, *Coffin v. Left Hand Ditch:*

The climate is dry, and the soil, when moistened only by the usual rainfall, is arid and unproductive; except in a few favored sections, artificial irrigation for agriculture is an absolute necessity....

. . . .

We conclude, then, that the common law doctrine giving the riparian owner a right to the flow of water in its natural channel upon and over his lands, even though he makes no beneficial use thereof, is inapplicable to Colorado. Imperative necessity, unknown to the countries which gave it birth, compels the recognition of another doctrine in conflict therewith.[96]

1938, *People v. Letford:*

It is a matter of common knowledge that, due to climatic conditions, except in a few limited areas, agricultural crops cannot be produced in Colorado except by irrigation of the land. Also it was early evident, and still is obvious, that the economic and industrial development of an arid state is directly dependent on its water supply.[97]

1986, *County Commissioners v. Denver Water:*

The effects of drought on water supply in Colorado are well known. The impact of drought on municipalities has resulted in lawn watering restrictions, moratoriums on service, and other restrictions on use to conserve water. A drought in the 1950's was so severe that the Board restricted use by temporarily creating a "Blue Line" beyond which water service would not be extended, and within which service was not assured.

As a result of the drought crisis of 1976 and 1977, the Board adopted water restrictions and a Tap Allocation Program which established procedures and criteria to allocate new taps among the various entities under contract outside Denver which are served by the Board's water system.[98]

---

[95] Gregory J. Hobbs, Jr., *Colorado Water Law: An Historical Overview*, 1 U. DENV. WATER L. REV. 9, 10 (1997).

[96] *Coffin v. Left Hand Ditch Co.*, 6 Colo. 443, 446-47 (Colo. 1882) (citing Territorial Legislative Acts, § 32, 1864 Colo. Sess. Laws 58).

[97] *People ex rel. Rogers v. Letford*, 79 P.2d 274, 280-81 (Colo. 1938).

[98] *Bd. of County. Comm'rs v. Denver Bd. of Water Comm'rs*, 718 P.2d 235, 239 (Colo. 1986).

3. The Role of Adjudication and Administration

Prior appropriation is a doctrine of scarcity that curtails undecreed water uses and decreed surface and tributary groundwater junior water uses, in accordance with decreed priority, when there is insufficient water available to supply all uses.[99] Adjudication of water rights priorities, and engineering studies of diversions and uses in wet, average, and dry times, allow water planners and suppliers to determine whether present and future water demands can be met, and what water rights have a supply dependable enough to support new uses by acquisition and change of those senior water rights to the new uses through water market transactions.[100] Augmentation and substitute supply plans may operate to allow out-of-priority uses to continue if adequate replacement water is made available to the otherwise injured water rights.[101]

F. A Water Law and Institutional Bridge—John Wesley Powell

In his 1879 *Arid Lands Report to Congress*, John Wesley Powell identified principles of climate, necessity, law, and use remarkably similar to those the Colorado Supreme Court had announced in 1872:

> The ancient principles of common law applying to the use of natural streams, so wise and equitable in a humid region, would, if applied to the Arid Region, practically prohibit the growth of its most important industries.
>
> . . . .
>
> If there be any doubt of the ultimate legality of the practices of the people in the arid country relating to water and land rights, all such doubts should be speedily quieted through the enactment of appropriate laws by the national legislature. Perhaps an amplification by the courts of what has been designated as the *natural right* to the use of water may be made to cover the practices now obtaining; but it hardly seems wise to imperil interests so great by intrusting them to the possibility of some future court made law.[102]

---

[99] Gregory J. Hobbs, Jr., *Priority: The Most Misunderstood Stick in the Bundle*, 32 ENVTL. L. 37, 48 (2002).
[100] *See generally* Daniel S. Young & Duane D. Helton, *Developing a Water Supply in Colorado: The Role of an Engineer*, 3 U. DENV. WATER L. REV. 373-90 (2000).
[101] *Simpson v. Bijou Irrigation Co.*, 69 P.3d 50, 55 (Colo. 2003).
[102] POWELL, *supra* note 7, at 42-43.

1. Visions of Agrarian Democracy

Powell emphasized that priority of utilization, based on seniority of rights, should apply in times of short supply based on the "necessities of the country."[103] He would limit the water anyone could appropriate to water actually used; his caveat was that water ought to be tied to the land permanently, a position he reasserted when serving as a member of the Public Lands Commission.[104] Like Jefferson before him, he foresaw the West's future in terms of an enduring agrarian democracy. Instead, today's West is a rapidly urbanizing, multi-faceted democracy, but Powell had a major hand in the rise of western irrigated agriculture and the institutions that grew up around it. Western agriculture—beyond Powell's vision—has supported the rise of western urbanization and a water law that provides stability, reliability, and flexibility in the identification, protection, and change of water use rights.[105]

Like the Native Americans, who animated his ethnology work,[106] Powell saw the hand of the Great Spirit in the blessing and the working of water. He revered both the desert and the garden that is the American West. Son of a Methodist minister, his scientifically poetical writing invokes the redeeming power of the water drop: "It may be anticipated that all the lands redeemed by irrigation in the Arid Region will be highly cultivated and abundantly productive, and agriculture will be but slightly subject to the vicissitudes of scant and excessive rainfall."[107] Climate, flood and drought, the power of divinely-inspired human labor teamed with natural cosmic forces to make a settling place through science, engineering, law, individual and community enterprise, and enlightened public policy—Powell harnessed Stephen Long's desert view and William Gilpin's garden view[108] into a vision of government in service to the cause of western settlement.

---

[103] *Id.* at 43.

[104] DONALD WORSTER, A RIVER RUNNING WEST: THE LIFE OF JOHN WESLEY POWELL 378 (2001).

[105] The rise of the cities and of commerce, in addition to agriculture, requires a water law that recognizes security, reliability, and flexibility. "Security resides in the system's ability to identify and obtain protection for the right of water use. Reliability springs from the system's assurance that the right of water use will continue to be recognized and enforced over time. Flexibility emanates from the fact that the right of water use can be changed, subject to quantification of the appropriation's historic beneficial consumptive use and prevention of injury to other water rights." *Empire Lodge Homeowners' Ass'n v. Moyer*, 39 P.3d 1139, 1147 (Colo. 2001).

[106] WORSTER, *supra* note 104, at 371.

[107] POWELL, *supra* note 7, at 10.

[108] William Gilpin, Colorado's first Territorial Governor, promoted western settlement during a cycle of wet weather, proclaiming another of the western great false prophecies: "rain follows the plow." JONI LOUISE KINSEY, THOMAS MORAN AND THE SURVEYING OF THE AMERICAN WEST 110 (1992). After President Lincoln removed him as Territorial Governor after one year in office, Gilpin became a land development, railroad, and irrigation proponent. In numerous speeches and writings that received nationwide attention, he argued, "Colorado's dryness was an advantage, for irrigated farming was the most efficient form of agriculture...." THOMAS L. KARNES, WILLIAM GILPIN: WESTERN NATIONALIST 318 (1970).

2. The Public Interest

Powell saw the necessity of invoking the power of the national government to aid the farmer; otherwise, corporate monopolies—not animated by the public interest—would control the scarce water resource. His vision started with cooperative efforts, like those of the Mormons in Utah and the Union Colony in Colorado, to construct ditches from the streams to the land.[109] Inevitably, however, the settlers could not—within the limits of their own labor and finances—construct the reservoirs that would be needed to compensate for nature's yearly watershed rhythm of a flood of water off the mountains from spring snowmelt, then a drought when the heat of mid-summer requires crop water but the streams ebb low.[110]

Powell became a law and institution builder, serving as director of the U.S. Geological Survey after the short tenure of fellow western surveyor Clarence King.[111] He advocated the organization of irrigation and land use districts, and supported laws that would institutionalize the ability of western settlers to survive and enjoy living on the land.[112]

> A series of alternate droughts and flash floods during the late 1880's and early 1890's brought [western farmers to] the belated realization that they could not maintain their farms unless they stabilized their water supplies by building larger reservoirs and stronger dams and canals than those they had attained so far through private effort.[113]

With congressional funding, the U.S. Geological Survey produced a survey of potential reservoir sites and a short-lived piece of Powell-proposed legislation to withdraw reservoir sites from settlement under the Homestead laws,[114] so they would be available for use as needed in the future.[115]

Powell envisioned segmenting major rivers into a series of "natural districts" or "hydrographic basins" for the resolution of land and water problems; each district would own the water within its boundaries, and each landowner in the district would share in the water and water decision making.[116] Although his land reservation proposals caused a congressional furor and repeal of the reservoir site reservations, his vision of local water districts in charge of water rights and decision

---

[109] POWELL, *supra* note 7, at 11.
[110] *Id.* at 12-14.
[111] KINSEY, *supra* note 108, at 99.
[112] POWELL, *supra* note 7, at 40-45; WORSTER, *supra* note 104, at 479-86.
[113] DAVID LAVENDER, COLORADO RIVER COUNTRY 173 (1982).
[114] WILLIAM DEBUYS, SEEING THINGS WHOLE: THE ESSENTIAL JOHN WESLEY POWELL 214-15 (2001).
[115] KINSEY, *supra* note 108, at 98; WORSTER, *supra* note 104, at 356-58.
[116] WORSTER, *supra* note 104, at 494-495.

making—aided by national legislative and administrative policy—has been followed throughout the West, at least in part, through local district sponsorship and operation of reclamation projects.

G. Climate and Water Institutions

Water scarcity sparked Powell's proposals, as they mark the current western institutional landscape. Drought events of four years or more occurred in large regions of Colorado and the West during the years 1899-1902, 1933-1937, and 1952-1956.[117] Each of these climatologically-caused episodes corresponded to the enactment of major laws creating significant water institutions.

In 1902, Congress enacted the Reclamation Act, creating the U.S. Bureau of Reclamation.[118] Also in 1902, Kansas sued Colorado, commencing the era of interstate water allocation through United States Supreme Court equitable apportionment decrees and interstate water compacts.[119]

In 1937, the Colorado General Assembly created the Colorado Water Conservation Board,[120] the Colorado River Water Conservation District,[121] and the Water Conservancy Act,[122] under which the Northern Colorado Water Conservancy District became the first of the fifty-one water conservancy districts existing in Colorado today.[123]

In 1956, Congress enacted the Colorado River Storage Project Act,[124] putting into place a network of Colorado River reservoirs structured to support the operation of the 1922 Colorado River Compact.[125] The 1956 Act was inevitable—the years 1905 to 1929 were the longest recorded wet cycle[126]—and resulted in a significant overestimation of Colorado River water available for allocation to the Upper and Lower Basin Colorado River states.[127] The guarantee of a 75 million acre-foot per ten-year period running average to the Lower Basin left the Upper Basin states in

---

[117] *See* Nolan Doesken & Tom McKee, *Drought in Colorado*, 1 COLO. CLIMATE, Winter 1999/2000, at 13, 20.

[118] 43 U.S.C. §§ 371-390 (2002).

[119] *See Kansas v. Colorado*, 185 U.S. 125 (1902).

[120] COLO. REV. STAT. §§ 37-60-101 to -130 (2002).

[121] *Id.* §§ 37-46-101 to -151.

[122] *Id.* §§ 37-45-101 to -153.

[123] Colo. Water Resources Research Inst., *Colorado Water Conservancy Districts*, at http://waterknowledge.colostate.edu/cnsvancy.htm (last visited Jan. 12, 2004).

[124] 43 U.S.C. §§ 620a-620o (2002).

[125] *See id.*

[126] Doesken & McKee, *supra* note 117, at 20.

[127] David H. Getches & Charles J. Meyers, *The River of Controversy: Persistent Issues, in* NEW COURSES FOR THE COLORADO RIVER: MAJOR ISSUES FOR THE NEXT CENTURY 51, 56 (Gary D. Weatherford & F. Lee Brown eds., 1986).

dire need of a large storage system that could withstand at least a severe four-year drought.[128]

In turn, reaction to the implementation of the 1956 Act—through the construction of Glen Canyon, Flaming Gorge, Blue Mesa, and Navajo dams—helped to counter-produce the 1964 Wilderness Act,[129] as proposed dams at Echo Park and Marble Canyon dramatized the environmental call for creation of a national wilderness preservation system.

H. Reclamation

Harking to Powell's view of water scarcity and the need for redistribution of the natural hydrograph through reservoirs, the progressive era produced a marriage of the national forest preservation system with the reclamation program of irrigation development.

1. Hearings on the Reclamation Act

The 1901 congressional hearings on the Newlands and Shafroth bills[130] sounded loudly with the principle that forest watersheds must be protected in aid of western water development and use. Congressman Newlands of Nevada emphasized that the capacity of locally built direct flow ditches, to provide a stable irrigation supply, had reached its limit, and the existing settlers were in need of water storage they could not finance on their own:

> On all those streams lands have been taken up and reclaimed, but the limit of reclamation under the present system has been reached. These rivers discharge immense quantities of water during the early spring and summer months, but become attenuated threads during July, August, and September. The only method of further development of irrigation is by water storage.[131]
>
> . . . .
>
> The snows on the mountains are in a certain sense storage reservoirs for the water. The snows fall in immense quantities and great banks form in the ravines and the valleys, and as long as they are protected by the trees, the melting is not as rapid in the spring and summer months as it otherwise would be. When these trees are cut down the snow is exposed to the fierce rays of the sun, it melts rapidly, and the water rushes down in the early spring months. The destruction of the forests has limited

---

[129] 16 U.S.C. §§ 1131-1136 (2002).
[130] *The Reclamation and Disposal of the Arid Public Lands of the West: Hearings Before the House Committee on the Public Lands*, 56th Cong. (1901).
[131] *Id.* at 11 (statement of Hon. F.G. Newlands, of Nevada).

and cramped many of the existing irrigation systems of the arid regions. Settlements which in former years never suffered from drought are now suffering, not because there is not the same quantity of water in the streams, but because it comes at a time when it is not needed, on account of the melting of the snow hastened by the cutting down of the forests.[132]

Congressman Newlands invoked Powell's earlier admonition that private corporations could not be trusted to act in the public interest:

> Private capital will not undertake to build storage works unless there is a speculative profit. Investors wish to get a large area of land out of which they may make this profit by leading irrigation ditches over it, and the general tendency of such a course is to create land monopolies. The object of the people of the United States is to prevent land monopolies and promote settlement.[133]

Pointing to the over-appropriation of the South Platte by the direct flow ditches, Congressman Shafroth of Colorado urged federal funding of reservoirs to allow irrigation of newly developed lands and to stabilize the water supply of existing farmers:

> Now, the Platte River in Colorado has been appropriated eight times over, and on account of the increase of the population the claims on the waters of the Platte River have increased to eight times beyond what it is possible for the river with its ordinary flow to supply, and there is not a drop of water for any new lands.... [I]f you construct reservoirs and put them in direct connection with the reclamation of Government lands and designate that the water is to be utilized in that connection, the water turned into the stream from the reservoir can be taken out at a lower point and taken to the land the Government owns.[134]

Shafroth emphasized that the "laws of the irrigation States" recognized conservation of water for the improvement of lands.[135]

2. Forest and Water Conservation

The great American forester Gifford Pinchot also testified at these hearings that the forest reserves would support, not impede, present and future water uses:

---

[132] *Id.* at 31.
[133] *Id.* at 13.
[134] *Id.* at 33 (statement of Hon. John F. Shafroth, of Colorado).
[135] *Id.*

"The successful development of those lands, the continuance of their prosperity, and the extension of this irrigation system over the West depends absolutely on the preservation of these forests."[136]

Colorado was central to the public debate surrounding the creation of the national forests. Colorado Senator Henry Teller, who also served for a time as United States secretary of interior, contended for the conveyance of the public lands to state and local interests and fought against federal forest reserves.[137] President Teddy Roosevelt campaigned on the ground in Colorado for the forest reservations, arguing that withdrawal from homesteading and conservation of the forested watersheds was necessary for the development and use of water for farms and cities.[138] Fourteen million acres of forest reserve exist in Colorado today.[139] Roosevelt convinced many Coloradoans, despite Teller's adamant states' rights advocacy.[140] Key to the compromise[141] were provisions in the 1897 Forest Organic Act[142] adhering to state water law and allowing rights-of-way for irrigation canals, ditches, flumes, and reservoirs.[143]

The 1902 Reclamation Act[144] wedded the national government's role in water conservation to forest conservation. As a result of this progressive conservation marriage, the Bureau of Reclamation ("Bureau") has celebrated its one-hundred year anniversary. It has created more than six hundred dams and reservoirs, and it distributes water to more than 31 million urban and rural residents in the West, including one-fifth of the region's irrigation farmers on land that produces 60 percent of the nation's vegetables.[145] The Bureau's early, almost exclusive, irrigation focus inevitably shifted as the western United States proceeded into the World War I, Great Depression, World War II, and environmental eras.

---

[136] *Id.* at 65 (statement of Gifford Pinchot, chief forester, United States Department of Agriculture).

[137] DUANE A. SMITH, HENRY M. TELLER: COLORADO'S GRAND OLD MAN 229-30 (2002).

[138] *See* G. MICHAEL MCCARTHY, HOUR OF TRIAL: THE CONSERVATION CONFLICT IN COLORADO AND THE WEST 1891-1907, at 88 (1977).

[139] JUSTICE GREGORY J. HOBBS, JR., COLO. FOUND. FOR WATER EDUC., CITIZEN'S GUIDE TO COLORADO WATER LAW 25 (2003).

[140] *See McCarthy, supra* note 138, at 88.

[141] *Id.* at 57.

[142] 16 U.S.C. §§ 471-539 (2002).

[143] *Id.* §§ 524, 525.

[144] 43 U.S.C. §§ 371-390 (2002).

[145] Donald J. Pisani, Federal Reclamation in the Twentieth Century: A Centennial Retrospective 33 (2002) (unpublished manuscript, prepared for the U.S. Bureau of Reclamation Centennial Symposium, June 18-19, 2002). Powell had estimated that 30 million acres could be irrigated; the actual productive area today is closer to ten million. Shelly C. Dudley, The First Five: A Brief Overview of the First Reclamation Projects Authorized by the Secretary of the Interior March 14, 1903, at 30 (2001) (unpublished manuscript, prepared for the U.S. Bureau of Reclamation Centennial Symposium, June 18-19, 2002).

3. From the Early Projects to Complex Controversies

In the late 1920s, Southern Californians were as much interested in the power production and flood control benefits of the Boulder Canyon Project as they were in a water supply.[146] Dams, as energy producers and cash registers, helped the effort of the United States to emerge from the Great Depression and produce the power needed to win World War II and supply the growing cities after the war.[147] Today, Bureau dams have a total capability of producing 14.7 million kilowatts of electricity.[148]

The creation of jobs, power, and water for cities often worked at cross-purposes to the homestead ideal upon which the Bureau began, and, despite charges that it has tried to dominate and compete, cooperation with local interests and institutions has been a major tread of its step.[149] Congress interjected the Bureau into a web of pre-existing land and water laws that recognized the values and rights of private entrepreneurs, and expected the Bureau to operate as a business, recapturing investments, while producing economic and democratic miracles for the disenfranchised urban poor and soldiers returning to civilian life.[150]

Colorado benefited from early reclamation projects and suffered detriment to its interests from others, dramatizing the point that the Bureau was responsive to a national constituency that included competing regional and state interests. Among the first five authorized projects were the Gunnison (Uncompahgre) Project in western Colorado and the Sweetwater (North Platte) Project in Wyoming and Nebraska.[151]

The Uncompahgre Project resulted from the late 1890-early 1900s drought, rescuing and completing a project that local residents had started.[152] The Gunnison Tunnel, diverting Gunnison River water into the Uncompahgre Valley, six miles long with a carriage canal another twelve miles long, came on line in 1909.[153] In the ensuing decades, the Bureau "built additional diversion dams and either purchased private canals or constructed new ones, totaling approximately 470

---

[146] Jay Brigham, From Water to Water and Power: The Changing Charge of the Bureau of Reclamation 15 (2002) (unpublished manuscript, prepared for the U.S. Bureau of Reclamation Centennial Symposium, June 18-19, 2002).

[147] Pisani, *supra* note 145, at 15-16.

[148] Brigham, *supra* note 146, at 3.

[149] Pisani, *supra* note 145, at 14, 32.

[150] Patricia Nelson Limerick, One Hundred Years of The Bureau of Reclamation: Looking from the Outside In 11, 15-16 (2002) (unpublished manuscript, prepared for the U.S. Bureau of Reclamation Centennial Symposium, June 18-19, 2002).

[151] *See generally* Dudley, *supra* note 145 (discussing the Bureau's first five projects). The other three of the earliest projects were the Milk River (Montana), Newlands (Truckee, Nevada), and Salt River (Arizona) projects. *Id.*

[152] David Lavender, *supra* note 113, 175-77 (1982).

[153] Dudley, *supra* note 145, at 12.

miles."[154] By 1913, "the Uncompahgre Project canals delivered water to 37,000 acres while the private irrigation structures transmitted water to 13,600 acres.... Within the next decade, the acreage increased to 64,180 acres irrigated within the project."[155]

John C. Fremont's 1842 surveying expedition produced a seven-part strip map of an overland, watered route by way of the North Platte through South Pass.[156] The North Platte River from Chimney Rock through Scott's Bluff and Ft. Laramie was a critical portion of the Oregon Trail's opening into the mountain West.[157]

The Bureau's Sweetwater Project benefited these portions of the North Platte valley in Wyoming and Nebraska.[158] It included the construction of Pathfinder Dam, named for Fremont, and the Fort Laramie and Interstate canals. Water deliveries started in 1908.[159] By the mid-1920s, the Bureau constructed over two thousand miles of canals and laterals, bringing water to about two hundred and twenty thousand acres in Wyoming and Nebraska.[160] The Bureau added Guernsey Dam at Goshen Hole, Wyoming, and created Lake Alice and Lake Minatare in Nebraska.[161] Under the Warren Act,[162] allowing contracting of water with private water users for supplemental water on their lands, irrigated acreage increased another one hundred thousand acres.[163]

Early reclamation projects resulted in an embargo on Colorado's development of the waters of the Rio Grande and North Platte Rivers and contributed palpably to (1) interstate water litigation in the U.S. Supreme Court; (2) successful negotiation of numerous water compacts; (3) construction of ever-larger waterworks by the Bureau and others; and (4) the essential and enduring role of the states, local water districts, and municipalities. All of these embedded arrangements resulted from adaptation of a changing West to the reality of western aridity.

---

[154] *Id.*

[155] *Id.* at 13.

[156] WILLIAM E. HILL, THE OREGON TRAIL: YESTERDAY AND TODAY 32-38 (1994) (containing copies of the Fremont-Preuss maps).

[157] *See generally* MERRILL J. MATTES, THE GREAT PLATTE RIVER ROAD: THE COVERED WAGON MAINLINE VIA FORT KEARNY TO FORT LARAMIE 378-521 (1969) (presenting the important role the Platte River Road played in opening the West).

[158] *See* Dudley, *supra* note 145, at 17-18.

[159] *Id.* at 18.

[160] *Id.*

[161] *Id.*

[162] 43 U.S.C. §§ 523-525 (2002).

[163] Dudley, *supra* note 145, at 17-18; Alan S. Newell, Did the Secretary Sell Us 'Blue Sky'? Inclusion of Warren Act Contractors in the North Platte River Project 2-3 (2002) (unpublished manuscript, prepared for the U.S. Bureau of Reclamation Centennial Symposium, June 18-19, 2002).

I. Interstate Disputes and Their Resolution

In the same year Congress passed the Reclamation Act, Kansas sued Colorado for impeding the flow of the Arkansas River into Kansas. Kansas was a riparian state; Colorado, a prior appropriation state; the United States, the owner of huge federal lands from and through which the vast percentage of western water flowed.[164] In the course of the litigation, which resulted in two opinions,[165] Kansas claimed its law required Colorado to by-pass all water to it; Colorado claimed its law could keep any water from flowing into Kansas; and the United States claimed that all unappropriated western water had been reserved for development and distribution through the 1902 Reclamation Act.[166]

The United States Supreme Court rejected all three theories in favor of case-by-case original jurisdiction for the equitable apportionment of waters between states that share an interstate stream system.[167] The Court held that each state could choose its own water law, could not impose its choice on another state, and the national government's interest in reclamation of arid lands could not supplant state water law selection.[168]

Having failed to establish a reservation of western water for the reclamation program, the United States used its property power over federal lands to embargo permits for crossing of federal lands necessary to build non-federal water projects upstream of Pathfinder Dam in Wyoming and Elephant Butte Reservoir in New Mexico.[169] This embargo, and the looming loss to Wyoming in an equitable apportionment case,[170] spurred Delph Carpenter of Colorado to formulate the "compact idea" resulting in the era of interstate water compact negotiation and ratification.[171]

Professor Daniel Tyler explains in his biography of Delph Carpenter that this water compact brainstorm derived from Carpenter's understanding of drought and "river culture":

---

[164] *Kansas v. Colorado*, 185 U.S. 125, 138 (1902).
[165] *Id.*; *Kansas v. Colorado*, 206 U.S. 46 (1907).
[166] 206 U.S. at 85.
[167] *Id.* at 117-18.
[168] *Id.* at 92, 97; *accord Simpson v. Highland Irrigation Co.*, 917 P.2d 1242, 1247 (Colo. 1996) (referencing and summarizing the U.S. Supreme Court's 1907 decision). The Supreme Court pointed out that section 8 of the Reclamation Act requires the secretary to proceed "in conformity" with state laws. *Kansas v. Colorado*, 206 U.S at 93.
[169] William A. Paddock, *The Rio Grande Compact of 1938,* 5 U. Denv. Water L. Rev. 1, 13 (2001); *see* Daniel Tyler, Silver Fox of the Rockies: Delphus E. Carpenter and Western Water Compacts 119, 154, 169, 314 n.58 (2003).
[170] *Wyoming v. Colorado*, 259 U.S. 419 (1922).
[171] Tyler, *supra* note 169, at 119.

The culture of rivers and streams is dictated by geographical location. Upstream residents tend to manifest an attitude of superiority. Their connection to reliable water is guaranteed, especially during periods of drought. Their major concern comes from the fact that most western states accept the principle of first in time, first in right. Economic development downstream, where warmer temperatures encourage agriculture and population growth, results in a prior use of water and therefore a potential legal claim to that water in times of scarcity. Downstream residents worry excessively about upstream transfers of water out of the river basin and upstream consumption that diminishes downstream flows at critical times.[172]

Experience with interstate water litigation taught Carpenter three great lessons. When the United States Supreme Court exercises its original jurisdiction to resolve an interstate water dispute, (1) the doctrine of equitable apportionment governs; (2) what is an equitable apportionment in one decade may not be so in another; and (3) the upstream state can lose to a downstream state whose development occurs first, if not now then later.

Carpenter had two primary fears: California would preempt Colorado by its capacity for early development, and the federal government—through the Bureau—would command all western rivers to the detriment of individual states.[173] However, by the time the Supreme Court recognized Wyoming's interstate Laramie River priority, leaving only 15,500 acre-feet per year for additional Colorado use,[174] Carpenter had convinced the powerful League of the Southwest to endorse the compact idea for the Colorado River, and Congress had enacted legislation for a seven-state Colorado River Compact Commission,[175] whose chair became Commerce Secretary Herbert Hoover.

The Colorado River Compact of 1922 institutionalized, as a matter of state and federal law, the allocation of Colorado River water.[176] Because of reliance on the longest wet cycle in recorded Colorado history (1905 to 1929),[177] the Upper Basin states of Colorado, New Mexico, Wyoming, and Utah are shorted in dry times by the guarantee of a 75 million ten-year running average of water delivery at Lee Ferry for the Lower Basin States of Arizona, California, and Nevada.[178] This

---

[172] *Id.* at 8.
[173] See James S. Lochhead, *An Upper Basin Perspective on California's Claims to Water from the Colorado River*, 4 U. Denv. Water L. Rev. 290, 291, 299 (2001).
[174] *Wyoming v. Colorado*, 259 U.S. at 496.
[175] Lochhead, *supra* note 173, at 294.
[176] Colorado River Compact, Colo. Rev. Stat. § 37-61-101 (2002).
[177] Doesken & McKee, *supra* note 117, at 20.
[178] Lochhead, *supra* note 173, at 319.

realization led to the alliance Colorado Congressmen Ed Taylor and Wayne Aspinall forged with western state congressional colleagues to build reclamation projects in the Upper Basin and throughout the West—projects to assist in the operation of the compacts and assure local water supply for agricultural, municipal, commercial, power production, and recreation.[179]

J. State and Local Water Boards, Districts, Municipalities, Ditch and Reservoir Companies—Their Enduring Role

The Great Depression drought of the 1930s propelled water development as a major means for rehabilitating America. Colorado's successful effort to forge a permanent water arrangement with the United States through the Great Divide flushed up construction and operation of the Colorado-Big Thompson Project, with water features tapping the headwaters of the Colorado River to benefit water uses on the western and eastern slopes of Colorado.[180]

In 1937, the Colorado General Assembly gave birth to the Colorado Water Conservation Board,[181] the Colorado River Water Conservation District ("Colorado River District"),[182] and the Water Conservancy Act.[183] The Northern Colorado Water Conservancy District became the first of the now-current fifty-one conservancy districts in Colorado.[184] The Colorado River District was the first of three conservation districts established by the Colorado legislature, the other two being Rio Grande Water Conservation District[185] and Southwestern Water Conservation District.[186]

A primary motivator for the establishment of state and local boards and districts was that the Reclamation Act required the Bureau to contract with local entities to obtain repayment for part of federal water project construction and operation costs.[187] The conservancy districts—empowered by the legislature to receive public funds from a property tax mill levy, make assessments, and charge fees for water use[188]—undertook the water project sponsorship and repayment role. Along with

---

[179] *See* STEVEN C. SCHULTE, WAYNE ASPINALL AND THE SHAPING OF THE AMERICAN WEST 25, 68 (2002).

[180] *See generally* DANIEL TYLER, THE LAST WATER HOLE IN THE WEST: THE COLORADO-BIG THOMPSON PROJECT AND THE NORTHERN COLORADO WATER CONSERVANCY DISTRICT 4, 19-25 (1992) (describing the development and construction of the C-BT project).

[181] COLO. REV. STAT. §§ 37-60-101 to -130 (2002).

[182] *Id.* §§ 37-46-101 to -151.

[183] *Id.* §§ 37-45-101 to -153.

[184] Colorado Water Resources Research Institute, *Colorado Water Conservancy Districts, at* http://waterknowledge.colostate.edu/cnsvancy.htm (last visited Jan. 12, 2004).

[185] COLO. REV. STAT. §§ 37-48-101 to -195 (2002).

[186] *Id.* §§ 37-47-101 to -151.

[187] *See, e.g.*, 43 U.S.C. § 485h(c) (2002).

[188] COLO. REV. STAT. §§ 37-45-121 to -131 (2002).

the conservancy districts, the conservation districts—assigned with a regional responsibility for water development and basin protection in separate major watersheds within the state[189]—became fixtures for state and national assertion of local water interests.

The Colorado Water Conservation Board—whose representatives are from all regions of the state, and are appointed by the governor and confirmed by the senate[190]—became the coordination and planning reservoir for marshalling Colorado's interest in the development and use of its scarce water resource.[191] The state and division engineers continued their historic role of administering the decrees of Colorado courts confirming the priorities of water use rights.[192] The Colorado Groundwater Commission oversaw the permitting of ground water withdrawals from designated deep groundwater basins.[193]

Across the state, towns and cities, water and sanitation districts, irrigation districts, mutual ditch and reservoir companies, homeowner associations, and individual businesses each have a local constituency and responsibility for water planning and delivery. Although criticized at times for acting undemocratically and for a narrow interest, each of these organizations—with the governor, the legislature, and the courts also performing their assigned roles—focuses on conserving water for community uses, a very important public interest also pursued by the Native American and Hispanic peoples—and western visionaries like John Wesley Powell. These institutions—and the result of pressure and counter-pressure among constituent groups—shape and reshape the water customs and values of the people.[194]

K. The 1956 Colorado River Storage Project Act and Wilderness Preservation, Counter-Twins

The annual native flow of the Colorado River can vary between 4.4 million acre-feet in drought times to 21.9 million acre-feet in wet years.[195] The Colorado River Compact guarantees a delivery of 75 million acre-feet measured at Lee Ferry to the Lower Basin over any ten-year period.[196] Only by storing water can the Upper Colorado River Basin states "even come close to meeting their allotted annual uses and discharging their Lee Ferry obligations."[197]

---

[189] *See, e.g., id.* § 37-45-102(1).
[190] *Id.* § 37-60-104(1).
[191] *See id.* § 37-60-106.
[192] *Id.* § 37-92-301.
[193] *Id.* § 37-90-107.
[194] *See* HOBBS, *supra* note 139, at 19.
[195] Getches, *supra* note 127, at 56.
[196] COLO. REV. STAT. § 37-61-101 Art. III(D); HOBBS, *supra* note 139, at 23.
[197] Edward W. Clyde, *Institutional Response to Prolonged Drought, in* NEW COURSES FOR THE COLORADO RIVER: MAJOR ISSUES FOR THE NEXT CENTURY 113 (Gary D. Weatherford and F. Lee Brown eds., 1986).

In 1956, Congress enacted the Colorado River Storage Project ("CRSP") Act[198] to assist the Upper Basin states in developing their allocation of water, producing hydropower, and ensuring Compact deliveries, among other uses that, as a result of the 1968 Colorado River Basin Act, include fish, wildlife, and recreation.[199] Particularly in times of drought, the Aspinall Unit on the Gunnison River in Colorado—together with Navajo Dam in New Mexico, Glen Canyon Dam in Utah, Fontenelle Dam in Wyoming, and Flaming Gorge Dam in Utah—operate as a "savings account," so that the citizens of Colorado and the other Upper Basin states can develop and use the water allotted to them by the Compact "without fear of being 'called out' at some time by the demands of the Compact."[200]

The proposal to build a dam on the Green River at Echo Park near the Colorado-Utah border—and another at Marble Canyon just east of the main gorge of the Grand Canyon below Lee Ferry—gave birth to the compromise of constructing Glen Canyon Dam and also helped Congress pass the 1964 Wilderness Act to flow forth from Congress.[201]

> In late 1955 and early 1956, Howard Zahniser of The Wilderness Society worked unceasingly at trying to insert a proviso into the CRSP that would protect the sanctity of the park system from future reclamation projects. Conservationists also insisted upon a second provision protecting Rainbow Bridge National Monument from the huge reservoir that would be created by the proposed Glen Canyon Dam. After another round of negotiations on Capital Hill, Zahniser gained assurance from Upper Basin leaders like Aspinall and William Dawson of Utah that they would support the provisos in return for the cessation of conservation-organization opposition to the CRSP. At long last, the way seemed clear to passage.[202]

Water storage to assist state use of water compact allocations, park protection, and wilderness preservation—these are the three essentials of the CRSP compromise that forged beneficial use and preservation, not just beneficial use, to the maturing western experience. Just as the reclamation movement tapped Native and Hispanic American water use roots, so the wilderness movement tapped a resonant core of awe and respect in Americans. Wilderness has fundamentally shaped our American character. Preservation of its remaining vestige is a great national

---

[198] Colorado River Storage Project Act, 43 U.S.C. §§ 620-620o (2002).
[199] Colorado River Basin Act, 43 U.S.C. § 1501(a) (2000); *Bd. of County Comm'rs v. Crystal Creek Homeowners' Ass'n.*, 14 P.3d 325, 333, 339-340 (Colo. 2000).
[200] *Crystal Creek Homeowners' Ass'n*, 14 P.3d at 334; HOBBS, *supra* note 139, at 20-21.
[201] *See* NORRIS HUNDLEY, JR., THE GREAT THIRST, CALIFORNIANS AND WATER, 1770s-1990s, at 307-309 (1992).
[202] SCHULTE, *supra* note 179, at 66.

achievement, the argument for which included the water quality and quantity benefits of preserving natural watersheds.

The movement for preservation started with the great nineteenth century western surveyors themselves—and the artists, photographers, botanists, and geologists who accompanied them—but most importantly the citizens of the United States. Congress intended the surveys of George Wheeler, Clarence King, Ferdinand Hayden, and John Wesley Powell to provide the location and resource nexus for settlement of the West.[203] But, the people of the United States through the work of artists, journalists, and popular magazines, such as Harper's Weekly,[204] also saw how vast, beautiful, varied, and stupendous this land is, carved of sporadic, surging rivers and trickling drops; sun; wind; and plenty of parching days.

The paintings of Thomas Moran, the sketches of William Henry Holmes, and the photographs of W.H. Jackson were direct products of the Powell and Hayden surveys. These works led the way for the establishment of those jewels of the park system, including Yellowstone, Grand Canyon, and Mesa Verde National Parks—and with the tremendous added value of John Muir's hiking, writing, wandering, and advocacy, Yosemite.[205]

---

[203] Robert W. Karrow, Jr., *George M. Wheeler and The Geographical Surveys West of the 100th Meridian 1869-1879*, in EXPLORATION AND MAPPING OF THE AMERICAN WEST: SELECTED ESSAYS 121-124 (Donna P. Koepp ed., 1986).

[204] Harper's Weekly—which modestly called itself "A Journal of Civilization"—described Denver as an oasis-community created in the desert a little over 25 years after the 1858 gold strike at the junction of Cherry Creek and the South Platte River:
> If the city were less substantial in appearance than it is, if it possessed certain glaring peculiarities, it would be much easier to describe it. But it so belies its age, and seems so much older than it really is, that one falls to taking for granted that which should be surprising. Wide, shaded, and attractive-looking streets, handsome residences surrounded by spacious grounds, noble public buildings, and the many luxuries of city life, tempt one to forget that Denver has gained all these excellencies in less than twenty-five years. Every tree that one sees has been planted and tended; every attractive feature is the result of good judgment and careful industry. Nature gave Denver the mountains which the city looks out upon; but beyond those hills and the bright sky and the limitless plains, she gave nothing to the place which one has only to see to admire. The site originally was a barren waste, dry and hilly. Never was it green, except perchance in early spring, and not a tree grew, save a few low bushes clinging to the banks of the river. Surrounded on the east, south, and north by the extended prairie lands, fast being converted into productive farms, and having on the west the mountains with their treasures of gold, silver, coal, iron, and lead, Denver is the natural concentrator of all the productions of Colorado. From it are sent forth the capital, the machinery, and the thousand and one other necessities of a constantly increasing number of people engaged in developing a new country.

THE WEST: A COLLECTION FROM HARPER'S MAGAZINE 52-53 (1990).

[205] *See generally* KEVIN J. FERNLUND, WILLIAM HENRY HOLMES AND THE REDISCOVERY OF THE AMERICAN WEST 102-122 (2000); WILLIAM HENRY JACKSON & JOHN FIELDER, COLORADO 1870-2000 (2000); John Muir, *Our National Parks*, in JOHN MUIR: THE EIGHT WILDERNESS DISCOVERY BOOKS 457-605 (1992); THOMAS J. NOEL & JOHN FIELDER, COLORADO 1870-2000 REVISITED: THE HISTORY BEHIND THE IMAGES (2001); Paul D. Sheats, *After Yosemite: John*

San Francisco tapped Muir's beloved Hetch Hetchy Valley for municipal storage. Muir's reaction to what he viewed as a moral outrage sounds a high and clear tone of the liberty bell that Americans can hear—and appreciate—among all the tones we hear from the lyric and rhythm of Nature and its influence on our national character.

> That any one would try to destroy such a place seems incredible; but sad experience shows that there are people good enough and bad enough for anything. The proponents of the dam scheme bring forward a lot of bad arguments to prove that the only righteous thing to do with the people's parks is to destroy them bit by bit as they are able. Their arguments are curiously like those of the devil, devised for the destruction of the first garden—so much of the very best Eden fruit going to waste; so much of the best Tuolumne water and Tuolumne scenery going to waste. Few of their statements are even partly true, and all are misleading.
>
> Thus, Hetch Hetchy, they say, is a "low-lying meadow." On the contrary, it is a high-lying natural landscape garden.[206]

Nearly four million acres of wilderness exist in Colorado today because Coloradans joined with other citizens of the United States to pass the wilderness acts, starting with the 1964 Act.[207] Congressman Wayne Aspinall, as chairman of the House Interior Committee—a procurer of water projects for Colorado—played a key if reluctant role.[208] Echo Park Dam had been a part of plans for the Colorado River Storage Project, but Congress removed it from the CRSP because of wilderness advocate opposition in favor of preserving Dinosaur National Monument.[209]

Wallace Stegner's Wilderness Letter of December 3, 1960 speaks to the preservation chamber of America's heart, just as John Wesley Powell's water writings address the beneficial use chamber of the same heart:

> We need wilderness preserved—as much of it as is still left, and as many kinds—because it was the challenge against which our character as a people was formed. The reminder and the reassurance that it is still there is good for our spiritual health even if we never once in ten years set foot in it. It is good for us when we are young, because of the incomparable sanity it can bring briefly, as vacation and rest, into our

---

Muir and the Southern Sierra, in JOHN MUIR: LIFE AND WORK 245-264 (Sally M. Miller ed., 1993); DOUGLAS WAITLEY, WILLIAM HENRY JACKSON: FRAMING THE FRONTIER 105-141 (1998); THURMAN WILKINS, THOMAS MORAN: ARTIST OF THE MOUNTAINS 106-135 (2d ed. 1998).
[206] John Muir, *The Yosemite, in* THE EIGHT WILDERNESS DISCOVERY BOOKS 715 (1992).
[207] 16 U.S.C. §§ 1131-1136 (2002); *Sierra Club v. Yeutter*, 911 F.2d 1405, 1408 (10th Cir. 1990).
[208] *See* RODERICK NASH, WILDERNESS AND THE AMERICAN MIND 215-219 (1967).
[209] *Id.* at 219.

insane lives. It is important to us when we are old simply because it is there—important, that is, simply as idea.[210]

Colorado, the state of the Great Divide—mother of rivers—headwaters of the Platte, Arkansas, Rio Grande, and Colorado Rivers has an enduring legacy of water preservation, conservation, and beneficial use.

L. 2000-2003 Drought, Testing the Limits

1. The Interstate Water Caps

In the South Platte, Arkansas, Rio Grande, and Colorado River watersheds, Colorado has approached the limits of its interstate water allocations.[211] The Colorado Water Conservation Board uses an estimated four hundred thousand acre-feet of water available for development under its Colorado River Compact and Upper Colorado River Compact apportionment.[212]

Normally, Colorado rivers generate an annual average of sixteen million acre-feet of water.[213] In the drought year 2002, they produced approximately four million acre-feet.[214] Colorado lived in 2002 on six million acre-feet of storage water released from reservoirs.[215] About 2000 reservoirs exist in Colorado.[216]

Colorado's current population is over 4.5 million persons.[217] In 1971, agriculture accounted for 92 percent of the state's water deliveries for consumptive use; today, that figure is 85 percent.[218] The difference represents market transfers, primarily to domestic and municipal use, which accounts for 10 percent of Colorado's deliveries for beneficial use.[219]

---

[210] Wallace Stegner, *Wilderness Letter*, in MARKING THE SPARROW'S FALL: WALLACE STEGNER'S AMERICAN WEST 112 (Page Stegner ed., 1998).

[211] *See* HOBBS, *supra* note 139, at 13.

[212] *Id.* at 23.

[213] *Id.* at 20.

[214] *Id.* at 22.

[215] *Id.*

[216] *Id.* at 21. The reliance of the United States on storage is shown by an illustration that storage capacity increased from less than 50 million acre-feet in 1925 to 450 million acre-feet in 1990. WAYNE B. SOLLEY, U.S. GEOLOGICAL SURVEY, ESTIMATES OF WATER USE IN THE WESTERN UNITED STATES IN 1990 AND WATER-USE TRENDS 1960-90, at 2 (1997), *available at* http://www.waterwest.org/reading/readingfiles/fedreportfiles/wateruse.pdf.

[217] HOBBS, *supra* note 139, at 4.

[218] *Id.* at 7.

[219] *Id.*

2. Conservation and New Uses

Together with demand-reducing measures, such as water restrictions and surcharge pricing, reservoirs with adequate storage rights are crucial to the state's ability to endure drought, such as the one Colorado has just experienced. A water right is a right to share in the public's water resource.[220] Conservation is indispensable—in all its forms—in stretching a scarce resource. The measure, scope, and limit of a water right is beneficial use.[221] Beneficial use without waste or speculation is the core of our western water law doctrine. In times of scarcity, juniors defer to seniors, and the water market operates to transfer senior priorities to those who want to make a new use or firm up a junior use.[222] Augmentation plans allow out-of-priority diversions to operate if adequate replacement water is supplied to senior water rights that would be injured otherwise.[223]

The Colorado General Assembly has adopted an instream flow law for fish and wildlife protection,[224] and has enacted a recreational in-channel diversion law for rafting and boating.[225] Surely, these laws are reflections of our maturation as westerners. They take their place in the priority system, with the opportunity to firm their use, through water market transfer of senior rights and water storage and release. These legal mechanisms have their institutional counterparts: the Water Conservation Board for the instream flow program; cities, conservancy districts, and other local governments, with consultation by the Water Conservation Board, for recreational in-channel diversions.[226]

3. Water Planning and the Public Interest

A true mark of western water being a scarce public resource is how long and how often we have institutionalized its conservation and use. This is apparent in legal assignments made to national, state, and local public agencies—from the U.S. Geologic Survey to the Bureau of Reclamation, from the Water Conservation Board to the Upper Gunnison Water Conservancy District, from the City and County of Denver to the Town of San Luis.

The public institutions, created by legislative bodies at all levels, have the duty, in the public interest, to plan for and secure a firm water supply, responsive to environmental laws as well as all other applicable laws, to the best of their ability. Environmental institutions and citizen groups help shape how, when, if, and why

---

[220] *See id.* at 13.
[221] *Id.* at 7.
[222] *See id.* at 15.
[223] *See id.* at 16.
[224] COLO. REV. STAT. §§ 37-92-102, -60-122.2 (2002).
[225] *Id.* §§ 37-92-102(5)-(6), -92-103(4).
[226] *Id.* §§ 37-92-102(3), -102(5).

additional water works will be built, but they do not have the public's water supply responsibility and will not be answerable for a lack of planning and failure to undertake needed actions. Public officials, on the other hand, will be held accountable.

As a result of severe drought at the outset of the twenty-first century, public officials at all levels are engaged in drought planning and response. As a result of the 1976-1977 drought and a dry year in 1981, Colorado's governor initiated the development of a comprehensive drought management plan.[227] "The Colorado plan is effective because it incorporates three primary components: a monitoring system, an impact assessment system, and a response system. The State is currently attempting to give greater emphasis to mitigation in its plan."[228] This effort has redoubled as a result in the most recent drought.

4. Adjusting the Water Laws

In its 2003 session, the Colorado General Assembly added additional flexibility to Colorado water law, extending administrative authority in the state engineer for water banking, changes of water rights, substitute supply plans, emergency water plans, loans of water including for instream flow purposes, prohibition of new covenants that restrict the use of drought-tolerant vegetative landscapes, state technical assistance for water usage and billing systems, and water rights for conservation easements, consistent with the laws for water court adjudication of water rights and state engineer enforcement of them.[229] The legislature also provided for financial mitigation to counties that suffer tax revenue loss from the removal of agricultural water from their jurisdiction.[230] The assembly has directed the Water Conservation Board to undertake a statewide assessment of water supply, water demand, and water development strategies; project alternatives are to include social, economic, and environmental impacts and a consensus-building

---

[227] Donald Wilhite, National Drought Mitigation Center, Improving Drought Management in the West 17 (June 1997), *available at*
http://www.waterwest.org/reading/readingfiles/fedreportfiles/drought.pdf.

[228] *Id.* at 18.

[229] S. 03-073, 64th Gen. Assem., 1st Reg. Sess. (Colo. 2003) (substitute, temporary, and emergency water supply plans); H.R. 03-1001, 64th Gen. Assem., 1st Reg. Sess. (Colo. 2003) (prohibiting new restrictive covenants limiting use of drought tolerant vegetation, providing technical assistance for customer water use and billing systems, allowing State Engineer approval of temporary changes of water rights); H.R. 03-1008, 64th Gen. Assem., 1st Reg. Sess. (Colo. 2003) (water rights for conservation easements); H.R. 03-1318, 64th Gen. Assem., 1st Reg. Sess. (Colo. 2003) (water banks to all seven water divisions); H.R. 03-1320, 64th Gen. Assem., 1st Reg. Sess. (Colo. 2003) (loans of water rights for instream flow use in drought emergencies); H.R. 03-1334, 64th Gen. Assem., 1st Reg. Sess. (Colo. 2003) (temporary interruptible water supply agreements during time of drought emergency).

[230] S. 03-115, 64th Gen. Assem., 1st Reg. Sess. (Colo. 2003) (financial mitigation to counties for removal of agricultural water);

approach.[231] These short- and long-term measures have their bud in the most recent drought but their root in the long, ongoing process of adapting to the arid lands. Surely, the arena of reducing water demand and increasing the efficiency of water application and use deserves additional action.

We must not forget the contributions of the professional community, including climate scientists—meteorologists, hydrologists, climatologists, among them—who help us gauge, analyze, and forecast based on past and current data, so we can prepare for what we must do to conserve supply and reduce demand. Our heritage is the same as all of those who have preceded us here. We must work the water well, and we must also leave it alone to do its shaping.

M. Conclusion

In one ironic sentence, Bernard DeVoto summed up the problem and experience of the way west-such as Lewis and Clark realized after they had bushwhacked their way with a lot of supreme effort, and luckily, to the mouth of the Columbia with the help of Native Americans, Sacagawea, the Shoshone, and the Nez Perce: "The point it indicated was clear and precise: the route they had taken west was certainly not the shortest and probably not the best one."[232]

I would add, how else goes the course of western civilization? Weather and water politics, in the wild cycle of their beneficial seasons, will always be with us.

---

[231] S. 03-110, 64th Gen. Assem., 1st Reg. Sess. (Colo. 2003) (Water Conservation Board funding, section 14).
[232] BERNARD DEVOTO, THE COURSE OF EMPIRE 507 (1952).

GOOD COLORADO HEADWATERS EDUCATION

Good we don't have to buy the weather,
Good isn't for sale and just happens whenever.
Predictions, though good and getting better,
Are wildly inaccurate when the best worst weather
Hits so suddenly you can't tell where the pitch
Comes from.

I prefer weather to politics,
I mean, at least, when you sear your lips
Or an will wind spanks your bottom, you can
Rightly say, "Wait just a minute, it'll change"—
Colorado axiom—any politics charging straight
Off the Divide is worth standing to for.

Sure you have to hunker down when thunder
Booms and lightning catches between a vortex
Pit-of-gut instinct and a gearing rain that may never
Touch ground. "Norm" is only a mathematical
Possibility. Yell, Hail! and run. Your average-
Staked tent blows down any minute.

Greg Hobbs
6/7/2003

Mesa Verde Journal
Prater Canyon Box Elder Reservoir Survey by Wright Paleohydrological Institute In Cooperation with the Colorado Historical Society and the National Park Service (also published with "The Role of Climate in Shaping Western Water Institutions" as an appendix, reprinted with permission)
May 2–4, 2003

May 1, 2003

Bobbie picks me up at the new Idaho Springs High School where the Colorado Supreme Court has heard oral argument on two criminal cases in front of students from a number of area high schools.

Bobbie and I drive through four major watershed headwaters on their way to Cortez: the Platte, the Arkansas, the Rio Grande, and the Colorado. The route is I-70 to Eisenhower Tunnel (Platte watershed), Eisenhower Tunnel to Leadville (Colorado River watershed into Arkansas River watershed), Leadville to Wolf Creek Pass (Arkansas River and Rio Grande watersheds), and Wolf Creek Pass to Cortez (Colorado River watershed—San Juan, Pine, Piedra, La Plata, and Mancos Rivers sub-watersheds).

Arrival and check into Comfort Inn at 10:00 p.m. We are met by Terri Ohlson.

May 2, 2003

Some engineer has set the clock radio in Greg and Bobbie's room to go off at 5:00 a.m. Promptly at 5:00 a.m. the radio comes on!

Breakfast is at six. The survey team early arrivals arrive for breakfast.

7:00 a.m. the team assembles in the Comfort Inn parking lot. Ken and Ruth Wright welcome all of us. Jack Smith, former Chief Archeologist at Mesa Verde National Park, briefs us on Park etiquette. In short, the etiquette is you may find and pick up artifacts but put them back where you found them. No collecting!!

Ken explains that this is the "intellectual day." The "heavy lifters" come tomorrow.

Doug Ramsey, a soil scientist, and Dick Wiltshire, U.S. Bureau of Reclamation civil/geotechnical engineer, load up a mobile core-drilling rig loaned by the Bureau of Reclamation.

We are off to Mesa Verde—sky high canyon home of the Anasazi. Ruth explains on the way:

The Pueblo I occupation was 750-900; the Pueblo II, 900-1150; and Pueblo III, 1150-1300. The Box Elder Reservoir in Prater Canyon was likely in operation from 750 to 950 A.D., during the Pueblo I period primarily. Its location and existence became known after the year 2000 Bircher fire burned off the piñon, juniper, and sagebrush. A fast and furious wind burned fiercely 27,000 acres.

The Box Elder Reservoir is named for the unusual box elder trees that are in the stream channel near the reservoir. Box Elder is the fourth Mesa Verde reservoir the Wright Paleohydrological Institute has surveyed. Two are mesa top reservoirs: Far View Reservoir (also known as Mummy Lake) on Chapin Mesa (A.D. 950-1180), and Sagebrush Reservoir on an unnamed mesa west of Chapin Mesa (A.D. 950-1100). The third is a canyon-bottom reservoir, Morefield Reservoir in Morefield Canyon (A.D. 750-1100).

We pass through Morefield Canyon and wind over tricky switchbacks into Prater Canyon.

Our first view of Box Elder Reservoir, site 5MV4505, is from high on the Prater Canyon ridge. No doubt about it. There's a big berm on the channel side of a circular-shaped landform. We see burned/ghostly white box elder trees in the channel at the upper end of the reservoir site.

This may be an "intellectual day" for some of us, but Doug Ramsey and Dick Wiltshire get right to work on setting up the drill rig and start drilling and extruding cores—they're at it all day with the help of Ernie Pemberton, formerly head of the Bureau of Reclamation's Sedimentation Branch; John Rold, former Colorado State Geologist; and David Breternitz, retired archeologist.

Bobbie has sharp eyes. She spots a sheer-white small and elegantly shaped arrowhead lying on the south slope of the berm.

We set out with archeologist Jim Kleidon to find P-I and P-II sites in the vicinity of the reservoir. We walk up the west slope of the canyon to the north end of the reservoir site. We find a P-II site (900-1100). Jim explains that the potsherds we see all over the ground are pottery pieces of P-II black and white and corrugated pottery. This is site 5MV3159.

Bobbie finds what we call a "hammer stone." It's made out of igneous rock and has a chipped out portion in the center for tying on a handle. It is broken, split right down the middle from top to bottom. We examine with awe this tool of 1,100 years ago, and put it back in place.

We return to the surface of the reservoir body—now just a large mound because of sedimentation over the centuries. The soil experts are excited. They point to cored material that is clearly the result of sediment transport and compression within the reservoir body. The cores taken so far are down to 11 feet.

Ken signals we are going back over the ridge to Morefield Canyon. Terri Ohlson and Jack Smith have hiked over the ridge between Prater Canyon and Morefield Canyon—to the east—to see how long it takes to walk between the two reservoirs.

Driving up the bottom of Morefield Canyon, we see Terri and Jack walking up the road towards us. They've proved the point. Even though they found, then lost, the ancient Anasazi trail near the top of the ridge, it took only an hour and a quarter to cross over. Forty-five minutes probably would do it for those familiar with the trail—and strong from constantly walking where they needed or wanted to go—a thousand years ago.

We see the Morefield Reservoir mound, site 5MV1931. Ken and Ruth, with the help of Jack Smith, conducted field investigations here in October 1995, May 1996, and May 1997, excavating an exploratory trench with a permit from the Park Service.

The mound is 200 feet in diameter, rises 16 feet above the valley floor, is 21 feet deep, and has a long berm-looking structure extending from it north up the valley floor. The whole thing looks like an inverted frying pan. Soil samples and potsherds showed that clay and sand were carried into the reservoir from the stream channel.

The Anasazi mucked out the sediment as best they could, throwing the material onto a growing embankment. The clay sealed the bottom of the reservoir from leakage. The mound rose over the centuries, so what probably began as a hole dug into the channel to intercept shallow groundwater became on off-channel reservoir as the intermittent streambed routed itself around a rising embankment.

To get water into the reservoir required a feeder ditch/canal. Bobbie and I walk up the elevated berm-like structure from the reservoir north. The stream channel is to our west. We clearly see large numerous stones lying at the surface—the size of a large cowboy hat, and larger. They are aligned and clearly appear to have been placed, not washed in. Here is evidence of the ditch/canal structure cutting northward to intercept the stream channel!

Bobbie and Ken (who has joined us) walk back and forth among the stones, showing me the canal's alignment. 1,400 feet of it!

Ken says there was no irrigation used here. This was a drinking water supply. The Anasazi at Mesa Verde were dry land farmers, using valley bottom alluvial land and terraces to grow their corn, storing it in nearby granaries they built of rock. They knew of droughts. They tried to keep up to two years of corn in storage.

The potsherds in the reservoir trench showed the Anasazi dipped the water out and carried it away in water jars, which sometimes broke in the effort to bring water back to their families. Deer antlers, sticks, and baskets were used to muck out the reservoir.

There's a great kiva near the Morefield Reservoir. House ruins in the vicinity show a population of nearly 500 people. They must have been proud of their reservoir, and very worried that it took so much work to keep it scooped out and to lengthen the canal. As the berm grew, they had to shift their diversion point again and again to intercept the shifting stream channel. They must have prayed for the rain to come and the water to enter the canal without washing it out.

I have with me a copy of the Wright Final Report of the Morefield Reservoir investigation, dated January 1998. It has a chart of tree ring data that show an annual average precipitation of 18 inches per year from 800 to 1100 A.D.—not much different from today in the Mesa Verde region, but there were good wet years and droughts. The Anasazi farmers, like today's, always perched between a sudden flood and enduring scarcity. The reservoir likely operated from 750 to 1100 A.D.

It's getting near to lunch, and we better get back to Prater Canyon!

A tailgate lunch with a famished crew is what we enjoy. The Boise State University history professor from Idaho, Todd Shallat, peppers the sandwiches and canned ice tea with questions: "Did the ducks fly in to sit on the reservoir water and the Anasazi eat them?" Archeologist David Breternitz answers they ate the corn they grew and turkeys they kept. But, what about the ducks? says Todd. (Bobbie and I saw duck-headed petroglyphs on several hikes to Grand Gulch twenty years ago—Todd is onto something).

After lunch, Jim Kleidon leads us down canyon and we climb a southeast-facing slope. The rocks of house structures and the sink spot of kivas are clearly visible. Potsherds dot the landscape. Site 5MV3146. Jim did the post-Bircher fire survey of the ruins, identifying previously hidden additional houses and where they needed to be protected against erosion. Ute Indian teams then came in to place protective checks to divert water away from them. 275 new sites found at Mesa Verde after the fire!

Jim shows us how the houses were aligned west to east with the kivas dug on the south side. The midden—or waste pile—is down slope. These are the archeological treasure houses that reveal the discarded tools of a people working to survive in a hard but familiar homeplace.

We can see how they perched themselves on the southeast-facing slopes to take advantage of the light and warmth a winter-sinking sun parcels out to those who seek it well.

Jim says the large P-II community here—though smaller than the population of Morefield Canyon—probably was home to 300 people.

We spend hours marveling at the privilege of a dawning understanding. These were smart people who used the native materials—and their craft at making clay and stone tools—to grow and store corn and conserve water to survive and live. Their places of prayer, the kivas, could also have served as winter homes, out of the wind and cold.

We arrive back to the Box Elder core-drilling. Dick Wiltshire and Doug Ramsey have been prodigious workers! The soil samples in long rows are spread out on a white sheet and boxed for later lab analysis of the reservoir profile, as best it can be determined from the cores, to show how deep and for how long this water body served these people.

At 4:00 p.m. we pile our sore feet and wind-chapped faces back into the vehicles and unpile at the Comfort Inn. A short snooze, wake to dinner at the Mexican Fiesta, and retire to a fiery western sky. Day one is done, the intellectual day, bundled up to our persistent memories.

May 3, 2003

Same clock radio goes on at the same time, 5:00 a.m., breakfast at 6:00 a.m., depart at 7:00 a.m. These engineers know how to organize a survey!

The "heavy lifters" are here. They turn out to be young people, strong and confident. They will do the hand augering and handle the precise surveying and global positioning instruments. They include engineers, geologists, biologists, and hydrologists: Jason Alexander, Eric Bikis, Chris Brown, David Foss, Pete Foster, Matt Gavin, Kurt Loptien, and Ryan Unterreiner.

Dr. Mary Gillam, a Quaternary geologist and soils stratification expert, also joins the team.

Ken announces the assignments for this day's work on the Prater Canyon Box Elder Reservoir survey. Peter Monkmeyer, Chairman of the Civil Engineering Department, University of Wisconsin—who was with us yesterday—will team up with Jason to see whether hand augering in the channel bottom will reveal groundwater. The surveyors will determine the channel parameters and locate natural and cultural features, the building blocks of an accurate map. The soils and sedimentation experts will ascertain the depth of the reservoir and the variety of its deposits. The archeologists will confirm the identity of cultural features and artifacts.

Greg will work with Jim Kleidon and Ernie Pemberton to identify the diversion point and canal alignment, if evidence of a canal can be found. Bobbie will accompany Eric Bikis and Jack Smith to fix, by GPS, the location of special cultural artifacts, like those Bobbie found yesterday. Jack will then accompany Jason in the afternoon to the abandoned Prater Brothers' homestead sites up the canyon, to auger for groundwater in the abandoned wells.

Ruth will continue photographing the work of all the teams, and Ken and Terri will continue with overall coordination and logistics. Todd will press his questions. He is editing the Wright report on the four Mesa Verde reservoirs for publication in a professional journal later this year.

We are at full strength and eager to get to work! At Prater Canyon we rivet and disperse to our assignments.

I set out with Jim and Ernie, walking north of the reservoir body. We have the map of the October 2002 field survey of the Wright Paleohydrological Institute, which this day's work will supplement. We check out "Ernie's ditch alignment." Ernie has hypothesized an alignment that takes us on a northern path from the reservoir's body onto an alluvial fan of material washed down from the canyon walls over the centuries.

Will we find cultural evidence similar to that in Morefield Canyon along the trace of an ancient ditch to a diversion point on the stream? Finding evidence will be difficult. It looks like a thousand years of washed-down soil has buried whatever may have been.

Approximately a hundred yards north of the reservoir's upper end, we encounter a gully that cuts the alluvial fan with a slice towards the channel. We see the tops of stones aligned in an up-canyon direction! Jim thinks they may have been placed there—tentative evidence of ditch reinforcement and demarcation. We walk on.

Thirty feet farther on we see a number of large stones flanking the western slope of the stream channel. Ken and Ruth join us. We show them this stone grouping. Jim lights up. He is finding P-I gray ware shards on the embankment. Large stones apparently arranged for erosion control, and potsherds—this is physical evidence of ditch/embankment armoring. Similar to Morefield Canyon, here in Prater Canyon is proof of an off-channel reservoir and canal—carefully tended water features operating at the same time in two canyons by people who could easily communicate and learn from each other by walking over the ridge.

Jim and I walk straight on. We find more scattered stones, too large to have been washed here, how many more are buried beneath? We reach the channel just below its confluence with a tributary channel running in from the northeast. Here's the likely diversion point into the canal.

We walk west up the main channel among the box elder trees. No more large placed stones on the bank, not a one! Jim and I believe we have confirmed that Ernie's tentative canal alignment is matched with on-the-ground cultural proof. We leave the gradient check to the surveyors (the Morefield canal had a one-percent gradient running from the diversion point to the reservoir).

Now we need to find the habitations of people who could have built and maintained this reservoir and canal. It's got to be a P-I site, as all the sherds Jim found along the ditch alignment were P-I. Nearby is a P-II site on the western canyon slope; there's another P-II site directly across on the eastern slope. Where's the P-I?

We climb up the western canyon wall. Jim is thinking out loud. P-I sites could be buried beneath the P-II structures, including the large down-canyon village we visited yesterday.

We climb to a site that perches way up near the top of the western canyon wall. Jim surveyed this site after the 2000 Bircher fire. Site 5MV3190. It's a glorious spot with a comprehensive view of the reservoir below and a southeast facing down-canyon view. We find many P-I sherds matching the type Jim found along the canal alignment.

We look directly out on the reservoir site below where the drill crew is busy drilling cores and laying out the telling proof of how these people stored their drinking water. I can see the paths those people walked, carrying their water pots, to fill them when the water was there, returning to their lofty homes in the sun. And how they must have thirsted when the reservoir was near-empty, watching and waiting for the skies to drop the weight of clouds into their storage bowl!

Jim and I see Bobbie walking amongst the ruins down below us. We join her. She's been to a P-II site across the canyon with Jack Smith. They found an axe! Now she is looking for the hammer stone she found the day before. Jim and I recall it being at the P-II site northwest of the reservoir at the edge of the burned-out forest.

Bobbie finds the hammer stone again! The site marker reads 5MV3159. I go get Eric from the reservoir site. He locks in the coordinates with his global positioning unit.

    N   37 14.471

    W 108 25.214

    Elevation 7289—hammer stone.

We go back to the reservoir berm to position in the arrowhead lying where Bobbie found it yesterday, site 5MV4505.

    N   37 14.585

    W 108 25.228

    Elevation 7289—arrowhead.

We go across canyon to the P-II ruins on the east side of the channel downstream from the reservoir where the axe head is lying. Site 5MV3033. We lock it in.

    N   37 14.471

    W 108 25.214

    Elevation 7257—axe.

It's lunchtime at the tailgates!

At lunch, Ken asks Greg and Bobbie if they will accompany Jason up to the Prater Brother homesteads for groundwater testing. The hand auguring in the vicinity of the reservoir, down to 10 feet, has not reached ground water. Will augering at the old well sites up-canyon show and ground water?

Jack Smith had planned to go with Jason, but isn't feeling well. It's a two-mile hike each way.

Jack briefs us before we start off. Brothers Albert and William Prater had adjacent homesteads in the canyon between 1900—before Mesa Verde National Park was created (1906)—to the late 1920s when the Park bought them out. They grazed cattle and sheep. In 1974, Jack tested the water in the lower Prater well. It was about ten feet from the surface.

We hike up-canyon on an old road that disappears half way up. The canyon is lined on the east side with beautiful rim rock. We spot the first green tree—likely a Douglas fir—we've seen in Prater or Morefield Canyons in two days. The 2000 Bircher fire was devastating.

We pass the lower well. The windmill structure, without its turning wheel, stands forlornly in the middle of a deserted field. We reach the upper Prater homestead site. Two busted windmill wheels lie apart from each other. We see the charred remains of wooden foundations and fence posts. The well has caved in, forming an open pit about four feet deep, so Jason has a good start at the augering. Site 5MV3129, Middle Well.

He reaches a depth from surface of 10 ft.8 inches. We hear a sucking noise as Jason pulls out a core of peat—he's gone through quite a bit of it—but no groundwater, just a heap of moist peat.

The day is growing late, and we need to be back by 4 p.m. to the vehicles, so we don't have time to test in the vicinity of site 5MV2896, Lower Well.

When we return to the reservoir site we learn that the coring work has shown that that the reservoir is 20¼ feet deep—very close to the depth of the Morefield Reservoir.

The wind has been lashing us all afternoon, and we are exhausted. The core drilling team is still at work when we leave with Terri, Jack, and Peter. We join the group for dinner at 7 p.m., but Ken is worried. Jack Smith doesn't show for dinner.

May 4, 2003

We arrive for the wrap-up symposium on Chapin Mesa at the Recreation Hall in the old CCC camp. We learn that Jack slipped and fell last night and is still in the hospital recuperating. To our great relief, apparently he's all right.

The teams report their findings. Archeologist David Breternitz, Professor Emeritus, Archeology Department, University of Colorado, sums up. We have confirmed that Box Elder Reservoir is a P-I site in Prater Canyon, the construction of which commenced somewhat later than the Morefield Reservoir. Both were in operation at the same time, although the Morefield Canyon Reservoir was longer-lived. Plainly the people in both canyons were in communication and learned from each other. Because the great kiva is in Morefield Canyon—David says the people from Prater Canyon "probably went to church over there."

Ken thanks all the members of the team for their work and says that a written report of the findings and a map will follow.

We say goodbye to each other, knowing we have shared a great privilege, to see—on their ground—how the organizational skills of these Pueblo people helped them live in a harsh environment they probably loved for its elevated light.

Bobbie and Greg visit the Chapin Mesa Museum and the Far View Reservoir and villages on their way out of the Park.

Like Sagebrush Reservoir, Far View Reservoir is on top of a mesa and was not fed by an intermittent stream channel. Instead, it intercepted rainstorm runoff from compacted soils and perhaps a collection ditch. You can see an inlet structure to the reservoir that likely conveyed water, and a separate set of stairs for the people to dip their water pots.

Driving out of the Park at the top of Prater Canyon, we see a big turkey cross the road right in front of us and head down through the burned-out oak brush. These faithful life-sustaining birds the Anasazi domesticated are still here! We hear this pilgrim sounding off for a good five minutes before disappearing across a high meadow into the skeleton forest beyond.

We wind down out of the Park. Good views of the Mancos River bottom lands below, where farmers are planting this year's crops.

On the way home, we visit the BLM's Anasazi Heritage Center outside of Dolores. We see a photograph of David Breternitz on the wall! We've been in the company of famous archeologists these past two days.

We drive over Lizard Head Pass through Telluride, up and over the Dallas Divide, the glorious San Juan and Uncompahgre Mountains surround us.

It's snowing on Vail Pass. We arrive home Sunday night after 11 p.m. The lights of Denver are a long way from the silent mound of the Box Elder Reservoir. And we are glad, so glad, to have its location and purpose fixed in the context of the long—yet still unfolding—community of Colorado.

Book Review: *Silver Fox of the Rockies*[1]
University of Denver Water Law Review, reprinted with permission
Spring 2003

Daniel Tyler, *Silver Fox of The Rockies: Delphus E. Carpenter and Western Water Compacts* (University of Oklahoma Press: Norman, 2003).

Professor Dan Tyler tells a remarkable story of a remarkable man: Delph Carpenter, a small-town water lawyer who became a national statesman of rivers.

Architect of the "compact idea" for settling interstate water allocation disputes, Carpenter was born to a nineteenth-century pioneering family in Horace Greeley's Union Colony, founded in 1870. Carpenter grew up working water with his father from the irrigation ditches that tap the Poudre River, which flows east from its source in what is now the Rocky Mountain National Park.

Carpenter's life mirrored the Great Divide he revered. He loved the shining mountains and the Great Plains that take one inevitably to them. He drew from their strength as a husband, father, lawyer, legislator, and craftsman of treaties. When litigating for Colorado against Wyoming in the United States Supreme Court, for example,[2] he climbed to the source of the Laramie River to understand the lay of the land and how the waters flow. He wanted to leave his name on the mountains he had climbed with the district water commissioner:

> Carpenter wanted precise information on the Laramie River's origins, but he also enjoyed the adventure of planting the first American flag on these unnamed peaks. Having deposited a record of their ascent in a Prince Albert tobacco can at the summit, Carpenter later asked the U.S. Geological Survey to recognize these mountains henceforth as the Carpenter Peaks.[3]

---

[1] 6 U. DENV. WATER L. REV. 566 (2003). © University of Denver Water Law Review 2003. Greg Hobbs is a Justice of the Colorado Supreme Court. He is the author of the *Citizen's Guide to Colorado Water Law*, recently published by the Colorado Foundation for Water Education.
[2] *Wyoming v. Colorado*, 259 U.S. 419 (1922).
[3] Tyler, SILVER FOX OF THE ROCKIES at 163.

There are no Carpenter Peaks. But Carpenter's work is indelible in the day-to-day, year-in-year-out administration of four great rivers from source to mouth—the Platte, the Arkansas, the Rio Grande, and the Colorado. His signature and mark are upon the 1922 Colorado River Compact, the 1922 La Plata River Compact, and the 1923 South Platte River Compact. His groundwork prepared the way for the 1938 Rio Grande River Compact, the 1942 Republican River Compact, the 1948 Arkansas River Compact, and the 1948 Upper Colorado River Compact.

Carpenter was a local northern Colorado ditch company lawyer and one-term state senator who became the state's equitable apportionment litigator in the United States Supreme Court. His decade-long, scorching struggle against Wyoming from 1911 to 1922 converted him from a state-of-origin, win-at-all-costs litigator into a patient and tireless negotiator of durable interstate agreements.

Ironically, Carpenter became a peacemaker because the reality of water scarcity and necessity—upon which the prior appropriation doctrine turns—applies with equal logic to interstate rivers, if litigation in the United States Supreme Court is the only device for resolving water disputes between states.

Colorado had won against downstream Kansas in their 1907 equitable apportionment case, on the basis of Colorado's settled equity in continuing established water uses over prospective Kansas water uses.[4]

When Wyoming brought the same argument to bear against Colorado, Carpenter initially resorted to claiming sovereignty over waters originating in the headwaters state. He knew the argument was likely a loser, and while the Supreme Court was busy—taking evidence and briefs, hearing oral argument, ordering further briefs, convening re-argument, and then pondering its decision for years—Carpenter was busy formulating the "compact idea."

With clarity, scholarship, and a profound understanding of Carpenter's keen passion and intellect, Professor Tyler explains that Carpenter's water compact brainstorm derived from his understanding of "river culture":

---

[4] *Kansas v. Colorado*, 206 U.S. at 117-18; David W. Robbins and Dennis M. Montgomery, *The Arkansas River Compact*, 5 Univ. Of Denv. Water L. Rev. 58, 67 (Fall 2001).

The culture of rivers and streams is dictated by geographical location. Upstream residents tend to manifest an attitude of superiority. Their connection to reliable water is guaranteed, especially during periods of drought. Their major concern comes from the fact that most western states accept the principle of first in time, first in right. Economic development downstream, where warmer temperatures encourage agriculture and population growth, results in a prior use of water and therefore a potential legal claim to that water in times of scarcity. Downstream residents worry excessively about upstream transfers of water out of the river basin and upstream consumption that diminishes downstream flows at critical times.[5]

Experience with interstate water litigation had taught Carpenter three great lessons. When the United States Supreme Court exercises its original jurisdiction to resolve an interstate water dispute, (1) the doctrine of equitable apportionment governs, (2) what is an equitable apportionment in one decade may not be so in another, and (3) the upstream state can lose to a downstream state whose development occurs first, if not now then later.

Carpenter had two primary fears: that California would preempt Colorado by its capacity for early development and that the federal government through the Bureau of Reclamation would command all western rivers to the detriment of individual states.

Carpenter's fears were real. In the Kansas/Colorado suit, the Supreme Court—citing section 8 of the 1902 Reclamation Act deferring to state water law—rejected the government's contention that Congress had reserved all unappropriated western waters for use as the United States saw fit.[6] Yet the Government proceeded to embargo Colorado from getting federal right-of-way approvals necessary for additional water development of Rio Grande River and Platte River water, in favor of assuring water supply for the federal Elephant Butte Project in New Mexico and the Pathfinder Project in Wyoming.[7]

---

[5] Tyler, SILVER FOX OF THE ROCKIES at 8.
[6] *Kansas v. Colorado*, 206 U.S. at 92-93.
[7] Tyler, SILVER FOX OF THE ROCKIES at 8, 119, 154, 169, 314 n.58; William A. Paddock, *The Rio Grande Compact of 1938,* 5 UNIV. OF DENV. WATER L. REV. 1, 13 (Fall 2001).

California's demand for a mainstream Colorado River dam for flood control, power production, and irrigation water was long, loud, and compelling, and its Congressional delegation insistent. In this maelstrom, Carpenter refined and forwarded his principle of interstate comity based on the Constitution's compact clause[8] and federalism guarantees.[9]

To Carpenter, "comity" meant that states sharing an interstate stream system would apportion the waters between themselves in perpetuity, respecting each other's legitimate present and future needs. Of course, Carpenter knew that Congressional assent was necessary to make the apportionments legally effective and enduring.

By the time the Supreme Court recognized Wyoming's interstate Laramie River priority, leaving only 15,500 acre-feet per year for additional Colorado use,[10] Carpenter had convinced the powerful League of the Southwest to endorse the compact idea for the Colorado River, and Congress had enacted legislation for a seven-state Colorado River Compact Commission, whose Chair became Commerce Secretary Herbert Hoover.

Professor Tyler's story of Delph Carpenter is a marvelous biography of national significance, culminating with particular resonance in the telling of Carpenter's key Colorado River Compact role. Following Professor Donald Pisani's foreword and Professor Tyler's introduction, this biography includes chapters devoted to (1) Lineage and Love Letters; (2) Education and the Beginnings of a Career; (3) The Making of an Interstate Stream Commissioner; (4) The Colorado River Compact: Phase I; (5) The Colorado River Compact: Phase II; (6) The Struggle for Compact Ratification; (7) Last Years as Interstate Streams Commissioner; (8) Vindication; and (9) Carpenter and the Compact Legacy. Extensive notes and a bibliography document Professor Tyler's ten-year, successful effort to bring Delph Carpenter to life.

---

[8] U.S. Const., Art. I, sec. 10; Art. VI, clause 2.
[9] Carpenter was a "literal, strict constructionist" in his view that the Tenth Amendment to the U.S. Constitution "provided parameters for his recognition of limited state sovereignty and a guarantee of states' rights against illegal federal usurpation... Although an interstate compact would diminish state sovereignty to some extent, it would supersede state laws and assure signatory states the comity necessary to avoid conflict (war) in the Supreme Court." Tyler, SILVER FOX OF THE ROCKIES at 19-20.
[10] *Wyoming v. Colorado*, 259 U.S. at 496.

Carpenter was sick at the time of his greatest achievement. Advocacy and negotiation wore him down. He suffered from Parkinson's disease aggravated by stress.

Aided by the first-ever access to Carpenter's personal and professional papers—made available by the Carpenter family—Professor Tyler tells how a stern-minded adversary of the federal government became a close personal friend of the future president and former state opponents in reaching monumental agreements.

These agreements are essential to the needs of a growing and diverse western United States. In the twenty-first century, rapid western urbanization—and the need to protect all creatures who share this harsh and magnificent environment we love and depend on—will test the durability of the river compacts.

Because the states and their citizens have placed great reliance on the guarantee that their water compact apportionments will be available to them for beneficial use when needed, continued decision-making within the compact framework appears to be a well-counseled choice.

Ultimately, Delph Carpenter learned that there is no substitute for hard work and good will. His love for the land of the Great Divide and his dear wife, Dot, welled up in these verses:

> From the blackest clouds come the brightest rains
> The tree that is most exposed to wind and storm is the strongest.
> The best fish come from the purest waters.
> Circumstances must be turned and are not anxious to turn themselves.[11]

---

[11] Tyler, SILVER FOX OF THE ROCKIES at 50.

Inside the Drama of the Colorado River Compact Negotiations: Negotiating the Apportionment[*]
Colorado River Project Symposium, Water Education Foundation
Santa Fe, New Mexico
September 17–19, 2003

Script by Justice Hobbs
From Minutes and Record of the Colorado River Commission
negotiating the Colorado River Compact of 1922,
made available by Colorado State Archives and Denver Public Library

Editorial assistance on the script by Karla Brown, Executive Director,
Colorado Foundation for Water Education

Introduction[*]
by Professor Daniel Tyler[*]

The seven commissioners and Secretary of Commerce did not come to Santa Fe through pure happenstance. Selection of each individual for the purpose of negotiating a Colorado River Compact was the culmination of events dating back to the earliest years of the twentieth century.

In the spring of 1905, the lower Colorado River flooded near Yuma, Arizona. Despite attempts to keep the river between its banks, it roared through a recently constructed headgate that had been cut to deliver water through Mexico to the Imperial Valley. For almost two years the raging river followed this course, creating the Salton Sea and inundating many of the 160,000 acres farmed by a population of nearly 15,000. The Southern Pacific Railroad stemmed the flow in 1907 and returned the river to its channel. But during two harrowing years, frightened Californians determined to find ways to construct a flood control dam and an All American Canal on the Colorado River somewhere above Yuma. They had their eyes on Boulder Canyon.

Even with the Reclamation Act of 1902 in place, funding costly reclamation projects was difficult. World War I encouraged food production and brought prosper-

---

[*] Reprinted with permission of Profession Daniel Tyler and the Water Education Foundation.

ity to the Imperial Valley, but residents were increasingly nervous about the volatile Colorado River. Levees on the lower Colorado were barely holding. Another flood was likely. When the war ended and the federal government announced plans to settle veterans in the Southwest along the Colorado River, Californians stepped up their efforts to influence a willing Reclamation Service to design and construct the works necessary to tame the river. They also encouraged other state, local, and private entities to join with them.

The League of the Southwest was the result. Born in 1917 and made up of representatives of eight western states (Arizona, California, Colorado, New Mexico, Oklahoma—later replaced by Wyoming—Nevada, Texas, and Utah) and municipal, cultural, and commercial organizations, the League's goal was to establish a power base capable of sustaining a partnership with the federal government. Numerous meetings were held in southwestern cities, where resolutions were passed urging the federal government to assist in controlling the refractory Colorado River through storage and flood control projects.

The Reclamation Service was delighted to comply, but the Upper Basin states balked at the possibility of a large dam on the lower Colorado River. They argued that the first works should be constructed on the upper Colorado in order to prevent adverse claims by California and Arizona, where agriculture and population settlements were more advanced. Friction developed, exacerbated by Reclamation director Arthur Powell Davis, who confidently expressed his opinion that an excess would remain in the river even after the seven river basin states took all the water they needed. He wanted to build a dam at Boulder Canyon.

By 1920 it was apparent that California's desire for rapid dam construction was clashing with the Upper Basin's fear of future restrictions on their own development. The West's general adherence to litigation in matters of interstate water conflict was based on the doctrine of prior appropriation. If California got its dam, and put to beneficial use large quantities of water, slower growth in the Upper Basin states would always be subject to already established rights along the Lower River. This is what the upper states referred to as an intolerable "servitude."

When the League's members met in Denver in 1920, they were looking for a way out of the stalemate. Colorado Governor Oliver Shoup asked his interstate water commissioner, Delphus E. Carpenter, to come up with a plan that would secure protection for the Upper Basin states to develop at their one pace, and set the stage for a construction plan that would please the Lower River. What Carpenter presented to delegates was his idea of using the states' treaty-making powers, as defined in the Constitution, to draw up an interstate compact that would determine how Colorado River water would be distributed prior to construction of works.

This was a watershed moment. Delegates approved Carpenter's suggestion unanimously, probably because there appeared to be no other way out of their dilemma. The concept of a congressionally approved interstate compact was already being implemented by Carpenter in negotiations with Nebraska on the South Platte River. What Carpenter learned from the *Kansas v. Colorado* (1907) decision, and what he had personally experienced during almost a decade of trying to protect Colorado's right to Laramie River water in *Wyoming v. Colorado* (1922), led him to search the Constitution for a way that states could legally settle interstate water conflicts without jeopardizing their future or compromising their state's rights in the federal system of government. Article I, section 10 provided the basis on which all interstate compacts could be negotiated.

Shortly after the Denver meeting adjourned, Carpenter sent samples of draft legislation to governors of each of the seven Colorado River states. It authorized the states' executives to appoint commissioners entrusted with the responsibility of negotiating a Colorado River compact between the states and the United States, subject to the approval of Congress. For the most part, each state adopted Carpenter's language. Congress, meanwhile, passed legislation giving the seven states the right to commence negotiations. President Warren G. Harding signed the act into law in August 1921.

Four months later, Harding chose his Secretary of Commerce to be the government's representative. Herbert Hoover, a Californian, was not Carpenter's first choice, but his strong international record and his reputation as an impartial negotiator earned him the confidence of the seven commissioners as they began negotiations in Washington, D.C. in January 1922.

Following Justice Hobbs' script, I've added a few words about each of the seven commissioners and the special interests that skewed their participation at Colorado River compact negotiations in Washington and Santa Fe during 1922.

(Compact Commission files on stage. Chairperson Hoover at head of table, Upper Basin Commissioners on one side to the left of Secretary Hoover, Lower Basin Commissioners on the other to the Secretary's right. Except for edits that place the text in context, the expressions are those of the negotiators, presented here as if they were in one continuous session. For reference, the script internally shows which meeting of the 27 negotiating sessions each excerpt is from. Slides running on screen to the left of the stage show photos of original Commissioners and Hoover dam during introduction and at closing. Hand-held signs show which negotiating session the Commissioners are in, as the docudrama proceeds.)

Federal Representative:

The Honorable Herbert Hoover, Secretary of Commerce, portrayed by Bennett Raley, Assistant Secretary for Water and Science, Department of the Interior

State Representatives:

Arizona: Mr. W.S. Norviel, State Water Commissioner, Phoenix, portrayed by Herb Guenther, Director, Arizona Department of Water Resources

California: Mr. W. F. McClure, State Engineer, Department of Public Works, Sacramento, portrayed by Arthur Baggett, Chair, California State Water Resources Control Board

Colorado: Mr. Delph E. Carpenter, Commissioner for Colorado on Colorado River Commission, Greeley, portrayed by Justice Greg Hobbs, Colorado Supreme Court

Nevada: Mr. James G. Scrugham, State Engineer, Carson City, portrayed by Jim Davenport, Chief, Colorado River Commission of Nevada

New Mexico: Mr. Stephen B. Davis, Jr., Commissioner for New Mexico on Colorado River Commission, Las Vegas, N.M., portrayed by Phil Mutz, Upper Colorado River Commission, New Mexico

Utah: Mr. R.E. Caldwell, State Engineer, Salt Lake City, portrayed by Wayne Cook, Executive Director, Upper Colorado River Commission

Wyoming: Mr. Frank E. Emerson, State Engineer, Cheyenne, portrayed by John Shields, Interstate Stream Engineer, Wyoming

1st Meeting, January 26, 1922, Washington D.C.

Secretary Hoover:
(authoritative, competent, welcoming, patient voice, looks at each of the Commissioners right in the eye individually at times, sometimes as if the Secretary sees some distant utopian but orderly horizon)

I am glad to have the honor of welcoming the Commissioners to Washington for this initial meeting of the Commission.

This Commission has been established primarily to consider and, if possible, agree upon a compact between the seven states of the Colorado River Basin. This compact shall provide equitable division of the water supply of the Colorado River and its tributaries among the seven states. If achieved, the Compact will be subject to ratification by their state legislatures and Congress.

The sole object of the federal government is to secure development of the Colorado River in the interest of all. It is fortunate that there is little established right on the river and that we have almost a clean sheet with which to begin our efforts.

Yet, the problem is not as simple as it might appear. There is possibly ample water in the river for all purposes—if adequate storage is undertaken. However, there will not be sufficient water unless we develop some definite program of water conservation.

Populations depending on the Lower River are in extreme jeopardy from floods. In fact, flood control has become vital to their very existence.

Mr. Carpenter:
(self-possessed, bordering on the arrogant, but is constantly aware that this great enterprise must be successful and he bears a heavy burden to accomplish this)

Mr. Secretary, it affords me great pleasure to nominate Secretary Hoover as permanent chairman of this Commission.

Mr. McClure:
(somewhat aloof, makes a sour look once in awhile, sometimes appears to be absent in his presence)

I second the motion.

Mr. Scrugham:
(exudes integrity and competence, really seems to be listening, his delivery of thought is paced and intelligent)

It has been moved and seconded that Secretary Hoover be the permanent Chairman of this Commission. All in favor say "aye."

(All say "Aye")

Mr. Scrugham:

The motion is carried.

Secretary Hoover:

I think it would be desirable for us to hear the views of each Commissioner concerning the problems before the Commission.

Mr. Carpenter:

The prime object of this Commission is to settle, in advance, those matters which otherwise would be brought into court. The extent to which this Commission may recommend the place and position of water storage and other structures is a matter that some of us feel should be developed later as the case proceeds. The main objective of this conference is to settle title to the river before structures are placed thereupon.

Secretary Hoover:

It may develop in the course of our inquiry that there is a deficiency of water in the Colorado River unless we assume adequate storage. There may even be a surplus—if storage is provided. It would seem a great misfortune if we did not give to Congress and the country a broad project for development of the Colorado River.

Mr. Scrugham:

There is no question that the people of the Southwest, particularly those states most directly interested in the Colorado River, look to this Commission for definite recommendations for action.

Mr. Davis:
(sidelong glances to Carpenter once in a while as if to ratify a secret or pre-arranged understanding of the implications of the legal points; a judge, as Carpenter is a lawyer, he speaks carefully and authoritatively, sometimes displays a distinct advocacy to Upper Basin position, stepping out of a judge's more neutral, listening role)

I can say, if we deal in generalities and lay down a general plan the details of which will be worked out later, we will have a much simpler task than if we attempted to work out an entire scheme. Each state should use their maps and what reports they have and make a full statement outlining the situation of each state.

Mr. Norviel:
(evidently nervous about what he has to accomplish for his state, but persuasive and passionate, well-spoken, exudes thorough knowledge, caught in the middle between the skillful Coloradan Carpenter and the seemingly passive but potential nemesis to Arizona, Californian McClure)

Arizona is particularly interested in the Colorado River and its development at the earliest possible date. Conditions are serious in the lower part of the river for both Arizona and California.

Mr. Caldwell:
(enthusiastic, an optimist, wants a deal, sure it can be done)

I believe there is enough water in the river for all interests. In addition, it is my firm belief that it is the duty of this Commission to fully consider the water rights in the river and allocate the waters accordingly.

Mr. McClure:

Mr. Chairman, your remark that there will not be enough water for all unless it is conserved, was quite apropos. Currently, the state of California has the largest monetary interest in the Colorado River because of our extensive development in the Imperial Valley. However, this area has already experienced a deficiency of water during the irrigation season.

Mr. Emerson:
(very aware of his prior clashes with Carpenter, but thinking he has a common bond with the Coloradan because of Wyoming's position as a headwaters source state, practical but also comes across as a youthful boomer, all is possible and growth and development is the key)

Wyoming shares Colorado's position in sitting upon the lid, the headwaters, of the United States. The Imperial Valley certainly needs protection from the Colorado River to save itself from submersion, and to prevent the breaking of those great levees that are maintained yearly at very great expense. However, while the needs of the Lower River are quite apparent, we must have assurance that we may go ahead with our development at such time as it becomes feasible. I believe myself, that each state, through its Engineer or Commissioner, should present to the Commission what it thinks are the possibilities for the future—as well as what rights have been established in the past.

Secretary Hoover:
(nodding in agreement)

I think Mr. Emerson has hit upon one of the fundamental tasks in the Commission's work—specifically that we must understand the claims of each state. This is critical if we are to determine whether there is a sufficiency or deficiency of water in the river.

I would suggest that Mr. McClure and Mr. Emerson serve on the committee addressing the volume of water available, in cooperation, of course, with Mr. Davis of the Reclamation Service.

Mr. Norviel, Mr. Caldwell and Mr. Scrugham should serve on a committee addressing the water requirements of the various states; and Commissioner Carpenter and Judge Davis should consider the legal matters to be laid before the commission.

6th Meeting, January 30, 1922, Washington D.C.

Secretary Hoover:

You have before you Table A, provided by the Reclamation Service, and Revised Tables B and C, provided by the Committee on Water Requirements. *(supplied to audience for reference, Commissioners have these tables before them).*

The Committee on Water Requirements reports that a total of 14,264,500 acre-feet will be required for present and future consumptive use of irrigation water in the seven basin states. Adding 3,280,000 acre-feet of water to be supplied for irrigation in Mexico, this equals a total of 17,664,500 acre-feet of demand annually for consumptive use.

In terms of annual supply, the reports of the U.S. Geological Survey for the years 1902-1920 show an annual average of 17.3 million acre-feet of water in the Colorado River at the Yuma, Arizona gauging station.

Mr. Davis:

Based on these findings, I respectfully submit the following proposition: (1) that all states waive their priorities for use of water in the Colorado River; (2) that a permanent Commission be established, known as the Colorado River Commission; and (3) the Commission shall have power to authorize the states to irrigate additional acreage, so long as there is no injury to the existing irrigated acreage in each state.

Secretary Hoover:

I ask for your vote on this proposition.

Arizona?	yes
California?	yes
Wyoming?	yes
Nevada?	yes
New Mexico?	yes
Colorado?	no
Utah?	no

Secretary Hoover:

The motion fails.

I propose that a permanent commission be established to determine an equitable division and allotment of all unappropriated water, and no division shall be determined until the construction of one of the major dams is assured.

(much consternation and mumbling amongst the Commissioners)

I see that it will be impossible to obtain the unanimous approval of all the Commissioners to this proposition.

7th Meeting, January 30, 1922, Washington, D.C.

Secretary Hoover:

I believe the time has come to get the various viewpoints into the record. Do you think it possible for us to secure any agreement on mutual acreage limitations, subject to expansion after a term of years as water supply proves itself?

Mr. Caldwell:

Nothing that I have said should be taken as indication that Utah will accept acreage limitations at any time, nor that I consider it the proper basis for allocating the waters of the Colorado River.

Mr. McClure:

The water supply figures submitted by the Reclamation Service may be substantially correct. Based on their information, can we arrive at statements from which to work?

Mr. Caldwell:
(looking directly at McClure, a rise to his voice, somewhat bitingly, with a hint of "shall we take this fight outside?" tone)

Mr. McClure, you seem to imply that my last statement has been put forward in an attempt to stall this proceeding. I wonder if I understand what you mean.

Mr. McClure:
(backing up, but not quite apologetic)

I mean as far as making progress at this meeting is concerned.

Mr. Caldwell:
(conciliatory, matter of fact)

I simply do not believe we can make progress on acreage limitations at this meeting.

Mr. Emerson:

All Wyoming wants is this: if a large reservoir is constructed on the Colorado River, then such construction and associated water use shall not establish a priority water right, and therefore shall not preclude or interfere with water development in Wyoming, as it becomes feasible.

Mr. Davis:
(judge puts on advocate's hat, puts on air of being offended by Lower Basin attitude, and reinforces Carpenter's initial Upper Basin hard line)

We say we have such and such irrigable acres in the upper states. But we have been asked to cut down and give up the right to irrigate certain acres up there. Still, we get nothing in exchange. It seems to me that the attitude of the lower states ought to be one of extreme liberality towards the upper states.

(addressing Hoover) They want a big project in the Lower Basin, but they want the Upper Basin to make water delivery guarantees. If we can't get sufficient acreage guarantees for the Upper Basin, I think these negotiations fail.

Secretary Hoover:
(shows alarm to the danger that bad feeling and wrangling will take the effort down, wants to steer the discussion to Carpenter's Compact framework—about to be presented—to get the negotiations back on track)

Mr. Carpenter has been preparing a compact proposition. Will you let us have your proposal?

Mr. Carpenter:
(starts out with maximum force of headwaters position, tone of rhetorician, then alters to diplomatic, statesmanlike tone as negotiations go along)

Certainly, Mr. Chairman. We propose that the construction of any and all reservoirs or other works in the Lower River shall in no manner arrest or interfere with the subsequent development of the territory of any of the upper states or their use of water. Further, these Lower River structures shall not have and cannot assert or claim any prior or preferred right or title to the use of these waters to the detriment of the upper states.

From the outset, we have been presented with the physical fact that 60 percent to 70 percent of the waters that pass by Yuma, Arizona originate in the mountains of Colorado. Can we, in fact, use all this water in our own territory? No, we cannot. The major part will always flow out to other states. However, the upper states do have the inherent right to use the water rising and flowing within their territory, as necessary, for their self-preservation and development, at least to the extent that they do not injure their neighbors below.

Secretary Hoover:
(taken aback by Carpenter's "headwaters at all costs" proposition in the face of what he thought to be the Coloradan's statesmanlike capability)

Does not your proposal imply that an equitable division of water is for you to perpetually take all the water you want? If we are to get equitable division, there are perhaps two bases upon which it could be approached. First, on how much land is to be irrigated. Second, on the percentages of water to be allocated.

Mr. Carpenter:
(somewhat arrogant and pompous lecture to Chair)

As the Commission is well aware, acreage limitations necessarily bring in issues related to the origin of the water. Origin is a concept that runs throughout international law, specifying that the nation of origin has inherent privileges and benefits that may be denied the lower nation.

Secretary Hoover:
(giving Carpenter the dagger eyes, pushes back at him to assert authority of chair)

Then it comes to this: the upper states want to take all the water they can and be declared immune from litigation by the other states.

Mr. Carpenter:
(indignant but abashed)

We are entitled to freedom of attack from below. We cannot be forced to just watch the waters flow away from us.

Secretary Hoover:
(turns away from and ignores Carpenter, turns to Carpenter's greatest adversary in the negotiations, Arizonan Norviel, who has a competing proposal)

I would like to know what Mr. Norviel's opinion is of Mr. Carpenter's proposal.

Mr. Norviel:
(scornfully, also not looking at Carpenter, but pointedly at Hoover, especially McClure and Scrugham, as if to warn them of the Upper Basin danger to derail Lower Basin plans for a large project on the Lower River)

He always comes back to the same point—the Upper Basin states cannot be limited by anything and are entitled to all that the Maker of the World has put before them, without regard to the rights of anybody else.

Mr. McClure:
(seems to have woken out of a weary lethargy, then gains rhetorical steam)

I must be dull of comprehension, Mr. Chairman, but Mr. Carpenter seems to me to take the position that Colorado must be protected to an extent that would make her absolutely safe—regardless of other interests. California clearly recognizes the rights of those who put water to beneficial use. Yet, California does not desire, nor would she make claims that injure her neighbors.

(looking directly at Carpenter and challenging him) I would like to know what character of assurance Mr. Carpenter would demand from the lower states?

Mr. Carpenter:
(sees he is forcing bad feeling and is highly aware of the need to moderate his tone and approach)

We ask, simply, that construction of any water structures shall in no manner interfere with water development in the upper states.

Mr. Emerson:
(enthusiastic, wants to be sure the talks move forward and Carpenter doesn't have a blank check to speak for the Upper Basin)

Well, I hope to see a plan that all seven states can subscribe to.

Mr. Scrugham:
(statesmanlike, obviously credible, constructive tone)

One fundamental problem is that projects on the Lower River cannot be successfully financed—unless the Lower Basin states can rely on a certain amount of water delivery necessary for their needs. Unless Mr. Carpenter can modify his statements about the natural rights of headwaters states, I do not believe that this commission can come to any agreement.

Mr. Caldwell:
(diplomatic, wants to strike a balance, but is wary about giving away position of Upper Basin)

I confess very frankly that my leaning is toward the idea advanced by Mr. Carpenter. But, I do not want to be in the position of throwing the Commission into a deadlock at this time.

Mr. Davis:
(looks at Carpenter to shore him up, then at Hoover)

Mr. Carpenter's proposal would amply protect the interests of New Mexico.

Mr. Norviel:
(Arizona counterpoints Carpenter to seize the bargaining initiative)

I have a new proposal, that all priorities between said states, with respect to their use of Colorado River water, excepting the Gila River, are specifically waived, *provided* that each state shall be free to develop the additional new acreage, without detriment to existing irrigated lands:

Wyoming	543,000 acres
Colorado	1,018,000 acres
Utah	456,000 acres
New Mexico	483,000 acres
Nevada	82,000 acres
Arizona	676,000 acres
California	481,000 acres

(sidelong glances to McClure and Scrugham)

Provided that adequate storage be created at one of the major dam sites in the Grand Canyon.

Provided that a permanent commission be created with power to grant waters for additional acreage without detriment to the acres stated above for each state.

Secretary Hoover:

Mr. Carpenter, would there be any hope of agreeing subject to an adjustment of acreage?

Mr. Carpenter:

I have my serious doubts about our legislature looking with favor upon an acreage limitation.

Mr. Norviel:

We might add without objection a word "may" which would make the clause read: "Provided that adequate storage *may* be created at one or the major dam sites in the Grand Canyon."

Secretary Hoover:

All those in favor of Mr. Norviel's proposal say "Aye."

Arizona?	Aye
California	Aye
Nevada	Aye

Those opposed, "No."
(forceful, loud negatives)

Colorado	No
New Mexico	No

Utah	No
Wyoming	No

Secretary Hoover:
(frustration on the verge of controlled despair)

The motion is lost. We have not been able to get to any agreement on a general single idea for a compact. Therefore, this session has no result except to define differences. The question arises, is it worthwhile to have another session? Or shall we make the declaration now that we are so hopelessly far apart that there is no use in proceeding?

Mr. Norviel:
(sensing he has pushed back at Upper Basin too far, wants to state his willingness to listen warily, however, to what might come next, fearful of breaking off negotiations)

I do not think we should foreclose our meetings at this time. I think that we should hold the matter open, subject to call of the chairman.

Mr. Scrugham:
(very candid, with a sense of great potential historical loss)

I believe that we have made a failure thus far.

Mr. Caldwell:
(rises half out of his seat in an appeal not to lose hope)

It may not be nearly so hopeless as you think. I certainly would like to suggest that Mr. Norviel and Mr. McClure do not take home to their states the idea that they met here commissioners unwilling to be generous and helpful.

Mr. McClure:
(grumpy, not seeming to catch that the Upper Basin states have a lot at stake in keeping the talks going)

That is exactly the attitude we are getting.

Mr. Carpenter:
(Carpenter sounds like, "Okay, I've stated the position expected back home, now let's get down to the real work")

I know that to some members of this commission, this seems to have been a fruitless conference. However, I am free to say—to me, this has been a very profitable conference and we are nearer a common accord than I expected when I arrived in

Washington. I think it would be the height of crime to the people who sent us here to adjourn permanently now.

Secretary Hoover:
("yes, we can do it" tone, let's go West)

I suggest the next meeting take place in the Southwest.

11th Meeting, Bishop's Lodge, Santa Fe, New Mexico, November 11, 1922

Secretary Hoover:
(getting down to brass tacks)

I understand that two or three commissioners have formulated suggested agreements.

(turning to Norviel) Mr. Norviel, for a better understanding of your proposal, might we not reduce it to five central principles: (1) the Colorado River is to be regarded as the entire watershed including the Imperial and Coachella Valleys; (2) that throughout the basin, the principle of prior appropriation should rule; (3) new appropriations could be made by each state from the waters of the Colorado River for a period of time, but you have left this period blank in your proposal; (4) these new appropriations would have a priority of appropriation, but with a ranking of the preference of the various uses; and (5) there would be a limitation on Colorado and Utah about how much water could be taken from the Colorado River for use outside the natural basin. Is that correct?

Mr. Norviel:
(addressing Hoover)

Yes, sir, that is correct. The vital principle of the whole thing is to apply the principle of prior appropriation. We respect all present rights. We have provided for a fixed period of time for making new appropriations. A permanent commission would be established. The commission shall fix the period of time for making the new appropriations. We have segregated the classes of the new uses. First, river control, the next use is municipal or domestic, the next is agriculture and the last is power. Each of these in their use takes precedence over those of lesser preference. As between the same type of uses, priority of appropriation would prevail.

Secretary Hoover:

I think California is next in line. Would you, Mr. McClure, like to offer any proposal?

Mr. McClure:

No, sir, not at this time.

Secretary Hoover:

Then we come to Colorado.

Mr. Carpenter:
(summary of Carpenter's written proposal read to the commissioners before discussion ensues)

On behalf of Colorado, I have prepared a draft compact founded upon the division of the entire flow of the river, based on an average annual river flow at Yuma from 1902 to 1921, being approximately 17.4 million acre-feet. Colorado, New Mexico, Utah, and Wyoming would agree that consumption of water within the Upper Basin shall never reduce the mean or average flow of the Colorado River at Lee's Ferry, over any ten consecutive-year period, below a 6,264,000 acre-feet annual average. In addition to this minimum average, there would be annual delivery by the Upper Basin of one-half of the Mexican delivery requirement.

Secretary Hoover:

A correct statement would be that the Lower Basin shall be apportioned a percentage of ten-year average flows equal to 36 percent of the flow at Yuma?

Mr. Carpenter:

Yes, we take into account the inflows above Yuma and below Lee's Ferry. They are to be deducted from the one-half supply due the Lower Basin and the resultant net figure will be given to pass at Lee's Ferry.

Secretary Hoover:

Mr. Caldwell, your proposal?

Mr. Caldwell:

My draft provides for partition of the water between the basins very much as outlined by Mr. Carpenter's draft. I propose that the total and aggregate of all priorities of rights running to the Lower Basin shall never be in excess of six million acre-feet per annum. The Upper Basin shall be permitted unrestricted use within its boundaries of tributaries arising within its territories and flowing into the Lower Basin. Above Lee's Ferry, not less than six million acre-feet of reserve storage shall be constructed to protect against periodic dry years and annual waste to the Gulf of California. Storage of water on the Colorado River system would not establish a priority water right, and therefore shall not preclude or interfere with water development, as it becomes feasible.

Mr. Emerson:
(looking at Norviel)

As I understand it, Mr. Norviel's form of pact proposes no definite allocation between states. Without some definitive allocation strategy, from the Wyoming standpoint, I can't conceive that we could sign any such agreement.

Mr. Norviel:

As to the division of the basin into two divisions, it isn't, as I conceive it, what we were appointed for. It doesn't arrive at any conclusion, and, as it is stated, it leaves the states of the two divisions to work out their own salvation on whatever plan they may choose in the future.

Mr. Emerson:
(appealing to Norviel to do what can be done for an allocation between the Upper and Lower states)

Mr. Norviel, it seems to me, the success of this endeavor depends upon whether we can solve the problem we have in hand now. If you look at this thing in a big way, it is a conflict between the states of the Lower River and the states in the Upper River. If we can solve that conflict—why, that is the biggest thing we can do.

Mr. Norviel:
(offended at suggestion he hasn't proposed a viable solution)

If you will read carefully the suggestion I make, I think you will find there is a solution there as clear as a clear sky.

Mr. Davis:
(challenging Norviel face to face)

I understand Mr. Norviel's proposition to be this: that there be a straight race for development for a certain unnamed period. At the end of that period, there will be priority for whatever water has been put to beneficial use. Yet, there is nothing whatever said as to what should be done after that period. We need to have a guarantee of water to each of the individual states.

Mr. Norviel:
(addressing Davis)

The period of time may be extended, or left to the next generation.

Mr. Carpenter:
(rejecting Norviel's proposal, as summarized by Davis, in its entirety)

The state of Colorado could not look with favor upon any plan which would degenerate into a mere contest of speed whereby an unfortunate unnatural growth would be forced upon one basin in order to keep pace with what might be a natural development in another basin. Neither can we look with favor upon permanent control by a super-government. Priority is a worthless expression unless enforced. To enforce it would require the intermeddling of a super-power, created, if you please, by surrender of local power. Secondly, when you proceed to reduce the adjustment to one of a definite fixing of quantities, or limitations of use state by state, you proceed to a degree of refinement that is hazardous and calls for knowledge which no man possesses at this time.

Proceeding upon that hypothesis or conclusion, it becomes a problem of seeing if it could be worked out on a division basis, with those divisions having been fixed by nature. We have a great catchment basin pouring down into a funnel neck, the canyon. Below that is territory to receive that water. For these reasons, it appears more prudent to strike at the root of the whole problem by looking at allocation based on divisions.

Mr. Emerson:
(looking to Hoover to give a signal)

As I look at it now, the allocation between these two great divisions is practical and no doubt the simplest solution. It will be proper if it goes far enough. Judge Davis would like to see the matter go further, to have an allocation of water made to each of the individual states. When we do that we are getting into more refinement and...

Mr. Scrugham:
(interrupting quickly on Emerson's comment)

More danger of failure to secure approval of the pact by the interested states. I suggest, Mr. Chairman, that you call for a vote of each representative of each state, yes or no, on the principle of division of water between the Upper and Lower Basins.

Mr. Norviel:
(exasperation that he can't seem to get priority of new uses established as the common point for the compact)

Let's first find out whether that is what we are here for!

Secretary Hoover:
(appealing to Norviel not to obstruct progress in the negotiation)

Is not this a question, Mr. Norviel, of whether we go back to our previous elaborate discussions on apportionment to each state? I think most all of us have, more or less, mentally abandoned the notion that we could ever agree upon an apportionment to each state.

Mr. Norviel:

I can conceive no way to administer it.

Secretary Hoover:
(turning to the Californian for help)

What is your impression, Mr. McClure?

Mr. McClure:

Mr. Chairman, two weeks ago I spent a full day attempting to outline some definite allocation between the states, going back to the minutes of our sixth meeting in Washington and looking all through the tables, and gave it up in despair. As desirable as it may be to allocate definite amounts to the different states, I think it quite an impossible task at this time.

Secretary Hoover:
(firmly takes hold of discussion)

I suggest, Mr. Norviel, that we abandon the discussion of apportionment based on acreage or any other individual state-by-state apportionment.

Mr. Norviel:
(resigned tone of voice)

I have gotten away from that.

Secretary Hoover:
(with a hint of "thank you" to the Arizonan)

Then we come to whether it is possible to make a division by groups of states.

Mr. Norviel:
(not wanting to seem like he is giving up)

The same question comes up regarding the administration of the water.

Secretary Hoover:

In what sense do you think it has to be administered if we just confine it to a division at Lee's Ferry?

Mr. Norviel:
(focusing on bottom line of guaranteed water delivery to Lower Basin)

Well, under Mr. Carpenter's plan, as he suggests an average of ten years, this year there might be an abundance of water and he might send 30 million acre-feet. That would satisfy for the next five or six years, and he wouldn't have to send down any additional water. So how it would be administered I can hardly understand. In dry years when everybody needs water, the Upper Basin could hold back all of it. Then, at some point in the future, within the ten-year period, they can use flash floods to make up the amount they held back.

Mr. Davis:
(addressing Norviel)

Isn't this an objection in detail, Mr. Norviel, rather than an objection to the general principle?

Mr. Norviel:
(ignoring Davis, addressing Hoover)

Mr. Carpenter's proposed division is founded, as I take it, or perhaps borrowed, from reports prepared by the Geological Survey and Reclamation Service. They made an exceedingly careful study of the supply of water and the acres currently cultivated and to be cultivated. They divided the basin into two divisions and arrived at the conclusion that the water could be divided, 35 percent above and 65 percent below at Lee's Ferry, not considering, as I take it, any of the inflow in the Lower Basin. Now, Mr. Carpenter wants to directly reverse the percentages to benefit the Upper Basin, and he fixes a ten-year period to make up for lack of water deliveries whenever they want to hold water back.

Mr. Davis:
(ignoring Norviel's rebuff, addressing Norviel directly again)

What I was trying to get at, Mr. Norviel, was this: without discussing the percentage division, whether 50-50, 60-40, or whatever it may be, will you discuss the principle?

Mr. Norviel:
(directly to Davis, warns of dangerous future wrangling among the states)

I am willing to discuss it, whether it is satisfactory or not. But, it leaves the work undone. That would leave us in Arizona to go into the Upper Basin and, I suppose, have to sit in their discussions and help them arrange the distribution of their water! And, it leaves Arizona also in the Lower Basin to assist in the distribution of the water between the states in that basin.

Mr. Carpenter:
(slightly sarcastic, but quickly going into an appeal to Arizona's interest in getting a Lower Basin storage project as soon as possible)

Mr. Norviel, may I bother you? What is uppermost in the thoughts of all your people is the possibility of immediate large construction, isn't it? The sooner you can get it the better, both for Arizona and California.

Mr. Norviel:
(firm affirmation)

Of course!

Secretary Hoover:
(seizing the opportunity to make a breakthrough)

Is the percentage too small, is that the objection?

Mr. Norviel:

Well, that is one of the objections. Of course we want to be in a position where we would not necessarily be dried up for five years and flooded for the next five years.

Mr. Carpenter:
(plainly showing that issue of amount of guaranteed water delivery is negotiable)

Yes, we will fix the minimum flow to take care of that.

Secretary Hoover:

We have all seen the figures from Reclamation Director Davis. Interpreted back from Yuma. The historical average flow is about 16.5 million acre-feet at Lee's Ferry, of which four million acre-feet is presently needed for consumptive use in the Upper Basin and 7.2 million acre-feet for the Lower Basin, including a half supply for 800,000 acres to Mexico.

12th Meeting, Bishop's Lodge, November 12, 1922

Mr. Davis:

Inasmuch as Mr. Norviel is not prepared to state his position tonight regarding the division of water between the two basins, might it not be well to go ahead and ascertain the position of the other states?

Secretary Hoover:

I think so.

Mr. McClure:

The 50-50 division appeals to me as a fair base for discussion.

Secretary Hoover:

Gentlemen, the proposition set before us is a general principle regarding the allocation of water between the upper and lower states specifying a 50-50 division. This is not a committal as to details or quantity—just the principle.

Utah?	Aye
Nevada?	Aye
New Mexico?	Aye
Wyoming?	Aye
California?	Aye
Colorado?	Aye

Mr. Norviel:
(with conspicuously-folded arms, not voting)

Arizona abstains.

13th Meeting, Bishop's Lodge, November 13, 1922

Secretary Hoover:

Last evening we left off discussing whether we could accept a general principle of a division between the upper and lower states as the primary basis of compact. Mr. Norviel wanted to await this morning before he came to a decision as to whether we could discuss it in principle, without any obligation at all as to detail.

Mr. Norviel:
(tries to seize back the lead by appearing to make a great concession)

Mr. Secretary and Gentlemen of the Commission. We from Arizona are perfectly willing to accept in principle the division of the basins. I say in this that we do not do so reluctantly, nor do we do so with avidity. We do it calmly, facing a serious proposition. For we feel in this principle that we are conceding a right that is ours by all established rules of law and precedent. However, we will accept the principle and try to adjudicate the matters on the basis of a division as suggested, a division of the waters.

Secretary Hoover:
(civil engineer and diplomat coming to the fore)

That will bring us to a discussion of detail. What is passing through my mind, if I might suggest it simply as a matter for discussion, is the concept of the river as a series of retaining vessels with a large vessel, or several vessels, in the lower division. The primary object of the lower division is to secure into this receptacle a sufficiency of water to give them a constant flow of eight or nine or seven million acre-feet per annum. That being the case, their desire must be to keep this receptacle filled to a point of security. The ten-year average could keep those vessels filled up to regulate flow downstream.

Mr. Carpenter:
(wary expression of understanding about Lower Basin needs)

The visitation of famine strikes primarily the source states, the states of origin. It seems to me incumbent upon the lower states to be reasonable in the demand of guarantee. The suggestion you make presupposes the construction of reservoirs in the lower countries, and along with it there should be concurrently the construction of reservoirs in the upper territory to permit the deliveries as you suggest. The suggestion I have made leaves that matter to be worked out entirely by the two divisions.

Mr. Norviel:
(responsive tone of good will)

I am very glad to hear that argument from our friend at the top of the hill, for it puts us in a better situation. I see no reason why we cannot include a minimum flow to be included with the average. That will give some satisfaction and stabilization of the water that comes to us. I think perhaps that ought to be discussed now and fixed upon.

Mr. Carpenter:
(aghast at the suggestion that he could be viewed as a partisan)

It is not within the range of my thought to even conceive of a condition where the upper states would strip the stream and deliberately paralyze the country below.

Secretary Hoover:

When we consider the question of storage, not only seasonal flows year to year, but also the flow over a term of years, we are coming towards equalization.

15th Meeting, Bishop's Lodge, November 14, 1922

Mr. Norviel:
(slipping back into contentiousness)

I can't conceive of any security without a minimum flow, and I see no harm in making the proposition at this time to the upper division.

Mr. Carpenter:
(responding in kind contentiously)

Isn't your attitude that no matter how terrible a drouth, or how great the affliction thrust upon the upper territory—which is the only occasion whereby a water shortage would arise at Lee's Ferry—isn't it always your disposition to get assurance for your dry deserts below, and ask us to bear the brunt of that visitation of drouth, which paralyzes us just as, or more, than the lower country? If I am in error that this is your frame of mind, well and good, I beg your pardon.

Mr. Norviel:
(recognizing he has pushed back too far)

You are forgiven for all your sins up to date as far as I am concerned. The assurance we ask is no more than our legal rights. We only want what is ours.

Mr. Carpenter:
(matter-of-fact recognition that Norviel needs to come away with preserving Arizona's right to the Gila)

You want the Gila River because it arises in your territory.

Mr. Norviel:

If you have any chance to appropriate water out of the Gila River, it is yours. Whatever appropriation we could make out of the Colorado of the unused water is ours. That is all we ask.

16th Meeting, Bishop's Lodge, November 14, 1922

Mr. Norviel:

You propose a reservoir above Lee's Ferry. But, if the storage is in the Upper Basin, you retain the water to our detriment. The storage must be in the Lower Basin.

Mr. Carpenter:

No, you misunderstand. If a large reservoir were constructed at or in the vicinity of Lee's Ferry, it would be essentially a reservoir for the delivery of water to the lower region. It could be nothing else. No other use could be made of it except the mere generation of power or floating of boats, and we could get no irrigation benefit from such a structure. That was my thought in the compact I suggested, although I don't believe I expressed it fully enough to bring it out clearly. It would accomplish first of all the saving of humanity and property with incidentally rich benefits to run to the lower territory, which would be entirely proper. In return for this, some day the upper territory might look to you folks for reciprocity in the matter of the upper development. Do I make myself clear?

Mr. Norviel:
(very measured signal to all the negotiators, these antagonists may now have an understanding of the bottom line that will carry the day, storage to guarantee delivery to the Lower Basin and a perpetual apportionment between the Upper and Lower Basins)

I think you do.

17th Meeting, November 15, 1922

Secretary Hoover:
(pushing to get over the hump of what the delivery guarantee shall be)

It appears that the result of these deliberations and our recommendation is to establish 16 million acre-feet as a sort of an average mean at Lee's Ferry. The Upper Basin proposes to guarantee delivery of 65 million acre-feet on a ten-year average, and the Lower Basin proposes 82 million acre-feet. Of course the business of the chairman is to find middle ground. So I am wondering if the upper states will make it 7.5 million acre-feet per annum, 75 million acre-feet ten-year average.

20th Meeting, Bishop's Lodge, November 19, 1922

Secretary Hoover:
(addressing McClure)

You were not here this morning when we came to this Mexican question. The question is whether or not the two basins should equally bear the present burden of Mexico. Have we got something, Mr. Davis?

Mr. Davis:

We do not admit or recognize that there exists any obligation on the United States, or any state, to deliver water or allow water to flow to Mexico for use upon lands in that republic. But, if by international agreement or otherwise, an obligation to deliver any such water shall be established, in that event the burden of supplying such water shall be equally borne by the upper and lower divisions.

Secretary Hoover:

Then there is the Indian tribes article. "Nothing in this compact shall be construed as affecting the obligation of the United States to the Indian tribes."

All in favor say "Aye."

(All say "Aye.")

22nd Meeting, Bishop's Lodge, November 22, 1922

Secretary Hoover:

Gentlemen, informal meetings have occurred outside of our sessions to break the logjam. I now have a draft of an apportionment proposal: (a) There is hereby apportioned in perpetuity to each basin, for its exclusive beneficial consumptive use, 7.5 million acre-feet of water per annum, which shall include all water necessary for the supply of any rights which may now exist; (b) The Lower Basin is given the right to increase its beneficial consumptive use by the further quantity of one million acre-feet per annum.

Mr. Norviel:

Would it hurt in any way if we could prefix the words "In addition to the waters apportioned in (a)" to the words "the Lower Basin is given the right"? I don't want to disturb anything now, but if that would clarify it in any way, I think I would like to have it.

Secretary Hoover:

Mr. Carpenter, have you any views?

Mr. Carpenter:
(signaling agreement resolutely)

No objection.

24th Meeting, Bishop's Lodge, November 23, 1922

Secretary Hoover:

Gentlemen, I have as follows the draft language regarding assurances for minimum delivery flows by the Upper Basin. Article III(d) would read:

> The States of the Upper Division agree that they will not cause the flow of the River at Lee Ferry to be depleted below an aggregate of 75,000,000 acre-feet for any period of ten consecutive years reckoned in continuing progressive series, beginning with the first day of July next succeeding the ratification of this compact.

26th Meeting, Bishop's Lodge, November 24, 1922

Mr. Emerson:

Can we change the time of year to the first day of October?

Secretary Hoover:

All those in favor say "Aye."

(All enthusiastically say "Aye.")

The motion carries unanimously.

27th Meeting, Bishop's Lodge, November 24, 1922

Secretary Hoover:
(with a great deal of pride in mutual and historical accomplishment)

I have a resolution to propose:

> "The members of the Colorado River Commission have had constantly before them the great menace by annual floods to the lives and property of the people of the Imperial and Palo Verde Valleys in California, and the Yuma Valley in Arizona, and the anxiety of their thousands of citizens:

> Therefore, they earnestly recommend and urge the early construction of works in the Colorado River to control floods, and that such construction be made subject to the Colorado River Compact."

All in favor say "Aye."

(All enthusiastically say "Aye.")

Mr. Carpenter:

We have completed the task assigned to this commission, which is the first example of interstate diplomacy in the history of the United States on so large a scale. Through all the days of our toil, our chairman has been kind, generous, and patient. And we assure you that wherever you may go, whatever you may do, you will carry through life the fond esteem and admiration and love of all of us; and if any us survive you, ours will be a fond recollection.

Secretary Hoover:

I am much overcome by that kind expression. The Commission has had a unique blending of talent. The engineers have had more hard things to say about the lawyers than the lawyers have been able to say back. But I think the engineers will agree that we would have got nowhere if it hadn't been for the lawyers. Congratulations to each and all of you! We are adjourned.

Biography of Negotiators
by Professor Dan Tyler

UPPER BASIN STATES

Frank C. Emerson (Wyoming): Because of his youthful looks, Emerson is known as the "boy commissioner." He was a tenacious adversary to Mr. Carpenter during the *Wyoming v. Colorado* litigation, but he also has great respect for Carpenter's broad-ranging views. His principal interest is the Green River, the Colorado's northernmost and largest tributary, which rises in the Wind River Mountains of southwestern Wyoming. Although irrigation development has been slow along the Green, largely due to the high altitude, Emerson believes that many acres remain to be reclaimed, not only for farming, but for the livestock industry as well. And consistent with the view of other Upper Basin representatives, Emerson looks forward to the day when hydroelectric plants will be built along the Colorado's headwaters, their product used to drive railroads, and to develop the oil shale, coal, and other mineral deposits.

Stephen B. Davis, Jr. (New Mexico): Davis, associate justice of the New Mexico Supreme Court, who is occasionally ill during negotiations, is mostly concerned with the San Juan River, which originates in Colorado and flows across the northwest corner of New Mexico into Utah. He is also interested in the Gila and Little Colorado rivers, both of which originate in New Mexico. There are times during compact discussions when his Upper Basin loyalties are affected by a proprietary concern over two of the rivers Arizona claims as exclusively hers, but, for the most part, Davis and Carpenter, both attorneys, are usually in sync on compact issues.

R. W. Caldwell (Utah): Engineer Caldwell shares Mr. Emerson's interest in industrial development and in the Green River, but he is also excited by the prospects along the upper Colorado—referred to until 1921 as the Grand River. Heavy runoff of these two rivers has made possible extensive irrigation, and Mr. Caldwell believes that thousands of additional acres can be developed if sufficient water is preserved to his state for the future. Because of potential development of mineral rights, he is also a strong advocate of his state's ownership of the banks of the Colorado River within its borders.

Delphus E. Carpenter (Colorado): Of the seven commissioners, attorney Carpenter is the most experienced in interstate water negotiation. He comes to Washington confident that the upper states need to oppose restrictions in their water use for two reasons: (1) beneficial water use in Wyoming, Utah, Colorado, and New Mexico is limited by topography, altitude, and climate; and (2) much of the water used in the Upper Basin will flow back into the river as return flow for the Lower Basin. Carpenter is somewhat self-centered and arrogant, and his behavior results in open criticism from Hoover. But during the year of off-and-on negotiations, he learns how to be a very effective negotiator. His great respect for Hoover allows a synergy to develop between these two men that ultimately produces results, but his impassioned defense of states' rights nearly causes negotiations to collapse.

LOWER BASIN STATES

Winfield S. Norviel (Arizona): State water commissioner and attorney by training, Norviel is clearly the most determined and indefatigable negotiator at the table, even though he has a reputation as a very private person. Because 90 percent of Arizona's land lies within the Colorado River basin, and because his state is eager to secure the hydroelectric power that will promote agriculture and mining, he will fight doggedly to obtain guarantees for Colorado River water, while demanding every drop in the Gila River for Arizona. His position as Arizona's representative is most precarious. As compact negotiations begin in Washington, he is an appointee of Governor Thomas Campbell, but three weeks prior to the more extensive negotiations in Santa Fe, Campbell is replaced by Governor George W. P. Hunt, whose principal objective is to secure construction of a High Line Canal from the Colorado River to central Arizona. Norviel's dilemma is how to preserve the confidence of Campbell, while showing his new boss that he is a tough negotiator.

W. F. McClure (California): State engineer McClure is a sour-looking, quiet, and sometimes detached representative. A former lay preacher with a penchant for quoting the Bible, he is less an innovator than an evaluator of others' suggestions. Because he hails from northern California, he is frequently accused of lacking interest in the proceedings and not knowing as much about the lower Colorado River as he should. Imperial Valley residents are not happy with him, and Mr. Hoover has to work hard to bring him into the discussions.

James G. Scrugham (Nevada): Also an engineer, and one who will be elected governor of Nevada, Scrugham is primarily interested in hydroelectric power. There aren't many acres in Nevada's desert that can be reclaimed for agriculture, and most of those are along the Virgin River as it nears the Arizona border. But despite his unique focus, Mr. Scrugham is an intelligent and thoughtful participant in the negotiations, winning the respect of his colleagues through low-key, understated commentaries.

FEDERAL REPRESENTATIVE

Herbert Hoover: Trained as an engineer, Hoover is precise and data-oriented. He is also a profound believer in democracy, an advocate of efficiency in the federal government, and a proponent of flood control, distribution of electricity to rural areas, and conservation of natural resources. He sees the importance of connecting the nation's waterways into a comprehensive and integrated plan in which transportation, flood development, and reclamation will be coordinated. He believes in preserving the federal system and promotes government as the umpire, rather than policeman, of the economic life of the nation. The synergy he develops with Mr. Carpenter emerges from their mutual faith in the pioneer spirit of Americans.

Note: This play was presented at the opening of a conference that later proved to be instrumental in negotiating the "Quantification Settlement Agreement" for California's reduction of Colorado River water use from 5.2 million acre-feet per year to its compact entitlement of 4.4 million acre-feet of water.

Hobbs Note: These tables are taken from the sixth meeting of the Colorado River Compact Negotiations. All information and notations that follow are the Commission's.

Table A
AREAS AND WATER REQUIREMENTS
(Reclamation Service Data)

State	ACRES			ACRE FEET OF WATER	
	Irrigated 1920	Probable Additional	Water use Ac.ft. per acre	Probably used on acres irrigated	Probable additional required
Wyoming	367,000	543,000	1.5	550,500	814,500
Colorado	740,000	1,018,000	1.5	1,110,000	1,527,000
Utah	359,000	456,000	1.5	538,500	684,000
New Mexico	34,000	483,000	2.0	68,000	966,000
Nevada	5,000	2,000	2.5	12,500	5,000
Arizona	501,000	676,000	3.0	1,503,000	2,028,000
California	458,000	481,000	4.4	2,015,800	2,116,400
Total U.S.	2,464,000	3,659,000		5,797,700	8,140,900
Mexico	190,000	610,000	4.4	836,000	2,684,900
Grand Total	2,654,000	4,269,000		6,633,700	10,824,000

Note (1) All data involve estimation in varying degree. The acre-feet of past use are in the nature of guess, but the water used is not included in run-off data used in estimates for the future. Figures for additional acres assume construction of storage and feasible canals.

Note (2) Figures of water requirement are intended to be "consumptive use" except for California and Mexico, for which figures of total diversions are used because return flow is not available for reuse.

Inside the Drama of the Colorado River Compact Negotiations

TABLE B (REVISED)
REPORT OF COMMITTEE ON WATER REQUIREMENTS ON TOTAL NUMBER NEW ACRES CLAIMED IRRIGABLE FOR WHICH WATER IS ASKED BY STATES IN COLRADO RIVER BASIN TO BE IRRIGATED FROM COLORADO AND TRIBUTARIES.

	Acres-new	Acre-ft. Duty	Acre feet Diversion	Acre-feet Return	Acre ft. per a. con. use	Acre feet consumptive use
Wyoming	580,000	2-1/2	1,450,000	1	1-1/2	870,000
Colorado	1,515,000	2	3,030,000	7/10	13/10	1,969,500
	310,000	1	310,000	0	1	310,000
Utah	1,000,000	3	3,000,000	1/2	2-1/2	2,500,000
New Mexico	1,400,000	2-1/2	3,500,000	3/4	1-3/4	2,450,000
Nevada	82,000	3	246,000	1	2	164,000
Arizona	1,172,000	3-1/2	4,102,000	1-1/2	2	2,344,000
California	481,000	4	1,924,000	0	4	1,924,000
Total U.S.	**6,540,000**		**17,562,000**			**12,531,500**
Mexico	620,000	4	2,480,000	0	4	2,480,000
	7,160,000		20,042,000			15,011,500

TABLE C (REVISED)
REPORT OF COMMITTEE ON WATER REQUIREMENTS ON CULTIVATED ACRES OF STATES IN COLORADO RIVER.

	Cultivated acres old	Acre feet duty	Acre feet diversion	Acre feet return	Acre feet loss	Acre feet consumptive use
Wyoming	400,000	2-1/2	1,000,000	1	1-1/2	600,000
Colorado	850,000	2	1,700,000	0.7	1.3	1,105,000
Utah	188,000	3	564,000	1	2	376,000
Nevada	35,350	3	106,050	1	2	70,700
New Mexico	57,000	2-1/2	142,500	3/4	1-3/4	99,750
Arizona	521,500	3-1/2	1,825,250	1-1/2	2	1,043,000
California	458,000	4	1,832,000	0	4	1,832,000
U.S. Old	2,509,850		7,169,800			5,126,450
U.S. New	6,540,000		17,562,000			12,531,500
Total U.S.	**9,049,850**		**24,731,800**			**17,657,950**
Mexico Old	200,000	4	800,000	0	4	800,000
Mexico New	620,000	4	2,480,000	0	4	2,480,000
GRAND TOTAL	**9,869,850**		**28,011,800**			**20,937,950**

Symposium Proceedings September 2003

Note: In analyzing the foregoing "Revised Tables B and C" to determine if there is now sufficient surplus water to irrigate "New Acres" claimed by all the States and at he same time allow for any allocation that may be given to Mexico, it is necessary to include both "Cultivated Acres Old" (See Revised Table C) and "Acres New" for California and Mexico as "New Acres." This is due to the fact that the present diversion point for irrigation in California and Mexico is below the Gauging Station at Yuma, at which point the total flow of the Colorado River is recorded and an average annual run-off of 17,300,000 acre feet is shown.

	Acres	Acre-ft. Duty	Acre feet Diversion	Acre-feet Return	Acre ft. Loss.	Acre feet consumptive
Total "New Acres," see Revised Table B	7,160,000		20,042,000			15,011,500
"Cultivated Acres Old," see Revised Table C,						
California	458,000	4	1,832,000	0	4	1,832,000
Mexico	200,000	4	800,000	0	4	800,000
	7,818,000		**22,674,000**			**17,643,500**

The foregoing table shows that the present available surplus of 17,300,000 acre feet average run-off will, on the claims of the various States and any allowance that may be accorded to Mexico, have to water 7,818,000 acres for which the diversion or duty will be 22,674,000 acre feet and the Consumptive Use will be 17,643,400 acre feet.

The discussion with reference to the foregoing tables also raised the question as to whether, in the light of the difference between new acreage as estimated by the Reclamation Service in Table A and as claimed by each State as irrigable in Table B, there would be sufficient water in the Colorado to meet the demands of the various states.

Prior Appropriation and Instream Flow: The Struggle to Integrate Instream Flow Rights into Western Water Law
Western Regional Instream Flow Conference
Copper Mountain, Colorado
October 9, 1998

Thank you for your invitation. The snowstorm of this past weekend, though bright and shortening autumn days are back, is a reminder that winter lies in our immediate future.

Mountain stream flows are normally at their lowest in September and early October. Rush of past season snowmelt has passed, though the forest—acting as a natural sponge and reservoir—continues to leach its bounty back to the stream. Darkness daily grows. Darting through the riffles, trout gather in the remaining pools and hunker into the fading light.

On both sides of Vail Pass, the ski season can hardly wait to see what nature will provide. Ingenious pumps and nozzles blow snow and dollars into Colorado's recreational economy.

Trout and people. On these mountains, through these streams, borders are drawn, borders are crossed. Translations emerge.

Hear of this from the tongue of our great western poet, William Stafford:

WALKING THE BORDERS

Sometimes in the evening a translator walks out
And listens by streams that wander back and forth
Across borders. The translator holds a mint
On the tongue, turns it over to try
A new side, then tastes a wild new flavor,
A flavor that enlivens those fading languages
Of cursing and calling each other those names
That destroyed millions by swinging a cross
Like an ax, or a crescent curved like a knife,
Or star so red it burned its way over the ground.

> The wild new flavor fades away too,
> But lingers awhile along borders for a translator to savor
> Secretly, borrowing from both sides, holding
> For a moment the smooth round world
> In that cool instant of evening before the sun goes down.
>
> William Stafford, *The Way It Is: New and Selected Poems by William Stafford* (1998).

Borders are drawn, borders are crossed. Before 1973, instream fish flows and diversions for snowmaking were unknown to Colorado and its law. Today, it is well accepted that water rights can be established for both types of beneficial use. Water court decrees, and their administration by state water officials, secure the place of each. That both types of use have come into being testifies to the evolving values and customs of the people of the state and of the United States.

Colorado's 1973 legislature pioneered the integration of instream flow water rights through delegation of authority for appropriation, without diversion, by the state's Water Conservation Board for "preservation of the natural environment to a reasonable degree." The Colorado Supreme Court disagreed with certain water user groups that this statute was unconstitutional. The court gave particular attention to the preservation of life forms that need water and of the ability of the Water Conservation Board to consult and utilize expert opinion:

> The legislative objective is to preserve reasonable portions of the natural environment in Colorado. Factual determinations regarding such questions as which areas are most amenable to preservation and what life forms are presently flourishing or capable of flourishing should be delegated to an administrative agency which may avail itself of expert scientific opinion.
>
> *Colorado River Water Conservation Dist. v. Colorado Water Conservation Board*, 594 P.2d 570, 576 (Colo. 1979).

Nearly 8,500 miles of Colorado streams have minimum stream flow appropriations on them. Some observers point out that these water rights are junior in priority. Sure, they are! So are the snowmaking water rights. So is every new water right that finds its way into use in Colorado. That's the very point and virtue of prior appropriation water law.

Water rights in Colorado become vested through actual beneficial use. Decreed prior vested water rights are secure in their administration vis-à-vis new or changed uses. Recognizing the value of marketable water rights for instream flow within Colorado, the legislature in 1986 permitted the Water Conservation Board to purchase or accept the donation of senior vested water rights for change of use to minimum stream flows and lake levels.

Thus has Colorado been faithful to borders it drew long ago and borders it continues to cross. You recall Michelangelo's finger of God touching the finger of a human being. Translation: we are body and spirit together. We look to our own needs, and we are capable of respecting the needs of other life forms. The customs and values of a people are reflected in its water law.

In 1872, the Territorial Supreme Court of Colorado upheld irrigation as a beneficial use:

> When the lands of this territory were derived from the general government, they were subject to the law of nature, which holds them barren until awakened to fertility by nourishing streams of water, and the purchasers could have no benefit from the grant without the right to irrigate them.
>
> *Yunker v. Nichols*, 1 Colo. 551, 555 (1872).

In 1979, the Colorado Supreme Court upheld preservation of the natural environment as a beneficial use:

> While we agree that the standards set forth call for evaluations by biologists rather than assessments regarding public health or economics, we cannot agree that the standards are not such as could be implemented by agencies having specific expertise regarding the preservation of flora, fauna and other aspects of the natural environment.
>
> *Colorado River Dist. v. CWCB*, 594 P.2d at 576.

A century between these opinions, Colorado's law of nature speaking in both of them; for the meantime, Colorado had passed from a territory of homesteaders to a more inclusive state of working people of all persuasions whose hobbies include gardening, skiing, fishing, and translating the song of running water into William Stafford's language of poetry.

HOME STATE

You can see mountains propped there,
A little bit blue. Rivers yearn through
Those canyons, and storms punctuate
Even the summer days.

Sometimes whole sides of the world
Lean against where you live.
Just being there is a career.
And the danger is in forgetting.

That sometime you might go away.
William Stafford, from *The Way It Is: New and Selected Poems by William Stafford* (1998).

A beauty of the law of the United States is that each state may choose its own water law. Each decides how to address the integration of instream flow rights. California has relied on the public trust doctrine; Colorado on its prior appropriation system; Oregon on what I believe to be a reservation paradigm.

Since the 1866 Mining Act, Congress has recognized the ability of the states to choose. Certainly, federal law continues to shape if and how new or enlarged water projects can be constructed. The National Environmental Policy Act, Clean Water Act, Endangered Species Act, Federal Land Policy and Management Act, and other federal regulatory laws will demand that instream flows are taken into account.

At the same time, vested water rights are valuable water rights to be honored. Interstate compacts approved by Congress are also the law of the land. The challenge of the past and the future is joined to our present. How we honor the rights of people and of nature is our western heritage. In the October 4, 1998 issue of the *Denver Post* appears an article in which I had the privilege to say so. As always, the newspapers will exercise their editorial rights.

Thank you!

How Like a River, The Evolution of Western Water Law
The Colorado Water Workshop, Western State College
Gunnison, Colorado
July 26, 2000

Geography and Experience

It's the natural order of geography for a river to keep on moving—and for those who would understand rivers, to walk in their path, sometimes pushing against the current, sometimes going with the flow. Western water law has always been changing—and remaining the same. From the earliest days of the states and territories, it's been so.

There's no contradiction in this. Law courts exist to decide actual cases, based on constitutions and statutes—state and federal—in light of the facts of each case and prior precedent, with a peek at the future, always hoping the decisions made at the time are as good as they can be. Oliver Wendell Holmes said, "The law embodies the story of a nation's development through many centuries, and it cannot be dealt with as if it contained only the axioms and corollaries of a book of mathematics."[1]

Mountains and rivers—like the lives of all creatures living among them—don't lend themselves neatly to a tape measure. You have to experience stretching your legs and your heart to understand depth and distance. Water law incorporates geography and experience.

Major Currents

For all his knowledge of the western landscape, his audacious physical and political explorations, his commitment to progressive planning and management, his fascination with irrigated agriculture as the enduring heritage of the western movement, pioneer river runner John Wesley Powell could not have foreseen the multi-dimensional role of water in future economies of the settled West. He predicted in his 1879 Arid Lands Report, for example, that, "All of the waters of all the arid lands will eventually be taken from their natural channels, and they can be utilized only to the extent to which they are thus removed, and water rights must of necessity be severed from the natural channels."[2]

---

[1] *Holmes*, The Common Law 1 (1881).
[2] John Wesley Powell, *Lands of the Arid Region of the United States* 42 (Harvard Press 1983 reprint) (1879).

The western states have discovered that they lack the means, the right, and the will to dry up all the streams. Downstream states, Native Americans, federal reservations, the utility and joy of a flowing stream for fishing and boating and walking along through urban drainage ways and rural meanderings—in sum, the changing values and customs of the people at work and at play—have intruded.

Major active currents of western water law are: (1) Congress severed water from the title to public lands and provided for the territories and states to establish water rights under their own laws;[3] (2) the western states chose prior appropriation as their basic water allocation and administration law for waters of the natural stream;[4] (3) under prior appropriation law, water remains a public resource, the states continue to create property rights to the use of this resource, and beneficial use is the basis, measure, and limit of these water rights;[5] (4) in times of short supply, state water officials have a duty to curtail junior water rights in favor of senior water rights;[6] (5) the reserved water rights of the United States and of Native American tribes are entitled to recognition and administration along with all other rights in order of their adjudicated priority;[7] (6) interstate water compacts and equitable apportionment decrees allocate water between the states, with congressional approval, and are enforceable;[8] (7) new water demand is created predominantly by the public sector, namely municipalities and special districts that serve the West's municipal and commercial growth;[9] (8) federal environmental laws significantly constrain new development of surface water resources, shifting water supply planning towards increased reliance on groundwater, changes of water rights from their prior uses, and conservation measures;[10] (9) the changing values and customs of the people of the West and of the United States include clean and flowing water for recreation, instream flow, and restoration of disturbed riverine habitat;[11] (10) optimum use, efficient water management, and priority administration are fundamental adaptive principles of western water law, increasingly important to meeting water needs in the twenty-first century.[12]

---

[3] See *California Oregon Power Co. v. Beaver Portland Cement Co.*, 295 U.S. 142, 163-64 (1935); *California v. United States*, 438 U.S. 645, 662 (1978).
[4] See, *e.g., Coffin v. Left Hand Ditch Co.*, 6 Colo. 443, 447, 449 (1882); *State v. Southwestern Colo. Water Conservation Dist.*, 671 P.2d 1294, 1304-08 (Colo.1983).
[5] See *Williams v. Midway Ranches Property Owners Ass'n, Inc.*, 938 P.2d 515, 521-23 (Colo. 1997).
[6] See *Navajo Development Co. v. Sanderson*, 655 P.2d 1374, 1377, 1380 (Colo. 1982).
[7] See *Winters v. United States*, 207 U.S. 564, 577 (1908); *United States v. City and County of Denver*, 656 P.2d 1, 17-18 (Colo. 1982).
[8] See *Kansas v. Colorado*, 514 U.S. 673, 693-94 (1995); *Simpson v. Highland Irrigation Co.*, 917 P.2d 1242, 1246, 1248 (1996).
[9] See, *e.g., City of Thornton v. Bijou Irrigation Co.*, 926 P.2d 1, 39 (Colo. 1996).
[10] See *Riverside Irrigation District v. Andrews*, 758 F.2d 508, 514 (10th Cir. 1985); *Chatfield East Well Co. Ltd. v. Chatfield East Property Owners Ass'n*, 956 P.2d 1260, 1270 (Colo. 1998).
[11] See *Water in the West: Challenge for the Next Century*, Report of the Western Water Policy Review Advisory Commission at 5-11, 6-11 to 6-14 (1998).
[12] See *Santa Fe Trails Ranches Property Owners Ass'n v. Simpson*, 990 P.2d 46, 54 (Colo. 1999).

Adaptive Law of Beneficial Use

State constitutions and statutes do not generally confine the content of the term "beneficial use." Instead, beneficial use tracks the economic and community values of the people. The western states are the most rapidly urbanizing region of the United States.[13] Citizen demand for water-related amenities in all forms drives the direction of water law and policy. The list of recognized beneficial uses now includes irrigation, stock watering, domestic, municipal, commercial, industrial, power generation, fire protection, flood control, residential environment, recreation, fish and wildlife culture, release from storage for boating and fishing flows, snowmaking, dust suppression, mined land reclamation, boat chutes, fish ladders, nature centers, augmentation of depletions for out-of-priority diversions, and minimum stream flows for preservation of the environment to a reasonable degree.[14] The list is growing as new and changed uses are proposed for state permits and judicial decrees.[15]

Instream flow use has been the most dramatic innovation. Thirteen western states now recognize instream water rights in some form.[16] Colorado is but one example. In 1965, reiterating longstanding rejection of riparian water law, the state supreme court proclaimed that "maintenance of the 'flow' of the stream is a riparian right and is completely inconsistent with the doctrine of prior appropriation."[17]

Fourteen years later, the court jumped the boundaries: "it is obvious that the General Assembly in the enactment of S.B. 97 certainly did intend to have appropriations for piscatorial purposes without diversion. We hold that under S.B. 97 the Colorado Water Board can make an in-stream appropriation without diversion in the conventional sense."[18]

---

[13] The American West is home to nearly one-third of the population of the United States. The western states have grown approximately 32 percent in the past 25 years, compared with a 19 percent rate in the rest of the nation; by the year 2025, the West will likely add another 28 million residents. See *Report of the Western Water Policy Review Advisory Commission* at 2-14.

[14] See Gregory J. Hobbs, Jr., *Colorado Water Law: An Historical Overview*, 1 U. DENV. WATER L. REV. 1, 9 (1997).

[15] See the monthly Colorado Water Court Resumes at the Colorado Courts Web Site (www.courts.state.co.us).

[16] See Janet C. Neuman, "Protecting Instream Flows In Prior Appropriation States: Legal And Policy Issues," Natural Resources Law Center Program "Water and Growth in the West," University of Colorado School of Law (2000). See also *United States v. New Mexico*, 438 U.S. 696, 711-13 (1978).

[17] See *Colorado River Water Conservation Dist. v. Rocky Mountain Power Co.*, 406 P.2d 798, 800 (Colo. 1965).

[18] See *Colorado River Water Conservation Dist. v. Colorado Water Conservation Board*, 594 P.2d 570, 574 (Colo. 1979).

Thus, prior appropriation law can evolve to protect environmental values through enforceable water rights that are subject to the exercise of senior rights.[19] The action of the legislature in assigning this unique program to the State of Colorado, acting on behalf of the people to obtain a water right in priority, was key to the Colorado Supreme Court's ruling of constitutionality.

Restoring Riverine Habitat

The 1998 Report of the Western Water Policy Review Commission included among its recommendations a goal of ensuring "sufficient instream flows to achieve and protect the natural functions of riverine, riparian, and flood plain ecosystems."[20] Those interested in assuring a long-term stable place for instream flow recognize that "it is critical to choose strategies that will actually get water back into the river, free from call, during the periods of greatest need."

How might this be accomplished? The preferred and surest way is through management within the water rights system, by "allowing conversion of senior consumptive rights to instream flows, either by the rights holders themselves, or in the marketplace, and with solid protection for keeping those flows instream, either as an official senior water right, or using some other device."[21]

Federal Constraints and Water Supply Alternatives

Through such laws as the Clean Water Act,[22] the Endangered Species Act,[23] and the Federal Land Policy and Management Act,[24] United States policy favoring western water development has shifted to environmental protection and preservation.

The necessity to obtain a Clean Water Act section 404 dredge and fill permit for a dam or diversion work that taps surface water has placed federal agencies in a regulatory role over additional western water development. This has spurred increased use of tributary and nontributary groundwater, change of agricultural rights to municipal use, water exchange projects, and augmentation plans. State adjudications increasingly involve these water supply and water management techniques.[25]

---

[19] *Aspen Wilderness Workshop Ltd. v. Colorado Water Conservation Bd.*, 901 P.2d 1251, 1260 (1995).
[20] *Report of the Western Water Policy Review Advisory Commission* at xx (1998).
[21] *Neuman*, at 13-14.
[22] 33 U.S.C. §§ 1251-1387 (1994 and Supp. 1995).
[23] 16 U.S.C. §§ 1531-1544 (1994 and Supp. 1995).
[24] 43 U.S.C. §§ 1701-1784 (1994 and Supp. 1995).
[25] See Gregory J. Hobbs, Jr., *Colorado's 1969 Adjudication and Administration Act: Settling In*, 3 U. Denv. Water L. Rev. 1, 15-17 (1999).

Existing reservoirs have become even more critical to meeting western water needs—as new reservoirs face a long, difficult, and uncertain permitting course. Since water rights are perfected under prior appropriation law only by application of water to beneficial use, the obligation to obtain required federal approvals and permits directly affects whether water users are in a position to obtain absolute decrees. Until the structures are built to turn water to beneficial use, a water right cannot be perfected.[26]

. . .

> So long ago my father led me to
> The dark impounded orders of this canyon,
> I have confused these rocks and waters with
> My life, but not unclearly, for I know
> What will be here when I am here no more.[27]

---

[26] See *Dallas Creek v. Huey*, 933 P.2d 27, 37 (Colo. 1997).

[27] Thomas Hornsby Ferril, *Time of Mountains*, in POETRY OF THE AMERICAN WEST 119, 122 (Alison Hawthorne Deming ed., 1996).

Tribute to Marc Reisner
The Colorado Water Workshop, Western State College
Gunnison, Colorado
July 26, 2000

Marc Reisner died this past Friday. Papers across the country eulogized him for writing *Cadillac Desert* (Viking Penguin Inc., 1986), which they described as "a seminal work about the environmental cost of western water projects."

You will recall that Mr. Reisner and I were invited by you to debate the *Cadillac Desert* thesis at the Gunnison Water Workshop on July 22, 1991. I recall him being affable and entertaining. My thesis was that every occupant of the arid regions of the Americas, north and south, had diverted and stored water.

Between 1989 and 1991, Bobbie and I visited Machu Picchu, Tikal, and Chaco Canyon. We had seen the evidence in dikes and ditches, headgates, wing-walls, catchments, and reservoirs constructed out of stone and earth. In the jungle, on the desert, up and down the valleys, round the highlands, these pre-Columbian civilizations were built upon water storage and irrigated agriculture. I pointed out that the lesson of our ancestors, native and immigrant, is that we must be efficient in use, store in times of plenty, conserve for times of want.

Mr. Reisner took no issue with this. His thesis was that building new dams under the Reclamation program for irrigation and hydropower development could no longer be justified. He delighted in pointing out that the new water needs were for cities, recreation, and environmental restoration. Projects that did not serve these purposes were dinosaurs.

In *Cadillac Desert*, Reisner pointed to the proposed Narrows Project on the South Platte River as an example of an irrigation project that the State of Colorado attempted to pursue despite warnings of its State Engineer that the dam probably wouldn't hold water because of suspect geological conditions, was below many of the cities and farmers who might benefit from the reservoir, and did not enjoy the support of many knowledgeable persons in the South Platte Basin. He wrote that the project seemed more about keeping water away from the cities by putting it into unneeded agriculture use, than it was about serving proven needs.

Reisner scorned Colorado's support in the 1960s of a scheme to divert waters of the Columbia River into the Upper Colorado River Basin states in order to make up for the shortfall in the Upper Basin's assumed 7,500,000 acre-foot annual allocation caused by a miscalculation of historical native supply at the time of the 1922 Compact. He complimented the Colorado-Big Thompson Project as an example of one of the best projects built by the Bureau of Reclamation. From its inception in the 1930s, that project was built to serve agricultural, municipal, industrial, and recreational uses, with features to protect water uses in the basin of origin.

Cadillac Desert is still a wonderful read. It is funny, aggravating, insightful, outrageous, full of gossip and political intrigue—not complimentary enough of the West's dependence on the water infrastructure to serve the new as well as the pre-existing uses of water, yet at its core fundamentally truthful: the customs and values of the people of the West and of the United States have evolved from a "dam every river again and again" thesis of the public good to a desire to raft and fish every river again and again and keep the dams off of them.

Blessings on Marc Reisner. May he rest in peace. He held the mirror up to us and again we saw the best and worst of us.

We Coloradans know enough of rivers and the joy and utility of rivers to recognize that our most important treasure is not the minerals of the mountains but the mountain snows and the spring flows. We can celebrate our differences yet unite in our dedication to community, a community that takes account of natural vistas and habitat, a community that serves the needs of humanity without forcing other creatures out of our hearts and off the planet.

Throughout Colorado, we are reclaiming the rivers that run through our towns and cities for walking paths, bikepaths, and herons. We flock out of the cities to go fishing and boating and when we contemplate our mortality we hear the waters sing to us and our ancestors:

Hear again the wonderful poem of Thomas Hornsby Ferril:

FISHING UPSTREAM WITH MY FATHER

> So much spoke to me of your death,
> The urn-shaped flowers of mountain heath,
> Canyon darkling sallow umber
> Shading into autumn slumber,
> Yet some deep feel of joy to be
> Began to pulse and pulse in me

As I began to wade and talked
To us of river floors we'd walked.

Under that sad but warming sky
I was precise as casting a fly
In where I let your ashes fall
From our Big Rock pool in the canyon wall
To the meadow's undercutting shelf
Where the stream curved back to meet itself
And almost did, each ripple burning
Into foretelling of returning.

I let a bright Gray Hackle whip
A peacock loop from the springing tip
Of my rod and watched it coil, uncoil
Over this now and over all
The nows and nows and nows to come
And the line felt good against my thumb,
And we gave that day to the river more
Of us than it had known before.

Thomas Hornsby Ferril and the American West, edited by
Robert C. Baron, Stephen J. Leonard, and Thomas J. Noel
(Fulcrum Publishing, Golden, Colorado and the Center of the
American West, University of Colorado at Boulder, 1996).

Yes, our legal system protects existing water rights and it is we, the community, each generation in its turn, who also bear the responsibility for making the best decisions we can in all we do that affects each other and the environment.

Delight for Waterbugs, A Colorado Education
WaterNews, Northern Colorado Water Conservancy District, reprinted with permission
April 2003

I love the Ferril poem about the Divide-swimming waterbug. She/he skates the golden ripples of a Colorado sunset, where the headwaters begin, regardless of oceans.

WATERBUG

I climb to a lily-pad lake
at the top of a mountain pass,
some of the water flows to the east,
some of it goes west.

Look how that struggling waterbug
is pushing sundown back
on golden golden ripples
of the lake.

Which ocean will he blunder to?
He does not know, nor I,
but I can feel the wonder
of the blue bandanna sky.

Thomas Hornsby Ferril, from *Anvil of Roses*.

On the Divide, there's nothing but summit vistas and the sky. Getting there is a water education—up the river, up the tributaries, up the rivulets, through the tundra forest, through the purple aster fields, through the bogs, up to that lily pad lake, to stand at the top. High and pure, full of hope.

Going downstream is also a water education. Headgates, ditches, and reservoirs take water out of the stream to farms, cities, and businesses. We wouldn't be living in Colorado without them. It's possible to document the history of our state—and its changing values—by studying how we use the state's greatest treasure, its water. Much more utilitarian, this story is still full of hope.

The new Colorado Foundation for Water Education, established by the Colorado legislature in 2002, has just published the *Citizen's Guide to Colorado Water Law*. I hope this trail map through our state's water law mirrors the need and respect we all share for Colorado's water. I had fun writing it. Colorado's water law, like its history, is based on repeated personal experience.

One of the great experiences I had as a water lawyer was taking a horse ride up over the Divide. Our leader that day in the mid-1990s was Homer Rouse, Superintendent of Rocky Mountain National Park. We started on the east side of the Divide and rode up Flat Top Mountain. By the end of the trail at Grand Lake, I wished with all my bottom I had walked.

It was a celebratory day. The City of Loveland had agreed to abandon the Eureka Ditch, a small diversion across a saddle of the Divide cut by east slope farmers in the nineteenth century. Just as Ferril wrote, it's impossible to know which way the drift goes when you're floating on the top of a Pacific water drop being tugged—almost imperceptibly—to the Atlantic.

Being tugged for use (first in time, first in right) is the priority doctrine. That's been Colorado's custom and law for waters of the natural stream since the territory's creation in 1861. Water use rights are valuable property rights in Colorado.

The creation of the Rocky Mountain National Park also created a 1915 federal reserved water right for the Park, but the Eureka Ditch had a prior water right protected by the constitution and laws of the United States and the state of Colorado.

So why did Loveland turn its transmountain diversion back to the beauty and the solitude of the Great Divide? Because that granddaddy of the great transmountain diversions, the Colorado-Big Thompson Project, made Homer Rouse's deal possible.

The deal was this: in creating Rocky Mountain National Park, Congress also provided for a water diversion tunnel from Grand Lake to the Thompson River. In 1955, water started flowing from Grand Lake (below the park's western boundary) through the Adams Tunnel into the Big-Thompson River drainage (below the park's eastern boundary). The 1937 repayment contract between the

Northern Colorado Water Conservancy District and the United States Bureau of Reclamation for construction and operation of the C-BT reserved three cubic feet per second of transmountain water for use by Rocky Mountain National Park. But the park wasn't using its full allotment.

Homer Rouse and other leaders and lawyers of the United States had studied Colorado law. In 1897, the Colorado legislature passed the state's first water exchange statute to legalize the many exchanges between reservoirs and ditches in the Cache la Poudre Basin prior to the twentieth century.

An exchange allows a water trade. The park had a contract right to C-BT water. The park proposed to use its C-BT water to replace the water Loveland would lose by ceasing its in-park diversion. The city, the Bureau of Reclamation, and the Northern Colorado Water Conservancy District all agreed.

Homer Rouse just howled. The Northern District's lawyer (me) collapsed off the horse at Grand Lake and couldn't move for ten minutes. Miserable me had a back-fanny strawberry mark about the size of a lily pad.

Like the new look on an old story, Colorado water law is one of adaptation and change, like the story of the now-gone Eureka Ditch. The oldest continuous prior appropriation water right in operation today is for the 1852 People's Ditch of San Luis. Hispanic settlers moving up from New Mexico onto the Sangre de Cristo land grant built this irrigation diversion from Culebra Creek to their farms.

Boulder residents Ken and Ruth Wright, working with the National Park Service and other paleohydrologists, have documented the existence of four reservoirs the Pueblo people used at Mesa Verde between 950-1180 A.D.

Today, Colorado's water law serves may uses. They include:

- Colorado Water Conservation Board instream flows
- Commercial
- Domestic
- Dust suppression
- Fire protection
- Fish and wildlife culture
- Flood control

- In-channel recreational diversions by local governments for rafting and kayaking
- Industrial
- Irrigation
- Mined land reclamation
- Municipal
- Nature centers
- Power generation
- Recreation
- Release from storage for boating and fishing flows
- Snowmaking
- Stock watering

The most basic principle of Colorado water law is beneficial use without waste. In an average year, Colorado streams produce 16 million acre-feet of water. Up to two-thirds of this water annually goes to downstream states because of interstate water allocation requirements under nine interstate compacts and two United States Supreme Court equitable apportionment decrees.

So, in normal years, Colorado lives on one-third of the water it produces naturally. In the drought year of 2002 (the worst drought since the 1700s), Colorado watersheds produced only 4 million acre-feet of water, one-fourth of the historical 100-year average of record.

To survive 2002, Colorado had to use 6 million acre-feet of storage water it had placed into reservoirs during good water years for times of scarcity. Like the water itself, reservoir storage is a precious Colorado resource. Releases from storage into the stream benefit recreation and the environment on the way to their diversion and use by cities, farms, and businesses downstream.

The old becomes the new. Colorado water law allows for a market in water rights, implemented through change-of-water-right decrees in the water courts. In the early 1970s, agriculture was delivered 92 percent of the water used in the state for beneficial use. Today, agriculture is delivered 86 percent, municipalities 10 percent, and all other uses five percent. This change reflects voluntary sale of agricultural water rights for municipal use. In the meantime, Colorado has grown from a population of 2 million to 4.25 million persons.

In the South Platte, Arkansas, and Rio Grande basins within Colorado, the state has reached its water allocation limits. The Colorado Water Conservation Board, for planning purposes, estimates that Colorado has only 400,000 acre-feet of its Colorado River Compact entitlement left to develop. How and when that water will be used depends on future decisions which affect all Coloradans.

We are united and divided by the greatest of all mountain spines, the one in our own backyard. The water we need to use and preserve will continue to sing and do its work long after we are gone.

Here's my version of Ferril's waterbug poem:

A DIVIDE

The mystery of a divide
is this, you can stand on opposites
and not lose your balance.

Draw a straight line from the sky
through the middle of your forehead,
half of you belongs to the other ocean.

Half your mind and half your heart,
you share downstream equally
and never drift apart.

The *Citizen's Guide to Colorado Water Law* is available through the Colorado Foundation for Water Education, Karla Brown, Executive Director, at 303-377-4433, karlab@cfwe.org

A Sonnet to a Problem River
High Country News (hcn.org)
July 8, 2002

Book review of G. Emlen Hall, *High and Dry: The Texas-New Mexico Struggle for the Pecos River* (University of New Mexico Press, 2002)

The Pecos River begins its 900-mile run high in the Sangre de Cristo Range of the Colorado and Northern New Mexico Rocky Mountains, and descends through New Mexico's lowlands "of Western myth and solid American values," as Emlen Hall writes in *High and Dry: The Texas-New Mexico Struggle for the Pecos River*. Finally, the author writes, the river bends its way across the Texas-New Mexico border into the "blasted heath" of west Texas.

Emlen Hall is a writer, gardener, University of New Mexico law professor, and lawyer who worked for New Mexico on litigation over the meaning of the 1948 Pecos River Compact. Ultimately, this sonnet to the unpredictable Pecos River is also a dirge about the failings of water administrators, engineers, and lawyers to comprehend a river they set out to divide.

The goal of the two-state compact was to wring the greatest use out of the "problem river." The Pecos "problem" was one of extremes: too much water in one year, too little in another, and a history of dam-destroying floods.

But the bigger problem was how to turn the compact's fair words into limits on New Mexico's diversions. That task took more than 15 years, the payment of $14 million in damages by New Mexico to Texas, and the appointment of a river master to gauge New Mexico's depletion. In the end, New Mexico paid nearly $41 million to buy and retire 25,472 acre-feet of water that had been irrigating 8,743.84 acres of land in the Roswell and Carlsbad areas. But even today, it's still unclear how New Mexico can deliver the amount of water to which Texas is entitled.

The ultimate Pecos challenge has been man's refusal to understand nature's basic river law: that surface stream and tributary ground water are connected and finite. When the Pecos breaks out of its high mountain stronghold into its middle reach, the river gains its base flow from tributary ground water seeping into the channel, bolstered by huge but unpredictable inflows from floods. The 1948 Pecos River Compact tried to deal with the unpredictable flows by requiring New Mexico maintain the "1947 condition" at the state line. That meant that New Mexicans, collectively, could not use any more water than they had consumed in 1947. Texas would get what was left over, whether it was a huge bounty or a few acre-feet due to drought. This seemed fair preservation of the status quo; so, with the consent of the two state legislatures and the United States Congress, the interstate apportionment occurred.

From then on, it was up to New Mexico, which meant it was up to the late, legendary state water engineer Steve Reynolds, to make sure New Mexican irrigators controlled themselves. Instead, New Mexico ignored well pumping in the Roswell area and promoted the drilling of new wells in the Carlsbad area. Finally, it refused to enforce the priority system against the holders of junior rights. When the Texas lawyers came calling, New Mexico argued that saltcedars were sucking up the missing water and that the compact guaranteed all of its water uses as of 1947, regardless of depletions they caused to state-line flows.

But the water masters sitting as hearing officers for the U.S. Supreme Court ruled that New Mexico had violated the compact, under-delivering 370,000 acre-feet of water to Texas from 1950 to 1983. The court rejected New Mexico's exceptions. Says Hall in summation: "If we acknowledge that ground water and surface water are interconnected, as they surely are, then the Roswell Basin estimates clearly show that New Mexicans went right on developing the Pecos River before, during, and well after the 1947 cut-off date set by the 1948 compact."

High and Dry is fascinating, enjoyable to read, and well-documented, but most of all, thoroughly surprising. Here's a lawyer who worked on the case confessing that a legal instrument approved by two states and the United States couldn't begin to constrain man's ability to strain a river to its vanishing point.

The sonnet? Read Hall's last chapter about working New Mexico acequia water to his garden for chile and basil. It's musical.

Lessons from History: How Drought Shapes Colorado Water Law and Policy

Headwaters: Colorado Foundation for Water Education, reprinted with permission
Fall 2003

As tree-ring and archaeological evidence shows, extended droughts are frequent visitors to the Rocky Mountain Region. In the short term, Coloradans are confronted with withered crops and dry stream channels. Yet in the long term, drought's lasting legacy is written in the history of Colorado's water laws and institutions.

New Settlers in an Arid Climate

Life in Colorado's arid environment quickly necessitated a new set of laws governing water use. In 1872, the Territorial Supreme Court moved Colorado water law in an entirely new direction, allowing diversions from the river and construction of ditches across public and private land. Water in Colorado became a public resource available for use by all private individuals and public agencies.

Reclamation Era

The years 1893-1905 witnessed multi-year cycles of severe drought in many areas of the West. In southwestern Colorado, 1899-1902 saw four consecutive years with less than 80 percent of average precipitation. Faced with an unreliable water supply, the West's largely agrarian society struggled to remain productive. In 1897 and 1899, Colorado adopted its first statutes allowing exchanges of water and changes of water rights between agricultural, municipal, and other users.

To promote continued settlement and development of the western United States, Congress passed the 1902 Reclamation Act, creating the Bureau of Reclamation. Today, the Bureau of Reclamation is best known for its construction of more than 600 dams, power plants, and canals across the 17 western states.

One of the first authorized Bureau projects in Colorado was the Gunnison (Uncompahgre) Project in western Colorado. The Uncompahgre Project, opened in 1909, now irrigates some 80,000 acres from Montrose to Delta. The Gunnison

Tunnel made the project possible, diverting Gunnison River water through 5.8 miles of solid rock into the Uncompahgre Valley.

Roosevelt's New Deal and Water Supply Projects to Soothe the Parched West

In October 1929, the Wall Street crash launched the nation into the worst depression in American history. Further intensifying the economic crisis, the most widespread and longest lasting drought in Colorado's recorded history dragged on from 1930-1940, famously known as the "Dust Bowl Years." Severe drought peaked in 1934 and 1935, culminating in 1939 with one of the driest years in recorded history, especially along the Front Range.

By March 1933, desperate to bolster the failing economy, Franklin D. Roosevelt called a special session of Congress to develop a series of programs known as the "New Deal." As part of these efforts, Congress gave the newly-created Public Works Administration $3.3 billion for construction of public works projects, including reservoirs.

By 1937, Colorado Senator Alva B. Adams and Congressman Ed Taylor helped secure reclamation funding from the Interior Department to construct, among others, the Colorado-Big Thompson (C-BT) Project. One of the first of its kind to provide both agricultural and municipal water, this project tapped the headwaters of the Colorado River by boring a hole through the Continental Divide. Presently, the C-BT Project delivers more than 200,000 acre-feet of water each year to northeastern Colorado for agricultural, municipal, and industrial uses, with Green Mountain Reservoir providing some 100,000 acre-feet of water annually for western slope use.

Creation of Local and Statewide Water Management Agencies

The Dust Bowl years motivated the Colorado State Legislature to find better ways to manage water locally. The 1937 Conservancy Law created a network of local and statewide water management agencies known as conservancy districts. Created to construct, finance, and manage water projects, today 51 conservancy districts operate in Colorado.

At the same time, the legislature established the Colorado River Water Conservation District, later followed by the Rio Grande and Southwestern water conservation districts, to assist in the development of water policy. Finally, on a statewide level, the Colorado Water Conservation Board was established in 1937 to coordinate the protection and development of the state's waters.

Drought in the 1950s

From 1950 to 1956, another drought hit the West, with some areas reporting conditions more severe than the Dust Bowl. In response, in 1956 the U.S. Congress enacted the Colorado River Storage Project Act to establish a savings account of reservoirs designed to help the Upper Colorado River Basin states (Colorado, New Mexico, Utah, and Wyoming) meet their Colorado River Compact entitlements. The resulting projects—the Aspinall Unit, Navajo, Glen Canyon, Fontenelle, and Flaming Gorge dams—today also provide substantial hydropower and recreational benefits. In 1962, Congress authorized the Frying Pan-Arkansas Project for southeastern Colorado water deliveries.

During the dry years of the fifties, farmers faced with dwindling surface water supplies looked to newly improved groundwater well-pumping technologies to keep their crops from failing. Well use blossomed. Particularly in the lower reaches of the South Platte River Basin, wells provided some farmers with what may have seemed like insurance against further drought. But many of these wells tapped groundwater tributary to surface water. This meant that in some years, pumping of these wells diminished the water available to senior surface water rights.

Not until 1965 did the Colorado legislature pass the Groundwater Management Act, which attempted to regulate groundwater use and well construction by requiring every new well in the state diverting tributary, nontributary, Denver Basin groundwater, or geothermal resources, to have a permit.

The 1950s drought also served as the worst-case scenario for municipal water supply planning in Colorado. However, the ongoing 1999-2003 drought has called into question whether this benchmark is still appropriate.

Planning for the Future

Coinciding with a sustained multi-year drought from 1974 to 1978, state lawmakers started to put efforts into planning for prolonged dry cycles. By 1981, Colorado initiated drought planning efforts at the state and local level incorporating monitoring, impact assessment, response, and mitigation systems. Colorado's "Drought Response Plan" came out of this dry cycle, as well as the formation of the "Water Availability Task Force," which continues to meet quarterly. These plans and organizations became particularly important in the year 2002, as stream flows hit record low levels.

It is still too early to say when the current drought will end, or how it will impact Colorado's current water law and policy. Significant new water legislation in 2003 has already developed some responses. Yet looking at historical trends reminds us that we do not operate in a vacuum, and that our ancestors wrestled with some of the same unknowns and challenges. Understanding what they did well and what they did poorly can serve as a useful tool for informing ourselves for the future.

Drought Duration	Region Impacted	Policy and Legal Changes
1865-1872	Statewide	1872: Colorado Territorial Supreme Court announces basic water law principles of water scarcity and public access to water sources for beneficial use.
1890-1894	Eastern Colorado	1897-99: Colorado General Assembly adopts first statutes allowing exchanges of water and changes of water rights between agricultural, municipal, and other users.
1898-1904	Southwestern Colorado	1902: Reclamation Act establishes the Bureau of Reclamation.
1930-1940	Statewide	1937: General Assembly creates Water Conservancy and Conservation Districts, and the Colorado Water Conservation Board. U.S. Congress authorizes construction of the Colorado-Big Thompson Project.
1950-1956	Statewide	1956: Colorado River Storage Project funds construction of Aspinall Unit, Glen Canyon, Flaming Gorge, Blue Mesa, Navajo, and Fontenelle dams. 1962: Congress authorizes the Frying Pan-Arkansas Project. 1965: Colorado Groundwater Management Act
1974-1978 and 1980-1981	Mountains and Western Slope	1981: Water Availability Task Force forms; Colorado Drought Response Plan developed

A Primer on Colorado Water Law
Trail & Timberline, Colorado Mountain Club, reprinted with permission
May/June 2003

Water scarcity in Colorado is a fact of life. The current drought in Colorado is causing citizens to pay attention, as never before, to one of the most technical areas of law in the state: the statutes and customs governing the distribution of water.

In 2002, Colorado rivers produced only four million acre-feet of water, compared to the historic annual average of 16 million acre-feet. As a result, last year Colorado had to use six million acre-feet of water it had placed into reservoirs in other years for use in the dry times.

Water is a public resource. Any area of the United States receiving less than 40 inches of precipitation annually is considered an "arid region." Since Colorado's annual average precipitation ranges from less than 10 inches of moisture on the plains to a little over 30 inches in the mountains, the state certainly qualifies for this category.

Early in the history of the West, Congress realized that water, a public resource, would have to be managed differently there than in the eastern United States, an area where water was abundant. Colorado became a territory in 1861. In the Mining Act of 1866, Congress provided that the customs and laws of the states and territories would govern water use within their boundaries.

Colorado chose the "prior appropriation" system as its basic water law for the allocation and administration of surface water and tributary groundwater (water that is connected to the surface stream). The earlier in time a person began appropriating and using water, the more senior the claim to that water is.

The Colorado Constitution

On admission to the Union in 1876, the people of Colorado adopted a constitution declaring that the water of every natural stream in the state is "the property of the public, and the same is dedicated to the use of the people of the state, subject to appropriation." The constitution further guaranteed the right to appropriate unappropriated waters for "beneficial uses." All persons and corporations were empowered, upon payment of just compensation, to obtain a right-of-way across public and private lands of others for the construction of ditches, canals, and flumes for carriage of water to its place of use.

Colorado has an active water market in the purchase and change of water rights, typically from agricultural to municipal use. In 1971, agriculture was delivered approximately 92 percent of the water used in Colorado. In 2002, agriculture was delivered 86 percent, municipalities 10 percent, and all other uses five percent.

Water Courts

Under Colorado's constitution and laws, water use rights are property rights. They are created by using unappropriated available water for a beneficial purpose; the earlier the date of appropriation, the more valuable the water right. Water rights are enforced in priority during times of short supply. Junior rights are curtailed until senior rights are satisfied.

Through an 1879 law, the courts are responsible for determining the priority dates for water rights. Court decrees identify the location, amount, and type of water use. The decrees include any conditions necessary to protect senior rights against injury. Because water is a public resource, even citizens who do not own water rights are allowed to participate in water court cases. Engineering testimony in water cases can be complex and contradictory, and proponents and opponents of a particular water rights claim can be highly adversarial.

Under a 1969 law, seven water divisions of the district court exist with special jurisdiction over matters concerning major watersheds. The water courts for the divisions are headquartered in Greeley (South Platte), Pueblo (Arkansas), Alamosa (Rio Grande), Montrose (Gunnison), Glenwood Springs (Colorado), Steamboat Springs (Yampa, White, North Platte), and Durango (San Juan, Dolores). The State Engineer, Division Engineer, and local Water Commissioners administer Colorado's water in accordance with water court decrees.

Changes of water rights are decreed by the water courts. Colorado water courts also decree out-of-priority diversions that allow new uses to be made in overappropriated stream basins if replacement water is provided to the water rights that would otherwise be injured.

Each water court publishes a monthly resume of applications. This is how the citizens of Colorado are informed of pending cases they might wish to monitor or participate in. Appeal from a water court judgment is directly to the Colorado Supreme Court.

Beneficial Uses

All water in Colorado is a public resource. Individuals, businesses, and public agencies may obtain a right to use water for "beneficial purposes." These uses originally included agricultural, domestic, municipal, commercial, and flood control. As the economy and values of Coloradans changed, statutes and court decisions recognized that beneficial use also includes fish and wildlife propagation, nature centers, mined land reclamation, and recreational in-channel diversions by local governments for boating and kayaking.

A unique 1973 law passed by the General Assembly allows the Colorado Water Conservation Board (CWCB) to appropriate minimum stream flows and lake levels for the preservation of the natural environment to a reasonable degree. "Instream flow water rights" now exist on 8,500 miles of Colorado streams. Under a 2002 law, the CWCB may also obtain senior water rights to add to the instream flows. The state and division water engineers and local water commissioners enforce the court decrees for the instream flow rights of the Water Conservation Board.

Progressive Conservation

In Colorado's early days, the state and federal public agenda was wholly pro-development. Water was a necessity of human life. It was taken from the streams and used without regard to environmental impact.

There were consequences. Mining districts came and went, leaving forests stripped for mills, housing, and firewood. Silt poured off with the snow melt, plugging ditches and reservoirs. Mining waste and human waste leached into streams, impairing other water uses.

By the close of the nineteenth century, the nation and Colorado began to shift from unmitigated use of natural resources to sustainable management of them. President Teddy Roosevelt and his forester, Gifford Pinchot, pushed to reserve forested lands from being homesteaded and conveyed to private ownership. Making water available to farms, cities, and businesses was a primary reason for the proposed forest reserves.

Fourteen million acres of forest reserves were created in Colorado. Today, 36 percent of Colorado remains in federal ownership, a heritage of the progressive conservation movement.

Reservoirs

Storage of water for later use was also a fundamental precept of progressive conservation. In an 1879 report to Congress, pioneering Colorado River runner John Wesley Powell stressed the necessity of public water storage. He also feared that powerful corporate monopolies would control the sale and use of water unless government intervened on behalf of the farmers.

In Colorado, farmers cooperatively established mutual irrigation companies and irrigation districts. The Colorado General Assembly followed with the creation of water conservancy districts and water conservation districts with the power to collect and spend public tax money to develop water for the use of Colorado citizens and business.

Reclamation reservoirs, along with many private and public non-federally financed reservoirs, exist throughout the state. Many cities own their own reservoirs. There are approximately 2,000 reservoirs in Colorado; they have the capacity to store 6.5 million acre-feet of water.

Interstate Water Compacts

Colorado is the mother of many rivers. In an average year, Colorado rivers produce 16 million acre-feet of water. But up to two-thirds of this water is legally committed by interstate law to downstream states. Colorado is a party to nine interstate compacts and two equitable apportionment decrees of the United States Supreme Court that allocate water to other states.

The nine interstate compacts are the Colorado River Compact, La Plata River Compact, South Platte River Compact, Arkansas River Compact, Rio Grande River Compact, Republican River Compact, Upper Colorado River Compact, Amended Costilla Creek Compact, and Animas-La Plata Project Compact. The equitable apportionment decrees are *Wyoming v. Colorado* and *Colorado v. New Mexico*.

The loss to Wyoming in the 1922 equitable apportionment case convinced Coloradans, notably its chief compact architect, Delph Carpenter, that the law of prior appropriation could not be applied to interstate rivers. Of greatest concern were California's thirst, size, and economic and political strength.

Congress and the states intended the 1922 Colorado River Compact to be a permanent and perpetual division of water between the upper and the lower basin on a beneficial consumptive use basis. The Lower Basin states (Arizona, California, and Nevada) could proceed with their development, while the Upper Basin states (Colorado, New Mexico, Utah, and Wyoming) could utilize their full share at any distant time, when ready. In the meantime, water not used in the Upper Basin is available to the Lower Basin under the law.

Colorado is nearing full compact utilization. This has occurred already in regard to the Arkansas and Rio Grande compacts. The Colorado Water Conservation Board estimates that only 400,000 acre-feet of water remain to Colorado for additional use under its Colorado River Compact entitlement.

Federal Reserved Water Rights

In 1908, the United States Supreme Court determined that the states could not deprive Native Americans of the water reserved to them expressly by Congress—or by implication—when the reservations were established. Reserved water rights also exist to serve the primary purposes of other federal reservations, such as national parks, monuments, and natural forests. For example, the Rocky Mountain National Park and the Cache la Poudre Wild and Scenic River have reserved water rights.

The Environment

The Great Depression, World War II, and post-war economic development encouraged the building of large mainstream dams throughout the West for water supply, power production, flood control, and recreation.

At the same time, magnificent canyons and free-flowing rivers were lost. American wildlands shrank dramatically. Citizens of the West and of the rest of the nation awoke to the need for preservation. A reservoir that would have flooded Echo Park in the Colorado-Utah Dinosaur Park country was halted after a fierce national debate spearheaded by the Sierra Club.

Negotiation between water and environmental interests and federal agencies led to designation of the Poudre as a Wild and Scenic River in 1986, passage of the 1993 Colorado Wilderness Act, and the North St. Vrain Protection Act in 1996. Colorado is cooperating with Utah, Wyoming, New Mexico, Nebraska, and the United States to conserve the endangered fishes of the Colorado River and the endangered birds of the Platte River.

Cooperation was notably absent when Denver attempted to obtain a dredge and fill permit under the Clean Water Act to construct the Two Forks dam. Many Coloradans, inside and outside of Denver, fought its construction. Historical conflicts between the east slope and the west slope re-emerged. While it did attempt to reach agreements with those opposing Two Forks, the Water Board found few allies for a project desired mainly by suburban cities and districts. In 1989, the Environmental Protection Agency vetoed the dam under a provision requiring a permit to deposit fill material in the streams.

Despite the Two Forks veto, growth has occurred exponentially in the Denver metropolitan area. Denver suburbs have turned to the use of deep exhaustible Denver Basin bedrock water and the purchase of farm water.

The Denver Basin bedrock water is not subject to Colorado prior appropriation law because it does not belong to a natural stream subject to the state constitution's water provisions. By act of the Colorado legislature, this deep underground water can be pumped by overlying landowners at the rate of one percent per year, assuming a 100-year life of this nonrenewable groundwater. But, in parts of the Denver Basin, wells are already going dry. The farmers and cities of the eastern plains largely depend upon the Ogallala aquifer, which is regulated by the Colorado Ground Water Commission and local management districts.

Colorado's Water Future

As the history of Colorado demonstrates, beneficial use and preservation are the two chambers of our western hearts, the two lobes of our brains. Our state and federal public land, land use, water, and environmental laws mirror these fundamental principles. Land use decisions will be instrumental in determining the look and feel of Colorado.

Local citizens will react to proposed diversions that threaten their economic livelihood and love for their home place. Conservation of animals, birds, and plants must be addressed. It is not possible to build a new water project without extensive public consultation and study of alternatives, including not building the project.

As Colorado approaches the day when it will be forced to live within its interstate apportioned water share, management will become even more necessary. Efficient means of diversion and storage, beneficial use without waste, and recognition of all purposes that Coloradans value have always been fundamental precepts of Colorado water law.

Water supply planners will be required to examine all options: among them, conservation, exchange, groundwater recharge, joint use projects, conjunctive use of groundwater and surface water, out-of-priority diversions through decreed augmentation plans, and the sale and purchase of water rights for use within the state.

Use of local water resources for local purposes will be the primary focus. Yet, Coloradans know that the state must share its water and financial resources as a whole. Eighty percent of the water supplies arise on the western slope. Over 80 percent of the population currently resides on the eastern slope. Rural areas throughout the state are experiencing significant population increase and will require municipal and recreational water supplies.

The farmland of Colorado is economically productive and beautiful to behold. Whether farms should be dried up to serve cities is a critical question for Colorado. Water rights are valuable property rights. The voluntary creation of farmland trusts and open space covenants, together with payment for the water rights through private and public funds, is an alternative for keeping water on the ground it has irrigated historically.

As Colorado struggles to live within its interstate apportioned share, water management will become even more necessary. Conservation will be indispensable. Efficient means of diversion and storage, beneficial use without waste, and recognition of all purposes that Coloradans value have always been fundamental precepts of Colorado water law. Now they are vital. The era of their fuller implementation is upon us.

Celebration of Colorado's Instream Flow Law
Trout Unlimited & Colorado Water Conservation Board
September 5, 2003

Thirty years ago, Colorado adopted its instream flow law. Since the founding of Colorado territory in 1861, Colorado's water law had favored the diversion of water out of the stream for irrigation, municipal, and industrial uses.

In 1965, the Colorado Supreme Court ruled that "maintenance of the 'flow' of the stream is a riparian right and is completely inconsistent with the doctrine of prior appropriation."

As the river flows, not so!

In 1979, based on the new statute, the court said the Colorado Water Conservation Board could make instream flow appropriations for fish flows. The legislative objective was "to preserve reasonable portions of the natural environment in Colorado."

. . .

When Powell, Hayden, Wheeler, and King embarked on the great western surveys in the nineteenth century, they brought along sketchers, photographers, and painters—Holmes, Jackson, and Moran, among them. They mapped the waters and the stunning clarity that lack of water imparts to the landscape. They fired the imagination of will-be-westerners. We are still settling in.

I came to Colorado for good in 1973. My professional career in water and environmental law commenced at the U.S. Environmental Protection Agency's new regional office. At the Colorado Attorney General's Office and in private practice, I concentrated on air, water, water quality, land use, and transportation law.

For the same 30 years that Colorado's instream flow law has existed, I have loved the way that water works and sings in the land of the Great Divide. In this, like all Coloradans, I am led by Pueblo people of Mesa Verde and the Hispanic settlers of the San Luis Valley. In the *Citizen's Guide to Colorado Water Law*, published in 2003 by the Colorado Foundation for Water Education, I have helped to tell how they—before the Anglo settlers—pioneered smart water conservation.

Working with water makes you want to sing. In the rhythm of the rivers, the West finds its most treasured experience.

COLORADO
MOTHER OF RIVERS

When I was young the waters sang
of being here before I am,
of falling sweet and soft and slow
to berry bog and high meadow.
And held me in her lap and cooed
the willow roots, the gaining pools,
and called me through bright dappled grass
and called me O, My Shining One;

And shaped a bed to lay me on
and played the flute so high and clear.
And shape the stones to carry me,
when I am young and full of fight
for roaring here and roaring there,
for pouring torrents in the air.
When I am young as mountain snow
in crag and cleft and cracked window;

I call the green-backed cutthroat trout,
I call the nymph and hellgrammite,
I call the hatch to catch a wind,
I call upon the mountain track;
I call the scarlet to the jaw
as morning calls her own hatchlings,
call Yampa, White, the Rio Grande,
San Juan, the Platte, the Arkansas.

Ev/Ann Long View
February 2004

In Greeley, I spoke to members of the Ditch and Reservoir Alliance at the end of their two-day conference. My topic: how water invented Colorado and the West.

I followed a member of the State Water Engineer's Office who, apologizing but doing his duty, explained why owners of water rights were now receiving a bill for water administration.

Since 1879—when the Colorado legislature only three years into statehood passed its first water rights administration statute—the General Assembly has funded state water officials from general tax revenues. But the tempestuous coincidence of the year 2002 500-year drought and the crash of the dot-com industry have squeezed the life out of many people-serving programs, public and private.

As with all rights, civil rights especially, the value of a water right resides in its enforcement by public officials, scrutinized by citizen vigilance, in times of scarcity and necessity.

The legislature has turned to water user fees to fund the priority administration of water rights, with a sunset clause in three years to review whether to renew this legislation. Other priorities of the community will never sunset, whether or not they are funded by taxes or fees.

The Graces will see to that.

The Graces are those in our lives who have watched over us. By their guidance, their gentle correction, their constant vigor, their teachings—mostly by the way they lived and so inspired us—they have set us free by setting us forth to go our way.

Many have passed, and so they pass with us as long as we shall breathe.

My talk done, Catherine, the daughter of Ev and Ann Long, came up to me to speak of her parents and how they had encouraged me in the days of my counselship for the Northern Colorado Water Conservancy District. Longs Gardens of Boulder, their business and their passion, they blessed the community of Colorado with gorgeous iris blooms and shared—with so many more than me—the love of all that water touches.

The Graces invent Colorado and the West.

I thanked Catherine, and said I'd written a poem, "Come On Back All You Graces," in tribute to her parents and others whose personal touch have carried the blessing of the Graces (others among them of the Northern, Beth and Gordon Dyekman, Vi and John Moore, Helen and Milt Nelson, Sam and Myrtle Telep, John and Bonnie Caneva, and Judy and Bill Farr). Could I have her e-mail to send the poem to her? She responded:

> 2/28/2004
> Greg,
>
> Thanks so much for sharing your beautiful poem. Mom and Dad would surely be honored to think they had any part in its inspiration!
>
> May the "Graces" come back to us all...
>
> Catherine

I wrote her back:

> 2/29/2004
> Catherine,
>
> The poem I wrote for your father nearly twenty years ago, it has no finish, apparently. Your coming up to me Friday reminded me of your mother just as powerfully, so this poem now shares the Ann Long View to the Ev Long view. Though gone, your parents continue to bless us. Thank you.
>
> Greg

THE EV/ANN LONG VIEW

    A man of grace
    and view at home equally
    on the Divide,
    in the garden or Board room,
    to him words and waters flow
    to Iris, people, vistas.

    I've seen him scan
    a page for every turn
    of phrase its place
    and accuracy,
    from the top of mountains, too, his aim—
    to the very source.

I pronounce this
"The Ev Long View."

And everywhere he could see
Ann was seeing, too,
for the two were root and source,
soil and water,
differing points of view
combining to a greater power,

Far within, everything they
would comprehend
and set free
to grow outside or fall
from a lofty precipice
or move along the furrow rows.

I announce this
"The Ann Long View."

COME ON BACK ALL YOU GRACES

Come on back all you graces,
come on back to me now,
come on back all you graces,
come on back to me now.

Courage, patience, humor,
plain speaking tolerance,
grit, passion, wit to believe
my own special insignificance.

Come on back all you graces,
come on back to me now,
come on back all you graces,
come on back to me now.

Those I've looked up to,
those who said go to it,
those who let go greatly when
they just knew it was time to.

Come on back all you graces,
come on back to me now,
come on back all you graces,
come on back to me now.

Yes, you can. Yes, you will.
And I'm so glad I could help.
Yes I believe you've got to
see, in your own way, through.

Come on back all you graces,
come on back to me now,
come on back all you graces,
come on back to me now.

Working with Water

Foreword to *Acquiring, Using, and Protecting Water in Colorado*, by Trout, Witwer & Freeman, P.C., published by Bradford Publishing Company
July 2004

Working with water is fun, and can often be a lot of hard work.

Consider the farmer who cleans out the irrigation ditch, straightens the furrow rows, sets the siphon tubes, and carefully changes them from row to row until the water's duty to the corn or garlic is done.

Consider the dedicated people of a city's public works department. They worry about storing, treating, and delivering the water for homes and businesses when it's needed, and returning the unused water to the stream clean enough for fish, swimmers, boaters, towns, and farmer's fields.

Consider the businesses that make consumer drinks or pour the water through the turning turbines for electricity or grow the greenhouse plants that grace the homes of citizens with flowers.

Consider the homeowners building in a rural subdivision. Each bought an open tract with plenty of vista, or forest canopy, to escape the city's forbidding din on weekends or to relocate their plugged-in business among the grace and glory of Colorado's splendid solitude.

Consider the out-of-state skier who has booked for her family a long-anticipated Thanksgiving vacation on the ski slopes, or the rafter in the summer sun riding the flowing current through a slotted red-walled canyon, or the urban kayaker scooting off a wave top crashing down an in-channel whitewater course.

Consider a greenway walk along the fisher heron's refuge path, where once a dumping ground for industrial refuse stunk with muck.

Consider the 18 downstream states that depend on water leached from melting snows high along both sides of the Great Divide.

Consider the native greenback cutthroat trout.

Now consider the ravages of a sustained drought.

That's what *Acquiring, Using, and Protecting Water in Colorado* is all about: conservation, distribution, and the beneficial use of scarce water in community.

Colorado has been about this task since the Puebloans of Mesa Verde built and operated their reservoirs between 750 and 1180 A.D.; since the establishment of Bent's Fort in American Territory on the north bank of the Arkansas River in the 1830s; since the migration of Northern New Mexico Hispanos onto a former Mexican land grant where the oldest continuous water right in Colorado, the San Luis People's Ditch of 1852, continues to perpetuate the Spanish acequia tradition; since the cry "Eureka!" sounded at the confluence of the Platte and Cherry Creek and Pikes Peak Region in the seminal Colorado year of 1858; since the first ditch to grow vegetables for the Front Range miners was cut into the banks of Clear Creek; since the First Territorial Legislature passed its first water law in 1861; and so along the current of Colorado's water use ever since into the future.

Laws express the customs and values of the people. The water law reflects how Colorado citizens choose to survive, and—hopefully—thrive in a vast and beautiful land that's dry and full of amazing creatures, mountains, mesas, plains, streams, and intermittent arroyos.

Water is a public resource. That's the fundamental precept of Colorado water law. Wherever it comes from—surface or groundwater, no matter what elevation, no matter what depth one must go to find it—water serves the people and the environment.

Water in our state operates under a set of firm and changing principles, adopted with the intent of being principled and the expectation of being applied justly. Accordingly, all three branches of Colorado government are involved in water and always have been. The people of Colorado etched the basic principles into the marble of the Colorado Constitution.

The Colorado General Assembly codifies the water law in a constant process to reflect the changing economy and desires of Coloradans, consistent with the constitution.

The water courts, to whom the legislature assigned this job, determine the priorities of each water right that shares the supply of the surface stream, or the tributary groundwater aquifers that feed the surface streams.

The State Engineer, the seven Water Division Engineers, and the local Water Commissioners administer the relative priorities of the water rights, according to the Water Court decrees, senior to junior to the limit of the available water.

The Ground Water Commission and the State Engineer control the issuance of well permits for the use of deep groundwater that heavy pumping might exhaust quickly because it's not recharged naturally.

And everywhere one goes in the throes of the early twenty-first century drought, Coloradans want to learn about and care for the water they love in their neighboring watershed backyard.

That's why this handbook about our water law is so important now. It's written for people who want to understand, in a common-sense fashion, what the relative few—the water engineers, attorneys, and managers—almost solely commanded until recently, not because they were greedy and tried to keep everyone else ignorant, but because we trusted them to get the job done and stayed out of their way.

Now getting the job done, because of many changes in state and federal law, requires the participation of the many among us whose full-time work does not involve the complexities of law, policy, natural science, engineering, and administration, which undergird the water law.

This book reveals straightforwardly 143 years of Colorado water law in terms of today's understanding and practices. You will visit a working piece of Colorado's history and culture in each page.

You will learn just how strapped Colorado is in meeting its water needs, and how relatively easy or terribly complex getting water for a new or changed use you might want to make can be.

You will see how the federal water quality, endangered species, and forest protection laws shape each major water development decision in our state. You will come to know how we are living on the water lines and the reservoirs that generations of the past built and handed over to us, and that conservation is a necessity.

You will gain insight into how Colorado's many water organizations function, and how existing water rights can be bought, sold, and leased. For over 100 years, Colorado water law has established a market for transferring water rights to new and different uses from their prior uses and points of diversion. Because beneficial use is the basis, measure, and limit of prior appropriation water rights, historic use of water rights must be defined and quantified before they can be changed to different uses, or the water taken out of the streams or aquifers at different points of diversion. The protection of other water rights is an essential feature of water court change-of-water-rights proceedings. Conditions designed to prevent an enlargement of the historic consumptive use made of the water right is typically a feature of any contemporary change decree. Often crucial to approval of the change is maintenance of historic return flow patterns upon which other water rights depend in whole or part for their supply.

You will grasp how an augmentation plan works to allow out-of-priority diversions and uses that could not otherwise occur under priority administration. This is possible through State Engineer-approved, temporary substitute water supply plans and water court-approved augmentation plans. These plans replace water to the stream in sufficient quantity and quality to satisfy the priorities of other water rights.

You will appreciate the difficult and essential job of the state and division engineers and the local water commissioners. They enforce the final decrees of the water courts, in accordance with Colorado's constitution, statutes, and case law precedent. Without enforcement, water rights lose the security and reliability to serve the needs of all who depend on them. Whether for a farm, city, business, recreation, or the environment, the value of a prior appropriation water right resides in the enforcement of its decreed priority in time of scarcity. The water officials also have the crucial job of delivering water out of state to comply with the nine interstate compacts and three equitable apportionment decrees that affect Colorado's right to use water.

You will discover, how in its 2003 session, the General Assembly adopted legislation for stored water banks in all seven water divisions, prohibited new residential covenants that restrict use of drought-tolerant landscape, authorized conservation easements for water rights, required financial mitigation to a county when transferring agricultural water permanently out of the county, and provided for interruptible water leasing from farms to cities and for instream flows during drought emergencies.

You will realize that many important questions await answers. Because water law tracks the customs and values of the people, new statutes and court decisions will continue to speak about how the basic principles of Colorado water law continue to adapt to changing times and changing uses.

At its core, this book explains how Colorado has responded to one of its most important public priorities: how to deliver water to humans for use while also protecting the environment. So, this book is necessarily about water scarcity and smart practices. Ultimately, of course, this practical handbook is a guide to those who need or want to understand the water law better. As the authors point out, this or any other guide does not substitute for good legal and engineering advice about a particular problem or case.

The authors conscientiously explore their understanding of Colorado water law. In doing so, they underscore how water is Colorado's most basic and important resource. In the drought year 2002, for example, Colorado citizens and the riparian environment lived principally on six million acre-feet of water released from stored reservoir water collected in the good years. Our mountain snow and infrequent rains normally produce an average of 16 million acre-feet of water per year. Up to two-thirds of that goes out to downstream states under the interstate water law. In 2002, Colorado produced only four million acre-feet, and much of that went to the other needy states.

Let's talk reality. Colorado is close to developing all the water to which it is entitled under interstate law. We are now up against our water limits, and conservation in all its forms will be required, including more efficient use and additional above-ground and underground storage projects.

Our inclusion of all points of view in contemporary water decision making is a great source of strength and a cause for great concern. Surely, in each and every generation, we have learned from cyclical drought that in scarcity is the opportunity for community. We must store wisely for the time and place of want.

We must realize much more carefully the basic maxim of Colorado water law, that the water is a public resource to be used beneficially, without waste. Let the hallmark of our generation be civilized action, not neglect.

Where We Are, Where We've Been
Colorado Water Newsletter of the Water Center of Colorado State University,
Ground Water Forum Issue, reprinted with permission
April 2004

A Few Words about Context

The conveners of this written forum on ground water asked me to review where we are and where we've been. I'm glad they didn't ask me where we're going. I honestly couldn't speak about that, as in my judicial capacity I await the next case and can do no other.

The strength of the judicial method—and of our merit selection system for judges—is that the water judges of this state aren't persuaded to engage in politics. The law, judicial ethics, and common sense prohibit us from making decisions based on political considerations. This is a very good thing, as we'd be very bad at that. There's plenty of opportunity for the General Assembly and the Governor to account for public policy and the synergy of politics; they're structured for that purpose.

The Canons of Judicial Ethics, nevertheless, allow judges to teach and write. And, since the invitation I accept is to review the state of the law bearing on this forum's examination—briefly, as best I might—I am privileged to join this educational context.

Written case opinions deal analytically, in much more detail, about the subject, so I recommend you read the Colorado Supreme Court's opinions in *Park County Sportsmen's Ranch, Empire Lodge*, and *Simpson v. Bijou*.

What's Uncommon about Colorado's Common Law

As Prescott Webb points out in his wonderful book of the western migration, *The Great Plains*, the people coming west in the mid-nineteenth century were radicals when it came to public land and water law. The aridity of this mountain/plains environment drove their audacity to invent a set of legal principles that differed markedly from the English and eastern American common law. Their insistence gained Congressional acceptance of these new principles, finding expression as the "Colorado Doctrine."

Nonetheless, these principles flowed directly from the western experience shared by Native Americans, Hispanos, Anglos, and African-Americans alike, in their order of western American progression: that the waters of the natural stream are a public resource to be conserved and carefully used.

The 2002 *Park County Sportsmen's Ranch* opinion contains a detailed discussion about the derivation of the "Colorado Doctrine" from the public lands experience (and also of tributary ground water hydrology; see the Appendix). So, I do no more than to re-state its basic principles, as seen through Colorado's historical lens:

> (1) Water is a public resource, dedicated to the beneficial use of public agencies and private persons wherever they might make beneficial use of the water under use rights established as prescribed by law;
>
> (2) The right of water use includes the right to cross the lands of others to place water into, occupy and convey water through, and withdraw water from the natural water-bearing formations within the state in the exercise of a water use right; and
>
> (3) The natural water-bearing formations may be used for the transport and retention of appropriated water.
>
> This new common law established a property-rights-based allocation and administration system that promotes multiple use of a finite resource for beneficial purposes.

The term "natural stream" contained in the prior appropriation provisions of Colorado's 1876 Constitution include tributary ground water, the pumping of which can affect the supply of the surface stream within 100 years. The 1951 *Safranek* decision of the Colorado Supreme Court announced this principle quite clearly.

Where We've Been

The *Safranek* opinion coincided with the unregulated drilling of numerous unregulated tributary ground water wells, most notably in the South Platte and Arkansas River Basins. The advent of the high efficiency pump, rural electric cooperatives serving farmers, and the "Eureka"-like discovery of a huge ground water treasure apparently available for the taking—without interference—left a dramatic marker on Colorado's future.

Plenty of agricultural production came from this, and many families came to depend on a water supply that, in many ways, was for a time seemingly firmer than far-senior surface diversions.

Nevertheless, the bedrock constitutional, statutory, and case law principles of prior appropriation remained the current by which Colorado flows to the future.

Equally as important, the natural science of hydrology and the tools of applied engineering—nature being the constant underpinning of these arts, for water is the stuff of dream, reality, and community consanguinity—continued to shape our understanding of the connection between the surface stream and the tributary aquifers.

The Out-of-Priority Pump Comes Home, Alas

A state committed to prior appropriation, vested water use rights, security, reliability, and flexibility in the use of its scarce water resource—as Colorado is—could not escape the inevitable intersection of the natural sciences and the legal artifice we know as the ground water law. Quite plainly, the law could not defy nature's way.

Maintenance of the stream conditions, as they existed on the date of the appropriation of unappropriated water, is a necessary corollary of any water use right, to be respected in order of priority.

Other states, like Arizona, California, and Texas, ignore the surface/ground water interconnection and the injury that junior well pumping can cause to senior surface or ground water rights. They allow any landowner to punch a well and possess the ground water without regard to the effect on a neighbor's senior water use.

But, from the outset, Colorado law—with Congressional approval—severed the water from the land, keeping the water always as a public resource, subject to the creation of use rights in water wherever water might appear, in mountain stream or within the deepest aquifer.

Empire Lodge and *Simpson v. Bijou* set forth the ground water law's progression quite clearly. The General Assembly introduced the augmentation plan provision of the 1969 act to assist the integration of surface and tributary water into the adjudication and administration of water rights. Again, this was a radical western innovation pioneered by Coloradans.

The operative principle is that one is free of priority administration, even though junior, if he or she replaces—by means of an approved augmentation plan—the depletions that would otherwise occur to the seniors' water supply due to the out-of-priority diversions.

The General Assembly adopted these conjunctive use principles in the 1969 Act and refined them through subsequent amendments, as stated in *Park County Sportsmen's Ranch*:

> (1) A natural stream consists of all underflow and tributary waters, § 37-92-102(1), 10 C.R.S. (2001);

(2) All waters of the natural stream are subject to appropriation, adjudication, and administration in the order of their decreed priority, § 37-92-102(1)(a) & (b);

(3) The policy of the state is to integrate the appropriation, use, and administration of underground water tributary to a stream with the use of surface water in such a way as to maximize the beneficial use of all of the waters of the state, § 37-92-102(2); and

(4) The conjunctive use of ground and surface water shall be recognized to the fullest extent possible, subject to the preservation of other existing vested rights in accordance with the law. § 37-92-102(2)(b).

While the State Engineer had temporary authority for the approval of augmentation plans in the early 1970s, the General Assembly repealed that authority after a brief time. The State Engineer then used the exchange statute, which contained authority for administrative approval of substitute supply plans, to approve out-of-priority depletions by surface and well users.

This practice amounted to the annual approval of what the Colorado Supreme Court in *Empire Lodge* and *Simpson v. Bijou* recognized to be augmentation plans, which the General Assembly by statutory amendment in the mid-1970s had deprived the State Engineer of authority over—in favor of the water court application, notice, water-user participation, and decree process.

One need not see any malevolence in the actions of three State Engineers in this regard. Another principle of water law expressed in the 1969 Act is maximum utilization. Tracking, accounting, and quantifying the impact of ground water depletions on senior water rights are sophisticated, resource-intensive efforts, replete with less than totally accurate predictions and results. But, as it turns out, the job is requisite.

When the water years are good, everybody gains. It took the early twenty-first century drought to bring the truth of the prior appropriation doctrine back out: it's still "first in time, first in right."

Where We Are

Where we are is where we began. When faced with the opportunity again to reiterate its long-standing commitment to prior appropriation and the integrated administration of tributary groundwater and surface water, the General Assembly by 2002 and 2003 legislation granted the State Engineer annual substitute supply authority. Getting approval of one of these annual substitute supply plans is contingent on replacing injurious depletions and the filing of long-term augmentation plan applications with the water court.

The General Assembly in the 2003 legislation (S.B. 2003-73) approved the State Engineer's Arkansas River well rules, resulting from the *Kansas v. Colorado* U.S. Supreme Court Compact litigation, and it gave the South Platte out-of-priority well operators three years in which to file their augmentation plan applications.

What is needed appears to include a fair and reliable method for calculating depletions and their effect on senior water rights, and the use of all available legal means to supply a firm supply of replacement water to those in need. But, at this juncture, I must yield to others.

And I thank you for the invitation to participate.

Additional Water Writings
1996-2004

Justice Hobbs also authored the following Colorado Supreme Court opinions and articles on water law.

Simpson v. Highland Irrigation Co., 917 P.2d 1242 (Colo. 1996).

Colorado Ground Water Comm'n v. Eagle Peak Farms, 919 P.2d 212 (Colo. 1996).

Bennett Bear Creek Farm Water and Sanitation Dist. v. City and County of Denver, 928 P.2d 1254 (Colo. 1996).

Dallas Creek Water Co. v. Huey, 933 P.2d 27 (Colo. 1997).

Williams v. Midway Ranches Property Owners Ass'n, Inc., 938 P.2d 515 (Colo. 1997).

Chatfield East Well Company, Ltd. v. Chatfield East Property Owners Ass'n, 956 P.2d 1260 (Colo. 1998).

Santa Fe Trail Ranches Property Owners Ass'n v. Simpson, 990 P.2d 46 (Colo. 1999).

Upper Black Squirrel Ground Water Management Dist. v. Goss, 993 P.2d 1177 (Colo. 2000).

Farmers Reservoir v. Consolidated Mutual Water Co., 33 P.3d 799 (Colo. 2001).

Empire Lodge Homeowners' Ass'n v. Moyer, 39 P.3d 1139 (Colo. 2001).

Bd. of County Commissioners v. Park County Sportsmen's Ranch, 45 P.3d 693 (Colo. 2002).

Vought v. Stucker Mesa Domestic Pipeline Co., 76 P.3d 906 (Colo. 2003).

Colorado Water Law: An Historical Overview, 1 U. DENV. WATER L. REV. 1 (1997).

Colorado's 1969 Adjudication and Administration Act: Settling In, 3 U. DENV. WATER L. REV. 1 (1999).

Priority: The Most Misunderstood Stick in the Bundle, 32 ENVTL. L. 37 (2002).

Citizen's Guide to Colorado Water Law, COLORADO FOUNDATION FOR WATER EDUCATION (second edition 2004).

Constitutional Perspectives

I AM THE FIRST AMENDMENT

I am freedom of religion, freedom of speech, freedom of press, freedom to assemble, freedom to petition the government for redress of grievances.

I am Moses, Jesus, Gandhi, Martin Luther. I am Joan of Arc, the Salem witches, the Hollywood writers summoned to appear before Senator McCarthy.

I am the man in Tiananmen Square staring down the gun barrel of a tank.

I am the Cathars burned at the stake, their mountain hideaways torn stone by stone by the French duke on orders from the Pope.

I am the Pope traveling to Communist Poland to be with his countrymen and women.

I am every man and woman who has said aloud, "This just isn't right!"

I am Jefferson yearning to have others see what is beyond the next mountain.

I am Lincoln full of strength for freeing others.

I am Roosevelt on the radio parting the drowning waters of fear.

I am Martin Luther King, Jr. praising the Lord and crying out for freedom in Selma, Alabama.

You can't plug me in or dial me up or shut me down.

You can't play me, display me, wrap me up in bubble wrap.

Every device that's ever been invented, every item that's ever been sold, every play or song or painting that's ever been born is my face and tongue and hand making, talking, inspiring, loving.

I am costly.

I am a young man gone down on land or sea or in the air to give the gift of living days so that others may.

I am Emily Dickinson shut up in her room because it wasn't seemly for women to be articulate publicly.

I am cheap, locked up, despised.

I am the bum in your street, the immigrant, the one they don't want in the Boy Scout Troop.

I am on your front porch wrapped in a rubber band, on the screen in the corner of your playroom, on your living room shelf.

I am what your children say to you and you to them.

I am what you don't like that others say and write.

I am you—whenever you may or may not want me, too.

A Tent is a Home for Fourth Amendment Purposes
People v. Schafer, 946 P.2d 938 (Colo. 1997)
Colorado Supreme Court – No. 97SA142
September 15, 1997

Headnote

The supreme court holds that a person camping in Colorado on unimproved and apparently unused land that is not fenced or posted against trespassing, and in the absence of personal notice against trespass, has a reasonable expectation of privacy in a tent used for shelter and personal effects therein.

Police officers of the City of Cortez conducted a warrantless search of a tent whose flaps were closed and its entrance zippered shut. The officers entered the tent while its occupant was away, opened a backpack which was within the tent, and extracted information from a notebook found therein. The District Court for Montezuma County ruled that the warrantless search lacked probable cause and exigent circumstances and suppressed testimony and other evidence gathered as a result of the illegal entry.

Taking notice of the long history of the use of tents for habitation in Colorado and the West, the supreme court determines, under the Fourth Amendment to the United States Constitution, that one's interest in a tent used for overnight or longer term stay is entitled to equivalent protection from unreasonable government intrusion as that afforded to homes and hotel rooms.

. . .

JUSTICE HOBBS delivered the opinion of the court.

This interlocutory appeal is brought by the prosecution, pursuant to section 16-12-102(2), 8A C.R.S. (1996 Supp.), and C.A.R. 4.1, from an order of the Montezuma County District Court granting the motion of defendant Scott E. Schafer (Schafer) to suppress evidence discovered as the result of a warrantless search of his tent and backpack. The District Attorney for the Twenty-Second Judicial District contends that the order should be reversed because Schafer lacked standing to challenge the search, or, alternatively, because exigent circumstances obviated the need for a search warrant. We affirm the district court's suppression ruling.

I.

On the morning of October 19, 1996, at approximately 10:00 a.m., an armed robbery took place at the Chief One Stop convenience store in Cortez,

Colorado. The clerk reported that the robber had fled the store on foot, heading east. Cortez police officers arrived at the scene and began to search the area based on the store clerk's description of the perpetrator. The police were informed by a friend of the clerk that a "transient" was camping in a tent behind Stromstead's Restaurant, about a half mile east of the Chief One Stop. Two police officers proceeded to the location of the tent, where they were joined by two other officers.

The district court found that the tent was standing on vacant land that was "junky, with broken glass, trash, and many dirt tracks/roads." Although the land was privately owned, it was publicly accessible and used by townspeople for parties. There were no fences or signs prohibiting entry onto the land. Schafer owned the tent and personal items therein, including the backpack.[1] Schafer was not present when the police officers arrived or at any time during the ensuing search. The flaps of the tent were closed and the entrance was zippered shut. The officers did not have a search warrant.

One of the officers opened the flaps and zipper and entered the tent, where he found clothes, a bedroll, and a backpack. The officer opened the backpack, removed an address book, and copied the name "Scott Robert Schafer" from an envelope therein.[2] He then returned the address book to the backpack, and the officers left without removing any object from the scene.

---

[1] The two-person sized tent and its contents were described by Schafer at the suppression hearing:
- Q: Okay. Whose tent is that?
- A: It's my tent.
- Q: And-how were you using it?
- A: As a place to live while I was passing through the area.
- Q: ... [W]as it you who put it there when it was there on the morning of October 19th, 1996?
- A: Yes, I did.
- Q: When did you put it there?
- A: The night of the 18th.
- Q: Okay. And did you leave the tent in that area at any time after you had set it up?
- A: Yes, in the morning on the-of the 19th I took off and went and had some breakfast and did a few things around town before I packed up and left for Montrose.
- Q: Okay. Before you left the tent, what did you do to it?
- A: I set it up and put everything inside.
- Q: Okay. And around what time did you get back to the tent?
- A: Oh, it was probably around-12:00, 12:30, 1:00 o'clock somewhere around in that area.
- Q: What did you do when you got back to the tent?
- A: I was getting ready to take off, go back to Montrose, so I opened up the tent and found everything was ransacked.
- Q: What property did you have inside the tent?
- A: I had two or three pairs of clothing, change of clothing. I had an address book. A day planner is what they call them I guess. And my packsack (sic). Sleeping bag. Pair of tennis shoes was in there too. Personal items in the packsack.
- Q: Was the packsack closed?
- A: Yes, it was.

Several months later, following a domestic violence complaint, Schafer was arrested in Montrose, Colorado for possession of a weapon which had been stolen in Montezuma County, in which Cortez is located. The police included Schafer's photograph in a photo lineup that was transmitted to Cortez. The clerk of the Chief One Stop identified Schafer as the person who robbed the store on October 19, 1996. Thereafter, Schafer was charged with aggravated robbery, in violation of section 18-4-302, 8B C.R.S. (1986), and carrying a concealed weapon, in violation of section 18-12-105, 8B C.R.S. (1986). Prior to trial, Schafer moved to exclude testimony and other evidence based on the warrantless search of his tent and backpack on October 19 in Cortez. The district court granted the motion for suppression, finding that "[Schafer] closed the tent and his knapsack. He clearly had a reasonable expectation that they would remain in that condition." The court further held that

> [n]o exigent circumstances existed for a search without a warrant, as the police were unaware of any connection between the occupant of the tent and the robbery for several months. Therefore there was no basis presented by the evidence to enter the tent, examine its contents and write down information.

The district attorney then brought this appeal, challenging Schafer's standing to raise the constitutionality of the search and asserting that exigent circumstances justified the warrantless entry and search. We uphold the district court's suppression order.

II.

We determine under the Fourth Amendment of the United States Constitution and its Colorado counterpart, Colo. Const. art. II, § 7,[3] that a person camping in Colorado on unimproved and apparently unused land that is not

---

[2] There is some confusion in the testimony as to whether the name on the envelope was that of Schafer or his brother. Either way, the name could be used to link Schafer to the tent and place him in Cortez at the time of the robbery.

[3] The Fourth Amendment to the United States Constitution provides:
> The right of the people to be secure in their persons, houses, papers, and effects, against unreasonable searches and seizures, shall not be violated, and no Warrants shall issue, but upon probable cause, supported by Oath or affirmation, and particularly describing the place to be searched, and the persons or things to be seized.

Article II, section 7 of the Colorado Constitution provides:
> The people shall be secure in their persons, papers, homes and effects, from unreasonable searches and seizures; and no warrant to search any place or seize any person or things shall issue without describing the place to be searched, or the person or thing to be seized, as near as may be, nor without probable cause, supported by oath or affirmation reduced to writing.

fenced or posted against trespassing, and in the absence of personal notice against trespass, has a reasonable expectation of privacy in a tent used for habitation and personal effects therein.

A.
Standing

The prosecution first contends that the district court erred in recognizing Schafer's standing to contest the search of the tent and backpack. In order to assert a Fourth Amendment violation, a defendant must show that he or she had "a legitimate expectation of privacy in the areas searched or the items seized." *People v. Naranjo*, 686 P.2d 1343, 1345 (Colo. 1984). Whether a person has a legitimate expectation of privacy in a particular place or object is determined by considering the totality of the circumstances, including "whether an individual has a possessory or proprietary interest in the areas or items which are the subject of the search." *Id*.

The prosecution observes that "[a] defendant who does not reside on the premises, had no right to be on the premises, and does not have a possessory interest in the premises is not an aggrieved person and cannot complain of the unlawfulness of a search." *People v. Juarez*, 770 P.2d 1286, 1289 (Colo. 1989). However, *Juarez* does not apply for two reasons. First, Schafer owned the tent and the backpack and was using the tent for an overnight stay. Second, a possessory interest in the premises "may be established by one lawfully in possession at the time of the search, or by one reasonably believing he has a ... colorable interest in the premises or vehicle." *People v. Pearson*, 190 Colo. 313, 319, 546 P.2d 1259, 1264 (1976).

In Colorado, one who enters or remains upon unimproved and apparently unused land, which is neither fenced nor otherwise enclosed in a manner designed to exclude intruders, does so with license and privilege in the absence of personal or posted notice. Section 18-4-201(3), 8B C.R.S. (1986), provides:

> Except as is otherwise provided in section 33-6-116(1), C.R.S., a person who enters or remains upon unimproved and apparently unused land which is neither fenced nor otherwise enclosed in a manner designed to exclude intruders does so with license and privilege unless notice against trespass is personally communicated to him by the owner of the land or some other authorized person or unless notice forbidding entry is given by posting with signs at intervals of not more than four hundred forty yards or, if there is a readily identifiable entrance to the land, by posting with signs at such entrance to the private land or the forbidden part of the land.

Schafer was given no notice that he was trespassing on private land or that the owner thereof intended to exclude the public. Accordingly, he enjoyed "license and privilege" to enter, was in lawful possession of the tent and the personal effects therein, and has standing to contest the search.

B.

Tents as Habitation

The Fourth Amendment to the United States Constitution and its Colorado counterpart are intended to protect from unreasonable governmental intrusion one's legitimate expectation of privacy. *See People v. Oates*, 698 P.2d 811, 814 (Colo. 1985). The highest protection is afforded to one's residence; a search thereof without a warrant is presumptively unreasonable. *See People v. O'Hearn*, 931 P.2d 1168, 1173 (1997). In determining whether Schafer had a reasonable expectation of privacy in his tent, we take notice that tents have long been utilized as temporary or longer term habitation in Colorado and the West.

Carved out of the public domain secured to the United States by the Louisiana Purchase and the Treaty of Guadalupe Hidalgo, *see* Charles F. Wilkinson, *Crossing the Next Meridian* 34 (1992), thirty-seven percent of Colorado remains in federal ownership, consisting primarily of Bureau of Land Management, Forest Service, National Park and National Monument lands which are widely available for hiking, hunting, fishing, rafting, wildlife watching, and tent camping. Mel Griffiths & Lynnell Rubright, *Colorado* 161 (1983). Colorado's twenty-four federally designated wilderness areas, *see Sierra Club v. Yeutter*, 911 F.2d 1405 (10th Cir. 1990), are accessed solely by foot or horseback, usually for multi-day treks utilizing tents as the predominant mode of shelter. Colorado state parks, federal lands, and some private lands offer opportunities for long term camping as well as overnight or weekend visits. Because wind, hail, rain, or snow may strike without warning any day of the year, particularly in the mountains,[4] the

---

[4] Description of Colorado's natural beauty has often included its quickly changing weather:
> Being out-of-doors is a basic part of Colorado. Climate makes the landscape visceral, where the skin, not the eyes, is the primary mode of perception. You feel the heat of the sun or the bite of the wind on your face; winter wets and chills you to the core. Western weather changes rapidly; it is typically unpredictable. Sun-filled skies become thick with thunderclouds, gentle snows change to blizzards, a dry wash is inundated by a flash flood, sweltering heat turns to freezing temperature in hours. Captain John Bell in 1820 spoke of clouds filled with "electric fluid," and John C. Fremont remarked on entering "the storehouse of the thunderstorms." William Parsons, part of the Lawrence Party in 1858, said: "We had a thunder shower almost each day while we remained in the camp—and SUCH thunder as no other country ever saw. On such occasions it seemed as if the old mountain rocked to its very base. The lightning, as if let loose for holiday pastime, played among the deep gorges and rocky canons of the mountains with appalling splendor." The climate is volatile and violent: chinooks, avalanches, floods, lightning, hail, brutal sun. An 1875 summer hailstorm broke windows in railroad cars and made steel boilers look like they had smallpox. During a storm in the summer of 1990, thousands of Denver automobiles became pockmarked in a single ten-minute burst of pellets. The National Hail Research Experiment has its field headquarters located near Grover, Colorado.

Kenneth I. Helphand, *Colorado Visions of an American Landscape* 29-30 (1991).

typical and prudent outdoor habitation in Colorado for overnight or extended stay is the tent.

Tents have long served humans as a form of habitation in Colorado and the West. Lewis and Clark, their interpreter Charbonneau, his wife Sacajawea, and their child shared a tent of dressed buffalo skins as they traveled from Fort Mandan to the Rocky Mountains in search of a passage to the Pacific Coast:

> This tent is in the Indian stile, formed of a number of dressed Buffaloe skins sewed together with sinues. It is cut in such manner that when foalded double it forms the quarter of a circle, and is left open at one side here it may be attatched or loosened at pleasure by strings which are sewed to its sides for the purpose.
>
> *The Journals of Lewis and Clark* 92 (Bernard DeVoto ed., 1953)(entry of April 7, 1805).

The twenty-one member expedition of 1820 led by Major Stephen Long up the Platte River to the Continental Divide in Colorado was housed by means of "three tents, sufficiently large to shelter all our party...from the storm." *From Pittsburgh To The Rocky Mountains, Major Stephen Long's Expedition 1819-1820* 150-151 (Maxine Benson ed., 1988)(journal account of the Long Expedition compiled by Edwin James, entry of June 1, 1820). Long's report to Congress included a watercolor by Samuel Seymour depicting the expedition's tents, and another by T. R. Peale illustrating the conical-shaped hide lodges inhabited by the Otos, a Native American tribe they encountered on their journey of exploration.

Canvas tents sheltered surveyor/mapmaker Dr. Ferdinand V. Hayden and his party during four field seasons of the early 1870s in their preparation of the first Colorado Atlas.[5] Richard A. Bartlett, *Great Surveys Of The American West* 40, 80, and accompanying photographs (1962). When Red Mountain Town caught fire on August 12, 1892, canvas tents sheltered the homeless. Robert L. Brown, *An Empire Of Silver* 244 and accompanying photograph (1965).

From September of 1913 to April of 1914, coal miners and their families, approximately nine hundred persons, lived in labor union tents at Ludlow across the railroad tracks from three Colorado National Guard tents housing twelve troopers during the coal field strike. George S. McGovern & Leonard F. Guttridge, *The Great Coalfield War* 210-11, 213 (1972)(and accompanying photographs). The tent colony burned to the ground during the fatal conflict of Easter 1914 between the Guard and striking miners. *Id.* at 224-25. Seeking refuge from bullets, women and children suffocated in pits to which they had retreated underneath the tents.[6] *Id.* at 226-227.

---

[5] "More than any other explorer or survey leader, Hayden dramatized the West as a wonderland—a paradise for tourists. He created the Tourist's West.'" William H. Goetzmann, *New Lands, New Men, America and the Second Great Age of Discovery* 411 (1986).

[6] Five miners, one militiaman, two women, and eleven children died at Ludlow that day. Carl Ubbelohde, et al., *A Colorado History* 256 (rev. ed. 1976).

"Your Wilderness Home" proclaims the Scout Field Book through a chapter title which identifies the "ideal camp site" as being located "on the outskirts of a clearing in the forest. The trees give you *shelter* against the wind if you pitch your tents so that they are protected from the North and West." James E. West & William Hillcourt, Scout Field Book, Boy Scouts of America 143 (1948). Today, wilderness trekkers, families car-camping for the weekend, and many travelers passing through Colorado, make tents their home away from home.[7]

C.

<u>Reasonable Expectation of Privacy</u>

The Fourth Amendment "protects people, not places. What a person knowingly exposes to the public...is not a subject of Fourth Amendment protection." *Katz v. United States*, 389 U.S. 347, 351 (1967). Whether pitched on vacant open land or in a crowded campground, a tent screens the inhabitant therein from public view. Though it cannot be secured by a deadbolt and easily may be entered by those who respect not others, the thin walls of a tent nonetheless are notice of its occupant's claim to privacy unless consent to enter be asked and given. One should be free to depart the campsite for the day's adventure without fear of this expectation of privacy being violated. Whether of short or longer term duration, one's occupation of a tent is entitled to equivalent protection from unreasonable government intrusion as that afforded to homes or hotel rooms. *See United States v. Gooch*, 6 F.3d 673, 677 (9th Cir. 1993)(reasonable expectation of privacy existed for tent on state campground); *Alward v. State*, 912 P.2d 243, 249 (Nev. 1996)(person has reasonable expectation of privacy in tent while camping on BLM land).

An integral facet of Colorado's economy and allure is recreational tourism. Visitors and residents of Colorado who choose to stay in a hotel room, cabin, or tent away from their permanent abode presumptively enjoy Fourth Amendment protection. "A guest in Yellowstone Lodge, a hotel on government park land, would have no less reasonable an expectation of privacy in his hotel room than a guest in a private hotel, and the same logic would extend to a campsite when the opportunity is extended to spend the night." *Gooch*, 6 F.3d at 678. The scenic and historic town of Cortez, the gateway to Mesa Verde National Park and the

---

[7] The attraction of Colorado has included tourism and health since before statehood, which occurred in 1876:

Although the promoters of Colorado played down the lack of rainfall, frequently denied that the Great American Desert extended so far west, and emphasized the possibilities of irrigation when addressing themselves to prospective settlers, there was one area of the "sell Colorado" program where the lack of humidity was an asset: the field of health and tourism. The Rockies widen in Colorado, dividing into several ranges with high mountain parks between, providing an area, more than half the width of the state, whose high, dry climate earned it the title "The Switzerland of America."

Robert G. Athearn, *The Coloradans* 92 (1976).

locus of this case, depends significantly on visitation to Southwestern Colorado and the Four Corners region.

Ordinarily, a person who occupies land as a trespasser, or a person who should anticipate under the circumstances that privacy cannot reasonably be expected, does not justifiably rely upon the Fourth Amendment. *See United States v. Ruckman*, 806 F.2d 1471, 1473 (10th Cir. 1986) (person occupying natural cave on federal land does not have reasonable expectation of privacy); *State v. Mooney*, 588 A.2d 145, 153 (Conn. 1991)(presuming that space under a bridge abutment owned by state transportation department cannot be considered one's home).

Here, the district court found that Schafer was not in trespass because he was using his tent for camping on unimproved, publicly accessible land which was neither fenced nor posted, and he enjoyed a license or privilege to do so. The land was often used by local youth for parties and bore no indication that it was not available for camping, despite its rough appearance. Schafer had spent the previous night in the tent. There was no basis for the police officers to reasonably believe that the tent and the personal effects therein had been abandoned by their owner.

The officers conducting the entry and search relied solely on the characterization spoken to them by a friend of the robbery victim that a "transient" was camping on land behind the restaurant. No description or other identifying information tied the robber to the inhabitant of the tent. Without a warrant, the officers nevertheless unzipped the tent, opened the backpack, extracted the notebook, and recorded information contained on an envelope therein.

The prosecution informed the trial court that it intended to offer this information "as circumstantial evidence that [Schafer] was in town at the time" of the robbery. This it may not do. The district court was correct in excluding testimony and other evidence based on this warrantless search. Schafer was using the tent for camping and had secured it in a closed position. The officers discovered the information they seek to utilize in this regard solely by means of their unauthorized intrusion. The exclusionary rule functions to redress such deprivation of a constitutional right and to deter like official misconduct. *Cf. People v. Shinaut*, 940 P.2d 380, 383 (Colo. 1997).

D.

Probable Cause and Exigent Circumstances

The prosecution argues that the search was justified by exigent circumstances. Exigent circumstances have been found to support a warrantless search in three situations: where "(1) the police are engaged in a bona fide pursuit of a fleeing suspect, (2) there is a risk of immediate destruction of evidence, or (3) there is a colorable claim of emergency threatening the life or safety of another." *People v. Crawford*, 891 P.2d 255, 258 (Colo. 1995).

The prosecution asserts that this case fits within the second category, because a tent is readily moveable and the evidence therein can be effectively "destroyed" or removed for law enforcement purposes from the jurisdiction. However, this exception to the warrant requirement demands that the threat of evidence destruction be real and immediate: "[t]he mere fact that evidence is of a type that can be easily destroyed does not, in itself, constitute an exigent circumstance." *People v. Marez*, 916 P.2d 543, 547 (Colo. App. 1995). The characteristic mobility of luggage does not justify dispensing with the Warrant Clause. *See Chadwick*, 433 U.S. at 13.

Here, the danger of evidence destruction was not immediate. The tent and its contents were in existence when the police arrived and would have remained so had surveillance been maintained. Instead, the four police officers chose to search the tent and backpack rather than posting one of them to wait until a person—who might or might not have matched the store clerk's description of the suspect—returned to the tent. The robbery occurred at approximately 10:00 a.m., and the police officers arrived at the tent site soon thereafter. Schafer returned, struck the tent, and left about noon the same day.

Even when exigent circumstances exist, a warrantless search must be based on probable cause. *See People v. Miller*, 773 P.2d 1053, 1057 (Colo. 1989). The only link between the convenience store robbery and the tent was a statement by the victim that the robber had headed east on foot, combined with a statement by her friend that a "transient" was camping behind a local restaurant east of the convenience store. These statements do not establish probable cause to believe that the tent might contain either the suspect or evidence relating to the robbery.

The record does not support a finding of probable cause that the suspect might be found inside the tent. We have identified factors which might justify a warrantless search for a suspect as including the following:

> (1) a grave offense is involved; (2) the suspect is reasonably believed to be armed; (3) there exists a clear showing of probable cause to believe that the suspect committed the crime; (4) there is a strong reason to believe that the suspect is in the premises being entered; (5) the likelihood exists that the suspect will escape if not swiftly apprehended; and (6) the entry is made peaceably.
>
> *O'Hearn*, 931 P.2d at 1175 (quoting *People v. Miller*, 773 P.2d 1053, 1057 (Colo. 1989)).

The police observed no one in the vicinity of Schafer's campsite and they had no reasonable belief that the robbery suspect was the camper or was inside the tent. If the officers had been looking for the suspect, an inquiry to determine the presence of a person, rather than a search of the empty tent and the closed backpack, would have sufficed.

The district court determined that probable cause and exigent circumstances did not exist. We have reviewed the record and ascertain no evidence of their existence. After hearing testimony by five witnesses, the district court found that no facts justified the warrantless search and that Schafer had a reasonable expectation of privacy in his tent and backpack. These findings are supported by the record and will be upheld. *See People v. D.F.*, 933 P.2d 9, 14 (Colo. 1997).

III.

Accordingly, we affirm the ruling of the district court suppressing testimony and other evidence based upon the warrantless search of Schafer's tent and backpack, and we return the case for further proceedings consistent with this opinion.

Note: Although the prosecution could not use the evidence produced by the unlawful search of Schafer's tent, he was later convicted of the convenience store robbery based on the eyewitness identification and other admissible evidence.

Teacher Should Not Have Been Fired for Showing Film to High School Senior Logic and Debate Class
Dissent from Board of Education of Jefferson County v. Wilder, 960 P.2d 695 (Colo. 1998)
Colorado Supreme Court – No. 97SC292
June 29, 1998

Note: The majority of the Court upheld the Jefferson County School Board's determination firing the Columbine High School teacher for showing a "controversial film" without the school principal's clearance.

Justice Hobbs, Dissenting

[Excerpt]

I respectfully dissent. I agree with the Court of Appeals that Wilder's dismissal by the Jefferson County School Board (Board) was arbitrary, capricious, and legally impermissible. In his professional judgment, Wilder determined that showing the film *1900* to his logic and debate class of seventeen- and eighteen-year old young adults would be appropriate and not controversial... A teacher with twenty-five years of service in Jefferson County, Wilder was unjustly fired and should be reinstated.

I.
The Facts of This Case

A.
1900

1900 is a 255 minute film, directed by Bernardo Bertolucci, depicting events in Italy between 1900 and 1945, perhaps the most violent and transforming half-century in human history. Persons living in western mainland Europe during this period personally experienced two world wars, socialism, fascism, communism, and the liberation of their countries from dictatorship. Bertolucci's film shows families and family members, rich and poor, and how they endured or disintegrated during this time.

The film is generational, epic, artful. Born on the same day in 1900 on the same estate, two boys, one rich—the landowner's grandson (played by Robert

DeNiro)—and one poor—a peasant's grandson (played by Gerard Depardieu)—grow up and grow old together. Though they are natural adversaries by economic and social class, they become lifelong friends.

The movie begins with the old padroni/grandfather (played by Burt Lancaster) celebrating his grandson's (DeNiro's) birth by taking bottles of wine into the field to share with the peasant workers, one of whom is his lifelong friend and the grandfather of the other boy (Depardieu). The film ends in 1945, upon the liberation of Italy, with the trial of a citizens' court wherein Depardieu's peasant character spares the life of DeNiro's landed character.

In between occurs the rise, cruelty, and fall of fascism portrayed through the character of the estate's foreman (played by Donald Sutherland). As the film progresses, he kills a cat and then proceeds to kill humans for personal and political purposes.

The peasant workers liberate the estate they have labored on their whole lives, as the country is simultaneously being liberated by the allies from the fascists. Sutherland's black-shirted character confesses, as long suspected by the peasants, to murdering two persons, a boy who has taken the fascist's black gloves to try them on, and a widow whose estate the fascist and his lover covet. Having manipulated these murders to gain power and property for himself, and having falsely accused others, the fascist is executed by a peoples' court at the foot of his victims' gravestones while an accordion plays and the people dance.

DeNiro's character is tried by the peoples' court and found guilty of being the padroni, the padroni's son, and the padroni's grandson. An act of grace spares him. Depardieu's character declares that the padroni is forever dead but the person of this last padroni must live, so to constantly remind the people of their victory.

Having been spared, instead of thanking Depardieu, DeNiro says to his face that the padroni is not dead. The two of them fall immediately to wrestling as they have done, in sport and in conflict, throughout their lives. In the last scene of the film, old with age, they wrestle on a country path with slices of their youth and old age flashing against the rural landscape they treasure.

The film contains brief scenes showing nude persons or suggesting that acts of sex are occurring or have occurred. However, these scenes universally occur in the context of a much longer narrative and are markers of passing moments in the protagonists' lives. They are not shown in shocking or erotic detail. For example, the two pubescent boys are shown fully clothed doing push-ups on the ground, suggesting experimentation with masturbation. They are not shown masturbating. When they briefly expose themselves to each other in a separate scene they are commenting evidently on the fact that one is circumcised and one is not.

When they are young adults, the DeNiro and Depardieu characters get into bed with a woman DeNiro has paid. This scene is shot from the foot of the bed and does not show any sex act. The woman is forced to have an alcoholic drink and goes into an epileptic fit. Her fit drowns out any notion of eroticism, and the entire scene functions to show the corruption of a rich man's power over a young peasant woman. The drug use scene is brief, and again is evidently utilized to show the corruption of money in an urban setting apart from the values of a farming community. This scene does not glorify the use of drugs.

The scene of the fascist played by Donald Sutherland killing the cat with his head shows blood on his head but not the agony of the cat. This scene is later paralleled by the fascist killing the boy who is eavesdropping on the fascist and his lover. The fascist swings the boy by his feet in the air so that his head hits the wall, killing him. The boy's death is not shown in gory or agonizing detail. Nonetheless, this scene convincingly portrays the cruelty of fascism.

Contrary to the board's and the majority's portrayal, *1900* is not a patently offensive movie. It deals with the fascist counterpart to Nazism in the same era as *Schindler's List*. Wilder's students were unable to see the whole film and debate its viewpoints because the principal confiscated it upon the complaint of a parent.

B.

<u>1995</u>

Wilder, who first began his teaching career in Jefferson County in 1970, was an innovative teacher known for helping students develop their critical thinking skills and utilizing a wide variety of instructional aids. A faculty evaluation during his third year at Columbine describes him as follows:

> I am convinced that he is a uniquely talented and diverse educator. He is a warm, sensitive teacher who is extremely supportive of his students. He has a special skill in prompting students to participate in classroom discussions without fear of judgment and ridicule from their peers. His classroom techniques are many and diverse. He is a skilled educator who is constantly challenging his students to develop their critical thinking skills. He uses a wide variety of techniques to foster student participa-

tion in class. He is constantly making the subject matter relevant to today's society. He uses the chalkboard, audio-visual materials, class hand-outs and student presentation frequently. His ever changing classroom technique keeps students involved and interested to the point where there weren't any visible discipline problems.

Evaluations throughout his career up to his termination contained similar comments. However, at times he was late to his classroom or excused himself from the classroom to use the phone while students were doing assignments. He explained that these instances were due to having to pay attention to problems at home stemming from illnesses of both his daughters and from his wife's resulting emotional fragility. Wilder's evaluations at times caution him to improve on his classroom attendance, and he was admonished for allowing students to have food in the classroom; but he was not required to pursue a remediation plan, nor was he administered any other form of discipline during his long tenure with the school district. Students praised his teaching and his concern for them... .

The school district fired Wilder after he showed *1900* to his senior year logic and debate class in March of 1995. *1900* has an "R" rating. Newspaper advertisements for films rated "R" shown in the communities of the school district bear the following advisory in capital letters: RESTRICTED, UNDER 17 REQUIRES ACCOMPANYING PARENT OR ADULT GUARDIAN. Wilder's students were all either seventeen or eighteen years of age. *1900* is available for rent in the "drama" section of Denver metropolitan area video stores.

Wilder and many other teachers had been using films as instructional aids in their classes at Columbine High School. Because the school district had only a handful of films listed as an official part of the curriculum and the list had not been updated since the mid-to-late 1980s, the teachers individually selected those films which they believed would forward the content of their courses in accordance with the school district's curriculum. Some of those films were "R" rated. Some teachers used parental permission slips in connection with using such films in the classroom, others did not. Only one teacher had cleared an "R" rated movie by prior written notice to the principal, *Schindler's List*. In that case, parental permission was particularly needed because the students had to travel to a local theater to see the movie.

Neither the school district's written policy, nor Columbine's more informal policy contained a specific requirement that "R" rated films be reviewed with the principal prior to their use. Rather, these policies addressed the use of "controversial learning resources."

The school district's written policy INB stated that:

> Controversial issues include matters characterized by significant differences of opinion usually generated from differing underlying values, beliefs and interests, which produce significant social tension and which are not necessarily resolvable by reference to accepted facts. Matters usually become controversial not so much due to disagreement about facts, but as to the interpretation or values to be applied to facts.

Policies INB and INBR (INB's procedural counterpart) turned upon the responsibility of the classroom teacher to decide in the first instance whether the material he or she intends to use is a controversial learning measure. In the teacher's doing so, policy INB stated that:

> Due consideration must be given to the maturity and ability of the students, standards of the community, and sound professional judgment.

. . .

Wilder's normal practice was to circulate a general parental permission slip to his students at the beginning of the school year; these included an advisory that "R" rated films might be shown in the class....

Before showing *1900* to his students, Wilder previewed the opening fifteen to twenty minutes with the class, and asked them whether they wanted to proceed with viewing the movie. The class decided in favor of this. Wilder had chosen the film because, in the preceding weeks, he and the students had shifted from "early Greek ideas, Aristotle, Plato" to the 20th Century: "I decided to focus on a half-dozen key ideas. And those key ideas were socialism, fascism, democracy, feudalism, and something about individual freedom...." He did not consider these themes or the film to be controversial....

Nevertheless, before showing the fifteen to twenty minute preview, Wilder explained and cautioned the students that the film contained graphic realism at times. On the second day, one of the students asked whether they should be seeing this film. Wilder replied that anyone who was disturbed could put his or her head down at the particular scene or be excused and do an alternate assignment in the library. After three to five days of showing and discussing the film in class, one of the students spoke about several of the scenes with a parent. The parent called the principal. The principal confiscated the film. He watched it by fast-forwarding to certain scenes. Upon viewing scenes he thought might be considered "controversial," he forbade the class from continuing to view and discuss it, suspended Wilder, replaced him with a substitute teacher, and prepared—for disciplinary purposes—a twenty minute edited version of "controversial" scenes from the 255 minute film. Wilder's termination followed a grievance which he filed for being placed on administrative leave.

Columbine's principal caused the students of the logic and debate class to complete a written questionnaire concerning the film; the overwhelming majority considered it to be appropriate. Only two objected. Several students testified regarding their belief that the film was appropriate, for example:

"Q. Did you have an opinion about whether the movie was appropriate to what you were discussing?

A. Yes, I believe it was very appropriate to what we were discussing.

Q. Why do you believe that?

A. Well, since we were discussing socialism and fascism, the movie was pertinent to what we were discussing. It was illustrating all the aspects of that, and what went on during that time....

Q. Did you see—was there anything in the movie that offended you?

A. No.

Q. Why? That might not be a very good question, but why do you feel that there was nothing offensive in the movie?

A. I can see the same kind of things on TV, prime time television. I'm—I was 17. I'm 18 now. I can go to the movie theater and see the same—the same thing."

Film critic and teacher Howie Movshovitz of the Denver Post and KCFR Public Radio testified that the twenty minute version of the film prepared by the principal did not fairly present the film. Movshovitz stated that the scenes alleged to be offensive, taken in context, were not titillating but were utilized to illustrate the themes of class differences and morality, people going too far: "It's not about sex. It's about corruption, I think, personal corruption."

Dr. Kearns, a professor of English at the University of Northern Colorado, testified as an expert witness that the movie was appropriate for seventeen- and eighteen-year-old persons to watch in a course on debate since the very nature of a debate class is to look at various viewpoints. In his opinion, the film was not controversial when shown in the context of this course and age group, was appropriate for its intended purpose, met the school district's general curriculum guidelines, and was not offensive to community standards....

[II]B.

Vagueness of the Policies

. . .

I would hold that the operative terms "controversial learning resources" and "controversial issues" are so vague that an ordinary person must guess as to their meaning, making the danger of arbitrary and capricious enforcement exceedingly high. Policy INB defines a "controversial learning resource" as "subject to disagreement" and defines a "controversial issue" as "characterized by significant differences of opinion usually generated from differing underlying values, beliefs and interest." The policy gives no indication of whose yardstick measures "controversial."

The public schools teach children from a diversity of families and backgrounds, many of whom undoubtedly have "differing underlying values, beliefs and interests." The Board's view of its policy forces the teacher to guess at what might fall within this policy. Potentially every novel taught in English class, potentially every picture, film, or book taught in a world history class, and potentially every matter raised in a course on logic and debate could be "controversial" in the sense of being "subject to disagreement" or "characterized by significant difference of opinion." That is what makes them worth teaching.

. . .

Art inspires thought by rooting in the heart the image of justice versus injustice. Bertolucci's film inspires and instructs. To the extent that community standards are a benchmark of the policies' implementation, this film was not offensive to community standards. The "R" rating is utilized throughout America as a theater, video store, and newspaper-published guideline for whether a particular age group may view a film without an accompanying adult. The Board did not proscribe "R" rated movies or require their clearance per se, letting stand the movie rating guide as a community standards indicator. The principal and the Board based their termination of Wilder on a twenty minute film which the principal had assembled, not Bernardo Bertolucci's film.

Were one to underscore the socially instructive highlights of Betolucci's film, the twenty minute excerpt instead could have included scenes showing the women of the village standing up against fascist soldiers, the act of grace in sparing a friend's life despite political advantage to be gained in killing him, and the joy that rich and poor people alike take in living despite evils which exist in society.

This nation was founded on disagreement and born of a diversity of ideas, peoples, and religions. Our public schools, at their best, generate interest and excitement in learning, instill democratic values, and prepare today's youth to become thinkers and problem-solvers....

When we strip teachers of their professional judgment, we forfeit the educational vitality we prize. When we quell controversy for the sake of congeniality, we deprive democracy of its mentors. The students of Wilder's class learned a valuable lesson at the expense of the teacher's job: one person's expression of ideas in the interest of critical thought and learning may be another person's "controversy."

I would uphold the judgment of the court of appeals for Wilder's reinstatement....

I am authorized to say that Justice Martinez and Justice Bender join in this dissent.

Note: The Colorado Supreme Court upheld Wilder's discharge by the principal of Columbine High School and the Jefferson County School Board on a four-to-three vote. The year following the Court's decision, two seniors of the same high school—studying how to hate in the privacy of their homes apparently without the knowledge of their parents—effectuated their plan to execute teachers and fellow students, killing more than a score of them. Wilder was three years gone from Columbine by that time.

Protection of Victim Under Rape Shield Act Justified Trial Court's Order Prohibiting Publication of In Camera Transcript Pending Rape Shield Hearing
In re: The People of the State of Colorado v. Kobe Bean Bryant, **94 P.3d 624 (Colo. 2004)**
Colorado Supreme Court – No. 04SA200
July 19, 2004

Headnote

In an original proceeding, the Supreme Court upholds an order by the District Court for Eagle County in a criminal prosecution against Defendant Kobe Bean Bryant for allegedly sexually assaulting a woman. The order prohibits revealing publicly the contents of *in camera* rape shield hearing transcripts of June 21 and June 22, 2004. The court reporter mistakenly sent the transcripts by electronic transmission to seven media entities, by using an electronic mailing list intended only for transmission of the District Court's public proceedings.

The Supreme Court holds that the District Court's order against revealing the contents of the June 21 and 22 *in camera* proceeding transcripts is a prior restraint, but it is constitutional under the specific facts and context of the case. The Supreme Court determines that the State has an interest of the highest order in this case in providing a confidential evidentiary proceeding under the rape shield statute, because such hearings protect victims' privacy, encourage victims to report sexual assault, and further the prosecution and deterrence of sexual assault.

The Supreme Court narrows the District Court's order by striking that portion of the order that required recipients of the transmission to delete the electronic transmission and destroy any copies. The Supreme Court further orders the District Court to: (1) make its rape shield rulings as expeditiously as possible and promptly enter its findings of facts and conclusions of law thereon; (2) determine if some or all portions of the June 21 and June 22 transcripts are relevant and material and, therefore, admissible under the rape shield statute at trial; and (3) enter an appropriate order, which may include releasing to the recipients of the original transmission and the public a redacted version of the June 21 and June 22 transcripts that contains those portions that are relevant and material in the case, if any, and maintains the ongoing confidentiality of portions that are irrelevant and immaterial, if any.

. . .

JUSTICE HOBBS delivered the opinion of the court.

. . .

Pursuant to C.A.R. 21, we accepted jurisdiction in this original proceeding to review an order by the District Court for Eagle County in a criminal prosecution against Kobe B. Bryant for allegedly sexually assaulting a woman.

In accordance with section 18-3-407(2), 6 C.R.S. (2003), ("rape shield statute")[1] the District Court, on June 21 and 22, 2004, held *in camera* proceedings regarding the "relevancy and materiality of evidence of specific instances of the victim's...prior or subsequent sexual conduct, or opinion evidence of the victim's...sexual conduct." § 18-3-407(2)(a).

On June 24, 2004, the court reporter mistakenly sent the transcripts of the *in camera* proceedings by electronic transmission to seven media entities ("Recipients") via an electronic mailing list for subscribers to public proceeding transcripts in the case, instead of using only the electronic mailing list for persons authorized to receive transcripts of *in camera* proceedings. There is no dispute that this was an error, and no dispute that the Recipients would otherwise not have received the transcripts.

The District Court's October 31, 2003, order previously entered in this case prohibits court personnel from disclosing to any unauthorized person information that is not part of the court's public records:

> Court personnel shall not disclose to any unauthorized person information relating to a pending criminal case that is not part of the public records of the court and that is likely to create a grave danger of imminent and substantial harm to the fairness of the trial proceedings.

Upon discovering the transmission mistake, the court reporter immediately notified the District Court, which promptly issued its June 24th order to the Recipients:

> It has come to the Court's attention that the *in camera* portions of the hearings in this matter on the 21st and 22nd were erroneously distributed. These transcripts are not for public dissemination. Anyone who has received these transcripts is ordered to delete and destroy any copies and not reveal any contents thereof, or be subject to contempt of Court.
>
> So Ordered this 24th day of June 2004.

Four days later, the Recipients filed their original proceeding petition, asking that we exercise jurisdiction to review the District Court's order and set it aside as an unconstitutional prior restraint against publication, in violation of the First Amendment to the United States Constitution and article II, section 10 of the

---

[1] In this opinion, we use the term "victim" as it is used under the rape shield statute. It implies nothing with respect to the veracity of the charges.

Colorado Constitution. Keeping the District Court's order in effect for purposes of our accelerated review, we have received answer briefs from the Colorado Attorney General on behalf of the District Court and from the District Attorney for Eagle County. The Recipients filed their reply brief. We now enter our decision.

We determine that the District Court's order is a prior restraint against publishing the contents of the transcripts. We also determine that, narrowly tailored, the prior restraint is constitutional under both the United States and the Colorado Constitutions. The state has an interest of the highest order in this case in providing a confidential evidentiary proceeding under the rape shield statute, because such hearings protect victims' privacy, encourage victims to report sexual assault, and further the prosecution and deterrence of sexual assault.

For purposes of this opinion we assume that the District Court could rule that some of the contents of the June 21 and June 22 *in camera* hearings may be relevant and material and therefore admissible at the public trial. The state's interest will be served by preventing the further dissemination and any reporting of all or any portion of the contents of the *in camera* transcripts that are not relevant and material under the rape shield statute. We strike that portion of the District Court's order that requires Recipients to delete the electronic transmission and destroy any and all copies of the *in camera* transcripts. Consistent with the First Amendment and the state's interest, we therefore order the District Court to: (1) make its rape shield rulings as expeditiously as possible and promptly enter its findings of facts and conclusions of law thereon; (2) determine if some or all portions of the June 21 and June 22 transcripts are relevant and material and, therefore, admissible under the rape shield statute at trial; and (3) enter an appropriate order, which may include releasing to the Recipients and the public a redacted version of the June 21 and June 22 transcripts that contains those portions that are relevant and material in the case, if any, and maintains the ongoing confidentiality of portions that are irrelevant and immaterial, if any.

Although we believe the District Court's order is also sufficiently clear and narrow on this point, we emphasize that our judgment applies only to the contents of the June 21 and June 22 *in camera* transcripts. Publication of information the media has obtained or obtains by its own investigative capacities is not limited by the District Court's order or our judgment, even though such information may also be spoken of or referred to in the transcripts.

I.

Facts and Procedural Background

By its Complaint/Information dated July 18, 2003, the state of Colorado alleges that Defendant Bryant, on June 30, 2003, committed forcible sexual penetration of a woman in Eagle County, Colorado, against her will, in violation of sections

18-3-402(1)(a), -402(4)(a), 6 C.R.S. (2002) a class 3 felony. The District Court has scheduled the trial to begin on August 27, 2004.

This criminal prosecution has received extraordinary media attention from the outset, fueled by Defendant Bryant's international reputation as an all-star professional basketball player and the sexual assault charge made against him. In order to facilitate public access to the proceedings in this case, the Eagle County District Court—through the State Court Administrator's Office—has maintained an electronic scheduling archive on the Colorado Courts' webpage that contains links to publicly accessible documents.[2]

Among these publicly accessible documents is the June 17, 2004, memorandum addressed by the District Court to "Members of the Media." It states that the District Court will hold hearings at the Eagle County Justice Center on the Bryant case on Monday, June 21, and Tuesday, June 22, 2004, a portion of which will be open to the public and a portion closed: "The courtroom will be open for the opening portions of this proceeding ... the remainder of the proceeding will be conducted in closed court." June 17, 2004 Memorandum to Members of the Media, at http://www.courts.state.co.us/exec/media/eagle/seating/june_21-22_memo.doc.

The June 18, 2004 "Amended Scheduling Order For June 21st and 22nd Hearing" lists eight items that will be held in open court and five items that will be held *in camera* after completion of the open matters. The *in camera* items are listed as:

1. Oral argument re: Defense Motion to Strike Testimony of Dr. Baden.

2. Other issues with regard to endorsed expert witnesses.

3. Continuation and Completion of Rape Shield Evidence.

4. Further proceedings concerning Crime Victim Compensation Records, including Defense Motion for Use at Trial.

5. Any other outstanding issues.

As the scheduling order intimates, the District Court has held prior *in camera* proceedings involving rape shield evidence, and transcripts of them have not been available except to the parties and persons authorized by the District Court to have and review them. The court reporter mistakenly transmitted the transcribed *in camera* proceedings for June 21 and 22, along with the transcribed public proceedings for June 21, to the Recipients. The notation "** IN CAMERA PROCEEDINGS **" is marked on every page of the transcript containing information from the closed portions of the proceedings. The mistake occurred because the

---

[2] Colorado Judicial Branch, *People v. Bryant Media Information*, at http://www.courts.state.co.us.

court reporter maintained an electronic list for media entities subscribing to transcripts of the public proceedings in the case.

Our review of the transcripts under seal demonstrates that the pages bearing the label "** IN CAMERA PROCEEDINGS **" are concerned with evidence and arguments relating to the victim's sexual conduct before and after her sexual encounter with the Defendant Bryant.

As recited in their "Emergency Petition for Immediate Relief in the Nature of Prohibition or Mandamus and for Issuance of a Rule to Show Cause Pursuant to C.A.R. 21" filed with us on June 28, 2004, Recipients were preparing stories about the *in camera* proceedings when they received notification of the District Court's June 24, 2004, signed order preventing further release of the contents of the *in camera* transcripts.

We exercised our original jurisdiction on June 29, 2004, and ordered expedited briefing. Recipients contend that the District Court's order is an unconstitutional prior restraint violating the First Amendment. The Attorney General and the District Attorney for Eagle County contend that the order is not a prior restraint, or alternatively, that it is a constitutional prior restraint.

The District Court's order and the original proceeding before us involve only the *in camera* proceeding transcripts for June 21 and June 22, and do not concern any information the media may have obtained through its investigative capacities.

We determine that the District Court's order prohibiting further release of the contents of the *in camera* proceeding transcripts is a prior restraint, but properly narrowed, is not unconstitutional. In conducting our analysis, we first examine the applicable First Amendment law; then, we turn to the state's interest of the highest order in protecting the transcribed *in camera* proceedings from public dissemination, as set forth in Colorado's rape shield statute.

II.

First Amendment Prior Restraint Law

The First Amendment limits the choices the government may make in its efforts to regulate or prohibit speech, but it does not bar all government attempts to regulate speech, and it does not absolutely prohibit prior restraints against publication. *Neb. Press Ass'n v. Stuart*, 427 U.S. 539, 570 (1976); *Hill v. Thomas*, 973 P.2d 1246, 1252 (Colo. 1999), *aff'd*, 530 U.S. 703 (2000).

The term "prior restraint" describes "administrative and judicial orders *forbidding* certain communications when issued in advance of the time that such communications are to occur." *Alexander v. United States*, 509 U.S. 544, 550 (1993). Prior restraint of publication is an extraordinary remedy attended by a heavy presumption against its constitutional validity. *CBS, Inc. v. Davis*, 510 U.S. 1315, 1317

(1994) (Blackmun, J., in chambers); *N.Y. Times Co. v. United States*, 403 U.S. 713, 714 (1971). "The thread running through [the prior restraint cases] is that prior restraints on speech and publication are the most serious and the least tolerable infringement on First Amendment rights." *Neb. Press*, 427 U.S. at 559.

To justify a prior restraint, the state must have an interest of the "highest order" it seeks to protect. *Fla. Star v. B.J.F.*, 491 U.S. 524, 533 (1989); the restraint must be the narrowest available to protect that interest; and the restraint must be necessary to protect against an evil that is great and certain, would result from the reportage, and cannot be mitigated by less intrusive measures. *CBS, Inc.*, 510 U.S. at 1317 (citing *Neb. Press*, 427 U.S. at 562).

The decisions of the United States Supreme Court teach that free discussion of public policy issues and criticism of public officials cannot be restrained. *See Near v. Minnesota*, 283 U.S. 697, 717, 722 (1931). Accordingly, the courts cannot enjoin newspapers from publishing contents of a classified federal government study on United States war policy. *N.Y. Times*, 403 U.S. at 714. Nor can a speculative concern about the impact of pre-trial publicity on prospective jurors justify a prior restraint. *Neb. Press*, 427 U.S. at 563, 570. Nor can a judge who allowed reporters to attend the trial of a juvenile—notwithstanding a state statute closing such trials—prohibit the news media from publishing the juvenile's name or photograph. *Okla. Publ'g Co. v. Dist. Court*, 430 U.S. 308, 311-12 (1977). Additionally, potential harm to an economic interest is not sufficient to justify a prior restraint. *CBS, Inc.*, 510 U.S. at 1318.

In cases dealing with the conflict between truthful reporting and state-protected privacy interests, the Supreme Court—when reviewing the validity of sanctions following publication—has held unconstitutional a civil damages award entered against a television station for broadcasting the name of a rape-murder victim it had obtained from publicly available courthouse records. *Cox Broad. Corp. v. Cohn*, 420 U.S. 469, 472-73, 496-97 (1975). Likewise, two newspapers learned the name of a juvenile offender from talking to witnesses and subsequently published the name, despite a state statute forbidding such publication. *Smith v. Daily Mail Publ'g Co.*, 443 U.S. 97, 99-100 (1979). The Supreme Court held that the indictment of the two newspapers for violating the statute was unconstitutional. *Daily Mail*, 443 U.S. at 105-06. The Supreme Court also invalidated a sanction imposed for publication of an article identifying judges whose conduct was being investigated, despite the state's provision for confidentiality in judicial discipline proceedings. *Landmark Communications, Inc. v. Virginia*, 435 U.S. 829, 831, 845-46 (1978).

Nevertheless, the Supreme Court has recognized that protecting the privacy of rape victims is a highly significant state interest, requiring courts to consider both the First Amendment and the compelling privacy interests in the particular factual context of the case in reaching their decisions. *Fla. Star*, 491 U.S. at 530, 537.

"We continue to believe that the sensitivity and significance of the interests presented in clashes between First Amendment and privacy rights counsel relying on limited principles that sweep no more broadly than the appropriate context of the instant case." *Id.* at 533.

In *Florida Star*, the Sheriff's Department publicly posted a police report containing a sexual assault victim's name. *Id.* at 527. Under the circumstances, the Supreme Court determined that a civil damages award against the newspaper for revealing the name violated the First Amendment. *Id.* at 541. But the Court said it was not holding that "truthful publication is automatically constitutionally protected, or that there is no zone of personal privacy within which the state may protect the individual from intrusion by the press, or even that a state may never punish publication of the name of a victim of a sexual offense." *Id.* at 541.

We therefore turn to Colorado's rape shield statute, which serves purposes the Supreme Court identified in *Florida Star* as being of the highest order.

III.

Colorado's Rape Shield Statute

Rape is among the most intimate and personally-devastating invasions a person may experience in his or her lifetime.[3] It typically produces emotionally-destructive reverberations for the victim and the victim's family long after its occurrence. It can destroy the ability of a person to enjoy his or her sexuality with another.

The price of making a sexual assault victim's testimony available to courts of law historically exposed the victim to detailed questioning about his or her sexual relationships with others on the theory that a person who consented to a sexual relationship in the past was more likely to have consented in the case at hand. This tactic of "putting the victim on trial" attempts to characterize the accuser as a person who consented to the alleged unlawful sexual conduct. *See People v. McKenna*, 196 Colo. 367, 371-72, 585 P.2d 275, 277-78 (1978). Due to the likelihood or possibility that this defense will be invoked, exposing the victim's most intimate life history to public view, victims often are deterred from reporting the crime, or having reported it, from following through in the role of complaining witness. *Id.* at 372, 585 P.2d at 278.

At the time the Colorado General Assembly enacted the rape shield statute, many sexual assaults were never reported because victims of rape were often ashamed, humiliated, or terrified about the specter of their most private hurt being publicly

---

[3] The crime formerly described as rape, from which the rape shield statute obtained its name, is now defined by statute as various forms of sexual assault.

revealed.[4] Therefore, the offenses could not be prosecuted under the state's criminal laws. In 1975, the FBI reported that forcible sexual assault was one of the most under-reported crimes, with the estimated actual rate of occurrence ranging from 80 percent to 350 percent more than the number reported.[5] M. Ireland, *Reform Rape Legislation: A New Standard of Sexual Responsibility*, 49 U. Colo. L. Rev. 185, 186 n.4 (1978) (citing Fed. Bureau of Investigation, Uniform Crime Reports 22-24, 37, 42 (1975)). "Rape crisis centers tend[ed] to support...that at least 90 percent of actual rapes [were] never reported." N. Gager & C. Schurr, *Sexual Assault: Confronting Rape in America* 91 (1976).

The FBI acknowledged in its Uniform Crime Reports that law enforcement administrators recognize that their sexual assault statistics are low because "fear and/or embarrassment on the part of victims" deter them from reporting the crime. N. Gager & C. Schurr, *supra*, at 1 (citing excerpt from a Uniform Crime Report from 1968-1973). One of the main reasons why so few sexual assaults were reported was fear of court harassment and embarrassing publicity. *Id*. at 93; National Institute of Law Enforcement and Criminal Justice, U.S. Dept. of Justice, *Forcible Rape* 21 (March 1978) ("National Institute") ("The victim who fears that her past sexual activities may be exposed in public is less likely to report her rape and pursue prosecution."). In addition, many victims have reported that "involvement with the criminal justice system has been almost as bad as the sexual assault itself." National Institute, *supra*, at 34.

Today, the issues of underreporting are still present. The United States Department of Justice reported in 2002 that "[m]ost rapes and sexual assaults [are] not reported to the police.... Sixty-three percent of completed rapes, 65 percent of attempted rapes, and 74 percent of completed and attempted sexual assaults against females [are] not reported to the police." U.S. Department of Justice, Bureau of Justice Statistics, *Rape and Sexual Assault: Reporting to Police and Medical Attention, 1992-2000* (Aug. 2002). Yet, to prosecute perpetrators of sexual assault and deter others from committing this crime, the state usually requires the victim's testimony to prove its case beyond a reasonable doubt.

---

[4] In *People v. McKenna*, 196 Colo. 367, 372, 585 P.2d 275, 278 (1978), we cited the following works that support the Colorado General Assembly's legislative public policy basis for the rape shield statute: M. Ireland, *Reform Rape Legislation: A New Standard of Sexual Responsibility*, 49 U. COLO. L. REV. 185 (1978); N. Gager & C. Schurr, *Sexual Assault: Confronting Rape in America* 145 (1976); National Institute of Law Enforcement and Criminal Justice, U.S. Dept. of Justice, *Forcible Rape* p. ix (March 1978); G. Delsohn, *Police are Baffled by Rape Increase*, Rocky Mountain News, June 18, 1978, at 5.

[5] In an article written in 1978, the *Rocky Mountain News* reported that Denver, Colorado had one of the highest sexual assault rates in the nation. Delsohn, *supra*, at 5. The article also stated that "most women still are fearful of being ridiculed and persecuted for reporting a rape." *Id*. The police and counselors stressed that "[w]omen must overcome their reluctance and report rapes...." *Id*. at 58.

Because a defendant may seek to inject irrelevant details about the victim's personal sexual conduct into the case, the Colorado General Assembly has enacted a carefully-crafted judicial mechanism that allows the prosecution and defense—in private, that is, "in camera"—to explore and argue about the relevancy and materiality of evidence tendered to the trial judge for admission at the public trial of the case. *McKenna*, 196 Colo. at 373, 585 P.2d at 279; see § 18-3-407, 6 C.R.S. (2003).[6]

This statute deems the prior or subsequent sexual conduct of any victim to be presumptively irrelevant to the criminal trial. *See People v. Murphy*, 919 P.2d 191, 195, 197 (Colo. 1996). It sets forth a detailed procedure by which a defendant

---

[6] Victim's and witness' prior history—evidentiary hearing. (1) Evidence of specific instances of the victim's or a witness' prior or subsequent sexual conduct, opinion evidence of the victim's or a witness' sexual conduct, and reputation evidence of the victim's or a witness' sexual conduct shall be presumed to be irrelevant except:

(a) Evidence of the victim's or witness' prior or subsequent sexual conduct with the actor;

(b) Evidence of specific instances of sexual activity showing the source or origin of semen, pregnancy, disease, or any similar evidence of sexual intercourse offered for the purpose of showing that the act or acts charged were or were not committed by the defendant.

(2) In any criminal prosecution under sections 18-3-402 to 18-3-405.5, 18-6-301, 18-6-302, 18-6-403, and 18-6-404, or for attempt or conspiracy to commit any crime under sections 18-3-402 to 18-3-405.5, 18-6-301, 18-6-302, 18-6-403, and 18-6-404, if evidence, that is not excepted under subsection (1) of this section, of specific instances of the victim's or a witness' prior or subsequent sexual conduct, or opinion evidence of the victim's or a witness' sexual conduct, or reputation evidence of the victim's or a witness' sexual conduct, or evidence that the victim or a witness has a history of false reporting of sexual assaults is to be offered at trial, the following procedure shall be followed:

(a) A written motion shall be made at least thirty days prior to trial, unless later for good cause shown, to the court and to the opposing parties stating that the moving party has an offer of proof of the relevancy and materiality of evidence of specific instances of the victim's or witness' prior or subsequent sexual conduct, or opinion evidence of the victim's or witness' sexual conduct, or reputation evidence of the victim's or witness' sexual conduct, or evidence that the victim or witness has a history of false reporting of sexual assaults that is proposed to be presented.

(b) The written motion shall be accompanied by an affidavit in which the offer of proof shall be stated.

(c) If the court finds that the offer of proof is sufficient, the court shall notify the other party of such and set a hearing to be held in camera prior to trial. In such hearing, the court shall allow the questioning of the victim or witness regarding the offer of proof made by the moving party and shall otherwise allow a full presentation of the offer of proof including, but not limited to, the presentation of witnesses.

(d) An in camera hearing may be held during trial if evidence first becomes available at the time of the trial or for good cause shown.

(e) At the conclusion of the hearing, if the court finds that the evidence proposed to be offered regarding the sexual conduct of the victim or witness is relevant to a material issue to the case, the court shall order that evidence may be introduced and prescribe the nature of the evidence or questions to be permitted. The moving party may then offer evidence pursuant to the order of the court.

may request that a court make an exception to this general rule. According to this procedure, the defendant must submit a written motion stating that the defendant "has an offer of proof of the relevancy and materiality of evidence of specific instances of the victim's ... sexual conduct." § 18-3-407(2)(a). The motion must be accompanied by an "affidavit in which the offer of proof shall be stated." § 18-3-407(2)(b).

If the court finds the offer of proof sufficient, it must hold an *in camera* hearing to determine whether the prior sexual conduct is "relevant to a material issue to the case." During the *in camera* hearing, the parties may call witnesses, including the victim. To the extent that the court deems the sexual conduct relevant to the case, this evidence will be admissible at the public trial. *McKenna*, 196 Colo. at 370-71, 585 P.2d at 276. However, the statute contemplates that contents of the *in camera* hearing and any transcripts thereof will remain confidential and under seal in the future, with the possible exception of use at the trial to impeach a witness' credibility or for some other admissible purpose.

In summary, Colorado's rape shield statute: (1) protects the sexual assault victim's privacy; (2) allows the accused person to explore facts, examine witnesses, present testimony, and challenge expert opinion to uncover material evidence potentially helpful to the defendant; (3) enables the trial judge in pre-trial proceedings to determine what shall be admitted or excluded at the public trial; (4) shelters all evidence in the *in camera* proceeding from being reported publicly; (5) keeps the evidence that is not material and relevant from being publicly reported in the future; and (6) serves the state's interest in prosecuting those accused of sexual assault and protecting the victims of sexual assault while affording defendants a fair opportunity to confront their accusers and hold prosecutors to the burden of proof at the public trial. *See People v. Murphy*, 919 P.2d at 194-95; *McKenna*, 196 Colo. at 372-73, 585 P.2d at 278-79.

IV.
Application to This Case

We determine that the District Court's order is a prior restraint because it prohibits specific entities possessing the *in camera* June 21 and June 22, 2004, transcripts from revealing the contents. *See Alexander v. United States*, 509 U.S. 544, 550 (1993).

We also determine that, narrowly tailored, the prior restraint is constitutional. The state has an interest of the highest order in this case in providing a confidential evidentiary proceeding under the rape shield statute, because such hearings protect victims' privacy, encourage victims to report sexual assault, and further the prosecution and deterrence of sexual assault.

We further determine that a narrowly tailored order can be fashioned in this case, and it is necessary to protect against an evil that is great and certain and would result from the reportage. *CBS, Inc. v. Davis*, 510 U.S. 1315, 1317 (1994).

1. The District Court's Order is a Prior Restraint on Publication of Lawfully Obtained Information

The Recipients contend that the District Court's order forbidding publication of the information contained in the *in camera* transcripts constitutes a prior restraint. In this respect, we agree with Recipients, and they are entitled to the heavy presumption against the constitutionality of a prior restraint. An accidental leak of privileged information does not necessarily entitle a court to punish or impose a secrecy order upon the media. *See, e.g., Landmark Communications, Inc. v. Virginia*, 435 U.S. 829 (1978); *Procter & Gamble Co. v. Bankers Trust Co.*, 78 F.3d 219 (6th Cir. 1996).

We also agree with Recipients that their acquisition of the transcripts was not illegal. Absent the prior court order, the statute, and the subsequent court order, Recipients would be free to publish the contents. *See, e.g., Bartnicki v. Vopper*, 532 U.S. 514, 528 (2001) (emphasizing and citing *N.Y. Times Co. v. United States*, 403 U.S. 713 (1971), for the proposition that a court must focus on the document's character and the consequences of public disclosure rather than the origin of the documents).

2. Facts and Context of This Case

The Supreme Court's precedent requires us to base our review on the specific facts and context of this case. Here, we ground our decision on uncontested facts derived from the following parts of the record: (1) the briefs filed with us; (2) the Colorado Courts' webpage entries; and (3) the sealed *in camera* transcripts that we rely upon but do not publish in this opinion. Additionally, we take notice of matters of common knowledge in this jurisdiction.

The pre-trial proceedings in this case are constantly monitored and reported by the press. Such media-intense activity has befallen a small mountain courthouse and has prompted a sizeable commitment of Colorado judicial resources. Among these is the constant updating of the Colorado Courts' webpage to provide the press and the public with contemporaneous and archive-accessible electronic documents and scheduling dates for pre-trial and trial activities.

The electronic technology being utilized helps to facilitate for Coloradans and the world a high-degree of access to the public proceedings in this case. Yet, while most aspects of the judicial role in proceedings are highly visible and responsive to the media's First Amendment-protected right to report news to the public, the District

Court closed the *in camera* rape shield hearings held on June 21 and June 22, 2004, following public announcement on June 17 and June 18 of their closure.

The District Court placed into effect reasonable procedures, in advance, to prevent the media from attending and reporting these proceedings. By a standing order entered in the case dated October 31, 2003, the District Court prohibited the parties, attorneys, and court personnel—including the court reporter—from publicly revealing the hearing contents. The District Court allowed only authorized persons, including witnesses, to attend the *in camera* hearings. To make the *in camera* evidence and arguments accessible to the court and the parties, so that the District Court could make its rape shield statute determinations, the court reporter transcribed the *in camera* proceedings, marking every page of the *in camera* transcripts with highly visible lettering: "** IN CAMERA PROCEEDINGS **." The court reporter then transmitted the contents of the *in camera* proceedings mistakenly by utilizing the wrong e-mail list.

Recipients, the few media entities on whose computer screens the electronic document appeared, obtained a private transmission placed under seal by the District Court. The District Court did not intend to make these transcripts publicly available, nor did the court reporter. The private and protected nature of these transcripts was manifest to the Recipients from the bold notation on each page and the District Court's prior orders and actions.

Recipients were in a position to receive this transmission from the court reporter only because the District Court's accommodation allowed them to contract for the court reporter's electronic delivery to them of public court proceedings in the case as soon as they were available.

When the court reporter realized the transmission mistake, she notified the District Court Judge who had presided over the *in camera* proceedings. The District Court Judge then ordered the Recipients not to reveal the contents of those transcripts and to destroy them. Such order preceded any publication of the transcripts. The *in camera* transcripts continue to remain under seal. Recipients were and are amply apprised of this.

The District Court's order pertains only to the contents of these transcripts. The District Court took the only remaining action available to uphold the protections afforded by the rape shield statute, which embraces all of the state interests at stake in this case. It ordered the Recipients not to reveal the contents of the transcribed *in camera* proceedings. Were the District Court to allow publication of the mistakenly transmitted transcripts, it would abrogate all of its duties under the rape shield statute, and its own prior orders.

3. Prior Restraint Necessary; Harm Great and Certain

Recipients do not dispute the constitutionality of excluding the public and press from the *in camera* hearings, nor do they challenge the requirement that the parties, witnesses, and court personnel must maintain the secrecy of the proceedings.[7] Rather, the Recipients argue in this case that at the moment the transcript arrived at their computers, they lawfully acquired the information and were entitled to publish it.

In conducting our analysis of whether the prior restraint is necessary to protect against an evil that is great and certain, would result from the reportage, and cannot be mitigated by less intrusive measures, we recognize that the Supreme Court has hypothesized that a valid restraint might occur in the intersection of First Amendment and privacy rights, but has not yet decided a case approving one.

A.
Florida Star and Other Applicable Cases

We reason from Supreme Court case examples that reject the argued basis for sanctions or prior restraint.[8] These include the posited-but-rejected justifications of: removing incentives for parties to intercept private conversations, *Bartnicki v. Vopper*, 532 U.S. 514, 529 (2001); minimizing the harm to persons whose conversations have been illegally intercepted, *Id.*; protecting anonymity of juvenile offenders and encouraging their rehabilitation, *Smith v. Daily Mail Publ'g Co.*, 443 U.S. 97, 104 (1979); and protecting the reputation of state judges and maintaining the institutional integrity of the court system, *Landmark Communications, Inc. v. Virginia*, 435 U.S. 829, 833, 842 (1978).

In many of these cases, the Court pointed to the strength of the interest asserted but held that it did not satisfy the high standard required by First Amendment law, or was not supported by empirical evidence. Nevertheless, the facts and context of this case justify the District Court's prior restraint against revealing the contents of the *in camera* transcripts.

In *Michigan v. Lucas*, 500 U.S. 145 (1991), the United States Supreme Court acknowledged the widespread adoption of rape shield statutes, and noted that the

---

[7] In *Globe Newspaper Co. v. Superior Court*, 457 U.S. 596, 601 (1982), the United States Supreme Court stated that "there is an unbroken tradition of openness in criminal trials," but one major exception involves sexual assaults.

[8] We recognize that many of these examples arose in cases involving after-the-fact punishment of speech rather than prior restraints. Nonetheless, they are instructive because if these reasons are not compelling enough to justify an after-the-fact restraint, they are certainly not sufficient to justify a prior restraint.

purpose behind them is "to protect victims of rape from being exposed at trial to harassing or irrelevant questions concerning their past sexual behavior." *Id.* at 146. The Court held that this state interest was sufficient to warrant excluding even relevant evidence of the victim's sexual history, if the defendant failed to follow the procedures outlined in the statute. The Court reached this holding after acknowledging that precluding this evidence limited the ability of the defendant to confront witnesses. *Id.* at 149. Nonetheless, the Court held that the state interest in protecting the victim was sufficient to justify the resulting imposition on the defendant's rights. The Court reasoned that "rape victims deserve heightened protection against surprise, harassment, and unnecessary invasions of privacy." *Id.* at 150. In subsequent cases, the Court has been explicit in addressing the privacy interest of sexual assault victims. In *Coker v. Georgia*, 433 U.S. 584 (1977), the Court stated that "short of homicide, [rape] is the 'ultimate violation of self'." *Id.* at 597.

Likewise, in *Florida Star v. B.J.F.*, 491 U.S. 524 (1989), the Supreme Court acknowledged the compelling interest of protecting a sexual assault victim's privacy.[9] In that case, a reporter obtained the name of a rape victim from a police report in a pressroom. *Id.* at 527. The name was not supposed to be in the pressroom, *Id.* at 528, and posted signs warned reporters not to copy or print the names of rape victims. *Id.* at 546 (Scalia, J. dissenting). Moreover, the newspaper had a policy not to print these names. *Id.* at 528. Nonetheless, the newspaper printed the name of the victim in a small blurb about the sexual assault in a police blotter. The victim sued, alleging that the newspaper was negligent per se in that it violated a statute making it a misdemeanor to publish the name of a sexual assault victim. *Id.* at 528-29.

The Supreme Court addressed whether the privacy of the sexual assault victim warranted the after-the-fact restraint on publication of lawfully acquired information. *Id.* at 526. The Court emphasized that the case involved a clash between privacy rights and First Amendment rights—both very important—and that this clash required a careful, case-by-case, fact-specific analysis. *Id.* at 530. The Court went on to say that the interests advanced by the statute in that case—the privacy of victims, the safety of victims, and encouraging victims to report

---

[9] We acknowledge that *Florida Star* involved penal sanctions for speech rather than a prior restraint. However, in *Smith v. Daily Mail*, the Court stated that "whether we view the statute as a prior restraint or as a penal sanction for publishing lawfully obtained, truthful information is not dispositive because even the latter action requires the highest form of state interest to sustain its validity." *Smith v. Daily Mail Publ'g Co.*, 443 U.S. 97, 101 (1979). Thus, the court's discussion necessitates the "highest form" of state interest—the identical requirement as a prior restraint.

crimes—were interests of the highest public order. The Court said that "[i]t is undeniable that these are highly significant interests."[10] *Id.* at 537.

While the Court acknowledged that the privacy interests involved were highly significant, it held that imposing damages on the newspaper for publishing the victim's name violated the First Amendment. The Court left open the possibility that "in a proper case, imposing civil sanctions for publication of the name of a rape victim might be so overwhelmingly necessary to advance these interests as to satisfy the *Daily Mail* standard."[11] *Id.*

In the case before us, the state's interest in protecting the victim's privacy is even stronger than in *Florida Star*. The Defendant Bryant is an internationally-recognized professional basketball player. The press has been covering every minute detail of this case, and most of this coverage has been published or broadcast nationwide. In addition, the reported news is typically posted on the Internet, and thus available to computer users world-wide. The *in camera* transcribed proceedings of June 21 and 22 address the prior and subsequent sexual conduct of the victim apart from her encounter with Defendant Bryant. A victim's sexual conduct is even more private than a victim's identity, which the Court held was of utmost importance in *Florida Star*.

Moreover, in contrast to *Florida Star*, the contents of the *in camera* transcribed proceedings were not publicly available, there was no burden on the press to determine whether it should risk publication and sanctions in light of the District Court's prior restraint order, and the specter of the press having to impose self-censorship was not an issue, as the transcripts were clearly marked private by the "In Camera" notation. In addition, this case is distinguishable from *Near, Landmark*, and *New York Times* because the contents of these transcripts do not implicate suppression of public policy debate or criticism of public officials. To the contrary, the testimony concerns conduct that is intensely private and personal.

---

[10] The Court also discussed that, given the choice of whether to hold the state liable for inadvertently releasing the information or holding the newspaper liable for printing the information, the better choice was to hold the state liable. This is because the state should implement policies and procedures for keeping the information secret and bear the punishment for disclosing the information. To punish the newspapers would cause self-censorship, which is disfavored by the First Amendment. *Fla. Star*, 491 U.S. at 535. Although one might note the similarity to the facts in the present case, in that in both cases the government inadvertently disclosed the information, the reasoning in *Florida Star* does not require us to invalidate the prior restraint simply because government error caused the problem. The fact that this information has not yet become public and is still sensitive and private leads to the conclusion that constitutionally permissible measures may be taken to maintain the secrecy of the transcribed *in camera* information.

[11] This standard is that "if a newspaper lawfully obtains truthful information about a matter of public significance then state officials may not constitutionally punish publication of the information, absent a need to further a state interest of the highest order." *Daily Mail*, 443 U.S. at 103.

In *Florida Star*, as the Supreme Court explored the tension between First Amendment rights and statutory rights to privacy, the Court noted that First Amendment rights are not absolute. Under the proper circumstances, the scale may tip in favor of the state's interest that protects the victim's privacy. *Fla. Star*, 491 U.S. at 530, 532-33. For the reasons discussed in this opinion, we hold that this is just such a case. In his dissent in *Florida Star*, *id*. at 542, Justice White emphasized the severity of sexual assault as compared to other crimes, as well as the fact that the ensuing publicity often multiplies the harm to the victim. He explained that even when the government attempts to protect the victim, "mistakes happen" and sometimes rape victims' personal information is inadvertently disclosed. *Id*. at 542, 547.

As Justice White observed: "The Court's concern for a free press is appropriate, but such concerns should be balanced against rival interests in a civilized and humane society. An absolutist view of the former leads to insensitivity as to the latter." *Id*. at 547 n.2. Here, where the mistake was caught before the *in camera* information was further disseminated, the balance must tip in favor of keeping the information private.

B.
Our Determinations Regarding the Harms in this Case

Under the circumstances and context of this case, any details of the victim's sexual conduct reported from the *in camera* transcripts will be instantaneously available world-wide and will irretrievably affect the victim and her reputation. She is entitled to rely on the protective provisions of the rape shield statute, which the state affords her in her capacity as complaining witness in a sexual assault prosecution. This includes the District Court's prohibition against the further release of the contents of the transcribed *in camera* proceedings.

Recipients have presented to us an affidavit attaching many press articles containing information about the victim's purported sexual activity before and after her encounter with Defendant Bryant. In addition, the probable cause order made public in this case contains hearsay references to DNA testing, the victim's clothing, and evidence that the victim had engaged in sexual activity with other persons. The argument is that the victim's privacy is already hugely compromised and publication of the *in camera* proceedings will not result in graver infringement on the victim's privacy.

We have reviewed the transcripts of these hearings and disagree. The applicable United States Supreme Court standard of review does not require us to disclose what is in the *in camera* proceedings versus what is already in the public domain. Doing this would contravene the rape shield statute by revealing what is in the transcripts and destroying the confidentiality of that information, before the trial court determines whether the information is relevant and material.

Rather, the applicable standard of review requires us to determine whether publication of these transcripts would cause great and certain harm to a state interest of the highest order. We conclude that it would.

First, the evidence and the opinion testimony presented at these *in camera* proceedings were taken under oath in a court of law. Reporting these court proceedings will add a level of official legitimacy and detail to the information that does not attend press reports—the ring of authenticity, the stamp of authority. Because sworn testimony is viewed by the law and the public as having greater value and credibility than press reports of unsworn statements, this will cause great and certain harm to the victim's privacy interest. Unsworn statements often contain a mix of fact, conjecture, rumor, and unconfirmed assertions that a person might not make under oath, or that lack evidentiary value or relevance.

We do not accept the proposition that the greater the press attention to a case the less important it becomes to keep *in camera* rape shield transcripts from being published. If the contents of these transcripts are reported, the world will have access to graphic detail of sworn evidence and opinion testimony about the victim's sexual conduct that the public trial of the case may not reveal, because the District Court may determine it to be irrelevant and immaterial under the rape shield statute. The very damage that the rape shield statute is designed to prevent—confirming through *in camera* court proceedings the details of this victim's sexual conduct that are not relevant or material—would thereby occur.[12]

Second, the state's interests of the highest order in this case not only involve the victim's privacy interest, but also the reporting and prosecution of this and other sexual assault cases. Revealing the *in camera* rape shield evidence will not only destroy the utility of this very important legal mechanism in this case, but will demonstrate to other sexual assault victims that they cannot rely on the rape shield statute to prevent public airing of sexual conduct testimony the law deems inadmissible. This would directly undercut the reporting and prosecution of sexual assault cases, in contravention of the General Assembly's legislative purposes.

Third, it is absolutely essential to our analysis that these transcripts are still private. Reportage of their contents would make all matters contained therein public. The court reporter's mistake handed to only a few media entities contains material that was plainly marked and intended to be kept private. The very purpose of such a marking is to make authorized readers aware that the information contained therein is restricted to use only in and for the proceedings in which the evidence and

---

[12] We also note that the victim's physical safety has apparently been jeopardized by the publicity in this case. In a pleading filed with the District Court on July 12, 2004, the victim's counsel stated that he had "met with the Los Angeles Federal Bureau of Investigations and Los Angeles County Sheriff's Office regarding what those agencies considered to be a credible [threat of a] plan to kill the victim in the Bryant case for financial gain."

argument thereon was taken. In this case, the confidentiality markings served to notify the non-authorized readers, Recipients, that this document remained under seal. Reportage of these transcripts would greatly and certainly magnify the harm of the mistaken transmission, to the immediate detriment of the victim and the state.

Taken together, the harms in making these *in camera* judicial proceedings public would be great, certain, and devastating to the victim and to the state. These harms justify the remedy we fashion in this case. "For even though the broad sweep of the First Amendment seems to prohibit all restraints on free expression, this Court has observed that freedom of speech...does not comprehend the right to speak on any subject at any time." *Seattle Times, Co. v. Rhinehart*, 467 U.S. 20, 31 (1984) (citations and quotations omitted).

If the District Court cannot prevent the release of the contents of the *in camera* transcripts while it expeditiously proceeds to make its relevancy and materiality determinations, as contemplated in the rape shield statute, the state will be unable to implement its interest of the highest order in providing a confidential evidentiary proceeding under the rape shield statute, because such hearings protect victims' privacy, encourage victims to report sexual assault, and further the prosecution and deterrence of sexual assault.

Accordingly, upon reviewing *de novo* the record in this case, including the *in camera* transcripts, we determine that indeed the District Court's order is a prior restraint against publication, which is presumptively unconstitutional under the First Amendment. However, given the circumstances of this case, the state's interest in keeping the *in camera* proceedings confidential is sufficiently weighty to overcome the presumption in favor of dissemination at this time. We also determine that this prior restraint is necessary to protect against an evil that is great and certain and would result from the reportage.

Specifically: (1) the transcribed *in camera* proceedings concern the relevancy and materiality of evidence of specific instances of the victim's sexual conduct prior to and after the alleged sexual assault, and opinion evidence related thereto; (2) the state of Colorado has not made these transcribed proceedings publicly available; (3) the District Court has not yet determined whether all or any portion of the matters reported therein consist of relevant and material evidence potentially admissible at trial in this case; (4) the Colorado rape shield statute presumptively declares inadmissible all evidence of a victim's prior or subsequent sexual conduct and related opinion evidence, unless the defendant proves at an *in camera* hearing that such evidence is relevant and material; (5) the transcripts of *in camera* rape shield hearings do not become public unless and until they are introduced at trial; (6) reporting publicly the contents of the *in camera* transcripts would cause great and certain harm to the state's interest in providing the rape shield hearing in this case, including the victim's privacy and safety interest, encouraging victims to report sexual assault, and prosecuting and deterring sexual assault; and (7) the

District Court's order, properly narrowed, is the only means available to protect this interest.

4. Narrowing the District Court's Order and Our Judgment

We have a duty under First Amendment law to narrow the District's Court order as much as possible.

In *Seattle Times*, a media entity was a party to the case and was prohibited by court order, as were all other parties, from publishing information it had gathered through use of discovery rules; the Supreme Court held that this form of restraint was not "the kind of classic prior restraint that requires exacting First Amendment scrutiny" and was not unconstitutional. *Seattle Times*, 467 U.S. at 33.

Although Recipients are not parties to this case, *Seattle Times* is somewhat analogous. Recipients have obtained transcripts that the state in no way intended to make public, and they received these transcripts under a confidentiality notice. Moreover, analogous to the pre-trial proceedings in *Seattle Times*, rape shield hearings are not "public components" of a trial. *Id.*

The facts of this case do not involve placing the transcripts in a "media bin" analogous to a publicly available police bulletin board or broadcast that could be publicly monitored. Recipients have no stake in the transcripts as a result of their investigative efforts. Due to the state's mistake, the transcripts appeared on their computer.

Yet, the state cannot undo the transmission; it has occurred. Ordinarily, the transcripts of an *in camera* rape shield hearing would remain under seal at all times, with the possible exception of actual use at trial to impeach a witness or for some other limited purpose. Here, although released by mistake and Recipients were not entitled to have them, Recipients do have possession of these transcripts.

The District Court ordered Recipients to delete the electronic transmission they received and destroy any copies made of them. We strike that portion of the District Court's order that required Recipients to delete the electronic transmission and destroy any and all copies of the *in camera* transcripts. We determine under the facts and context of this case that we must narrow the District Court's order and fashion a remedy that otherwise would not be applicable to a transcript of an *in camera* rape shield hearing. The government's interest of the highest order will be served by preventing the further dissemination and any reporting of all or any portion of the contents of the *in camera* transcripts that are not relevant and material under the rape shield statute.

Consistent with the First Amendment and the state's interest of the highest order, we order the District Court to: (1) make its rape shield rulings as expeditiously as possible and promptly enter its findings of facts and conclusions of law thereon; (2)

determine if some or all portions of the June 21 and June 22 transcripts are relevant and material and, therefore, admissible under the rape shield statute at trial; and (3) enter an appropriate order, which may include releasing to the Recipients and the public a redacted version of the June 21 and June 22 transcripts that contains those portions that are relevant and material in the case, if any, and maintains the ongoing confidentiality of portions that are irrelevant and immaterial, if any.

Finally, although we believe the District Court's order is also sufficiently clear and narrow on this point, we emphasize that our judgment applies only to the contents of the June 21 and June 22 *in camera* transcripts. Publication of information the media has obtained or obtains by its own investigative capacities is not limited by the District Court's order or our judgment, even though such information may also be spoken of or referred to in the transcripts.

V.
Order and Judgment

Accordingly, we uphold the prohibition against revealing the contents of the transcribed *in camera* proceedings of June 21 and 22, 2004, and affirm the District Court's order to that extent. We strike that portion of the District Court's order that requires Recipients to delete the electronic transmission and destroy any and all copies of the *in camera* transcripts. We further order the District Court to make its relevancy and materiality determinations under the rape shield statute as expeditiously as reasonably possible regarding the evidence it heard in the rape shield *in camera* proceedings, and promptly enter its findings of facts and conclusions of law thereon. In connection therewith, the District Court shall address whether any or all of the transcribed *in camera* proceedings of June 21 and 22 shall be made public or shall remain private, and enter appropriate orders.

Therefore, we uphold the prohibition against revealing the contents of the transcribed *in camera* proceedings of June 21 and 22, 2004, and discharge our rule to show cause, in part. We make our rule to show cause absolute, in part, by striking the provision for immediate deletion and destruction of the transcripts. We remand this case to the District Court for further proceedings consistent with this opinion.

JUSTICE BENDER dissents, and JUSTICE MARTINEZ and JUSTICE RICE join in the dissent.

Note: The dissent argued that much of the woman's sexual history had been reported previously, and any restraint against publication was not justified. The United States Supreme Court, despite the media's request, refused to overturn the Colorado Supreme Court's restraint of publication pending the trial court's decision on the relevancy and materiality of the rape shield testimony. The trial court did release a redacted transcript making much of the information public, as material and relevant to trial of the case.

Book Review: *The Colorado State Constitution: A Reference Guide*[*]
The Colorado Lawyer
December 2002

Book review of Dale A. Oesterle and Richard B. Collins, *The Colorado State Constitution: A Reference Guide* (Greenwood Press, 2002).

Courts, attorneys, the press, and the public will appreciate this unique guide to Colorado's constitution. University of Colorado law professors Dale Oesterle and Richard Collins start with a very useful historical account of Colorado's founding and its six attempts at drafting a constitution.

Colorado's successful 1875-1876 constitutional convention focused on the Illinois, Pennsylvania, and Missouri constitutions as models; but the convention also produced unique provisions, such as Article XV, Section 15, banning employees' waivers of their employers' liability; Article XVI on mining and irrigation; and Article XVIII, Section 6, on preservation of state forests. The delegates added provisions to curb legislator misbehavior and railroad monopolies, limit bills to a single subject, prohibit substantive provisions in appropriation bills, and give the Governor line-item veto power.[1]

Published sources about the derivation of Colorado's constitution are few. Colorado Supreme Court decisions most often cite the Convention Proceedings.[2] Oesterle and Collins also draw on the Hensel Thesis,[3] prominent Colorado histories,[4] decisions of the Colorado Supreme Court, and publications of the Colorado General Assembly's Legislative Council.[5]

---

[*] Reproduced by permission of the Colorado Bar Association from Volume 31, December 2002, p. 39, © Colorado Bar Association 2004. All rights reserved.

[1] See pages 1 to 25 of the *Guide* for an overview of Colorado's constitutional history.

[2] *Proceedings of the Constitutional Convention Held In Denver, December 20, 1875 to Frame a Constitution for the State of Colorado Together with the Enabling Act and the Address to the People Issued by the Convention, Published by Authority of Timothy O'Connor, Secretary of State* (Denver: Smith-Brooks Press, 1907).

[3] Donald Wayne Hensel, "A History of the Colorado Constitution in the Nineteenth Century," Thesis Submitted to the Faculty of the Graduate School of the University of Colorado, Department of History (1957) (available on microfilm from the UMI Dissertation Services, Ann Arbor, Michigan).

Colorado citizens have amended the Colorado Constitution 142 times, two-thirds by referral from the Colorado General Assembly and one-third by initiative. Oesterle and Collins consulted primary sources in commenting on these amendments. The *Guide* contains a useful list of the 21 most important amendments, including the 1902 and 1912 Home Rule amendments, the 1910 Initiative and Referendum amendment, the 1966 Judicial Selection amendments, the 1974 Reapportionment Commission amendment, the 1992 Taxpayer's Bill of Rights amendment, and the 2000 Public School Funding amendment. The authors do especially fine work in dealing with these important amendments.

The *Guide* proceeds to examine the Colorado Constitution provision-by-provision, as amended through the year 2000 election. A historical and legal commentary follows each provision, accompanied by footnote citations at the end of every Article. The attention the authors pay to Article II (Bill of Rights), Article X (Revenue), Article XI (Public Indebtedness), and Article XVI (Mining and Irrigation) is particularly valuable.

The Article II discussion compares Colorado's bill of rights to the federal Constitution's counterpart provisions and points out where the Colorado Supreme Court has afforded greater protection under the state provision. Notable examples are Section 4, religious freedom, and Section 10, freedom of speech and press. In most other respects, the Colorado Supreme Court has construed the state provisions consistent with federal precedent.[6]

The Article X commentary unpacks the provisions relating to uniform taxation, equalization, and exemptions; then focuses on Section 20's tax, spending, and revenue limitations. The authors predict that it will "take another decade or two of judicial precedent to work out all the kinks in TABOR." Pointing to the

---

[4] *E.g.*, Abbott, Carl, Stephen J. Leonard & David McComb, *Colorado: A History of the Centennial State, 3rd ed.* (Niwot: University of Colorado Press, 1994); Hafen, Leroy R., *Colorado and Its People: A Narrative and Topical History of the Centennial State* (New York: Lewis Historical Publishing Co., 1948); Noel, Thomas J., Paul F. Mahoney & Richard E. Stevens, *Historical Atlas of Colorado* (Norman: University of Oklahoma Press, 1994); Stone, Wilbur Fiske ed., *History of Colorado* (Chicago: S.J. Clarke, 1918); and Ubbelohde, Carl, Maxine Benson & Duane A. Smith, *A Colorado History, 7th ed.* (Boulder, CO: Pruett Publishing Co., 1951).

[5] These materials include Research Publications of the Legislative Council of the Colorado General Assembly, a continuing, numbered series that began in 1953 and also contain the Analysis of Ballot Proposals published for general elections.

[6] See pages 31 to 91 of the *Guide*.

95 percent pass rate of close to 1,000 local government referendums allowing spending of increased revenues, the commentary observes that "Colorado voters wanted the tax limits in TABOR but not necessarily the spending and revenue limits."[7]

The Article XI analysis sorts out the Colorado constitution's stringent limitations against state-incurred debt and pledging public credit to private interests. The prohibition of government aid to corporations in general and railroads in particular was one of the convention's "successes." The authors point to several breaches against the Constitutional Convention's apparent purpose by Colorado Supreme Court decisions identifying and upholding legislative "valid public purpose" and public authority finance exceptions.[8]

The Article XVI overview addresses the constitutional provisions establishing prior appropriation as the law of surface water and tributary ground water in Colorado, as limited by interstate compact and equitable apportionment delivery obligations to downstream states. This part of the commentary also notes the critique of environmental interests that Colorado water law "induces overuse in the present rather than conservation for the future by rewarding the first to take water and requiring its constant use."[9]

Alongside the annual publication of the Colorado Revised Statutes, this very readable work provides a handy starting point for research into the state constitution's derivation and meaning. The authors illuminate Colorado's political, legislative, and judicial history, often pungently. In the authors' view, Colorado's labor wars produced especially zany actions by governors and the Colorado Supreme Court.

The *Guide* demonstrates time and again how Colorado's penchant for citizen government continues to mark its principal governing document, requiring implementing legislation by the General Assembly, interpretation by the judiciary, and adjustment by the people. I consider this book a valuable asset for those who may have a Colorado constitutional question and those who would understand their state's legal heritage.

---

[7] See pages 250 to 263 of the *Guide*.
[8] See pages 264 to 279 of the *Guide*.
[9] See pages 336 to 346 of the *Guide*.

The Trial of the President
Doyle Inn of Court, Justice Hobbs' Group
Denver, Colorado
February 10, 1999

Script by Justice Greg Hobbs

Inspired by reading William H. Rehnquist, Grand Inquests, *The Historic Impeachments of Justice Samuel Chase and President Andrew Johnson* (New York: Quill William Morrow, 1993). Assistance on the script by Maggie Conboy and Kathy Chaney. Passages marked with quotation marks are excerpted from the record of the Congressional proceedings and from the Andrew Johnson impeachment Web site "Finding Precedent: The Impeachment of Andrew Johnson," Courtesty of HarpWeek, LLC at http://www.impeach-andrewjohnson.com.

The Players

Narrator William Rehnquist:	Greg Hobbs
Andrew Johnson:	Ed Bronfin
Thaddeus Stevens:	Brandi Pummell
John Bingham:	Kathy Chaney
Sergeant-at-arms:	Pat Ridley
Justice Samuel Nelson:	Hal Haddon
Chief Justice Chase:	Joe Jaudon
William Evarts:	Maggie Conboy
Edmund Ross:	Marie Kirk
Chorus (All)	

All players wear long frock coats, black ties, shirts, trousers, and top hats of the day (costumes by American Costume Company, 1526 Blake St., Denver, Colorado).

The Trial of Andrew Johnson on Impeachment
Before the Senate of the United States of America

Rehnquist:

At his first inauguration, at the outset of the Civil War, President Abraham Lincoln sounded the theme of reconciliation he would later urge as the basis for Reconstruction policy:

> We are not enemies, but friends. We must not be enemies. Though passion may have strained, it must not break our bonds of affection. The

mystic chords of memory, stretching from every battlefield, and patriot grave, to every living heart and hearthstone, all over this broad land, will yet swell the chorus of the Union, when again touched, as surely they will be, by the better angels of our nature.

Lincoln favored a full amnesty for the defeated citizens of the South on the condition that slavery be abolished and that every man take an oath to support the Constitution of the United States. The Radical Republicans were not satisfied with this. They wanted an ironclad oath of past as well as future loyalty to be sworn by anyone seeking to vote, as well as repudiation of the Confederate war debt. These principles were included in the Wade-Davis Bill, which Lincoln killed by a pocket veto in 1864.

Lincoln was assassinated five days after Lee surrendered at Appomattox Courthouse in May of 1865. Johnson inherited Lincoln's Cabinet. The Radical Republicans determined to take control over Reconstruction policy. The country experienced over the next two-and-a-half years an increasing confrontation between the Republican Congress and the Democratic President.

The Radical Reconstructionists of the majority party pressed universal suffrage for black Americans in the former Confederate states, although black Americans were not yet allowed to vote in the northern states. White southern leaders who had held high civil and military posts in the Confederacy were disenfranchised. Military rule prevailed as reconstructed southern governments were established to cement implementation of the radical agenda. Johnson suspected his cabinet member Edwin Stanton of conspiring with the Republican leaders to undermine his efforts to placate white southerners.

Johnson:

I sent Secretary of War Stanton the following message on February 21, 1868:

> "By virtue of the power and authority vested in me, as President, by the Constitution and laws of the United States, you are hereby removed from office as Secretary for the Department of War, and your functions as such will terminate upon the receipt of this communication.
>
> You will transfer to Brevet Major General Lorenzo Thomas, Adjutant General of the Army, who has this day been authorized and empowered to act as Secretary of War ad interim, all records, books, papers, and other public property now in your custody and charge.
>
> Respectfully yours,
Andrew Johnson"

I used to be a tailor, you know. I sewed the stitching tight on that scalawag Stanton!

Rehnquist:

The Congressional reaction to Stanton's dismissal was immediate. Thaddeus Stevens was the leader of the Radical Republicans. He sent a message to Stanton, that he should stand firm against the President. So reinforced, Stanton barricaded himself within his office. Stevens was sick unto death and supported himself feebly by a cane, yet he appeared on the floor of the House the following day with a resolution of impeachment.

Stevens:

"Resolved this day of February 22, 1868. That the Committee on Reconstruction be authorized to inquire what combinations have been made or attempted to be made to obstruct the due execution of the laws: and to that end the committee have power to send for persons and papers and to examine witnesses on oath, and report to this house what action, if any, they may deem necessary; and that said committee have leave to report at any time."

Rehnquist:

In more fiery terms, Stevens laid down the taunt and the gauntlet.

Stevens:

"Let me see the recreant who would vote to let such a criminal escape. Point me to one who will dare do it and I will show you one who will dare the infamy of posterity."

Johnson:

They say I am a drunkard, that I keep a harem, that I plotted with that villain Booth to assassinate Mr. Lincoln. Infamy! I have discharged all my duties and fulfilled all my pledges. Let them impeach and be damned!

Chorus—Stevens, Boutwell, Bingham, Hulburd, Farnsworth, Beaman, and Paine:

"Resolution providing for the impeachment of Andrew Johnson, President of the United States:

Resolved, That Andrew Johnson, President of the United States, be impeached of high crimes and misdemeanors in office."

Johnson:

My crime is this. I believe what Mr. Lincoln said at his first inauguration. These men want revenge, not peace. This is what I said of them on August 18, 1866, and hold as true today:

"We have in one department of the government every effort, as it were, to prevent the restoration of peace and harmony in the Union. We have seen hanging on the verge of the government, as it were, a body called, or which assumes to be, the Congress of the United States—but, in fact, a Congress of only part of the States. We have seen this Congress assume and pretend to be for the Union, when its every step and act tended to perpetuate disunion and make a disruption of the States inevitable. Instead of promoting reconciliation and harmony, its legislation has partaken of the character of penalties, retaliation and revenge."

Chorus—One-hundred and twenty-four members of the House:

"Be it resolved that: a committee of seven be appointed to prepare and report articles of impeachment against Andrew Johnson, President of the United States, with power to send for persons, papers, and records, and to take testimony under oath."

"Be it further resolved that the Committee to declare articles of impeachment against the President of the United States be George S. Boutwell, of Massachusetts; Thaddeus Stevens, of Pennsylvania; John A. Bingham, of Ohio; James F. Wilson, of Iowa: John A. Logan, of Illinois; George W. Julian, of Indiana; and Hamilton Ward, of New York."

Johnson:

Massachusetts, Pennsylvania, Ohio, Iowa, Illinois, Indiana, New York! I'm from Tennessee. They'll never forgive me for that. I was the only Senator from any of the Confederate States to declare my loyalty to the Union and continue to serve. But they want to make an example of me for welcoming Tennessee and all the rest of her sisters back to this one country. I said this to the citizens of Cleveland on September 4, 1866, and I hold it to be as true today:

> "I have been fighting traitors of the South. They have been whipped and crushed. They acknowledge their defeat and accept the terms of the Constitution. And now, as I go round the circle, having fought traitors at the south, I am prepared to fight them at the north."

Chorus—Majority of the House of Representatives:

"We report eleven articles to the Committee of the whole of the House of Representatives of the United States, in the name of themselves and all the people of the United States, against Andrew Johnson, President of the United States, in maintenance and support of their impeachment against him for high crimes and misdemeanors in office."

"We appoint the following Managers to appear at the bar of the Senate to conduct said impeachment: John A. Bingham, George S. Boutwell, James F. Wilson, Benjamin F. Butler, Thomas Williams, Thaddeus Stevens, and John A. Logan."

Johnson:

I lost my father at 3, I had no formal schooling, I was introduced to books at the age of 14 as a tailor's apprentice, I moved to eastern Tennessee at the age of 18, I married Eliza McCardle the next year, she taught me to write. I started speaking. I was elected alderman, mayor, state legislator, Congressman, Governor, Senator, Vice-President of the United States. Over two-thirds of this Senate is Republican. I'm a Democrat. I like these odds!

Rehnquist:

The vote on impeachment in the House was 126 to 47. Thaddeus Stevens made clear his view that the issue was whether Andrew Johnson was fit to serve as President, not whether he was guilty of an indictable offense. On Wednesday, March 4, 1868, the House Managers, with their spokesperson being John Bingham, appeared in the Senate to present the articles of impeachment.

Bingham:

"Mr. President, the managers of the House of Representatives, by order of the House, are ready at the bar of the Senate, whenever it may please the Senate to hear them, to present articles of impeachment and in maintenance of the impeachment preferred against Andrew Johnson, President of the United States, by the House of Representatives."

Johnson:

My high crimes and misdemeanors? I vetoed their bills. They passed them over my veto. The Reconstruction Act—it calls for martial law in the South, limits white southern voting rights, gives unlimited voting rights to African Americans, but only in the south.

The Army Appropriations Act—it includes a rider that requires the President to issue orders to military officers only through the General of the Army, who the President cannot remove except with the consent of the Senate. I signed this only because it would deny money to pay the Army. The Tenure in Office Act—it says I cannot remove any office holder whose appointment required Senate approval, unless the Senate consents. I believe each of these acts to be against the Constitution, which I swore a holy oath to uphold.

Sergeant-at-Arms:

"Hear ye! hear ye! hear ye! All persons are commanded to keep silence, on pain of imprisonment, while the House of Representatives is exhibiting to the Senate of the United States articles of impeachment against Andrew Johnson, President of the United States."

Rehnquist:

Whereupon the eleven articles of impeachment were read to the assembled Senators. The first eight dealt with violations of the Tenure in Office Act. A ninth dealt with Johnson sending orders to military officers without issuing them through the General of the Army, contrary to the Appropriations Act. The tenth, added by Benjamin Butler, dealt with Johnson's disparaging remarks about Congress in public speeches. The eleventh, drafted by Stevens, summarized the other ten articles and accused the President of failing to execute the Reconstruction Acts. This was considered the most serious charge.

Stevens was so sick he could not stand. Mr. Bingham therefore rose to read the articles of impeachment, culminating with the eleventh, which would be voted upon first.

Bingham:

Article XI.

"That said Andrew Johnson, President of the United States, unmindful of the high duties of his office, and of his oath of office, and in disregard of the Constitution and laws of the United States, did, heretofore, to wit, on the eighteenth day of August, A.D. eighteen hundred and sixty-six, at the city of Washington, and the District of Columbia, by public speech, declare and affirm, in substance, that the thirty-ninth Congress of the United States was not a Congress of the United States authorized by the Constitution to exercise legislative power under the same, but, on the contrary, was a congress of only part of the States, thereby denying, and intending to deny, that the legislation of said congress was valid or obligatory upon him, that said Andrew Johnson, except in so far as he saw fit to approve the same, and also thereby denying, and intending to deny, the power of the said thirty-ninth Congress to propose amendments to the Constitution of the United States, and, in pursuance of said declaration, that said Andrew Johnson, President of the United States, afterwards, to wit, on the twenty-first day of February, A.D., eighteen hundred and sixty-eight, at the city of Washington, in the District of Columbia, did, unlawfully, and in disregard of the requirements of the Constitution, that he should take care that the laws be faithfully executed, attempt to prevent the execution of an act entitled 'An act regulating the tenure of certain civil offices,' passed March second, eighteen hundred and sixty-seven, by unlawfully devising and contriving and attempting to devise and contrive means by which he should prevent Edwin M. Stanton from forthwith resuming the functions of the office of Secretary for the Department of War, notwithstanding the refusal of the Senate to concur in the suspension theretofore made by said Andrew Johnson of said Edwin M. Stanton from said office of Secretary of the Department of War; and, also, by further unlawfully devising and contriving, and attempting to devise and contrive means, then and there, to prevent the execution of an act entitled: 'An act making appropriations for the support of the army for the fiscal year ending June thirtieth, eighteen hundred and sixty-eight, and for other purposes,' approved March second, eighteen hundred and sixty-seven; and, also, to prevent the execution of an act entitled 'An act to provide for the more efficient government of the rebel states,' passed March second, eighteen hundred and sixty-seven, whereby the said Andrew Johnson, President of the United States, did then, to wit, on the twenty-first day of February, A.D. eighteen hundred and sixty-eight, at the city of Washington, commit, and was guilty of a high misdemeanor in office."

Rehnquist:

At 1:00 p.m. on Thursday, March 5, 1868, the Chief Justice of the United States entered the Senate chamber, accompanied by Senior Associate Justice Samuel Nelson, who thereupon administered the oath to the Chief Justice.

Nelson:

Mr. Chief Justice, please repeat after me:

"I (state your name) do solemnly swear that in all things appertaining to the trial of the impeachment of Andrew Johnson, President of the United States, I will do impartial justice according to the Constitution and the laws; so help me God."

Rehnquist:

Chief Justice Salmon Chase, as he did then, will now administer to you, the Senators of the United States who will sit as the judges of the guilt or innocence of the President of the United States, this solemn oath.

Chase:

Please stand and repeat after me:

"I (state your name) do solemnly swear that in all things appertaining to the trial of the impeachment of Andrew Johnson, President of the United States, I will do impartial justice according to the Constitution and the laws; so help me God."

Rehnquist:

Andrew Johnson did not appear at the trial; instead, five attorneys spoke for him. The President's answer was read into the record of the Senate on March 23. His attorneys requested 40 days to prepare; instead, the Senate ordered the trial began on March 30. Preliminary rulings made by the Chief Justice were subject to a vote of the Senate.

Seventeen times the Senate overruled the Chief Justice; members of the Cabinet were not allowed to testify for the President; defense evidence was excluded. The popular press screamed for the President's conviction. Thirty-six of the 54 Senators were needed for conviction. There were 42 Republicans and only 12 Democrats. As closing arguments were made, it appeared that the Republicans had lost six of their number. But they needed only the vote of the junior Senator from Kansas, Edmund Ross, to reach the needed two-thirds vote for conviction.

Edmund Ross:

I have received the following telegram:

> "Leavenworth, May 14, Kansas has heard the evidence, and demands the conviction of the president.
>
> D. R. Anthony, and 1,000 others."

I have delivered the following response:

> "Gentlemen:
>
> I do not recognize your right to demand that I shall vote either for or against conviction. I have taken an oath to do impartial justice...and I trust I shall have the courage and honesy to vote according to the dictates of my judgment and for the highest good of my country.
>
> To D.R. Anthony and 1,000 others
>
> E. G. Ross"

Rehnquist:

For the House Managers, John Bingham delivered a three-day summation for conviction. For Johnson's defense team, William Evarts responded with a four-day summation.

Mr. Bingham:
(Summation for House Managers)

"I protest, Senators, that in no mere partisan spirit, in no spirit of resentment or prejudice do I come to the argument of this grave issue. Yesterday the supremacy of the Constitution and laws was challenged by armed rebellion; today the supremacy of the Constitution and laws is challenged by executive usurpation and is attempted to be defended in the presence of the Senate of the United States.

On the 9th day of April, in the year of our Lord 1865—on that day, not without sacrifice, not without suffering, not without martyrdom, the laws were vindicated. Surely it is the pride of every intelligent American that none are above and none beneath the laws; that the President is as much the subject of law as the humblest peasant on the remotest frontier of our ever advancing civilization. Law is the only sovereign, save God, recognized by the American people.

I feel myself justified, entirely justified, in saying that it rests not simply upon the traditions of the people, but is embodied in their written record from the day when they fired the first gun on the field of Lexington to this very hour.

How is the proposition, so plain and simple, met by the retained counsel who appear to defend this treason of the President, this betrayal of the great trusts of the people? The proposition is met by stating to the Senate, with an audacity that has scarcely a parallel in the history of judicial proceedings, that every official may challenge at pleasure the supreme law of the land, and especially that the President of the United States, charged by his oath, charged by the express letter of the Constitution, that "he shall take care that the laws be faithfully executed," is nevertheless invested with the power to interpret the Constitution for himself, and to determine judicially whether the laws declared by the Constitution to be supreme are after all not null and void, because they do not happen to accord with his judgment.

This is the defense which is presented here before the Senate of the United States. That the President may judicially determine finally for himself whether the laws, which by your Constitution are declared to be supreme, are not, after all, null and void and of no effect, and not to be executed, because it suits the pleasure of his highness Andrew Johnson, first king of the people of the United States, in imitation of George III, to suspend their execution.

The whole defense of the President rests upon the simple but startling proposition that he cannot be held to answer for any violation of the written Constitution and laws of the United States. No matter what demagogues may say of it outside of this chamber, no matter what retained counsel may say of it inside of this chamber, that is the issue. It is all there is of it. It is what is embraced in the articles of impeachment.

I read now in the hearing of the Senate the decision of Chief Justice Marshall in the case of *Marbury v. Madison*, touching this alleged obligation of the heads of departments to take the will of the Executive as their law. Marshall says on page 158 of 1 Cranch:

It is the duty of the Secretary of State to conform to the law, and in this he is an officer of the United States, bound to obey the laws. He acts in this respect, as has been very properly stated at the bar, under the authority of law and not by the instructions of the President.

This illustrates the proposition with which I started out, that neither the President nor his Secretaries are above the Constitution or above the laws which the people enact.

I ask you, Senators, to consider whether I am not justifiable in saying that it is a tax upon one's patience to sit here and listen from day to day and from week to week to these learned arguments made in defense of the President, all resting upon his asserted executive prerogative to dispense with the execution of the laws and protect himself from trial and conviction before this tribunal, because he said that he only violated the laws in order to test their validity in the Supreme Court, when that very Court already decided 30 years ago that any such assumed prerogative in the President, that would enable him to sweep away all the legislation of Congress and prevent the administration of justice itself, found no countenance in the Constitution.

I submit to you that there never was a balder piece of effrontery practiced since man was upon the face of the earth. I care not if he be President of the United States; it is simply an insult to the human understanding to press any such defense in the presence of his triers.

Is the Senate of the United States, in order to shelter this great criminal, to adopt the bold assumption of unrestricted executive prerogative, the wild and guilty fantasy that the king can do no wrong, and thereby clothe the Executive of the American people with power to suspend and dispense with the execution of their laws at his pleasure, to interpret their Constitution for himself, and thereby annihilate their government?

Senators, I have endeavored to open this question before you in its magnitude. I trust that I have succeeded. Be assured of one thing, that according to the best of my ability, in the presence of the representatives of the nation, I have not been unmindful of my oath; and I beg leave to say to you, Senators, this day, in all candor, that, in my judgment, no question of mightier import was ever presented to the American Senate, and to say further, that no question of greater magnitude ever can come by possibility before the American Senate, or any question upon the decision of which greater interests necessarily depend.

Senators, if he has the power to sit in judgment judicially upon the Tenure in Office Act of 1867, he has like power to sit in judgment upon every other act of Congress. If the President may set aside all laws and suspend their execution at pleasure, it results that he may annul the Constitution and annihilate the government, and that is the issue before the American Senate.

Be it known, Senators, that your matchless constitution of government, the hope of the struggling friends of liberty in all lands, and for the perpetuity and the triumph of which millions of hands are lifted this day in silent prayer to the God of nations, can no more exist without laws duly enacted by the law-making power of the people than can the people themselves exist without air or without that bright heaven which bends above us filled with the life-giving breath of the Almighty. A Constitution and laws which are not and cannot be enforced are dead.

Yet we are debating here today whether a man whose breath is in his nostrils, the mere servant of the people, may not suspend the execution both of the Constitution and of the laws at his pleasure, and defy the power of the people.

I have dwelt thus long upon this point because it underlies the whole question in issue here between the President and the people, and upon its determination the decision of the whole issue depends.

It results that the willful violation of such acts of Congress by the President, and the persistent refusal to execute them, is a high crime and misdemeanor, within the terms of the Constitution, for which he is impeachable, and of which, if he be guilty, he ought to be convicted and removed from the office that he has dishonored.

I believe it is conceded on every hand that a crime or misdemeanor made indictable by the laws of the United States, when committed by an officer of the United States in his office, in violation of his sworn duty, is a high crime and misdemeanor within the meaning of the Constitution. If that be not accepted as a true and self-evident proposition by Senators, it would be in vain that I should argue further with them. And I might as well expect to kindle life under the ribs of death as to persuade a Senate so lost to every sense of duty and to the voice of reason itself.

I have said enough and more than enough to show that the matter charged against the President is impeachable. The charges are admitted substantially by the answer. Now what are his reasons? The President is concluded by his record and in the presence of the American people is condemned by his record. What are his reasons? Let the Senate answer when they come to deliberate. What evidence did he furnish this Senate, in the communication made to it, that Edwin M. Stanton had become in any manner disqualified to discharge the duties of that office? What evidence did he furnish the Senate that he had been guilty of any misdemeanor or crime in office? What evidence was there that he was legally disqualified, in the words of the statute? None whatever.

It results, therefore, Senators, that the President of the United States, upon his own showing, judged by his own record, suspended Edwin M. Stanton from the office of the Secretary of War and appointed a successor without the presence of any of the reasons named in the statute, and he is confessedly guilty before the Senate and before the world, and no man can acquit him.

I ask you to consider that we stand this day pleading for the violated majesty of the law, by the graves of a half million hero-patriots who made death beautiful by the sacrifice of themselves for their country, the Constitution, and the laws, and who, by their sublime example, have taught us that all must obey the law; that none are above the law; that no man lives for himself alone, but each for all; that some must die that the state may live; that the citizen is at best for today, while the Commonwealth is for all time; and that position, however high, patronage, however powerful, cannot be permitted to shelter crime to the peril of the republic.

It only remains for me, Ssenators, to thank you, as I do, for the honor you have done me by your kind attention, and to demand, in the name of the House of Representatives, and of the people of the United States, judgment against the accused for the high crimes and misdemeanors in office whereof he stands impeached, and of which before God and man he is guilty."

Mr. Evarts:
(Summation for the President)

"I am sure, Mr. Chief Justice and Senators, that no man of a thoughtful and considerate temper would wish to take any part in the solemn transaction which proceeds today unless held to it by some quite perfect obligation of duty.

Who will provide a chart and compass for the wide, uncertain sea that lies before us in the immediate future? Who shall determine the currents that shall flow from the event of this stupendous political controversy; who shall measure their force; and who shall assume to control the storms that it may breed?

Of the absolute and complete obligation which convenes the Chief Justice of the United States and its senators in this court for the trial of this impeachment, and of its authentic commission from the Constitution, there can be no doubt. So, too, of the deputed authority of these honorable managers, and their presence in obedience to it, and the attendance of the House of Representatives itself in aid of their argument and their appeal, there is little doubt. The President of the United States is here, in submission to the same Constitution, in obedience to it, and in the duty which he owes by the obligation he has assumed to preserve, protect, and defend it.

As, then, duty has brought us all here to this august procedure and has assigned to each of us his part in it, so through all its responsibilities and to that end we must each surrender ourselves to its guidance. Thus following, our foot steps shall never falter or be mislead; and leaning upon its staff, no man need fear that it will break or pierce his side.

But what do we behold here? Why, Mr. Chief Justice and Senators, all the political power of the United States of America is here. The House of Representatives is here as accuser; the President of the United States is here as the accused; and the Senate of the United States is here as the court to try him, presided over by the Chief Justice, under special constitutional duty attributed to him.

These powers of our government are here, this our government is here, not for a pageant or a ceremony; not for concord of action in any of the duties assigned to the government in the conduct of the affairs of the nation, but here in the struggle and contest as to whether one of them shall be made to bow by virtue of constitutional authority confided to the others, and this branch of the political power of the United States shall prove his master.

How have we come to this point? Why, Congress passed a law for the first time in the history of the government undertaking control by law this matter of removal from office; and they provided that if the President should violate it should be a misdemeanor, and a high misdemeanor, and now he has removed or undertaken to remove, a member of his cabinet and he is to be removed himself for that cause. He undertook to make an ad interim Secretary of War, and you are to have made for you an ad interim President in consequence!

That is the situation. 'Was the Secretary of War removed?' you inquire? No, he was not removed, he is still Secretary, still in possession of the department. Was force used? Was violence meditated, prepared, attempted or applied? No; it was all on paper, and all went no further than making the official attitude of which a judgment of the Supreme Court could be got. And here the Congress intercepting again and in reference to this great office, this great authority of the government instead of the liberty of the private citizen, recourse to the Supreme Court, has interposed the procedure of trial and impeachment of the President to settle by its own authority this question between it and the Executive.

The people see and the people feel that in this attitude of Congress there seems to be a claim of right and an exercise of what is supposed to be a duty, to prevent the Supreme Court of the United States from interposing its serene judgment in the collisions of government and laws upon either the framework of the government or upon the condition of liberty of the citizen. And they are not slow to understand...that this is a question between the omnipotence of Congress and the supremacy of the Constitution of the United States; and that is an issue on which the people have no doubt, and from the beginning of their liberties they have had a clear notion that tyranny was as likely to be exercised by a Parliament or a Congress as by anybody else.

The honorable managers have attracted our notice to the principles and the motives of the American Revolution as having shown a determination to throw off the tyranny of a king, and they have told us that people will not bend its neck to the usurpations of a President. That people will not bend its neck to the usurpations of anybody.

But the people of the United States know that their fathers went to war against the tyranny of Parliament, claiming to be great subjects of the king and ready to recognize his authority, preserving their own legislative independence, and against the tyranny of Parliament they rebelled and, as a necessity finally of securing liberty against Parliament, severed their connection with the mother country; and if any honorable member of either house will trace the working of the ideas in the convention that framed the Constitution of the United States, he will discover that inordinate power which should grow up to tyranny in the Congress was more feared, more watched, and more provided against than any other extravagance that the workings of our new government might be supposed possible to lead to.

If this is not a court, what is it? If this is not an altar of justice which we stand about, if we are not all ministers here of justice, to feed its sacred flame, what is the altar and what do we do here about it? It is an altar of sacrifice if it is not an altar of justice; and to what divinity is this altar erected? What but the divinity of party hate and party rage, a divinity to which we may ascribe the Greek character given of envy, that is at once the worst and the justest divinity, for it dwarfs and withers its worshipers. That, then, is the altar that you are to minister about, and that, the savage demon you are to exalt here in displacing justice.

Our learned managers, representing the House of Representatives, do not seem to have been at all at once to conceal the party spirit and the party hate which displayed itself in the hastening in the record, and in the maintenance of this impeachment.

Yes, indeed, this divinity of party that, when it possess a man, throw him now into the fire and now into the water, and he is unsuitable to be a judge until he can come again clothed and in his right mind to hear the evidence and administer the law.

But to come down to the words of our English history and experience, if this is not a court it is a scaffold, and an honorable manager yesterday told you that each one of you brandished now a headman's axe to execute vengeance, you having tried the offender on the night of the 21st of February already. I would not introduce these bold words that should make this a scaffold, in the eyes of the people of this country, and you headsmen brandishing your axes, but that honorable manager has done so, and have no difficulty saying to you that if you are not a court, then you are that which he described and nothing else if it be true that on the night of the 21st of February, upon a crime committed by the President at midday of that date and on an impeachment moving already forward to this chamber from the House of Representatives, you did hold court and condemn, then you are here standing about the scaffold of execution, and the part that you are to play is only that which was assigned you by the honorable manager Mr. Stevens, and he warned you, held by fealty to your own judgments, not to blanch at the sight of blood.

In approaching, then, the consideration of what constitutes an impeachable offense, within the true method and duty of that solemn and unusual proceeding and within the Constitution...Mr. Manager Butler has given us a very thorough and well-considered suggestion of what constitutes an impeachable offense:

We define, therefore, an impeachable high crime or misdemeanor to be one in its main consequences subversive of some fundamental or essential principle of government or highly prejudicial to the public interest and this may consist of a violation of the Constitution or law, of an official oath, or of duty by an act committed or omitted...by the abuse of discretionary powers from improper motives or for any improper purpose.

See what large elements are included in this. That was intended, in the generality of its terms, to avoid the necessity of actual and positive crime, but it has given us in one regard everything that is needed to lift the peccability of the technical offense of mere statutory infraction out of the region of impeachable offense...You must have the crime definite under law and Constitution, and even then it is not impeachable unless you affect it with some of the public and general and important qualities that are indicated in this definition of the learned and honorable manager.

So you will perceive that under these necessary conditions that judgment must be arrived at that there is no impeachable offense here which covers and carries with it these conditions.

We are treated to the most extraordinary view on the subject of violating what is called an unconstitutional law. Why, nobody ever violates an unconstitutional law, because there never is any such obstacle to a man's action, freedom, duty, right, as an unconstitutional law. The question is whether he violates law, not whether he violates a written paper published in a statute book but whether he violates law; and the first lessons under a written Constitution are and must be that a law unconstitutional is no law at all. The learned managers speak of a law being, possibly, capable of being annulled by the judgment of the Supreme Court. Why, the Supreme Court never annuls a law. There is not any difference in the binding force of the law after the Supreme Court has annulled it, from what there was before. The Supreme Court has no political function; it has no authority of will or power to annul a law. It has the faculty of judgment, to discern what the law is, and what it always has been, and so to declare it.

Apply it to an indictment under this very statute, and supposing the law is unconstitutional, for purpose of argument, what is the result? Is the man to be punished because he violated the law, and the Supreme Court has not as yet declared it unconstitutional? No, he comes into court and says, 'I have violated no law.' The statute is read; the Constitution is read; and the judge says, 'You have violated no law.' That is the end of the matter, and he does not want to appeal to the discretion of the court in the measure of punishment or to the mercy of the Executive in the matter of pardon. He has done what was right, and he needs to make no apology to Congress or anybody else.

We argue that if an act be unconstitutional we had a right to obey the Constitution, at least in the intent and purpose of a peaceful submission of the matter to a court, and that our judgment on the matter, if deliberate, honest, and supported by diligent application to the proper sources of guidance, is entitled to support us against an incrimination. To meet that, and to protect the case against the injury from the exclusion of evidence that tends to that effect, the honorable managers do not hesitate to say that the constitutionality or unconstitutionality of the law does not make the least difference in the world where the point is that an unconstitutional law has been violated, and for a President to violate an unconstitutional law is worthy of removal from office.

Now, mark the desperate result to which the reasoning of the honorable managers under the pressure of our argument has reduced them. That is their proposition, and the reason for that proposition is given in terms. If that is not so; if the question of constitutionality or unconstitutionality in fact is permitted to come into your considerations of crime, then you would be punishing the President for an error of judgment, or releasing him or condemning him according as he happened to have decided right or wrong, and that the honorable managers tell us is contrary to the first principles of justice.

We agree that it offends every principle of justice, that a President of the United States should be convicted when honestly, with proper advice, peacefully and deliberately, he has sought to raise a question between the Constitution and the law; and the honorable manager can escape from our argument on that point in no other mode than by the desperate recourse of saying that constitutional laws and unconstitutional laws are all alike in this country of a written Constitution, and that anybody who violates an unconstitutional law meets with some kind of punishment or other. This confusion of ideas as to a law being valid for any purpose that is unconstitutional has been exposed in an argument by one of the managers when he said, 'It is not the right of any senator in this trial to be governed by any opinion he may entertain of the constitutionality of the law in question.'

You may all of you think the law is unconstitutional, and yet you have got to remove the President!

That is pretty hard on us that we cannot even go to the Supreme Court to find out whether it is unconstitutional, and we cannot regard it on our own oath of office as unconstitutional and proceed to maintain the obligation to sustain the Constitution, and you cannot look into the matter at all, but the unconstitutional law must be upheld!

Can we summon now resources enough of civil prudence and of restraint of passion to carry us through this trial, so that whatever result may follow, in whatever form, the people may feel that the Constitution has received no wound! To this court, the last and best resort for this determination, it is to be left. And oh, if you could carry yourselves back to the spirit and the purpose and the wisdom and the courage of the framers of the government, how safe it would be in your hands? How safe is it that the structure of your work comports in durability and excellency with theirs?

Indeed, so familiar has the course of the argument made us with the names of the men of the convention and of the first Congress that I could sometimes seem to think that the presence even of the Chief Justice was replaced by Washington, and that from Massachusetts we had Adams and Ames, from Connecticut, Sherman and Ellsworth, from New Jersey, Patterson and Boudinot, and from New York, Hamilton and Benson, and that they were to determine this case for us. Act, then, as if under this serene and majestic presence your deliberations were to be conducted to their close, and the Constitution was to come out from the watchful solicitude of these great guardians of it as if from their own judgment in this high court of impeachment."

Rehnquist:

Senator Ross, the junior Senator from Kansas, voted to acquit. The conviction of Andrew Johnson fell one vote short on the eleventh article. A ten-day recess was taken. A vote was taken on article II. The result was the same, 35 to convict and 19 to acquit. The same occurred on article III.

Senator Williams then moved that the Senate sitting as a court of impeachment adjourn sine die. The motion was adopted by a vote of 34 to 16, no vote having been taken on eight of the articles of impeachment.

Johnson:

His party did not nominate Johnson for re-election. He was elected to the Senate in 1874 and died five months later.

Stevens:

I died three months after the President's acquittal.

Chase:

I unsuccessfully sought the presidential nomination of the Democratic Party in 1868.

Bingham:

I was responsible for drafting the first section of the 14th Amendment. I was appointed U.S. Minister to Japan in 1873 and served in this post for 12 years.

Evarts:

I was named Attorney General following the President's acquittal. I later served as Secretary of State under President Hayes and represented New York in the U.S. Senate from 1885 to 1891.

Ross:

I was not re-elected to the Senate. In my later years, I was appointed Territorial Governor of New Mexico.

Rehnquist:

Years later, the United States Supreme Court (Myers, 1925) declared The Tenure in Office Act unconstitutional.

Sources:

Trial of Andrew Johnson, Vols. I, II, & III (Washington: Government Printing Office, 1868).

John F. Kennedy, *Profiles In Courage* (New York: Harper & Brothers, 1956).

Samuel Eliot Morison, *The Oxford History of the American People* (New York: Oxford University Press, 1965).

William H. Rehnquist, *Grand Inquests, The Historic Impeachments of Justice Samuel Chase and President Andrew Johnson* (New York: Quill William Morrow, 1993).

Finding Precedent: The Impeachment of Andrew Johnson (courtesy of HarpWeek LLC), http://www.impeach-andrewjohnson.com/

Note: Justice Hobbs' group presented this play at the Doyle Inn of Court on the eve of the President Bill Clinton impeachment proceedings.